Theoretical Perspectives on Human Rights and Literature

D0224866

Routledge Interdisciplinary Perspectives on Literature

Theoretical Perspectives on Human Rights and Literature

**Edited by Elizabeth Swanson Goldberg
and Alexandra Schultheis Moore**

Foreword by Joseph R. Slaughter

 Routledge
Taylor & Francis Group

NEW YORK   LONDON

First published 2012
by Routledge
711 Third Ave, New York, NY 10017

Simultaneously published in the UK
by Routledge
2 Park Square, Milton Park, Abingdon, Oxon OX14 4RN

*Routledge is an imprint of the Taylor & Francis Group,
an informa business*

© 2012 Taylor & Francis

Typeset in Sabon by IBT Global.

First issued in paperback 2013

Library of Congress Cataloging-in-Publication Data
A catalog record has been requested for this book.

ISBN13: 978-0-415-70404-5 (pbk)
ISBN13: 978-0-415-89097-7 (hbk)
ISBN13: 978-0-203-80519-0 (ebk)

Dedicated to those on whose behalf human rights desire to speak, and to those whose utterances inspire deeper understanding of human vulnerability, connection, and possibility.

For Chloë, Samantha, and Marcelle

Contents

PART II:
Questions of Narration, Representation, and Evidence

PART III
Rethinking the "Subject" of Human Rights

Foreword
Rights on Paper

Joseph R. Slaughter

The front page of the 28 May 1961 edition of *The Observer* newspaper featured an unusual essay by Peter Benenson, a British Barrister and (as his biographers like to note) one-time tutee of the poet W. H. Auden. Benenson's article, "The Forgotten Prisoners," told very short stories of six men imprisoned by governments for their political or religious views; these "Prisoners of Conscience" (a term that would become a keyword in the twentieth-century human rights lexicon) had been selected by Benenson and his colleagues—"a group of lawyers, writers, and publishers in London"— as the subjects of their *Appeal for Amnesty, 1961* campaign, which evolved shortly thereafter into Amnesty International. In his article, Benenson made what must now seem a rather extraordinary claim about the generic technical innovations of his campaign's approach to "mobilis[ing] public opinion." "The technique of publicising the personal stories of a number of prisoners of contrasting politics is," Benenson claimed, "a new one. It has been adopted to avoid the fate of previous amnesty campaigns, which so often have become more concerned with publicising the political views of the imprisoned than with humanitarian purposes." In Benenson's formulation, the "personal story" of the religious or political "non-conformist" is not itself a political story; that is, the "personal story" is something worth defending in its own right.

The modern amnesty campaign emerged, at least in part, as a defense of literature, or literary values, forms, and figures of free expression, what Mümtaz Soysal characterized as "voices of the human imagination" in his speech accepting the 1977 Nobel Peace Prize on behalf of Amnesty International. Literature has a central place in Benenson's *Observer* article; indeed, in the examples he offers of the powerful effects of concentrating "world opinion . . . on one weak spot" through publicizing the personal stories of political prisoners, Benenson cites the cases of Hungarian poet and novelist, Tibor Déry, who had recently been released under pressure from "Tibor Dery committees" formed around the world, and of Spanish lawyer, sociologist, and essayist Tierno Galván ("and his literary friends"), who were acquitted of political crimes against Franco's government after foreign observers arrived to monitor the trials. Furthermore, of the six Prisoners of Conscience whose personal stories Benenson publicized, two (Constatin Noica, held in a Romanian prison, and Agostinho Neto, an Angolan held by Portuguese colonial authorities) were identified as poets and literary critics. Noica was later amnestied in August 1964, and the release of Neto—who was just the first of many Prisoners of Conscience adopted by Amnesty to go from prison (and poetry) to the presidency— was announced in the first annual Amnesty International report with the following caveat: "If a prisoner is released . . . after some publicity about conditions in a country, we can only note the coincidence. We cannot say that Amnesty was directly responsible. In the twelve months that Amnesty has been working, however, there have been enough coincidences to make us feel that what we are doing is having some influence" (cited in Amnesty International). We might want to repeat the cautious modesty of this claim in noting some of the intersections between literature and human rights; however, I can say that the essays in this collection show enough "coincidences" between the two to suggest that what literature does clearly has some influence on human rights.

The centrality of literary expression to the *Amnesty Campaign, 1961* reflects the professional interests of the committee of lawyers, writers, and publishers with whom Benenson worked, but it also emerges from Amnesty's narrow mandate to advocate on behalf of "Prisoners of Conscience," who were defined as "Any person who is physically restrained (by imprisonment or otherwise) from expressing (in any form of words or symbols) any opinion which he honestly holds and which does not advocate or condone personal violence."[1] Amnesty drew its charge from the Universal Declaration of Human Rights, especially article 18 (freedom of thought, conscience, and religion) and article 19: "Everyone has the right to freedom of opinion and expression; this right includes freedom to hold opinions without interference and to seek, receive and impart information and ideas through any media and regardless of frontiers." In its efforts to defend these "rights that exist on paper," Amnesty developed literary methods for mobilizing public opinion (the personal story) and focusing it on repressive regimes (the mass letter-writing campaign) that themselves depended heavily on paper. Both of those methods exercise precisely the rights of freedom of opinion and expression that are being denied the Prisoner of Conscience; in other words, the techniques entailed in defending freedom of expression are of the same kind as the modes of expression for which the political prisoner is being punished. In a sense then, at least some of the original Amnesty campaigns were defenses not just of individual writers but of the literary universe and its conditions of possibility more generally.

Literature and human rights may have intersected only recently as common or overlapping areas of scholarly inquiry, but the two have been bound up with one another in the field (so to speak) for a very long time. As a number of the chapters in this volume, and studies elsewhere, demonstrate, literary works and literary modes of thinking have played important parts in the emergence of modern human rights ideals and sentiments, as well as in the elaboration of national and international human rights laws. Such relationships are rarely quantifiable, which I think is probably a good thing for both literature and human rights—not only because it leaves the dynamic terms of their entanglements undetermined in mutually productive ways but also because it reminds us that we must resist the easy temptation to instrumentalize one in the service of the other, to bend one to the exigencies of the other. In other words, the terms of cooperation, coordination, and contradiction between literature (or cultural production more generally) and human rights remain open questions. That the influence of literature on human rights may be both immense and immeasurable is not just a reflection of the indefinable epistemic effects of what Gayatri Chakravorty Spivak has described as "the Humanities . . . without guarantees"[2]; it is the condition and wager of human rights work itself. In the early years of its existence, for example, Amnesty International properly refused to credit directly its letter-writing campaigns with the release of political prisoners. In the presentation speech awarding the Nobel Prize to Amnesty International, Aase Lionæs flirted with some inexact statistics on the percentage of prisoners freed to "provide some indication of the scope of the [organization's] work"; she concluded, following Amnesty's own lead, that such figures were impossible to calculate, arguing instead that it is "more important to consider Amnesty International's worldwide activities as an integral part in the incessant pressure exerted by all good forces on governments and on the United Nations Organisation." Like literature, letter writing too is an activity without guarantees; and like letter writing, literature (in its best moments) participates in mounting "incessant pressure" through its own "worldwide activities."

By any account, the *Appeal for Amnesty, 1961* campaign's emphasis on personal stories predates the so-called narrative turn in the social sciences and the ethical turn in literary studies—when narrative and ethics apparently turned into one another. Personal stories are the contemporary currency of human rights projects, and it seems difficult now—despite Benenson's insistence—to imagine the genre as new in 1961 or to imagine a time before personal stories and human rights campaigns. Indeed, from our perspective, it seems almost as difficult as imagining the introduction of a third character onto the stage of classical Greek drama as a revolutionary literary technological innovation—in a sense, Amnesty's efforts were similar: to introduce a third character (world opinion) into the two-person drama of political imprisonment, to interpose public opinion between the state and the individual. Nonetheless, looking back, it is possible to see that the rise of personal story politics and memoir culture in the 1970s and 1980s coincided with mass movements for decolonization, civil rights, women's rights, and sexual freedoms—many of whose participants would themselves become subjects of Amnesty's letter-writing campaigns. In fact, one of the primary tools of all those campaigns was the personal story— although, in contrast to Amnesty's official opinion, the personal was also (or always already) political.

The intellectual (and not just the emotional or political) attraction of Amnesty International's project for academics in particular might suggest that we should look more closely at the relationship between the development and popularity of human rights campaigns in the 1970s and 1980s and the turns taken by literary studies and the social sciences at the same time. What we call the World Republic of Letters in the second half of the twentieth century was at least in part shaped by the human rights campaigns defending the lives and rights of individual writers, but the campaign methods themselves seem likely to have had an influence on the generic shape of late-twentieth-century literature, and vice versa. We might discover, for instance, that human rights campaigns and methods like those popularized by Amnesty International and other organizations had more to do with steering the narrative and ethical turns than we suspect—that the dramatic turn to personal stories in the context of human rights struggles (broadly understood) helped to create and consolidate many of the literary tastes and methods—as well as the memoir culture—that remain with us today.

I have considered here only one very narrow but highly and historically influential way of thinking about the links between literature and human rights—the admirable chapters in this collection strike out in other important directions. Indeed, as a group, these chapters explore what we might call the necessary and incessant pressure of culture and the worldwide activities of literature on human rights thinking and practice.

NOTES

1. Peter Benenson, "The Forgotten Prisoners," *The Observer*, May 28, 1961. http://www.amnestyusa.org/about-us/the-forgotten-prisoners-by-peter-benenson/page.do?id=1101201.
2. Gayatri Chakravorty Spivak, "Righting Wrongs," *The South Atlanta Quarterly* 103, no. 2/3 (2004), 537.

Acknowledgments

The Editors gratefully acknowledge the vision and support of our editor, Liz Levine; the inspiration and solidarity experienced with the many colleagues who meet to discuss human rights and literature each year at the American Comparative Literature Association convention, especially the consistently warm, generous support of Joey Slaughter; and the unwavering patience, encouragement, and love of our families and friends.

A longer version of "'Literature,' the 'Rights of Man,' and Narratives of Atrocity: Historical Backgrounds to the Culture of Testimony" by Julie Stone Peters originally appeared in *The Yale Journal of Law & the Humanities*, Vol. 17 (2005): 253–283. Portions from the extended version are reprinted by permission.

"Enabling Fictions and Novel Subjects: The *Bildungsroman* and International Human Rights Law" by Joseph R. Slaughter is reprinted by permission of the copyright owner, The Modern Language Association of America.

Excerpt of Guillaume Apollinaire, "Shadow" from *Calligrammes: Poems of Peace and War (1913-1916)*. A Bilingual Edition (Berkeley: University of California Press, 2004), translated by Anne Hyde Greet, is reprinted by permission of the translator and the University of California Press.

Excerpt of Paul Celan, "There Was Earth Inside Them" from *Poems of Paul Celan*, translated by Michael Hamburger. Translation copyright © 1972, 1980, 1988, 2002 by Michael Hamburger. Reprinted by permission of Persea Books. Translation © the Estate of Michael Hamburger, 1988. Reproduced with permission of Johnson & Alcock Ltd.

Excerpt of Angel Cuadra, "In Brief" is reprinted by permission of the translator, Catherine Rodríguez-Nieto.

Excerpt of Robert Desnos, "Epitaph" is reprinted by permission of the translator, Carolyn Forché.

Zbigniew Herbert, "The Wall," translated, from the Polish, by John and Bogdana Carpenter is reprinted here with their permission.

Excerpt of "Suppose I make a timepiece of humanity" is reprinted by permission of the publisher from *The King of Time: Poems, Fictions, Visions of the Future* by Velimir Khlebnikov, translated by Paul Schmidt, edited by Charlotte Douglas, pg. 56, Cambridge, MA: Harvard University Press, Copyright 1985, by the Dia Art Foundation.

Excerpts of Wislawa Szymborska, "Hunger Camp at Jasło" and "Any Case" are reprinted by permission of the translator, Grazyna Drabik.

Excerpt of Vahan Tekeyan, "Forgetting" is reprinted by permission of the translator, Diana Der Hovanessian.

Introduction
Human Rights and Literature: The Development of an Interdiscipline

Elizabeth Swanson Goldberg and
Alexandra Schultheis Moore

Although the Universal Declaration of Human Rights (UDHR) was endorsed in 1948, and international law and practice of human rights have burgeoned in the interim, in many ways a conversation between literature and human rights has only just begun. It seems appropriate to pause, then, to ask why literary scholars should embrace human rights as an analytical lens, and what literary reading and critique can add to the aspirational field of human rights. In spite of ongoing debates about the framing of human rights via the construct of the nation-state, about its dependence upon the recognition of a rights-bearing individual whose legitimacy often, in fact, vanishes precisely at the moment she most needs the protective force of human rights, and about its complicity with the very power structures and violence it seeks to eradicate, the vision of creating conditions whereby persons and cultures may be free from persecution and deprivation remains a common denominator for advocates and critics of human rights alike. Whether or not the language of human "rights," with its nationalist and juridical parameters and moral idealism, is the most efficacious and ethical framework for the work of securing dignity for all peoples remains in question. Still, striving toward such a condition is never not urgent: as Elaine Scarry reminds us in *The Body in Pain*, the most important thing we must know about torture is "that it *is happening.*"[1] Generalizing from the scene of torture to preventable human suffering of both acute and chronic kinds, we must understand the role to be played by human rights, with its instrumentalization in international law and politics, in ending suffering and striving for human dignity and justice—even as we recognize its imperialist origins and complicities with global power and corruption. Our questions about the theoretical implications of interdisciplinary work in human rights and literature are posed within this aura of contestation, critique, and deep desire for social justice.

While the imbrication of the humanities and human rights is evident on the most basic etymological level, overt attention to interdisciplinary work in these two fields is relatively recent. Human rights academics and activists have for some time considered the significance of cultural texts in the struggle against human rights violations, and scholars in literary studies have always devoted critical energy to interpreting representations of suffering, yet their pairing as an interdiscipline is emergent. It is clearly rooted in questions and approaches developed over several decades in trauma, postcolonial, holocaust and genocide, and feminist studies, questions and approaches which also fueled and were fueled by the rise of the "personal story" in responding to social suffering, as Joseph Slaughter's Foreword to this volume explains, as well as the foothold human rights discourse and ideals gained in political and activist rhetoric in the late 1970s. In his important new history of how human rights achieved its current ideological dominance, Samuel Moyn underscores the importance of 1977 as its "breakthrough year": the year Amnesty International was awarded the Nobel Peace Prize, U.S. President Jimmy Carter made human rights a centerpiece of his governing moral framework in his Inaugural Address, and Charter 77 was published in Czechoslovakia.[2]

As an interdisciplinary scholarly field in the U.S., human rights and literature gained formal momentum after September 11, 2001. The shift in political, social, cultural, and intellectual landscapes at that point seemed suddenly both to obviate and to render imperative the connection in relation to changing understandings and practices of war, imprisonment, torture, and immigration. As human rights continues as the dominant discourse for addressing issues of social justice more broadly, scholars working at the intersection of human rights and literature, each galvanized perhaps by his or her own political moment and geographic location, are developing new and more effective tools for understanding the ethical, literary, and political implications of their shared intellectual foundations. Interdisciplinary scholarship in human rights and literature, finally, undertakes two mutually invested intellectual projects: reading literary texts for the ways in which they represent and render intelligible the philosophies, laws, and practices of human rights from multiple, shifting cultural perspectives and considering how stories, testimonies, cultural texts, and literary theories contribute to the evolution of such philosophies, laws, and practices. Significantly, both intellectual projects are profoundly implicated in—and have profound implications for—the realm of the political as located within the flows and jumps of global capitalism.

As Domna C. Stanton notes in her "Foreword" to the special issue of the *PMLA*, "The Humanities in Human Rights: Critique, Language, Politics," human rights and the humanities have a long, shared history. The proliferation of literary and cultural texts telling the stories of past and current human rights violations clearly necessitates an understanding of human rights philosophies and frameworks; less obvious, perhaps, is the extent to which the critical insights gained through literary readings in the past fifty years might be brought to bear in human rights contexts—in the field and in legal, activist, and scholarly sites—to open the foundations of shared rights norms to new interpretations. The essays in this collection explore this intersection from both perspectives. They examine ways in which human rights norms and concerns change the way we read familiar literature even as they shape new directions in the "world republic of letters"; and they bring the interpretative methodologies of literary criticism to bear on human rights to uncover the stories that normative rights discourses implicitly include and exclude. If, as Thomas Keenan suggests, "[e]thics and politics—as well as literature—are evaded when we fall back on the conceptual priority of the subject, agency, or identity as the grounds of our action," theoretical approaches to reading literarily can help return us to the necessary work of negotiating shared foundations of rights, suffering, and representation.[3]

One of the difficulties in defining the interdisciplinary field of human rights and literature is the nature of the "field" of human rights: it comprises law, politics, philosophy/ethics, sociology, anthropology, history, cultural and media studies, and journalism, yet is bound by structural and institutional components of the human rights regime. And of course, approaches to literature have been informed by multiple disciplines and cross-disciplinary approaches including, most relevantly in the late twentieth and early twenty-first centuries, history, philosophy, psychology, linguistics, economics (especially Marxist theory), political science, film and media studies, feminism, critical race studies, and queer theory. Requiring rigorous scholarship, nuanced interdisciplinary work contributes to efforts to move beyond the structuring of disciplines and departments which has produced both the rise of specialization as well as the compartmentalization of knowledge. Such compartmentalization of knowledge (and the teaching and learning practices that accompany it) must especially be disrupted if we are to tackle the complexly interwoven problems accelerating in our new millennium. The contributors to this volume share attention to the ways in which literary readings of human rights discourses (fictional, poetic, testimonial, legal, political, economic, journalistic, cinematic) may illuminate both the limitations of those discourses and the imaginative possibilities of alternative frameworks. We conceptualize such possibilities as substantive, in terms of the alternative potentialities occasioned by progressive work in human rights and in literary production, and as a kind of meta-narrative reflection on the forms that such interdisciplinary work has taken or may yet take. With this dual focus upon form and content in mind, then, we posit a human rights–oriented literary criticism that engages in several unique activities which are explored in this volume: it attends to what is shared by narratives of suffering while at the same time recognizing the particular situations and positions of those who suffer; it explores how narratives probe the limits of language, representation, and translation to depict their subjects adequately; it reflects awareness of the arguably "west-centric" history of human rights, taking account of representations of non-western approaches to human rights, and of economic and social rights as well as third-generation solidarity rights; and it engages in both reflection upon and critique of the theories of the liberal subject and the liberal democratic state that underlie the modern international human rights system.

Narratives of origins for such human rights–oriented literary criticism can be constructed in multiple ways. For instance, one may trace its growth historically, from the shared roots of modern human rights and literary expression/criticism in the eighteenth century, or in the contexts of key movements within literary studies and legal studies. The law and literature movement that crystallized in the 1970s and 1980s, alongside the accession of human rights as a leading discourse of moral idealism and social justice, presages some of the momentum and potential limitations of work in human rights and literature. Driven by shared interest in social justice as well as what Marjorie Garber and Julie Stone Peters have called "disciplinary envy,"[4] "[e]ach [discipline] in some way fantasized its union with the other: law would give literature praxis; literature would give law humanity and critical edge."[5] Peters reads in this "double [disciplinary] desire—for the other and for the other's projection of the self,"[6] the unintended consequences of "exaggerate[d] disciplinarity," a yearning for the real "emerg[ing] from the center of postmodern skepticism as a kind of return of the repressed."[7] The work materializing from this desire would purportedly bring important changes to both disciplines: the broadening of literary studies to include material effects, and of legal studies to include greater attention to theoretical and academic concerns. It is possible to see the emergence of human rights and literature as coeval with the transformation of the law and literature movement into "law, culture, and the humanities."[8] Notable among literary approaches of the past several decades that have contributed to this movement are (new) historical, narratological, holocaust and genocide, trauma, and postcolonial studies, aided by what scholar Mark Sanders and others have termed "the ethical turn," the reclamation of ethics as a central term of literary study in the wake of poststructuralist criticism and its interrogations of subjectivity.[9] Contributors to this volume work across this spectrum to develop substantive vocabularies, frameworks, and standpoints from which to examine the structural affinities of human rights and literature, their shared paradoxes, and the limits of legal and literary representability.

Beyond these origination points, the interdiscipline is built upon solid foundations recently produced by scholars who pose crucial questions from multiple disciplinary perspectives about the production and circulation of both human rights and literature in the modern context. Historian Lynn Hunt's *Inventing Human Rights* (2007) makes the case that modern human rights were articulated in the particular historical moment of the American and French Revolutions partly because of the enabling function of empathic responses fostered by the novel form which produced readers able to care for others outside of the limits of their social class, gender, race, and other situated particularities. Martha Nussbaum makes a similar claim for literature's humanizing effects on the reader: that literature enables us to "see

the lives of the different with [. . .] involvement and sympathetic understanding," to "cultivat[e] our humanity," and to learn the habits necessary
for "world citizenship."[10] Even as they formulate the powerful shared foundations of human rights and literary discourses, Hunt's and Nussbaum's
works focus our attention upon the critical problem of the west-centric
history of contemporary human rights, begging the question of whether
human rights can materialize in states without democratic systems of governance, in societies in which "the individual" is not the major category of
social organization, or in translation in local contexts that remain illegible
to the human rights regime. As Hannah Arendt famously described in *The
Origins of Totalitarianism*, one of the central paradoxes of human rights as
outlined in the Universal Declaration of Human Rights (1948) is that they
are available foremost to citizens, such that statelessness or marginalization within state formations challenges individual and collective claims to
rights precisely at the moment that persons and groups are most vulnerable
to the kinds of harms that such rights mitigate against. Similarly, expanding Arendt's question about the role of the nation-state in maintaining the
human rights regime to include the role of global capitalism, Talal Asad
asks whether normative human rights discourse is in fact "part of a great
work of conversion" which promises that when "redemption is complete,
rights and capital will be equally universalized." "But," he notes, "whether
universal capital or universal human rights will bring with it practical
equality and an end to all suffering is quite another question."[11]

Considering Asad's focus upon the affiliations between global capital(ism)
and human rights, we might consider one of the UDHR's framers, René
Cassin's, elegant diagram of the structure of the Declaration as a classical
temple in "Cassin's Portico" as emblematic of these limitations identified
in the modern human rights regime, inasmuch as his image resonates culturally with notions of rights as a secular morality based upon individualism and democracy. Cassin imagined rights resting on the cornerstones of
dignity, liberty, equality, and brotherhood and grouped into four stately
columns relating to the individual; to individuals in relation to one another
and social groups; to public and political rights; and to economic, social,
and cultural rights.[12] Engaging with this image of the structural relations of
rights as foundational to a symbolic space of sacred sanctuary, we must ask
what worshippers, adherents, or supplicants it produces, whom it excludes,
and what it promises in return for faith in its principles. One avenue of
response would recognize that, unfortunately, the divisions within Cassin's
idealized structure of the UDHR as a document that "could never be more
than an entryway to a better world"[13] were formalized in the separation of
the Covenant on Civil and Political Rights and Covenant on Social, Economic, and Cultural Rights (1966) which resulted in the prioritization of
civil and political rights and the marginalization of social, cultural, and
(perhaps most consequentially) economic rights. As several of the contributors in this volume note, invigorating economic rights discourse is one of the

foremost tasks for human rights in the face of accelerating global poverty, increasing inequity between rich and poor, and potentially catastrophic scarcity of basic resources.

Interpreting the structural relationships between different categories of rights presents specific challenges for literary studies, where readings of characterization and interiority (which seemingly align with notions of the autonomous individual's freedom) are often separated from those of historical and economic context. As Pheng Cheah has argued recently, the humanities, as the source of our understanding of what it means to be human, help us to "figure[e] the global as human" and thus "underwrite our understanding"[14] of globalization's ineluctable participation in the force fields of uneven capital development. The challenge for the humanities then is to "question this pre-comprehension of the human" and to provide an "account of the normativity of human rights that acknowledges their contaminated nature without reducing them to ideological reflections of global capitalism."[15] Both challenges must be met through the "radical reconceptualization of freedom," not as an escape from but as a desired condition within global capitalism.[16] Not only must we recognize the structural conditions that ground both the humanities and human rights regimes, but we must also read literarily, linguistically, rhetorically, and philosophically for the ways in which rights may be "violent gifts, the necessary nexuses within immanent global force relations that produce the identities of their claimants."[17]

We embrace the paradox imminent in Cheah's construction—"violent gifts"—as constitutive of human rights discourses more generally, as both Greg Mullins (in his contribution in this volume) and James Dawes, in his recent assessment of the field of literature and human rights, have noted.[18] If a gift is violent, is it still a gift? In what ways might the suffering that is often engendered by the protection of rights and redress of wrongs be considered gifts? If we return to the roots of "gift" in the Old English, where it originally signified "payment for a wife," but also was linked to "poison," and trace its journey through Middle to modern English, where in addition to its standard reference to something bestowed "gratuitously, for nothing," it also references a bribe or corrupt payment, we can discern the subtleties of corruption and exchange embodied in Cheah's construction of the gift, which then gestures toward the complexities and complicities inherent in the distribution, protection, and enforcement of human rights in the contemporary context.[19] We can also perceive through this etymology the important revision brought by this idea of "gifts" to the deeply held idea of "inherent rights" enshrined in the UDHR. For all the drafters' embrace of this idea, the truth is that in practice, human rights have in fact been "something bestowed" unequally by national governments and, to a lesser and more recent extent, international law. Too, Cheah's phrasing of the "violent gift" that contributes to producing the "identities of its claimants" evokes the important role of suffering—both one's own experience of suffering and recognition of the suffering of others—in the construction and metamorphosis of the self. This point suggests the strain of philosophical theory emergent from such thinkers as Giorgio Agamben, Judith Butler, and Emmanuel Levinas that underpins the ethos of human rights in the contemporary moment and that has particularly informed interdisciplinary work in literature and human rights, as we discuss below.

Implicit in the nature of paradox are the challenges of and to representation itself. To return to the contemporary paradoxes of state power, for instance, the rise of the neoliberal state in the post–Soviet era constitutes a new site of interface between global capital and global terror, a site with particularly important consequences for thinking about the full range of human rights in the post–9/11 era. The paradox of the neoliberal, democratic state as a force that *produces* terror in order to *fight* terror constitutes ground for the work of human rights and literature, which, in the context of the "war on terror," strives to deconstruct the newly mobilized language of terror and its application to extrajudicial actors, largely people of Arab and Muslim identity. Such deconstructive efforts across the spectrum of literary production and human rights activism reveal the terror produced by states in both their overt and covert military and policing options, as well as that produced by nation states, transnational corporations, and global financial institutions in the practices of global capitalism.

These issues of language in relation to contemporary discourses of terror are closely tied to the problems of representation, narratability, and embodiment which have been explored at length in the scholarly work of holocaust and trauma studies. These sub-fields are also foundational to the interdiscipline of literature and human rights. In the 1980s and 1990s, critics such as Shoshanna Felman, Saul Friedlander, Dori Laub, Hayden White, and others posed questions about how to represent the unthinkable, unspeakable, unrepresentable event of the Nazi holocaust. Indeed, some thinkers argued that this event quite literally could not be represented, nor the name *Shoah* even uttered, without committing further violence against both its victims and survivors. The range of positions on aestheticizing historical atrocity may be represented in the context of antipodal debates about Claude Lanzmann's film *Shoah* (1985) in which Lanzmann purposefully refuses to recreate images or narrative of the Nazi holocaust, presenting instead only interviews with individual survivors, bystanders, and perpetrators, and Stephen Spielberg's *Schindler's List* (1994), a classical Hollywood dramatization of the story of Oskar Schindler, a Nazi official who rescues 1,300 Jews, complete with high-octane stars and blockbuster cinematography. These positions occupy the ends of a broad spectrum of aesthetic strategies employed to represent atrocity that continues to require deep critical engagement on the part of scholars engaged with the ethics of representation in the context of human rights.

Importantly, work on trauma and representation over the past two decades has broadened analysis from the paradigmatic case of the Nazi

holocaust. Kali Tal, in *Worlds of Hurt* (1995), addresses the Nazi holo-
caust in her first chapter, and then analyzes narratives about the Vietnam
War and about sexual trauma (domestic violence and incest) suffered by
women. Laura Tanner's *Intimate Violence: Reading Rape and Torture in
Twentieth Century Fiction* (1994) addressed literary inscriptions of vio-
lence against women at precisely the moment that Julie Stone Peters and
Andrea Wolper were assembling their foundational collection *Women's
Rights, Human Rights: International Feminist Perspectives* (1995), and as
preparations were underway for the United Nations World Conference on
Women, Beijing, 1995, in which "women's rights as human rights" were
formally articulated in the Beijing Declaration and Platform for Action.
Each of these works pushes at the limits of how different experiences of
trauma and suffering may be articulated within and against a human rights
framework originally set up through the paradigm of the Nazi holocaust
and the limited definition of rights violations perpetrated by government
agents working in an official capacity in the public sphere, with the rights-
bearing subject constructed as an individual male.

The significance of witnessing and testifying to egregious human wrongs
suffered by a broad range of people and groups is taken up by literary
critics Kay Schaffer and Sidonie Smith in *Human Rights and Narrated
Lives: The Ethics of Recognition* (2004), a study of human rights claims
articulated in testimonials and narratives in the multiple spaces of the
courtroom, community, and literary production. Smith and Shaffer's work
reveals the testimonial and the closely related literary genres of autobiography and memoir as ripe forms of overlap between literature and human
rights. Beyond finding language sufficient to the telling of the experience
of atrocity, the primary question haunting modern testimonials has to do
with veracity. Is what the survivor relays "true" in the sense that it happened to her exactly in the way that she has claimed? As scholars working
in both literary and human rights studies have shown, such prioritization
of factual veracity occurs within the epistemological tenets of individualist
western notions, contexts, and applications of truth value. Indeed, some of
the most important recent rights work has occurred in legal, psychoanalytic, and literary testimonial forums in which such limits to the forms and
contexts of legitimated "truth-telling," including truth and reconciliation
commissions, have been challenged. In the literary context, Leigh Gilmore
has explored the potential of autobiographical literary forms to provide a
broader archive of the testimonial than the one currently bound within the
juridical model.[20] In addition, recent scholarship in human rights and literature has emphasized that the literary form and the testimonial it produces
depends on the model of subjectivity that underwrites it: the terms, relationships, contexts, epistemologies, and experiences through which the self
is made present to itself. A feminist contribution to this body of scholarly
work from Susan J. Brison considers the necessity of crossing boundaries
between self and other, developing a conception of a relational self, in order

to explain how trauma alters the terms through which the subject formerly knew and now must learn to know herself. Contributions by scholars in the field of trauma studies, such as Cathy Caruth, Shoshanna Felman, Dori Laub, and E. Ann Kaplan, also consider the theoretical possibility of representing the traumatic experience on both historic and individual levels from a psychoanalytic perspective.

Moving out from the relative truth value of and subjectivity constructed through individual survivor testimonials, the larger problem of representability emerges when artists, writers, and filmmakers who were not present at the historical event, who are not survivors, and who may well be removed by time or distance from the event attempt its representation in historical or artistic terms. The problem here has an ethical cast which Goldberg explores in her book, *Beyond Terror: Gender, Narrative, Human Rights* (2007), which considers problems of representing grave violations of human rights in literature and film: how to do justice to the memory of those who suffered, or who were lost to, the event? How not to do further violence to these humans, their loved ones, or their descendants by spectacularizing, eroticizing, or exploiting the representation of pain inflicted in a grave violation of human rights? How to create cultural images that will not perpetuate cycles of violence and revenge? Goldberg also argues for a critical examination of the warrant, often left unexamined, that narrativizing atrocity in the form of novel, testimonial, or film is in some way an effective means of creating a deeper consciousness in viewers about the event, and even of encouraging viewers to act in a way that would contribute to efforts to decrease the occurrence of such events in future. This subject is taken up by James Dawes, whose 2007 book, *That the World May Know: Bearing Witness to Atrocity*, combines analyses of literary texts with assessments from human rights and humanitarian aid workers in order to consider questions about who has the authority to speak on behalf of victims and survivors of atrocity, and about the uses to which such stories and testimonies are put.

Implicit in all of this scholarship is a need to respond to the critique Makau Mutua makes in *Human Rights: A Political and Cultural Critique* (2002; 2008) of a "grand narrative" of human rights literature based on the metaphor of "savages-victims-saviors" (SVS).[21] This paradigm, as Mutua argues, authorizes witness testimony over other forms of narration and, in its valorization of the hero-function, is often culturally coded to legitimize "western" humanitarian intervention. Drawn from the shared history of human rights and literature in the imperialist European eighteenth century, the SVS narrative, like that of political modernity, relegates those of the Global South to the "waiting-room" of History (which itself is constructed as a progressive narrative inseparable from the development of the nation-state and global capitalism).[22] Significantly, many literary scholars working in human rights and literature, including some represented in this volume, specialize in postcolonial studies and have grappled over time with the terms of Mutua's anti-imperialist critique of human rights. One response to this problem, in the spirit of "provincializing Europe," is to read for articulations of human rights in local and transnational contexts that uncover or produce alternative modernities, narratives, and ways of articulating political, economic, cultural, and social justice claims that fall outside the national-legal spheres of institutionalized human rights.

Reading literarily for narrative claims to human rights and to social justice raises the question of the speaking and embodied subject of narration. Literary scholars have brought diverse theories of subjectivity to bear on contemporary human rights discourses in response to the urgent need to grasp the characteristics that constitute the bearer of rights and how she is recognizable (to herself and others) discursively, philosophically, corporeally, ethically, and politically. Philosophers such as Agamben, Levinas, and Butler interrogate the limits of human freedom within and from the space of the political, as well as the problems of ethical interdependence and responsibility beyond the self. Here we quote from Judith Butler, who powerfully asks us all to acknowledge the extent to which we are "as much constituted by those [we] do grieve for as by those whose deaths [we] disavow, whose nameless and faceless deaths form the melancholic background for [our] social world, if not [our] First Worldism."[23] As Joseph R. Slaughter reminds us in his Foreword to this volume, the personal story holds the center of human rights work, and the personal story rendered literarily can illuminate the names and faces of those whom we cannot know, but with whom we are imbricated in the Levinasian sense, while also providing a site for the imaginative reflection of variously-constituted subjectivities. It also can help us to name productively our own complex subject positions with their relative powers and privileges in relation to others without succumbing to the paralyzing force of negative identity politics, seeking instead an ethical position from which to forge solidarity across difference.

Crucial to a human rights–oriented literary criticism is the insight that in Levinas's theory, we are not only constructed through but are also responsible to the other, in much the same way that as readers we are called by the text and the other worlds it represents. This responsibility may be reciprocal, in the sense that we are all constructed in this way and thus have this same responsibility—before acting on our own will—of responding to the call of the other; however, it is also unreciprocal, asymmetrical, because the call is not a kind of quid pro quo, a "do unto others." Instead, one has this responsibility for the other even if the other does not reciprocate. In *Witnessing: Beyond Recognition* (2001), Kelly Oliver offers another approach to this process through a resignification of witnessing, comprised of "address-ability and "response-ability" untethered from the antagonistic dichotomy of self and other, as "the basis for all subjectivity."[24] It is thus in the critical interpretative methodologies and theories through which we read literature, rather than in literature itself as a romanticized realm apart from the real, that we might begin to parse the implications of subjectivity as a political problem for human rights.

An ongoing challenge to the theorization of subjectivity and its relationship to discursive practice is the need to account for the embodiment
and performativity of specific subject positions. This need becomes all the
more telling when human rights violations themselves correspond to the
particularities of the subject's race, gender, religion, class position, and
other markers of identity. Theories of specific subjectivities, which must
themselves be rendered contingent and fluid, rather than static, deepen our
understanding of the relationship between literary forms—in their ability
to envision and inscribe such complex identity formations—and the poetics
of and political responses to suffering. Such theories must account for the
problem of narrative temporalities required to tell both individual stories
and complex social histories in the context of traumatic events marked as
rights violations. Narrative strategies such as magical realist or postmodern
jumps and juxtaposition of times/spaces/places/persons, or lyrical meditations upon the repetitious nature of traumatic experience, can help to make
intelligible the ineffable nature of time as it is haunted by individual and
historical violence and suffering. In a sense, temporality becomes another
boundary to be negotiated in theorizing the responsibilities that attend the
ethics of recognition of suffering across times and places.

In *Politics Out of History* (2001), another attempt to rethink the fundamental tenets of liberal political theory and subjectivity, Wendy Brown
addresses this problem of transhistorical responsibility in her reading,
through Derrida, of Walter Benjamin's angel of history:

> This is how one pictures the angel of history. His face is turned toward
> the past. Where we perceive a chain of events, he sees one single ca-
> tastrophe which keeps piling wreckage upon wreckage and hurls it in
> front of his feet. The angel would like to stay, awaken the dead, and
> make whole what has been smashed. But a storm is blowing from Para-
> dise; it has got caught in his wings with such violence that the angel can
> no longer close them. This storm irresistibly propels him into the future
> to which his back is turned, while the pile of debris before him grows
> skyward. This storm is what we call progress.[25]

Where is the scholar of human rights and literature, or the reader of human
rights discourses, in this tableau? As the history of the interdiscipline and
the more contemporary critiques of its imperializing tendency make clear,
the notion of History as progress potentially blinds us, as "inheritors of a
radically disenchanted universe,"[26] to the need to rethink the terms of our
political futures. "Justice," Brown argues through Derrida, "demands that
we locate our political identity between what we can only imagine and the
histories that constrain and shape that imagination."[27] If, as Chakrabarty
writes, "it may legitimately be argued that the administration of justice by
modern institutions requires us to imagine the world through the languages
of the social sciences, that is, as disenchanted,"[28] how can literatures of

human rights enable the possibility of enchantment, yet remain strictly attentive to the potential for political violence? It is again at this nexus of imagination and incorporation, of idealism and realpolitik, that the inter-discipline can do its best work.

Alternatives to the liberal individual subject and its attendant discourses of history, progress, and modernity are also evident in some non-western literary, cultural, philosophical, and religious textual and non-textual practices. From the perspective of our interdiscipline, as the "world repub-lic of letters" and human rights discourses expand, they demand great leaps of both literacy and translation to facilitate the share-ability of and thus response-ability to suffering. In his contribution to this volume, Greg-ory Price Grieve provides a trenchant example of the kind of translation skills required in his reading of diverse literary forms through a Buddhist approach to the (no-)self. In contradistinction to the liberal subject at the heart of normative human rights discourses, Grieve posits the *samsaric* sub-ject who is ever-changing yet anchored in the present through compassion and duty. Grieve's reading of the samsaric subject's translation of human rights concerns into and from other registers provides an example of how "story telling" across literary and philosophical traditions may expand the foundation of human rights beyond individual entitlement.

This ideal of translatable, shared discourses and practices, gesturing as it does toward solidarity, must in fact provide the foundation for an ethical politics of human rights, including the representational politics of human dignity and rights claims in multiple media. Facing the urgencies of millen-nial contexts—wars and disenfranchisement, environmental crisis, poverty and deprivation—while always keeping in mind the possibilities of radi-cal political actions and solidarities, we conclude with a note on possible futures for the interdiscipline. In *The Future of Human Rights* (2006), legal theorist Upendra Baxi argues similarly for the (re)generation of human rights discourses to give voice, and thus the potential for legal standing, to those whose suffering remains unacknowledged or unanswered. Advocat-ing interdisciplinary approaches to complex problems and possibilities, we note emerging work in a number of areas that build upon the theoretical foundations outlined in this volume.

As Sophia A. McClennen and Joseph Slaughter noted recently, "human rights everywhere are on the move,"[29] and this movement presents con-comitant challenges to our reading practices, necessitating careful work in translation across disciplinary, linguistic, and formal borders. Human rights in literature transgresses boundaries between English and Compara-tive Literary Studies, and thus can benefit from the developments in theo-ries of translation that have shifted the focus from questions of authenticity and veracity to the ways in which translation opens up new "circuits of connection" among both readers and texts without losing local specific-ity.[30] The globalization of literary studies in the context of human rights asks us to attend to different ways of being in the world, without sacrificing the possibility for shared ethics and political solidarities. This work will require the kind of situated translation of other conceptions of the subject as bearer of rights and duties of care as we see in Grieve's essay in this volume, as well as the approach McClennen outlines, that we "dispel and defer our focus on the self and its formation, in order to substitute the object/subject of human rights with attention to developing an ethically just comparative method."[31]

The challenge of negotiating these comparisons was made visible in discussion and voting on the United Nations' most recent major human rights document, the Declaration on the Rights of Indigenous Peoples, which was adopted in 2007 over the objections of Canada, Australia, New Zealand, and the United States. That it was four former settler colonies that still have fraught relations with their indigenous populations that voted in opposition to the Declaration speaks also to future directions in postcolonial theory. The Preamble of the Declaration notes "the urgent need to respect and promote the inherent rights of indigenous peoples which derive from their political, economic and social structures and from their cultures, spiritual traditions, histories and philosophies, especially their rights to their lands, territories and resources," and the Declaration includes repeated acknowledgment of indigenous peoples' collective standing, rights to alternative forms of development, and rights which invoke multiple temporalities. Scholars working in the relatively new field of postcolonial ecocriticism address the forms, literary and otherwise, through which rights to environmental cultural resources and practices and other so-called third-generation or solidarity rights are expressed and represented, keeping in mind the danger of sublimating the particularities of indigenous claims to a broad notion of "Green Romanticism."[32] Postcolonial ecocriticism and the interdiscipline of human rights and literature already share awareness of the paradoxes of ethnocentrism and the problem of enmeshment within global capitalism as ways to account for the inherent biases in their own structures. Moreover, when competition over scarce resources, ongoing effects of climate change, and the ravages of war underscore our eco-social connections, scholars working in areas typically devoted to social justice need increasingly to examine potential alliances between movements for social *and* environmental justice. Here we might follow the lead of writers such as Ken Saro Wiwa, Mahesweta Devi, Leslie Marmon Silko, and Alexis Wright, who have tackled these issues in their fiction and in their political activism.

A further area of inquiry that has generated recent scholarly work concerns the nominatively opposite end of the spectrum of human rights: those of the new world order and emergent technologies of disembodiment and re-embodiment that both generate the "posthuman" and necessitate changing conceptions and discourses of rights. In *Human Rights in a Posthuman World: Critical Essays* (2007), Upendra Baxi takes up this "problematic of rightlessness"–which Arendt first noted in her critique of the Universal

Declaration of Human Rights[33]—as it emerges through environmental, technological, and economic challenges to the sovereignty of human bodies, reason, and the state.

These evolving areas of inquiry also raise new questions about the relationship between humanitarianism and human rights, with an emphasis upon the function of "narratives of suffering" in both discourses. In their Introduction to *Humanitarianism and Suffering: The Mobilization of Empathy* (2008), Richard Ashby Wilson and Richard D. Brown trace the common origins of humanitarianism and human rights in natural law and the notion of inherent human dignity; however, they also make note of the divergence of the two discourses inasmuch as human rights is bounded as a juridical discourse, while humanitarianism remains a moral one. Thus, the humanitarian actor can imagine action based upon moral exigency, while the human rights activist must remain within the parameters of existing legal frameworks or seek to expand or change those parameters before taking action.

Fertile areas for research at the interdiscipline of human rights and the humanities, then, is the ethos shared by these discourses; the subjectivities (of both advocates for and subjects of human rights law or humanitarian aid) brought into being through their operations in the world; the narratives used to tell the tales that precipitate engagement and action; and the power relations or solidarities generated in the process. And, we would argue, it is incumbent upon scholars to continue to train their critical eyes upon the discourses of humanitarianism and human rights, considering the relations between these and alternative discourses—such as "the political" or "justice"—and making note of the ways in which dominant rights and aid discourses can crowd out other forms of solidarity and action, as Wendy Brown eloquently demonstrates in her essay, "The Most We Can Hope For: Human Rights and the Politics of Fatalism."[34] In this sense, reading in the humanities—reading that attends both to literature's invitation to imagine other worlds and other ways of being and that interrogates its own suppositions—remains a crucial balance for the pragmatic work of honoring and protecting the lives of all human beings.

MAPPING THIS VOLUME

There is no singular way to map the theoretical territory of the interdiscipline of human rights and literature, given its complex historical antecedents as well as the pressures—political, intellectual, aesthetic—of the present. We have not aimed to cover the globe nor the vast spectrum of human rights violations nor every literary form; rather, we have encouraged contributions and organized this volume in three main categories of theoretical scholarship in the field: the shared histories, philosophies, structures, and paradoxes of rights and literary imagination; the potential and limitations of literary language in writing rights; and, the problematics of defining the core bearer of rights, the subject. Our contributors work in different historical periods and literary genres as well as from different theoretical foundations. They share with us a desire to employ strategies of reading literarily to offer interpretations and critiques of writing human rights without abandoning their still evolving potential. In that spirit, we hope this volume serves as an invitation to further developments in the interdiscipline of human rights and literature.

NOTES

1. Elaine Scarry, *The Body in Pain: The Making and Unmaking of the World* (New York: Oxford University Press, 1985), 9.
2. Samuel Moyn, *The Last Utopia: Human Rights in History* (Cambridge, MA: Harvard University Press, 2010), 129 and the larger argument in Chapter 4 "The Purity of This Struggle."
3. Thomas Keenan, *Fables of Responsibility: Aberrations and Predicaments in Ethics and Politics* (Stanford, CA: Stanford University Press, 1997), 3.
4. Marjorie Garber, *Academic Instincts* (Princeton, NJ: Princeton University Press, 2001), 53–96, qtd. in Julie Stone Peters, "Law, Literature, and the Vanishing Real: On the Future of an Interdisciplinary Illusion," *PMLA* 120, no. 2 (2005): 448.
5. Julie Stone Peters, "Law, Literature, and the Vanishing Real: On the Future of an Interdisciplinary Illusion," 448.
6. Peters, "Law, Literature, and the Vanishing Real," 449.
7. Peters, "Law, Literature, and the Vanishing Real," 449, 450.
8. Peters, "Law, Literature, and the Vanishing Real," 451.
9. See Mark Sanders, ed., *Diacritics* 32, nos. 3/4 (2002), special issue on Ethics. See also Todd F. Davis and Kenneth Womack, eds., *Mapping the Ethical Turn: A Reading in Culture, Ethics, and Literary Theory* (Charlottesville: University of Virginia Press, 2001) and Marjorie Garber, Beatrice Hanssen, and Rebecca L. Walkowitz, eds., *The Turn to Ethics* (New York: Routledge, 2000).
10. See Martha Nussbaum, *Cultivating Humanity: A Classical Defense of Reform in Liberal Education* (Cambridge, MA: Harvard University Press, 1998), 88, 10, 67.
11. Talal Asad, "What Do Human Rights Do? An Anthropological Enquiry," *Theory and Event* 4, no. 4 (2000). http://muse.jhu.edu/journals/theory_and_event/v004/4.4asad.html.
12. Mary Ann Glendon, *A World Made New: Eleanor Roosevelt and the Universal Declaration of Human Rights* (New York: Random House, 2001), 172, 174.
13. Glendon, *A World Made New*, 174.
14. Pheng Cheah, *Inhuman Conditions: On Cosmopolitanism and Human Rights* (Cambridge, MA: Harvard University Press, 2007), 3.
15. Cheah, *Inhuman Conditions*, 3, 146.
16. Cheah, *Inhuman Conditions*, 112.
17. Cheah, *Inhuman Conditions*, 172.
18. See James Dawes, "Human Rights in Literary Study," *Human Rights Quarterly* 31, no. 2 (May 2009): 304–409.

19. The paradox of human rights as "violent gifts" is perhaps nowhere more clear than in the context of humanitarian action, which often does bodily harm in order to prevent or end the infliction of bodily harm. See especially David Rieff, *A Bed for the Night: Humanitarianism in Crisis* (New York: Simon and Schuster, 2003), and David Kennedy, *The Dark Sides of Virtue: Reassessing International Humanitarianism* (Princeton, NJ: Princeton University Press, 2004).
20. Leigh Gilmore, *The Limits of Autobiography: Trauma and Testimony* (Ithaca, NY: Cornell University Press, 2001).
21. Makau Mutua, *Human Rights: A Political and Cultural Critique* (Philadelphia, PA: University of Pennsylvania Press, 2002), 10.
22. Dipesh Chakrabarty, *Provincializing Europe: Postcolonial Thought and Historical Difference* (Princeton, NJ: Princeton University Press, 2000), 9.
23. Judith Butler, *Precarious Life: The Power of Mourning and Violence* (New York: Verso, 2004), 46.
24. Kelly Oliver, *Witnessing: Beyond Recognition* (Minneapolis: University of Minnesota Press, 2001), 7.
25. Walter Benjamin, "Theses on the Philosophy of History," in *Illuminations*, ed. Hannah Arendt, trans. Harry Zohn (New York: Schocken, 1969), 257.
26. Wendy Brown, *Politics Out of History* (Princeton, NJ: Princeton University Press, 2001), 139.
27. Brown, *Politics Out of History*, 147.
28. Chakrabarty, *Provincializing Europe*, 72.
29. Sophia A. McClennen and Joseph R. Slaughter, "Introducing Human Rights and Literary Forms; or, The Vehicles and Vocabularies of Human Rights," *Comparative Literary Studies* 46, no. 1 (2009): 17.
30. Sophia A. McClennen, "Human Rights, the Humanities, and the Comparative Imagination," *Comparative Literature and Culture* 9, no. 1 (March 2007), http://docs.lib.purdue.edu/clcweb/vol9/iss1/13 p. 13 (19).
31. McClennen, "Human Rights, the Humanities, and the Comparative Imagination," 8 (19).
32. See, for instance, Graham Huggan, ""Postcolonial Ecocriticism and Green Romanticism," *Journal of Postcolonial Writing* 45, no. 1 (2009): 3–14; Graham Huggan and Helen Tiffin, eds., *Postcolonial Ecocriticism*, New York: Routledge, 2009; Lawrence Buell, *Writing for an Endangered World: Literature, Culture, and Environment in the U.S. and Beyond* (Cambridge, MA: Harvard University Press, 2001); Bonnie Roos and Alex Hunt, eds., *Postcolonial Green: Environmental Politics and World Narratives* (Charlottesville and London: University of Virginia Press, 2010); and Laura Wright, *Wilderness into Civilized Shapes: Reading the Postcolonial Environment* (Athens, GA, and London: University of Georgia Press, 2010).
33. Upendra Baxi, *Human Rights in a Posthuman World: Critical Essays* (New Delhi: Oxford University Press, 2007), 27, 28.
34. Wendy Brown, "The Most We Can Hope For: Human Rights and the Politics of Fatalism," *South Atlantic Quarterly* 103, nos. 2/3 (Summer 2004): 451–463.

Part I

Histories, Imaginaries, and Paradoxes of Literature and Human Rights

1 "Literature," the "Rights of Man," and Narratives of Atrocity

Historical Backgrounds to the Culture of Testimony[1]

Julie Stone Peters

> "Un récit? Non, pas de récit, plus jamais[!]"
> —Maurice Blanchot, *La folie du jour*

In response to the horrifying state-sponsored atrocities of the past decades, our era has seen the rise of what is essentially a new phenomenon, quasi-judicial, quasi-political, quasi-theatrical in nature: the truth commission and other national and international venues in which victims may bear witness to what they have suffered, and in which the narration of atrocity may serve at once as testimony, redress, and public catharsis. In addition to truth commissions, there are international and national post-atrocity tribunals of various sorts, personal testimonials in public venues, televised confessionals, documentary films, internet sites featuring human rights victims telling their stories, all devoted to giving voice to those who have suffered.[2] While the truth commissions differ in significant ways from the international tribunals and these differ from victim testimony in more general media outlets, they (and other public displays of post-atrocity narrative) share an underlying aspiration to redress through storytelling. Narrative has come to be used instead of (or alongside) punishment or victim compensation: not as evidence (even where it is also used as evidence) but as a form of remedy, in and of itself. That is, narrative in human rights has come to have an independent legal-political function.

We are told that—even if they offer no other form of redress—truth commissions and other testimonial venues are necessary because trauma victims must tell their stories, that through narrative they create a memorial to suffering, that confession can redeem even the perpetrators. We are told that storytelling can bind the community, and thus serve as a force for healing, moving us past atrocity and into a healthy future. Institutions in which victims can speak "affir[m] the value of 'narrative' as well as of 'forensic' forms of truth."[3] "Narrative truth" contributes to "the process of reconciliation by giving voice to individual subjective experiences."[4]

Victims have a "right" to "tell their own stories," the "right of framing them from their own perspectives and being recognized as legitimate
sources of truth with claims to rights and justice."[5] Allowing victims to
tell their own stories offers them relief, we are told, even in the absence of
other forms of redress. Thomas Buergenthal, a judge on the International
Court of Justice and former member of the El Salvador Truth Commission, describes the victims' "silence and pent-up anger" before "finally,
someone listened to them." Their testimony produced "a record of what
they had endured." But "the mere act of telling what had happened was
[also] a healing emotional release."[6]

If the healing power of testimony seems to offer narrative closure for victims, it also offers narrative closure for society as a whole. Through "'narrative' . . . truth," nations can achieve "reconciliation, national healing, and
moral reconstruction."[7] Indeed, Homi Bhabha argues, such narrative is not
only an individual human right, whose exercise is necessary to the preven-
tion of further atrocity, but essential to our more general humanity:

> The right to narrate is . . . a metaphor for the fundamental human
> interest in freedom itself, the right to be heard, to be recognized and
> represented. . . . When you fail to protect the right to narrate you are in
> danger of filling the silence with sirens, megaphones, hectoring voices
> carried by loudspeakers from podiums of great height over people
> who shrink into indistinguishable masses. Once we have allowed such
> "walls of silence" to be built in our midsts and our minds, . . . we are
> compelled to return to the silent killing fields of the past and the pres-
> ent—be it Colonisation, Apartheid, the Holocaust, or Vietnam, Pal-
> estine, Afghanistan, South Africa, Rwanda, Kosovo—to try and give
> voice to those who were silenced.[8]

What lies behind claims about the value of post-atrocity narration are a set
of views influenced by ancient religious ideas about redemption through
confession and memorial, more modern political discourses of rights and
medical discourses of healing, as well as a view—borrowed from literary
and narrative theory of the past decades—that narrative ("subjective") truth
has a special value. These views were promulgated most directly by what
became known in the 1980s as the "law and literature movement," with
its 1990s offshoot, the "legal storytelling movement." These movements
entered into dialogue with less narrowly legal and more global sub-disci-
plines and theoretical movements: holocaust studies, with its discussion of
the nature and limits of the representation of atrocity and the paradoxes
of memorial; feminist criticism and critical race theory, with their discussion of the liberating force of counter-hegemonic narrative; Latin American
"testimonio" and trauma studies, with their discussion of the importance of
bearing witness and the curative power of truth. Under this optic, not only
could victim narratives be viewed as potentially subject to the interpretive

tools of literary criticism, but the narration of atrocity could also be seen as a good in itself, offering its own special form of redress through catharsis and of rectification through the truths of storytelling. There are many reasons for the proliferation of testimonial venues, not least the institutionalization of human rights in the late twentieth century. But this proliferation also owes something to the conversion of studies of legal and witness testimony into a storytelling imperative.

How we got here can be best understood by stepping back for a moment and looking at the intertwined histories of modern literature and modern rights, histories that are (as I will suggest) inextricably linked from the eighteenth century onward. Understanding these linked histories may help us not only to contextualize contemporary claims about the function of narrative in the representation of human rights abuses, but also to look critically at some of their strongest assumptions. I offer what follows not as a final word, but more in the spirit of a theory or set of hypotheses: a template for further exploration of, first, the mutually imbricated histories of literature and human rights and, second, the past decades' focus on narrative as a kind of post-atrocity remedy—the exercise of a fundamental right in the service of memory, truth, and healing.

THE EMERGENCE OF "LITERATURE" AND "RIGHTS"

Historiographic work of the past few decades has given us a better understanding of the genealogy of the modern concept of literature, which arguably achieved a recognizable modern shape only in the later eighteenth century. While the distinction between poetry (the making of imaginary stories) and history (the making of true stories) reaches back, of course, to the ancients, there was, until the later eighteenth century, as yet no inclusive class of works of imaginative literature distinct from other kinds of works. For sixteenth- or seventeenth-century writers, the term "literature" meant either the quality of being well-read (something like what we mean by "learning"), the capacity to read well (something like what we mean by "literacy"), or the collection of works representing learning—a broadly inclusive category comprehending, essentially, all human knowledge in written form. Jean de La Bruyère, for instance (writing c.1688), praises those who have "wit and pleasing literature."[9] Sir Francis Bacon lauds James I for being "learned in all literature and erudition, divine and human," possessing a conjunction as much of "divine and sacred literature as of profane and human."[10]

By some time in the eighteenth century, however, the term had come to refer to a narrower category of "polite letters," privileging classical texts (and those modeled on them) and segregating works worthy of preservation from the mass of cheap ephemera being circulated by the popular press: "literature" was opposed to the "whole heaps of trash" to be found in the ordinary booksellers' shops.[11] By the turn of the eighteenth century, the modern usage had (largely) emerged, in which fictionality takes a central place. The histories of literature produced in the last decades of the eighteenth century (*Les Siècles de littérature française* [1772], *Storia della letteratura italiana* [1772], Herder's *Über die neuere deutsche Literatur* [1767]) treat poetry, drama, and (notably) novels as a unique class—the works that define the national spirit.[12] "Literature" had become, primarily, the worthiest works of the vernacular *imagination*. Like art, literature was an object of "aesthetics" (a term first emerging during this period): to be set apart from the more prosaic works of science and of the popular press. Simultaneously (and, in a sense, constitutively), literary criticism was born in the coffeehouses and the news press, confirming the identity of "literature," legitimizing such new (or relatively new) genres as the novel, creating doctrines of literary judgment, and establishing the canon of works through which a national literature could recognize itself. From the vernacular criticism of the coffeehouse and news press, professional literary study was to emerge in the nineteenth century.

At the same time, the concept of "rights" was becoming central to political discourse. "Natural rights" in European political and legal theory can be traced back at least to the twelfth century, when various theorists began to develop the idea out of Roman natural law principles.[13] And modern notions of subjective natural and inalienable rights were, in a sense, fully formed in seventeenth-century political theory (for instance in Grotius, Hobbes, and Locke). But until the later eighteenth century, "rights" still tended to refer to specific privileges (for instance those specified in the *Magna Carta* or the English Bill of Rights). For Samuel Johnson, a "right" is a "just claim," "Property," "interest," "Power," "prerogative" (i.e. . powers specifically granted by law).[14]

That the modern concept of rights—rights possessed innately by virtue of one's humanity, inhering in the individual, grounded in reason and nature, neither granted by nor capable of obliteration by any earthly power—emerged in the late eighteenth century is, of course, a familiar story: usually told through such major political manifestos and programs as the Declaration of the Rights of Man and Citizen or the American Bill of Rights, or philosophical works like Thomas Paine's *The Rights of Man*. However, in the absence of a *discursive* history of rights—a history tracing the language of rights and its vicissitudes in the byways of the popular press and imaginative literature—it is hard to see fully the political, ethical, and—at the same time—*personal* purchase that rights talk gained in the last decades of the eighteenth century. "Say to yourself often," commanded the *Encyclopédie* article on "Natural Right": "I am a man, and I have no other truly inalienable natural rights than those of humanity."[15] The discourse of rights certainly did not displace the various other political vocabularies available to eighteenth-century writers and orators (duty, virtue, obligation to the public good). But its cultural force can be gauged by such parodies as Thomas Taylor's *Vindication of the Rights of Brutes* (1792) (a sign of the conventionality of the genre). ("The next stage of that irradiation which our enlighteners are pouring in upon us," wrote Hannah More derisively, "will produce grave descants on the *rights of children*.")[16]

As important, the discourse of rights was transformed, in the late eighteenth century, by its fusion with various doctrines of humanitarianism. Humanitarianism as a philosophical doctrine had been developing since the late seventeenth century, in arguments for the natural benevolence of humankind–as a humanist counter-discourse to Hobbesian arguments about the depravity of human nature. But, like rights, it became a part of popular discourse only in the later eighteenth century, with the absorption of moral theories of natural benevolence (propounded by such thinkers as the Earl of Shaftesbury and Francis Hutcheson), in reaction, in part, to various mechanistic theories of power as right, which accompanied the beginnings of industrialization.[17] Human beings were naturally driven by "irresistible compassion" to relieve the suffering of others. Natural human compassion gave rise to an equally natural human moral obligation: a duty to aid those whom one perceived to be in distress. "Nature hath implanted in our breasts a love of others," wrote Thomas Jefferson, "a sense of duty to them, a moral instinct, in short, which prompts us irresistibly to feel and to succor their distresses."[18]

The grounding of humanitarian principles in rights, and of rights in humanitarian principles, fused the sentimental with a political program. "The rights of man" were humane principles, entailing not just claims but *obligations*, and these not only toward the ordinary run of humanity but toward slaves, the poor, the young, primitives, eventually criminals, and various and sundry other downtrodden persons. Reading through Thomas Paine's *The Rights of Man* (1791–1792) or Mary Wollstonecraft's *Vindication of the Rights of Woman* (1792) suggests the extent to which humanitarian language—the language of compassion, pity, the succor of distress—inflected rights discourse. Rights and the humanitarian duty to aid were, in a sense, two sides of the very definition of what it was to be human: one had rights by virtue of one's humanity (as the *Encyclopédie* article proclaimed); and it was one's sense of obligation to another's suffering that proved one human ("humane," in the spelling that did not yet, in the eighteenth century, distinguish between species identity and moral identity).

The simultaneous emergence of the modern concept of "literature" and the modern concept of "rights" in popular discourse suggests a historical intersection between literature and human rights that I would like, here, to attempt to untangle. The most conventional account of this intersection might look at literary discourses as agents of rights talk, noting that certain texts we would consider "literary" were crucial vehicles for galvanizing the imagination of the newly constituted "public" in the eighteenth century, thus coming to serve as a foundation for modern rights claims (as well as proving symptomatic of tensions in the era's notion of rights). Another approach might focus on the *political* writings most central to the formulation of "rights" in the eighteenth century (rights treatises, public speeches, and the pamphlet literature that ultimately disseminated and normalized the rhetoric of rights), noting the extent to which the discourse developed in political writings was re-imagined through literary aesthetics and narrative. In the late eighteenth century, of course, the literary had not yet been segregated from the "scientific": the aesthetic was mingled with the political, the narrative with the discursive, fiction with non-fiction. Rights treatises could be indistinguishable from what we would think of as literary genres: Simon-Nicolas-Henri Linguet's *Mémoires sur la Bastille* (1783) or Count Mirabeau's *Des Lettres de cachet et des prisons d'Etat* (1778) or the scandalous *Les Fastes de Louis XV* (1782).[19] Scripture, history, and literary sources could all serve as evidence. In *The Social Contract: Or Principles of Political Right* (1762), for instance, Rousseau can cite Genesis, *The Odyssey*, and *Robinson Crusoe*, all within a few sentences of one another, as authorities on the nature of sovereignty.[20] In her *Vindication of the Rights of Woman*, Wollstonecraft can argue with Milton, Pope, Rousseau's portrait of Sophia in *Émile*, and "Moses' poetical story" of Adam and Eve over the capacity of women (as rational creatures) to be proper rights-bearers.[21] The critical analysis of narrative embedded in political treatises on rights was inseparable from the political claims of those treatises. It has often been noted that literary and legal rhetoric were once inseparable (see, e.g., Ferguson), and the same can be said for the rhetoric of rights. But "literature" and "rights" (unlike law) were also bound through their simultaneous modern institutional crystallization. It is on this relationship that I would like to focus.

EMPOWERING AND TRANSCENDING BOURGEOIS COMMERCE

Raymond Williams speculatively identified the transformation of the concept of "literature" with several concomitant material and institutional transformations: the passing of aristocratic authority and the rise of the bourgeoisie; the growth of print capitalism; changes in literacy; the development of ideologies of the nation (and hence of national literatures); and the professionalization of criticism. He argued that the creation of the modern category "literature" (imaginative, creative, and above all *human*) was a reaction to the specialization and mechanization of modern conditions of wage labor in industrial capitalism. Literature came to represent "truth" and "beauty" by way of negative contrast with "science" and "society," technical skill, "discursive" and "factual" writing, "popular" writing, and "mass" culture. Criticism became the central "humane" activity.[22]

   Williams's brief speculation on the production of "literature" as a modern category has been taken up and vigorously examined, over the past decade or so, in various studies of literary culture in the eighteenth and nineteenth centuries.[23] While some of these studies refine his claims or challenge particular points, his broader speculations essentially stand. These have been extended into various explorations of the relationship between the conceptual transformation of "literature" and a number of phenomena (largely situated in the eighteenth century): the production of the commercial system of letters; the development of the modern system of authors and readers (and the transformation, in the eighteenth century, of the concept of the "author" itself through the development of author copyright); the development of the modern vernacular literary canon as the "cultural capital of the bourgeoisie"; the increased prominence and power of women writers and readers; the rise of the bourgeois "public sphere"; the final centralization of national vernaculars and vernacular literatures and their use in the production of ideologies of the nation; the rise of journalistic and (eventually) professional literary criticism; and the institutionalization of vernacular literary study (all of these, of course, crucial to understanding the historical identity of contemporary literary study).

While there is an extensive critical literature on the development of the concept of rights in seventeenth- and eighteenth-century political theory, only recently has attention been paid to the underlying ideological framework of rights in the eighteenth century and its broader cultural valence: its relation to other cultural and ideological developments during the period; its discursive and rhetorical trajectories; its historical unconscious.[24] There are, however, certain recurrent themes that emerge from discussions of the modern idea of "rights" and that identify the discourse of rights with a set of related values and phenomena (controversially, in some cases, but nonetheless with a good deal of consistency): the new-found political power of the bourgeoisie; the rise of the "bourgeois public sphere" and of Enlightenment public culture; the concomitant modern separation of public from private; the increased role of ideologies of individual freedom (often accompanied by a liberal, contractarian paradigm); the development of liberal political and economic institutions, accompanying the development of mercantilism into laissez-faire industrial capitalism; the development of ideologies of benevolence based in the cult of "sympathy"; philosophical universalism accompanied (paradoxically) by political nationalism.

Identified with all of these, "literature" and "rights," at the same time, contributed importantly to each other's institutional evolution. The development of the idea of rights liberated writers from either aristocratic patronage or the market. Authors became the "natural proprietors" of their works (in the words of Jean-François de La Harpe, addressing the French National Assembly in 1790), with "natural" and "exclusive" rights in them.[25] At the same time, it liberated readers: for the concept of rights led to vernacular education for the working classes. Both author copyright and the spread of vernacular reading were essential to the reconstitution of "literature" as a category. At the same time, the development of the genres that became "literature" (and of a self-conscious "literary" public) created both the material and ideological conditions necessary to the discourse of rights, through the simultaneous stimulation of the print trade that disseminated the rights treatises and the development of a bourgeois reading public receptive to (and capable of financing) them.

If literature and rights were each essential to each other's institutional foundation, they also shared an ideological framework and a set of social functions that kept them bound in less obvious but no less important ways. The French Revolution (framed as a "rights" revolution) was explicitly a project for the liberation of the bourgeoisie from aristocratic tyranny, but rights discourse generally directed itself toward the political and social empowerment of an already commercially empowered population. At the same time, rights discourse helped internalize bourgeois commercial values, casting as innate those powers most necessary to a thriving market, unfettered by aristocratic or government privilege: the right to property; freedom from searches and seizures (necessary to the protection of property); freedom of religion (long associated, in Britain, with the merchant dissenters); equality of political representation; and equality under the law (equality, that is, by reference to the aristocracy, though not the un-propertied, slaves, or women). Rights were allied with commerce: Thomas Paine sang the virtues of commerce and understood the necessity of rights to what he saw as a properly functioning market.[26] The conception of freedom embedded in rights discourse (freedom from encroachment by the state) served the constitution of a power base independent of the feudal allocation of political, material, and cultural goods: freedom meant freedom to construct an alternative, non-aristocratic, commercial sphere of political and cultural control.

The burgeoning ideology of rights, however, not only drew on and served the liberation of the marketplace. At the same time, paradoxically, it depended for its legitimation (and hence the legitimation of the bourgeois rights-bearer) on ideas of aristocratic virtue, ostensibly autonomous from market values. "Rights," then, at once promised liberation from aristocratic privilege and cast a mantle of aristocratic dignity over their beneficiaries. Rights were "inalienable" and "sacred," essential to human dignity. Rhetorically (though not actually) liberated from property in the American context, rights served the "pursuit of happiness"—a goal apparently dissociated from the pursuit of riches and uniting the private and the public good. Eminence could be achieved through merit rather than birth, but was also (officially, at least) to be dissociated from commercial power. At the same time, rights served as a stay against the numerical power of the rabble. They granted their bearers freedom from the tyranny of the dangerous democratic majority (who might otherwise vote away the commercial freedoms and property privileges that protected that aristocratic dignity).

"Literature," similarly, as a modern formation, found its origin in the transfer of power and authority from the aristocracy to the commercial sphere, while at the same time suppressing its commercial foundations. In the literary sphere, the growth of bourgeois literacy and the concomitant development of print capitalism helped contribute to the displacement of aristocratic patronage by market-based public patronage. According to Williams and those who have followed him, the birth of modern "literature" (along with the birth of "art" in the modern sense) thus represented a bourgeois encroachment on aristocratic institutions, constituting a domain for non-aristocratic cultural production, cultural consumption, and cultural judgment.

As with "rights," however, the new aesthetic ideologies depended not only on the subjection of literature to the marketplace but also on the idea that it was autonomous from the market. The institutions through which literature secured its place reinforced this idea: literary criticism, the anthologizing of vernacular classics, and vernacular literary study all embraced a set of regulatory norms ("taste" and "judgment") that protected them from identification with the marketplace alone. This attempt to save literature from the taint of the marketplace produced the distinction between the productions of Grub Street (the imaginary territory of the new class of commercial literary hacks and other writers for hire) and "polite letters" (the territory of the bourgeoisie, aspiring to nobility as a way of distinguishing itself from Grub Street). The right to determine what constituted "polite letters" was an aristocratic-style privilege possessed not by the pamphlet-reading masses but by those of taste and judgment.

In this sense, literature was parallel to rights in its conceptual work: at once liberating culture from the monopoly of the aristocratic classes and allowing literature's new possessors to aspire to the aristocratic dignity and privileges associated with the realm of polite letters. Constructed in the capitalist culture market, "literature" emerged as a reaction to the degradations of that market. To draw on Pierre Bourdieu's framework, literature was created out of the opposition between exchange value and aesthetic value: "literature" as a category created a "field of restricted cultural production" opposing itself to "the field of large-scale cultural production" in order to create a new form of capital—cultural capital—autonomous from mass buying power. This cultural capital depended on an ideology of non-commercial merit similar to that in the sphere of rights. The modern "author" was, by definition, one who rose to prominence solely on his or (increasingly, her) own worth. The author could be rewarded by literary property for being a "genius" above the concerns of property.

THE TRANSCENDENT HUMAN: BEYOND UTILITY AND HISTORY

If print capitalism and bourgeois literacy were, in part, responsible for the creation of the modern category "literature," they also helped disseminate ideas about rights. It is by now a commonplace that the eighteenth century gave birth to a newly commercial bourgeois "public sphere" whose aesthetic judgment expressed itself both in such collective spaces as the coffeehouse and the news press and through the market. Here, "rights" and "literature" converged. Whether or not we are to believe Jürgen Habermas's claim that print and literacy were crucial to the rise of a newly "public" form of discourse with a particular set of political consequences, both "literature" and "rights" found their home in the treatises and pamphlets and imaginative genres that addressed themselves to "the public." Addressing this "public," theorists of rights cast themselves as serving "the public good" and identified themselves with a set of values insistently reiterated in the "public-minded" literature of the period: rationality, impartiality, politeness, public transparency, merit-based judgment. At the same time, "literature" identified itself with the discursive values of "public-minded" letters. Like rights, literature provided for polite, rational discourse. It was the product of merit-based participation, a vehicle for the (normatively male) writer's public visibility through his very invisibility (his autonomy from the trappings of rank and artificial power). It was a basis for an imaginary community of like-minded readers. As Jonathan Kramnick writes, the literary "public" stood for "the polite stratum of educated readers hovering above the toiling masses of vulgar illiterates," even if, in actuality, the consumers of "literature" and of pamphlet material on rights were often neither particularly literate nor particularly polite.[27]

Both "literature" and "rights," then, were stimulated by the concept of the "public": created simultaneously in the coffeehouses, clubs, and pamphlet literature (where the canon of letters was being constructed and the new ideology of rights propagated). But they were also to be consumed in private—ideally, in the private spaces of the bourgeois home—and to reproduce the intimate experiences of the private individual. Both rights and literature were associational (crucial to serving and constituting the idea of a collective public). And they were things that permitted the rights-bearer, literary producer, and literary consumer autonomy from a coercive collective sphere. Both "literature" and "rights" as concepts held to the belief in the liberating and redemptive power of public language (in the form of great works and revolutionary declarations)—a belief learned from the experience of print-based fame and print-produced revolution. But they also drew on and shaped crucial notions of freedom, autonomy, and privacy. For both literature and rights, national identity was founded, paradoxically, on the universality of the human. The universalist French Declaration of the Rights of Man and Citizen grounded national sovereignty (centered in "the Nation") in the "natural, inalienable, and sacred rights of man" (*Les declarations* 11), just as eighteenth-century anthologies and literary histories grounded claims for the coherence and superiority of a national literature in the "Universal Genius" of its greatest writers.[28]

At the same time, while contributing to crucial ideas about nation, empire, and universal humanity, the shared anti-utilitarian ideology of literature and rights meant that both could be seen as transcending politics in the vulgar sense. Literary content might be explicitly political, offering (for instance) a committedly partisan account of the French Revolution or the Napoleonic wars. But, as the *concept* of literature took shape—identifying enduring works of the human imagination as its normative product (with poetry, that most abstract and airy and distinctly un-useful form of humane pleasure, at its center)[29]—it began to be seen as necessarily transcending the politics of the present for a more abstract and enduring kind of ethics, largely indistinguishable from the precepts of humanitarianism. "Polite letters" was, at the same time, "humane letters."[30] Literature was, in this sense, representative of the aesthetic sphere more generally, ideally autonomous and (in Kant's crucial formulation) disinterested, even while it played a central role in shaping public attitudes toward political questions.[31] Schiller's *Letters on the Aesthetic Education of Man* is, arguably, paradigmatic here. For Schiller, precisely because art is disinterested (autonomous from the world of getting and spending), it is the thing that allows one to realize one's humanity—one's connection to a higher and more universal humanity than that of the everyday (commercial) world. Art redeems one from modern means–end utilitarianism, relieving one from the burden of competition and the praxis of life and preserving, in their ideal forms, such things as joy, truth, solidarity, and humanity. As Peter Bürger puts it, "The citizen who, in everyday life has been reduced to a partial function (means–ends activity) can be discovered in art as 'human being.'"[32]

Paradoxically, rights too began to be seen as distinct from the interestedness of politics, in the nineteenth century increasingly taking both their philosophical and legal character from their opposition to utilitarian policy arguments (as they continue to do today).[33] They were fundamental, neutral, general, disinterested, non-means-driven, autonomous from the particularities of exchange. They allowed you to realize your humanity— a higher and more universal humanity than that of the particular political sphere. As with art (for Schiller), it was through "the rights of man" that the citizen could become a "human being," without being thrust into the exigencies of the public sphere. It is from this division that the claim arose (common until perhaps the end of the twentieth century) that rights were *not* political, and indeed that their essential identity was their *distinctness* from politics. In this sense, while rights came to represent a variety of institutionalized legal norms—fought over in the political sphere—they also represented something of the aesthetic end of the legal: they were the beautiful truths (truths higher than the ordinary particulars of history) toward which politics might strive but which politics could never perfectly achieve.

To live in literature, or to experience oneself as the bearer of rights, then, was to rediscover one's humanity, apart from the world of commerce and politics. The language of the "human" embedded in both "literature" and "rights" helped to reinforce this universalist humanism, as well as to distance both domains still further from mechanistic notions of competition in the political, economic, or cultural spheres. Literature was to become the crowning discipline of the "humanities." "Rights" were "the rights of man," on their way to becoming "human rights." What distinguished literature from other kinds of writing was that literature could unite one with the rest of humanity, teaching not the particular but the higher and more universal human values embedded in natural sentiment, far from the brutalities of the market. What distinguished rights from other kinds of political claims is that they were based in universal human nature, not in political particulars, and could thus draw on moral claims cognizable through natural reason and sentiment.

Central to the humanist ideology underwriting both literature and rights were the explicitly "humanitarian" discourses that (as we have seen) were beginning to emerge at the end of the eighteenth century. These brought literary narrative into the service of rights claims and, in a sense, also brought rights into the service of literature by extending literature's humanizing role. Humanitarianism was grounded not only in a theory of natural human goodness, but also in theories of compassion that relied on a model of individual human sympathy through identification with the sufferer. This was an idea imported from aesthetics and literary theory, most particularly eighteenth-century interpretations of Aristotelian catharsis as a theory not of emotional purgation but of emotion-based social union through narrative identification. Pity, generated by narrative, was to serve as a mechanism for uniting humanity and stimulating charitable action through the sentimental bond. As Thomas Laqueur has shown (in his suggestive exploration of the "humanitarian narrative" of the late eighteenth century), humanitarianism was founded in notions of the narrative power of the suffering human body as the basis for moral response.

The discourse of rights, accompanied by the language of moral obligation, served as an imperative version of the lessons of sympathy that literature taught. Writing in 1772, Benjamin Franklin expressed the idea that narrative demands sympathetic response, referring to the "natural compassion to . . . Fellow-Creatures" that brings "Tears at the Sight of an Object of Charity, who by a bear [sic] Relation of his Circumstances" seems "to demand the Assistance of those about him."[34] Sympathetic identification was understood to be responsive to images, but still more to *stories* of suffering, that is, to visual, but still more to *narrative* stimuli, the kind of narrative stimuli that eighteenth-century culture produced in abundance: in the autopsy reports that Laqueur describes (unlike their predecessors, expanded into pathos-rendering narrative); in non-fiction narrative accounts of the period; but above all in "literature." That is, humanitarianism was a fundamentally narrative, or literary, ideology: the narratives of suffering central to literature taught one how to be human, and ultimately to rise above the dehumanizing forces of modernity.

The transformation of "natural rights" and "the rights of man" into "human rights" over the course of the nineteenth century[35] merely confirmed what was implicit in the development of late eighteenth-century rights discourse: rights were, in a world of commodity exchange, a desperate protection of the sacredness of the human. The conjoined discourse of rights and humanitarianism, then, continued to serve a function similar to that of literature. As a number of critics have argued, what dominated both the popular idea of literature and its institutional identity throughout the nineteenth century were grand visions of its humanizing role—very much a moral role, but a role that understood literature as a vehicle for uniting the classes in the harmonies of a shared culture.[36] As a result, literature (and its "true-narrative" offshoots) became the central vehicle for the great humanitarian and rights movements of the nineteenth century (one need only think of *Les Misérables* or *Uncle Tom's Cabin*). This was in part because its pleasure-value suited it to the task of popularizing humanitarian ideas, but also because its institutional ideology was harmonious with that of nineteenth-century humanitarian and rights talk: aiming to transcend both law and politics with an ideal form of justice, and sheltered from the depredations of utility or the degradations of mass culture.[37]

THE SUFFERER'S VOICE AND THE CULTURE OF TESTIMONY

Humane letters and human rights effectively preserved this core identity throughout the nineteenth and twentieth centuries, despite what was arguably an eclipse of the rights paradigm by a social engineering paradigm in the twentieth century, and despite the defiantly *engagé* stance of literary theory in much of the second half of the twentieth century. What is striking is the fact that, in the past few decades, the unconscious of this parallel formation has become manifest in the many claims for the power of narrative in the service of rights. Rights and literature grew up together, serving similar functions and united by a shared ideology. Now—in claims for the necessity of witness storytelling in public venues—the humanist literary can underwrite the human in human rights, overriding narratives of power struggle with narratives of suffering.

While one would not wish to draw too artificial a link between the conjoined ideological development of literature and rights and the contemporary deployment of narrative in the service of rights, there are distinct echoes. In today's truth commissions and tribunals, we have a reiteration of the belief in the rationality of the public sphere and its ability to transcend the chaos and violence of the rabble. We have a reiteration of the notion that private and individual traumatic experience must be brought into the public light. We have a reiteration of the view that the authentic narrative voice of the victim both allows the victim the relief of being heard and creates moral demands, which, speaking to the natural compassion of the audience, can bring about a general societal conversion. We have a belief that the victim's voice can be deployed in the service of a kind of ongoing catharsis that might restore social harmony. As in the eighteenth century, narrative is seen as the foundation for responsive action and social union that can transcend the alienation of modernity and return us to the human. Shared suffering, understood through narrative, reminds us of our common humanity and thus can redeem us from social trauma.

The tribunals and commissions are largely anti-utilitarian: treating the individual as more sacred than the good of the greatest number; less about what they can achieve than about the human dignity for which they stand. As in the eighteenth century, the redemptive humanism of narrative here is, like human beings themselves, an end in itself. Narratives of suffering are thus seen as sufficient to the righting of wrongs, whatever their consequences. In the aristocratic rejection of the eye-for-an-eye exchange entailed in punishment, given up for a kind of *noblesse oblige* grace (if you tell the truth, we may pardon you), there is a subtle reiteration of the counter-commercial, pseudo-aristocratic paradigms of eighteenth-century literature and rights, even while the institutions that offer such grace are technocratic machines offering their products (narratives of atrocity) to the consumers of sensationalist media.

Why now? It has been suggested that the proliferation of truth commissions and tribunals is a response to a moment of crisis for the law, produced by a sense of law's groundlessness, its radical contingency, especially when translated into the sphere of the super-state, with its never-fully-legitimized authority. In this context, the victim is responsible for providing an unquestionable ground for the exercise of legal power, and that ground is located in the performance of suffering. Suffering serves to authenticate a set of newly created and still-somewhat-tenuous legal claims in the domain of human rights (tenuous because difficult to legitimize, difficult to prove, and difficult to redress). The truth commissions and tribunals share a desire for a form of authenticity represented through the human voice: the voice of the victim offers a kind of truth that documentary evidence, reports, legal determinations cannot provide. Human rights creates a memorial—a sort of Church built on the "Word"—out of speech and the voice (with distinctly religious overtones: the law offers grace through a penitential ritual).

However, one might instead argue that, paradoxically, narratives of suffering also seem to offer renewed legitimacy to both literature and rights as institutions. Arguably, both literature and rights were, by the late twentieth century, in crisis, in part because the paradigms that originally defined them seemed exhausted. For literary study, one might see the crisis as arising from the obsolescence of the central historical function of literature: the maintenance of cultural legitimation independent of the aristocracy but unsullied by commerce. The essentially nation-based definition of culture (culture as national, public property, built on individual intellectual property) began to dissolve. "Culture," rather than serving as locale of conservationist consensus, could become a high-profile site of conflict—in, for instance, the "canon wars." The very definition of "literature" (as aesthetic, primarily imaginative writing) came under siege, as literary critics looked to "non-literary" texts (primarily philosophy and "social texts" in the 1970s and 1980s, primarily political, cultural, and legal texts in the 1990s and beyond). The aesthetic itself came under attack. In this context, turning toward non-literary texts was paradoxically an attempt to revitalize literature as a discipline by reaching past its decadence toward its foundations. Embracing rights—the most successful global moral discourse of the last half century—it could reassert its special role as protector of the human against the depredations of the utilitarian calculus.

As for human rights, its historical autonomy from mechanisms of exchange was challenged by its very institutional success in the late twentieth century. Rights became part of the technologies of the modern administrative state and super-state, not merely pure principles through which we recognize our humanity, or even general constitutional provisions or items of political exchange, but autonomous institutional machines (with staffs, big budgets, and acronyms): the UN Human Rights Council, the Human Rights Committee, Human Rights Watch (and so on). One might think of late twentieth-century rights culture, then, as recapitulating the original double move of eighteenth-century rights culture. On the one hand, in its labor- and capital-intensive institutionalization, it fully developed the latent promise of its free-trade, capitalist origins. On the other hand, in reaction to the dehumanizing features of such a development, it attempted to recapture the original humanitarian paradigm on which it was founded in the eighteenth century by reclaiming a narrative morality based in compassion, pity, and an aesthetics of suffering. The more technologized the institution of rights became, the more its proponents had to call on narrative and aesthetic values, recalling the "human" that would otherwise seem to be slipping away. The spectacularization of atrocity through the narration of suffering became a mechanism whereby rights culture could distance itself from its very institutional success and reclaim its humane origins. Thus, strangely, the culture of rights picked up some of the discarded humanism and aestheticism of literary study—a humanist aestheticism that was, paradoxically, underwritten by literary criticism's interventions into human rights narrative.

In this sense, however different the reasons for the narrative turn in human rights and the turn toward human rights in literary study, they are both institutionally redemptive projects. By channeling rights culture, literary critics not only give voice to the silenced victims of atrocity. They also reclaim literary study's foundering political role and thus redeem themselves from the terrors of insignificance. While human rights is busy redeeming the injustices of violence and history, it can, at the same time, redeem literary criticism from the guilt of aesthetic detachment. By channeling literary discourses, human rights theorists and institutional actors not only oppose the blunt machinery of the law (designed to camouflage its in-built injustices) with the truths of the victims' stories. They also reclaim the aesthetic-humanist heritage of rights and thus redeem themselves from the taint of technocratic trade.

There are many forms of idealization at work in the culture of testimony in which both literature and rights participate: idealization of victimhood, of "narrative" or "story" and its healing powers, and—above all—of the sufferer's individuated voice. In his *L'humanité perdue* (*In the Name of Humanity*) (1996), for instance, the French philosopher Alain Finkielkraut offers a critique of late-twentieth-century humanitarian projects and a plea for attending to the individual narrative of suffering. In Finkielkraut's view, the (Marxist and Fascist) ideological critique of sentimental individualism ended up producing the horrors of the twentieth century. Large-scale humanitarianism is an attempt at compensation: "It was in the name of ideology that we once refused to be taken in by suffering. It is in opposition to suffering and all the misery in the world that we now refuse to be taken in by ideology." But the humanitarian embrace of the task of combating suffering merely recapitulates the early twentieth-century ideological depersonalization of the human: "[The humanitarian generation] continues to think ideologically. [It] does not like men—they are too disconcerting—but enjoys taking care of them."[38]

Drawing on Hannah Arendt's critique of the anti-humanistic legal technologies of the modern state (in *The Origins of Totalitarianism* and *Eichmann in Jerusalem*), Finkielkraut denounces the dangerous generalization inherent in humanitarianism, founded on a sentimental idea of the unified "cry" of the suffering: "the rescuer without borders embraces all silent calls of distress, subjecting them to no preliminary cross-examination." In the first half of the twentieth century, "historical reason was used to stifle sentimental reason," explains Finkielkraut. "Now the heart, not history, guides the way, giving emotions their rights once again." "Victims call out in a single voice," he writes derisively, "and that voice does not lie."[39] While he repudiates, then, the simultaneously sentimental and impersonal technologies of twentieth-century humanitarian aid, Finkielkraut also takes an ironic stance toward the eighteenth-century culture of pity, quoting sympathetically Goethe's mocking description of humanitarianism (in 1787): "I must admit that I too consider it true that humanity will finally be victorious, but I also fear that the world will turn into a vast hospital and each of us will become the other's human nurse."[40] He notes Rousseau's sardonic comment on the fact that, while we give in to pity when we see our neighbors' throats cut under our windows, "man has only to put his hands to his ears and argue a little with himself, to prevent nature, which he has shocked within him, from identifying itself with the unfortunate sufferer."[41]

And yet Finkielkraut diverges from Arendt's arguments about the limits of compassion in ways that seem symptomatic of the present culture of testimony. For Arendt, one of the central lessons of the French Revolution was that pity, or the "sentiments of the heart," compelled by the representation of suffering, could inspire only a dangerously lawless humanitarianism.[42] For her, the narrowness of compassion lies precisely in its fixation on the individual story—its inability to see the whole. Compassion (the moral drive behind humanitarianism), she writes in *On Revolution*, "by its very nature, cannot be touched off by the sufferings of a whole class or a people, or, least of all, mankind as a whole." To deal with large-scale suffering, one needs politics rather than narratively induced and individually directed compassion:

> Because compassion abolishes the distance, the worldly space between men where political matters, the whole realm of human affairs, are located, it remains, politically speaking, irrelevant and without consequence. . . . As a rule, it is not compassion which sets out to change worldly conditions in order to ease human suffering, but if it does, it will shun the drawn-out wearisome processes of persuasion, negotiation, and compromise, which are the processes of law and politics, and lend its voice to the suffering itself.[43]

For Finkielkraut, on the other hand, what is dangerous in humanitarian action is its response to a whole class or people. For Finkielkraut, to respond to the class subordinates actual men to abstract humanity: "'Water! Water!'—this primitive cry is what passes for *logos* today, the cry of an undifferentiated mass of humanity." "This generation has turned off the sound on the cries of misery. . . . No need to listen, for the will to live is simple." In other words, rather than worrying (as Arendt does) that compassion produced by individual humanitarian narrative blinds one to the suffering of an entire class, Finkielkraut worries that the large-scale, technologically sophisticated response to the suffering of an entire class blinds one to the particular suffering of the individual. What is wrong, for instance, with the doctors who work for *Médicins sans frontières* is that they are busy trying to save lives:

> The global doctor . . . does not . . . car[e] very much . . . about who the suffering individual is—about his being or his reason for being, the world he wants to build, the causes of his persecution and suffering, the meaning he gives to his history and perhaps to his death. Save lives: that is the global mission of the global doctor. Attending to anonymous people in desperate situations, the humanitarian generation is motivated by principles of caution, not brotherly love.

The humanitarian "is too busy feeding rice to hungry mouths to listen to what these mouths are saying. Words do not concern him. He turns his attention to murdered populations, not to eloquent voices."[44]

Eloquent voices are, of course, precisely what the various truth commissions and tribunals purport to offer their audiences: victims and perpetrators get an opportunity to tell their stories and undergo either healing or the purgation of sin; audiences get to experience the pleasure of sympathetic identification without a concomitant demand for action: the atrocity is over, and sympathy is all that is required. (It is a perplexing by-product of the commissions that, while it is their task precisely to distinguish victim from perpetrator, they tend to blur this line, in the manner of most confessional-conversion modes: when the perpetrator tells his story and undergoes conversion, declares his repentance, reveals his own suffering for what he has done, he can be made one with the victims.) Critics have often complained that the work of both commissions and war crimes tribunals are "merely symbolic" (in their failure to punish the large numbers of people responsible for the atrocities, in their singling out of an exemplary few). But their proponents at the same time claim their symbolic function as their central virtue. Individual narrative becomes, simultaneously, the "telling of one's story" and humanitarian cultural memorial, answering to the recurrent post-holocaust call "never to forget" (in what, to my mind, is a significant undervaluation of forgetting).

Few would wish to stand against truth. And to create a space for victims to tell their stories seems, at the least, harmless enough, and potentially of supreme importance to the tellers. But whether or not post-atrocity narrative in fact serves truth or moral education is an open question. It is not my purpose, here, to reiterate the detailed critique of truth commissions and other testimonial venues that have found their way into the scholarly literature in recent years.[45] But it is worth recalling not only that they can be a poor substitute for prosecution, but also that their performances may not always achieve the authenticity and efficacy they seem to promise. The "unique" narratives of the victims are produced, in part, by the conventions of the tribunal and the demands of performance. And there is no evidence that hearing testimony alters moral choices in the moment of trauma and crisis. Back in 1754, Rousseau recognized the limits of a sense of moral obligation based on narrative stimulus ("Man has only to put his hands to his ears and argue a little with himself."). While elaborating the general arguments of eighteenth-century humanitarianism in his moral theory, Adam Smith (drawing on Hume) similarly saw how ephemeral were sentiments of humanity generated by narratives of catastrophe:

> Let us suppose that the great empire of China, with all its myriads of inhabitants, was suddenly swallowed up by an earthquake, and let us consider how a man of humanity in Europe . . . would be affected upon receiving intelligence of this dreadful calamity. He would, I imagine, first of all, express very strongly his sorrow for the misfortune of that unhappy people. . . . And when all this fine philosophy was over, when all these human sentiments had been once fairly expressed, he would

pursue his business or his pleasure, take his repose or his diversion, with the same ease and tranquility, as if no such accident had happened. . . . If he were to lose his little finger to-morrow, he would not sleep tonight; but . . . he will snore with the most profound security over the ruin of a hundred millions of his brethren.[46]

The epidemic of storytelling that has come to rights culture, and literary theory's implicit claim that it can offer rights a narrative foundation, may indeed be a curative return, one that both mobilizes compassion and serves as an art of healing. But it may be one that—precisely by drawing on the suppressed paradigm at the origins of humanitarian rights—merely offers hysterical repression a ritual expression. It may be a way of focusing on our little fingers at the expense of the global corpus (with its dreary impersonality), or at the expense of getting down to the complicated technical business of saving lives. It may be a sentimental and eviscerated displacement of other kinds of work: the rebuilding of cities and farms; the fixing of broken bodies; the sad policing of still-unquiet violence.

NOTES

1. This essay was originally published in 2005 (in a longer and more extensively annotated version). I have not attempted, here, to incorporate relevant new scholarship (e.g. Lynn Hunt, *Inventing Human Rights* [New York: W.W. Norton, 2007] and Samuel Moyn, *The Last Utopia: Human Rights in History* [Cambridge, MA: Belknap Press, 2010]), or to address the reconsideration of the relationship between aesthetics and politics in recent theory (most notably that of Jacques Rancière: see the essays in Beth Hinderliter et al., eds., *Communities of Sense: Rethinking Aesthetics and Politics* (Durham, NC: Duke University Press, 2009), but hope to do so in further work on these issues.
2. Useful general discussions of truth commissions include Rotberg and Thompson, Hayner, and Phelps.
3. Elizabeth Kiss, "Moral Ambition Within and Beyond Political Constraints: Reflections on Restorative Justice," in *Truth v. Justice: The Morality of Truth Commissions*, edited by Robert I. Rotberg and Dennis Thompson (Princeton, NJ: Princeton University Press, 2000), 70.
4. Alex Boraine, "Truth and Reconciliation in South Africa: The Third Way," in *Truth v. Justice*, ed. Rotberg and Thompson, 152.
5. André Du Toit, "The Moral Foundations of the South African TRC: Truth as Acknowledgment and Justice as Recognition," in *Truth v. Justice*, ed. Rotberg and Thompson, 136.
6. Thomas Buergenthal, "United Nations Truth Commission for El Salvador," *Vanderbilt Journal of Transnational Law* 27, no. 3 (Oct. 1994): 539.
7. Kiss, "Moral Ambition Within and Beyond Political Constraints," 70.
8. Homi K. Bhabha, "Literature and the Right to Narrate," University of Chicago lecture, October 28, 2000: http://www.uchicago.edu/docs/millennium/bhabha/bhabha_a.html (See Bhabha, *The Right to Narrate* [forthcoming]).
9. "Gens d'un bel esprit et d'une agréable littérature"; qtd Paul-Emile Littré, *Dictionnaire de la langue française* (Versailles: Encyclopaedia Britannica France, 1994), 4:3555.

10. Francis Bacon, *The Philosophical Works of Francis Bacon*, ed. John Robertson (Freeport, NY: Libraries Press, 1905), 43.
11. Alexander Pope, ed., *The Works of Shakespeare* (London: Jacob Tonson, 1725), 1: xvi.
12. See Raymond Williams, *Keywords: Vocabulary of Culture and Society*, 2nd ed. (New York: Oxford University Press, 1983), 185; and John Guillory, *Cultural Capital: The Problem of Literary Canon Formation* (Chicago: University of Chicago Press, 1993) who outlines three stages (123): (1) roughly the sixteenth through early eighteenth centuries, in which "literature" is a general term privileging classical texts (with a special subset, "poetry," for imaginative literature; (2) much of the eighteenth century, when "literature" means "polite letters" and now includes writing in the vernacular; and (3) the turn of the eighteenth century, in which "literature" takes on a more restricted sense, indicating (primarily) imaginative writing.
13. See Brian Tierney, *The Idea of Natural Rights: Studies on Natural Rights, Natural Law, and Church Law, 1150–1625* (Atlanta: Scholars Press, 1997), who argues for the twelfth-century origin of subjective, juridical, natural rights; Michel Villey, *La formation de la pensée juridique modern* (Paris: PUF, 2003), who discusses the origin of the idea in such thinkers as Jean Gerson or William of Ockham; and Richard Tuck, *Natural Rights Theories: Their Origin and Development* (Cambridge: Cambridge University Press, 1979), who identifies them as originating in the fourteenth century, and offers a detailed discussion of their seventeenth-century articulation.
14. Samuel Johnson, *A Dictionary of the English Language* (London: J. and P. Knapton et al, 1755).
15. *Encyclopédie, ou Dictionnaire raisonné des sciences, des arts et des métiers* (Paris: Briasson, 1751–1780), 5: 116.
16. Hannah More, *Strictures on the Modern System of Female Education* (London: T. Cadell and W. Davies, 1799), 1: 135.
17. On eighteenth-century doctrines of humanitarianism, see Norman S. Fiering, "Irresistible Compassion: An Aspect of Eighteenth-Century Sympathy and Humanitarianism," *Journal of the History of Ideas* 37, no. 2 (April–June 1976): 195–218 and Thomas L. Haskell, "Capitalism and the Origins of the Humanitarian Sensibility," *American Historical Review* 90, no. 2 (April 1985): 339–61 (Part 1) and 90, no. 3 (June 1985): 547–566 (Part 2). Haskell argues that the origins of the modern humanitarian sensibility lie in capitalist market principles of agency and causation, stimulated by industrialization, which laid a groundwork for humanitarian ideas of moral responsibility for social ills.
18. Thomas Jefferson, *The Writings of Thomas Jefferson*, ed. Andrew Lipscomb and Albert Ellery Bergh (Washington, DC: Thomas Jefferson Memorial Association, 1904), 14: 141.
19. See Robert Darnton, *The Literary Underground of the Old Regime* (Cambridge, MA: Harvard University Press, 1982), 140–147.
20. Jean-Jacques Rousseau, *On the Social Contract with Geneva Manuscript and Political Economy*, ed. Roger D. Masters, trans. Judith R. Masters (New York: St. Martin's Press, 1978), 48.
21. Mary Wollstonecraft, *Vindication of the Rights of Woman*, ed. Miriam Brody Kramnick (Middlesex: Penguin, 1982), 101–102, 107, 109.
22. Raymond Williams, *Marxism and Literature* (Oxford: Oxford University Press, 1977), 51.
23. John Guillory, for instance, has explored the place of "literature" as the "cultural capital of the bourgeoisie" in the broad history of literary canon formation. Jonathan Brody Kramnick looks at the development of the English

canon, the turn from amateur to professional criticism, the origins of modern literary study in the rise of literary expertise, the rise of the national literary tradition, and the separation of commercial from aesthetic value, in the first three-quarters of the eighteenth century.

24. In addition to Hunt's and Moyn's recent work, see Luc Ferry and Alain Renaut, *Philosophie politique: Des droits de l'homme à l'idée républicaine* (Paris: Presses Universitaires de France, 1985); Michael J. Lacey and Knud Haakonssen, eds., *A Culture of Rights: The Bill of Rights in Philosophy, Politics, and Law 1791–1991* (Cambridge: Cambridge University Press, 1991); and Costas Douzinas, *The End of Human Rights: Critical Legal Thought at the Turn of the Century* (Oxford: Hart, 2000).

25. Jean de La Harpe, *Adresse des auteurs dramatiques a l'assemblé nationale, Prononcée par M. de la Harpe, dans la Séance du mardi soir 24 Août* (Paris: n.p., 1790), 30.

26. Thomas Paine, *Thomas Paine Reader*, ed. Michael Foot and Isaac Kramnick (Middlesex: Penguin Books, 1987), 309–313, 233–234.

27. Jonathan Brody Kramnick, *Making the English Canon: Print-Capitalism and the Cultural Past, 1700–1770* (Cambridge: Cambridge University Press, 1998), 7.

28. For the literary association of universality and nationhood, see, e.g., Catharine Trotter's dedication to *The Unhappy Penitent* on Dryden as "The most Universal Genius this Nation ever bred." And see the discussion in Benedict Anderson, *Imagined Communities: Reflections on the Origin and Spread of Nationalism* (London: Verso, 1991).

29. See the discussion in Guillory, *Cultural Capital*, 117 (and generally his discussion of Grey's "Elegy").

30. According to the *Oxford English Dictionary*, the first use of the phrase "humane letters" in the modern sense is only in 1746, followed (in English usage) by the neo-Latin *"litterae humaniores"* in 1747 (both modeled after the somewhat earlier French *lettres humaines*).

31. The broader and more general creation during the period of "aesthetics"— an autonomous aesthetic realm, distinct from the economically or socially "useful"—has been discussed extensively, most notably by Peter Bürger in *The Theory of the Avant-Garde*, trans. Michael Shaw (Minneapolis: University of Minnesota Press, 1984) and Pierre Bourdieu in *The Field of Cultural Production: Essays on Art and Literature*, ed. Randal Johnson (Cambridge: Polity Press, 1993) and *Distinction: A Social Critique of the Judgement of Taste*, trans. Richard Nice (Cambridge, MA: Harvard University Press, 1984). As Bürger puts it, art could become the realm of non-purposive creation and disinterested pleasure, opposed to the life of society, to be ordered rationally, in strict adaptation to definable ends (42).

32. Bürger, *Theory of the Avant-Garde*, 48, and see 42–50.

33. For the (arguable) claim that rights became discredited political tools during the nineteenth century, see Jeremy Waldron, ed., *'Nonsense upon Stilts': Bentham, Burke and Marx on the Rights of Man* (London: Methuen, 1987), 13–18; and Douzinas, *The End of Human Rights*, 110–114.

34. Benjamin Franklin, *The Papers of Benjamin Franklin*, ed. L. W. Labaree and W. J. Bell, Jr. (New Haven, CT: Yale University Press, 1959), 1: 37.

35. Thomas Paine uses the phrase once in *The Rights of Man*, and it begins to be used occasionally in the nineteenth century in abolitionist, feminist, and economic contexts, but is used widely only in the 1940s (credit goes to Kenneth Cmiel for a helpful email on this history).

36. For the classic analysis along these lines, see Terry Eagleton, *Literary Theory: An Introduction* (Minneapolis: University of Minnesota Press, 1996),

15–46. For one of several recent revisionist accounts, see Hinderliter et al., eds., *Communities of Sense.*

37. See, for instance, Haskell, "Capitalism and the Origins of the Humanitarian Sensibility"; Thomas W. Laqueur, "Bodies, Details, and the Humanitarian Narrative," in *The New Cultural History*, ed. Lynn Hunt (Berkeley: University of California Press, 1989), 176–204; Gregory Eiselein, *Literature and Humanitarian Reform in the Civil War Era* (Bloomington: Indiana University Press, 1996); and William Morgan, *Questionable Charity: Gender, Humanitarianism, and Complicity in U.S. Literary Realism* (Durham, NH: University Press of New England, 2004). For a helpful essay on the relationship between narratives of pain and the growth of rights discourse in the abolitionist movement, see Elizabeth B. Clark, "The Sacred Rights of the Weak: Pain, Sympathy, and the Culture of Individual Rights in Antebellum America," *The Journal of American History* 82, no. 2 (Sept. 1995): 463–493.

38. Alain Finkielkraut, *In the Name of Humanity*, trans. Judith Friedlander (New York: Columbia University Press, 2000), 94, 91.

39. Finkielkraut, *In the Name of Humanity*, 91, 87.

40. Finkielkraut, *In the Name of Humanity*, 89.

41. Finkielkraut, *In the Name of Humanity*, 88.

42. Hannah Arendt, *On Revolution* (Middlesex: Penguin Books, 1973), 92.

43. Arendt, *On Revolution*, 85–86.

44. Finkielkraut, *In the Name of Humanity*, 89, 91.

45. See, for instance, Margaret Popkin, *Peace without Justice* (University Park: Pennsylvania State University Press, 2000); Mark Osiel, *Mass Atrocity, Collective Memory, and the Law* (New Brunswick, NJ: Transaction Publishers, 2000); and Robert I. Rotberg and Dennis Thompson, eds., *Truth v. Justice: The Morality of Truth Commissions* (Princeton, NJ: Princeton University Press, 2000).

46. Adam Smith, *The Theory of Moral Sentiments*, ed. D. D. Raphael and A. L. Macfie (Oxford: Clarendon Press, 1976), 136–137; and see David Hume, *A Treatise of Human Nature*, ed. L. A. Selby-Bigge and P. H. Nidditch, 2nd ed. (Oxford: Clarendon Press, 1978), 416.

2 Enabling Fictions and Novel Subjects

The *Bildungsroman* and International Human Rights Law

Joseph R. Slaughter

> The *as if* of the novel consists in [. . .] the establishment of an accepted freedom by magic.
>
> Frank Kermode, *The Sense of an Ending* (135)

> God may have died [. . .] but at least we have international law.
>
> Costas Douzinas, *The End of Human Rights* (9)

> Everyone has the right to recognition everywhere as a person before the law.
>
> *Universal Declaration of Human Rights* (Article 6)

LITERARY SUBTEXTS OF THE LAW

Like twins separated at birth by the accidents of British imperialism, two Watts (Ian and Alan) found themselves grappling with the battered legacy of the Enlightenment's emancipatory promise in the aftermath of World War II, converging on *Robinson Crusoe* as a literary marker of the emergence of rationalized individualism. The apprentice literary critic Ian Watt was writing at St. John's College, Cambridge what was to become his seminal work, *The Rise of the Novel*, in which *Crusoe* features as both the coming of age story of *Homo economicus* and "a monitory image of the ultimate consequences of absolute individualism."[1] Meanwhile, across the English Channel, Alan Watt, Australian delegate to the Third Social and Humanitarian Committee of the United Nations, was at the Palais Du Chaillot, Paris, revising the text of the *Universal Declaration of Human Rights* (UDHR) that would be adopted by the General Assembly on 10 December 1948.

During consideration of the UDHR's Article 29, Alan Watt proposed an amendment that would fundamentally reconfigure the international legal character of the relation between the individual and society. As drafted, the article declared: "Everyone has duties to the community *which enables him* freely to develop his personality." Watt's amendment construed a more integral relation between human personality and society: "Everyone has duties to the community *in which alone* the free and full development of his personality is possible."[2] Debate on this emendation centered around several problematics: its image of the human person, the terms of the individual's debt to the community for having developed what the UDHR elsewhere calls the "human personality," and the extent to which "the community" can take responsibility for the development of human personality.[3] It was to clarify these issues that the delegates invoked *Robinson Crusoe*, and Daniel Defoe took his official place among the unacknowledged legislators of the world.

Watt's proposal intended to moderate what many delegations perceived as the declaration's individualist excesses. However, concerned that the amendment endorsed a kind of social determinism, Belgium's delegate, Fernand Dehousse, expressed his objection with an *explication du Crusoe*: "It might . . . be asserted that the individual could only develop his personality within the framework of society; it was, however, only necessary to recall the famous book by Daniel Defoe, *Robinson Crusoe*, to find proof of the contrary." Mistaking Crusoe for the Enlightenment fiction of natural man, Dehousse found in Defoe's novel sociological "proof" that appeared to contradict what he regarded as an erroneous and potentially perilous emphasis on the community over the individual. Watt's amendment might imply "that it was the duty of society to develop the human being's personality; that principle, might, perhaps, be in harmony with the philosophy of certain countries, but it might equally well run counter to that of other peoples."[4] Playing Defoe as his universalist trump, Dehousse ironically defended the ahistorical, natural figure of human personality in the proto-language of cultural relativism.

Apparently persuaded by this interpretation, Watt withdrew his amendment. Subsequently, Alexei Pavlov sponsored it on behalf of the Soviets and contested Belgium's reading: "The example of *Robinson Crusoe*, far from being convincing, had, on the contrary, shown that man could not live and develop his personality without the aid of society." In fact, Pavlov noted, "Robinson had . . . at his disposal the products of human industry and culture, namely, the tools and books he had found on the wreck of his ship."[5] Defoe's book served the delegates similarly as an enabling fiction, a shared cultural product of human industry, salvaged from the shipwreck of western civilization, enlisted in their legislative project to facilitate "the advent of a world in which human beings shall enjoy freedom of speech and belief and freedom from fear and want" (UDHR). Although the delegates drew contradictory lessons from *Crusoe*, the literary dispute brought the UDHR to a resolution, alternative amendments were withdrawn, and, if a vote can be taken as evidence of such things, Pavlov's reading proved the more compelling to the interpretive community of the UN. Thus, with no objections and six abstentions, human personality entered international law as both the product and medium of social relations in Article 29: "Everyone has duties to the community in which alone the free and full development of his personality is possible."

Beyond adoption of the UDHR, 1948 was a watershed year in the reconfiguration of the international order, which saw the establishment of the Organization of American States; the declaration of the state of Israel and the appointment of the perennial "Palestine Question" on the UN agenda; the electoral victory of South Africa's National Party and its consequent legislation of apartheid; and the Berlin Blockade, which demarcated emergent lines of cold war conflicts. During the previous year, the General Agreement on Tariffs and Trade was signed and the Marshall Plan proposed. The "great era" of decolonization began inauspiciously with the partition of India and Pakistan, followed in 1948 by the independence of Ceylon and Burma, a process that would accelerate over the next two decades as imperial powers were forced to retreat from formal empire. By 1966, when the UN completed the International Bill of Rights with the International Covenant on Civil and Political Rights (ICCPR) and the International Covenant on Economic, Social, and Cultural Rights (ICESCR), the voting rolls of the General Assembly would more than double from the fifty-eight constituent members who adopted the UDHR.

Given the geopolitical climate and incipient ideological cold war chill in mid-1948, the fate of one fictionalized English castaway may seem rather beside the point. Indeed, the invocation of this "first novel" is unusual among the Third Committee's more predictable, if scattered, allusions to Locke and Rousseau, Lenin and Marx, but the interpretive dispute over Defoe's novel intimates the general terms of debate about the individual and its sociality that have consistently attended the articulation of human rights. Pavlov's social-materialist reading, in which "full" personality develops from the dialectical interaction of individual and society, rebuts Dehousse's libertarian reading of "possessive individualism," in which the "free" personality's development requires protection from society. Despite their differences, both extrapolated from *Crusoe* transcendent literary proof to substantiate their ideal of human personality development, an ideal that in the committee's deliberations had so far proved incapable of substantiating itself.

Human rights legal discourse and the novel genre are more than coincidentally, or casually, interconnected. Although literary criticism may intuit an intimate relation between the novel's rise and human rights, as Erich Auerbach did in 1946 when he attributed the emergence of "modern tragic realism" to the "convulsions" of the French Revolution (404),[6] rarely are those linkages named explicitly, except in passing, as Roberto Schwarz did when he suggestively identified a "combination of individualism and the Declaration of Human Rights" as the socio-political stipend of nineteenth-century novelistic realism.[7] Edward Said proposed, "Without empire . . . there is no European novel as we know it," and a similar codependency becomes evident when we examine the socio-historical and formal correspondences between international human rights law and the idealist *Bildungsroman*, whose hegemonic norms and forms are themselves "unthinkable without each other."[8] Tracking the figure and formula of human personality development, this chapter aims to excavate a neglected discursive genealogy of international human rights law that intersects with German Idealism and its particular nomination of the bourgeois, white male citizen to universal subject. The assumptions about that subject shared by normative human rights law and the idealist *Bildungsroman* manifest themselves in a common conceptual vocabulary, humanist social vision, and narrative grammar of free and full human personality development. Human rights and the *Bildungsroman* are mutually enabling fictions: each projects an image of the human personality that ratifies the other's vision of the ideal relations between individual and society.

The *Bildungsroman* is not the only cultural form that cooperates with human rights, nor is it the only form through which they may be imagined, but it is exemplary in the degree to which its conventions overlap with the image of human personality development projected by the law. It is beyond the scope of this essay to consider the ways in which other cultural forms interact with, and make imaginable alternative visions of, human rights; but clarifying the hegemonic complicity between the *Bildungsroman* and human rights might offer a methodology for thinking the formal and ideological human rights implications of other, non-hegemonic literary genres. Beyond elaborating a narratological alliance between human rights and the *Bildungsroman*, I suggest problems raised by the complicity of cultural forms in disseminating and naturalizing the norms of human rights, in making them both legible and commonsensical. Some of these problems are forecast in the notion of "enabling fiction" that I adapt from Rita Felski's feminist critique of the Habermasian liberal public sphere, whose "ideal of a free discursive space that equalizes all participants . . . engenders a sense of collective identity but is achieved only by obscuring actual material inequalities and political antagonisms among its participants."[9] Human rights' enabling fiction gives expression to certain laudable aspirations in its projection of what Ernesto Laclau and Chantal Mouffe call an "egalitarian imaginary," but the revolutionary rhetoric of liberty, equality, and fraternity tends to obfuscate the character of its implementation in "practices and discourses bearing new forms of inequality" as it becomes the hegemonic "common sense" of "liberal-democratic ideology."[10] Yet, as Laclau and Mouffe emphasize, the discourse of common sense becomes available for appropriation and the transformative re-articulation of the egalitarian imaginary by historically marginalized subjects (e.g., women and members of racial, religious, sexual, and class minorities) not comprehended practically within its original enabling fiction.[11] That is, the projection of a normative egalitarian imaginary not only sets the terms and limits of universality's coverage; it becomes the discursive condition of possibility for non-hegemonic re-articulations of universality's compass. In this regard, it is worth noting Friday's absence from the *Crusoe* debates. Although it would be a mistake to read the delegates' concern for Crusoe rather than his "man Friday" as endorsement of classical imperialism, their focus on the role of European cultural artifacts in Crusoe's socialization suggests something of the exclusions entailed and enacted in an enabling fiction of human rights that presumably aspires to promote the free and full personality development of so many Fridays.

TWO SUBJECTS OF HUMAN RIGHTS

Contemporary human rights law aims to mediate the relations between the individual and society's institutions. It takes two persons as subjects: the individual and the state, which historically is both the violator of human rights and the administrative unit that capacitates individuals as beneficiaries of human rights, as "person[s] before the law." Although the nonbinding UDHR appears concerned primarily with the human, this double subject is explicit in the two justiciable international covenants, where "States Parties" alternate with the human person as grammatical and legal subjects of rights. Thus, it is "The States Parties . . . [who] agree that education shall be directed to the full development of the human personality and [of] the sense of its dignity."[12] These alternating subjects of *contemporary* human rights formalize a paradox that commentators have noted since the *modern* predecessors of these rights were articulated after the eighteenth-century European revolutions[13]: in practice, human rights are not the natural rights of human beings as presocial creatures but the positive rights of citizens as incorporated creatures of the state.

Contemporary human rights law attempts to reconcile the continued historical primacy of the state and its needs with what the UDHR takes to be the aspiration of the human personality to consummate its manifest destiny in internationalized citizenship. If "forms are the abstract of specific social relations," the UDHR's articulation of the ideal social relations between individual and community or state intimates the form of human rights' undeclared developmental narrative.[14] The generic elements consist of two actants (the human person and the state), a probable conflict between them, a means of remediation in the human personality, and a temporal trajectory that emplots a transition narrative of the human person's socio-political incorporation into the regime of rights and citizenship.

The project of human personality development legislated in contemporary human rights might properly be described as novelistic. Indeed, literary theory written contemporaneously with the UDHR tended to describe the novel's primary virtue as its capacity to represent "particular individuals in the contemporary social environment."[15] Northrop Frye asserted that the genre's distinguishing mark and "chief interest" consist in the "human character as it manifests in society."[16] The development of human rights personality assumes a progressivist telos, a linearity that Robert Scholes and Robert Kellogg considered the central technical innovation enabling the modern novel. Published the year the UN completed the two Covenants, their *The Nature of Narrative* (1966) echoes our human rights formula in describing a modern sublimation of Aristotelian plot to character that makes the rounding of character itself the plot of "modern narrative": "The movement toward chronological plot . . . is part of the general movement to emphasize character . . . its episodic pattern allows for *free and full character development* without interference from the requirements of a tightly knit plot."[17]

The sociological name of Scholes and Kellogg's plot is *modernization*, presumably the narrative pattern of European civilization's transition to modernity that "repeat[s] itself in each life" as the teleological manifestation of the human personality.[18] This normative personalizing "transition narrative" projected by the UDHR not only patterns the novel, (auto)biography, and history but also "underwrote, and was in turn underpinned by," the institutions of the modern European nation-state, as Dipesh Chakrabarty observes.[19] The narrative of enlightenment articulates the individual within a "state/citizen bind as the ultimate construction of sociality."[20] Given their dual commitments to the welfare of the individual and to the Westphalian institution of state sovereignty, it is not altogether surprising that UN delegates turned to the novel as the supple cultural form most often implicated in modern problematics of both individualism and nation-state formation.[21] Although Crusoe cuts a rather ludicrous figure, as a bookkeeper of both self and state he resolves the conflict between individual and society through his meticulous narrative invoicing. Personal sovereignty becomes fabulously coextensive with the administrative geography of an island "state" cast outside ordinary civil time. Ironically, this antisocial, isolationist fantasy of complete congruity between human personality and political subjectivity provided the enabling fiction to underwrite the UDHR's ideal of sociality.

THE SOCIAL WORK OF THE *BILDUNGSROMAN*

The project of personality development conventionalized in the UDHR is native to theories of the *Bildungsroman* and eighteenth-century German Idealist solutions to the perceived conflict between the individual and society that describe a transitive grammar for the elevation of the individual to the universal. Each of these theories and solutions configures *Bildung*—a notoriously untranslatable word that denotes image and image making, culture and cultivation, form and formation—as a project of civicization, the cultivation of a presumably inherent universal force of human personality (*Bildungstrieb*) naturally inclined to express itself through the media of the nation-state and citizenship. For Wilhelm Dilthey, generally credited with formalizing the generic conception of the *Bildungsroman*, this novelistic plot obeyed a kind of natural law: "A lawlike development is discerned in the individual's life . . . on his way towards maturity and harmony."[22] Although Dilthey emphasized the genre's individualism, idealist sociological theory of *Bildung* was as invested in the emergence (and conservation) of a social order responsive to the human personality as it was in egoistic self-fulfillment, a fact reflected in the common names that *Bildungsroman* criticism usually gives to the "lawlike" process of subjectivation: *socialization, apprenticeship, assimilation, acculturation,* and *accommodation.* These terms share a progressive temporality in which the presumably cross-purposive compulsions of individualism and socialization, self-determination and social determinism, unfold and enfold in the development of the protagonist's (*Bildungsheld*'s) human personality. The idealist *Bildungsroman* has its own double subject; it imagines a relational individualism, a harmonious concordance of the person's universalist inclinations and the interpellative force of social relations, of which the person is a part and an effect.

The idealist *Bildungsroman* is a reconciliatory genre whose social work Franco Moretti famously characterized as "narrat[ing] 'how the French Revolution could have been avoided'"[23]—an appraisal that Swiss educational reformer Johann Pestalozzi issued before the revolution, warning in his "Education for Citizenship" of the potential for violent revolt if the "ruling classes" continued to deny the advantages of *Bildung* to the masses.[24] The 1789 French Declaration of the Rights of Man and of the Citizen (DRMC) similarly articulated, after the event, how the revolution could have been avoided and how future revolutions might be avoided. Both modern human rights and the *Bildungsroman* are reformist rather than revolutionary; their social-preservationist impulses conjoin in the UDHR, where safeguarding the free and full development of human personality intends to obviate collective violence as a legitimate mode of self-determination: "it is essential, if man is not to be compelled to have recourse, as a last resort, to rebellion against tyranny and oppression, that human rights should be protected by the rule of law."[25]

Many stalwart critics of the *Bildungsroman* maintain with Moretti a historicistic and Euro-centric view of the genre, eulogizing the loss of its synthetic social vision in the trauma of World War I.[26] Like the incorporative socio-political projects of modern human rights in the French and American contexts, their German Idealist counterpart of *Bildung* proffered a socio-aesthetic model of development and integration that served the emergent nation through two cooperating centripetal forces: centralizing the nation-state and centering its citizen-subjects.[27] The *Bildungsroman* conventionalized a narrative pattern for participation in the egalitarian imaginary of the new bourgeois nation-state, a plot for incorporation of previously marginalized people as democratic citizen-subjects. This account evokes Fredric Jameson's "national allegory," by which "All third-world texts are necessarily . . . *to be read as . . . the story of the private individual destiny* [that] *is always an allegory of the embattled situation of the public third-world culture and society*,"[28] in part because "Western" readers have tended to interpret contemporary postcolonial *Bildungsromane* through the lens of that allegory and because the "first meager shelf of 'Third World classics'" that Jameson proposed to *read as* national allegories "consisted almost exclusively of bildungsromane."[29]

Although it has allegedly ceased to have viable social work to perform for the Anglo-European white male (the ostensibly already incorporated and capacitated citizen), the *Bildungsroman* continues to serve, as Marianne Hirsch and others have recognized, as "the most salient genre for the literature of social outsiders, primarily women or minority groups."[30] Part of a larger transnational "memoir boom,"[31] the age of the "rise . . . of published life narratives" is also, not incidentally, the age in which human rights became the lingua franca of international affairs, as Kay Schaffer and Sidonie Smith have argued.[32] The last two decades have seen a surge in the Euro-American publication of *Bildungsromane* narrating the experiences of historically marginalized peoples (e.g., postcolonials, indigenous peoples, diasporic and immigrant populations, as well as metropolitan racial, ethnic, religious, gender and sexual minorities), who perhaps "for the first time find themselves in a world increasingly responsive to their needs."[33] The genre's proliferation—recently and in the previous two centuries—corresponds to periods of social crisis over the terms and mechanics of enfranchisement, the meaning and scope of citizenship. Historically, the *Bildungsroman* has served as a genre of demarginalization, even if the gap between who counted as demarginalizable and central subjects in the early examples appears, from our perspective, infinitesimal. The genre provides the normative literary technology by which social outsiders narrate affirmative claims for inclusion in the franchise of the nation-state, the story form of incorporation through which the historically marginalized individual is capacitated as a citizen-subject—that is, as "a person before the law." However, as the canonical genre of human rights incorporation, the *Bildungsroman* has the dual capacity to articulate claims of inclusion in the rights regime and to criticize those norms and their inegalitarian implementation. From the perspective of human rights, we might recognize the *Bildungsroman* not as the name of some typologically consistent literary artifact, an idealist strain of the realist novel that Jeffrey Sammons and Marc Redfield have argued was a nineteenth-century historical "phantom" anyway, but as the name of a function, the generic label that good reformists repeatedly give to texts that perform a certain kind of incorporative literary social work.

NARRATIVE SPONSORSHIP AND TAUTOLOGIES OF BECOMING

By epistemic coincidence, Georg Lukács anticipated the United Nations' human rights formula in an essay on Johann Wolfgang von Goethe's *Wilhelm Meister's Apprenticeship* (1795) published a year before adoption of the UDHR. Citing Goethe's novel as the genre's prototype, Lukács attributed Wilhelm's driving desire to play the role of Hamlet to "his insight that only the theatre will enable him fully to develop his human capacities. . . . Hence theatre and dramatic poetry are only *means* here to the free and complete development of the personality."[34] Although Lukács ultimately sees Wilhelm's quest for "the cultivation of my individual self, here as I am"[35] as unfulfillable, he nonetheless endorses its *Bildung* vision of what he described in 1920 as "an ideal of free humanity which comprehends and affirms the structures of social life as necessary forms of human community . . . [and] an occasion for the active expression of the essential life substance."[36] In his 1947 reading of the novel, Lukács is cynical about the prospects for holistic socialization in a capitalist world where the division of labor has atrophied the human personality and debased social relations. Instead he stresses the edifying function of culture and the emancipatory possibilities of the social simulacral theater.

Goethe's novel ends not with Wilhelm's theatrical self-fulfillment but with his return to the prosaic business of life, to the management of estates and capital, to the social recognition of his own biological fatherhood, to an arranged marriage that he accepts as his own desire, and to the revelation of the masonic Society of the Tower, a contrived plot (or plotting) device that claims to have secretly coordinated the events of Wilhelm's apprenticeship and pronounces his "freedom" in the name of Nature. Goethe's novel patterns a curious notion of development by which Wilhelm is habituated after the fact to what could not have been otherwise. He accepts the articles of apprenticeship prepared by the Society of the Tower as a narrative of development that he would have willed for himself if he had possessed the (self-)plotting agency that he supposedly acquires through socialization. The novel registers this social mastery as the voluntary affirmation of fatherly responsibilities, an affirmation replete with civic implications: "In this sense his apprenticeship was ended: with the feeling of a father, he had acquired all the virtues of a citizen."[37] The teleology of Goethe's story of *Bildung* brings Wilhelm to the point of public acceptance—translated into personal will—of what he must otherwise have been by the codes of biology, society, sponsorship, family inheritance and his patronymic: the father of Felix and a *meister Bürger*, a fully incorporated and capacitated citizen of the Society of the Tower, itself a surrogate for a proto-German state.

Goethe's novel underwrites the contingencies of personality development with the social security of the Tower, straitening the vagaries of a loose, linear plot of self-propulsion into the fatality of a tightly knit plot guided by the invisible hand of social sponsorship, converting the teleological drift of Wilhelm's social career into a tautological confirmation of himself just as he already was. The Tower stands surrogate for both nature and bourgeois society, guaranteeing Wilhelm's successful apprenticeship and producing a paradox in the temporality of development that is revealed to be simultaneously tautological (confirmative of the same: Wilhelm a biological and social father) and teleological (productive of difference: Wilhelm the *convinced and voluntary* biological and social father). The logical and temporal twisting of the developmental structure emplots the story of what Charles Taylor calls "responsibilization," the narrative process by which the *Bildungsheld* retroactively becomes responsible for the plot of personality development and so for fate and the state.[38] Imbricating "the principles of circularity and progress,"[39] this impossible tautological-teleological developmental complex engenders the formal, paradoxical structure of international human rights law and the narrative of human personality development that it charters.

POLITICAL POSSIBILITIES OF PARADOX

The curious temporality of development narrated in the idealist *Bildungsroman* configures a literary personality that has a political analogue in the paradoxical "historical figure" of Enlightenment civil subjectivity that Étienne Balibar finds emerging from the institution of popular sovereignty.[40] The modern democratic subject, he argues, is suspended between the French DRMC's titular natural rights of man and its positive rights of the citizen, configuring a citizen-subject who is at once law maker and law abider, a figure both before and after the law. The UDHR formally reanimates this citizen-subject in its articulation of a human personality that simultaneously preexists society and law *and* comes into being through social interaction and collective declaration of human rights. Ultimately, of course, these personalities are one and the same; underwriting and underwritten by human rights, the human personality is both natural and positive, presocial and social, their premise and promise. This (para)logical articulation exemplifies the formal shape and rhetorical architecture of contemporary human rights' fundamental enabling legal fiction, which presupposes that the person *is* a person in order to effect the person *as* a person.

Following Hannah Arendt's famous conclusion that, under a nation-state model of citizenship, statelessness amounts to a state of human rightlessness,[41] critics and advocates alike have made an industry of exposing such paradoxes to challenge the legitimacy and the egalitarian imaginary of human rights. Such publicity efforts to deploy the "politics of shame" by,[42] and on behalf of, those "suffering the paradoxes of rights" (in Wendy Brown's phrase) are clearly necessary, but they also do not dependably move people "into doing what they 'should.'"[43] These strategies often

underappreciate the degree to which inequality has been historically constitutive of the human rights regime and the ways in which the discourse
of the regime tends to pedestrianize paradox. Instead of merely exposing
the hypocrisy of rights, our analyses (both literary and socio-political) need
to go beyond the point at which this revelation is expected to embarrass
governments or human rights discourse in order to ask, with Brown, "How
might paradox gain political richness when it is understood as affirming
the impossibility of justice in the present and as articulating the conditions and countours of justice in the future?"[44] Instead of treating paradox
as a shameful limitation of human rights, we can attend to its productive
possibilities. Such a project must consider not only the content of human
rights discourse but also its logical and rhetorical forms, from which its
content is in fact inseparable—one form of which, I am arguing, finds its
fullest elaboration in the normative (and normalizing) literary technology
of the *Bildungsroman*. Recognizing that form(s) and formation(s) matter in
human rights, we can begin to respond to Giorgio Agamben's provocation:
"What is the *form of life* . . . that corresponds to the *form of law*?"[45]

LEGAL CONVENTIONS OF THE OBVIOUS

"Human rights are literally the rights one has simply because one is a human
being," both common sense and international legal scholar Jack Donnelly
tell us.[46] While the political condition of human rights may be paradoxical,
the form of their articulation tends toward the tautological. Commemorat-
ing the fortieth anniversary of the UDHR, John Humphrey—first director of the UN Human Rights Division and compiler of the first draft of
the UDHR—intimated this form in his assertion that "Everyone knows,
or should know, why human rights are important. They are important
because without them there could be no human dignity."[47] Humphrey suggests that human rights not only protect but effect human dignity. Indeed,
the UDHR repeats its preambular "*recognition* of the inherent dignity and
of the equal and inalienable rights of all members of the human family"
in a positive *declaration* in Article 1: "All human beings are born free and
equal in dignity and rights" (my emphasis). Human dignity thus precedes
and derives from human rights, warranting their recognition *and* emerging
from their declaration.[48]

Humphrey valorizes contemporary human rights' tautologies as con-
firmations of common sense. Since at least 1789, when the Marquis de
Lafayette put before the French National Assembly his proposal for a
déclaration des droits that would "*'dire ce que tout le monde sait, ce que
tout le monde sent'* (say what everyone knows, what everyone feels),"[49]
legislation of the obvious has been the rhetorical mode of the transcription of what the ancient Greeks called "unwritten law." The legal tautologies of contemporary human rights are rhetorical and formal remainders

of Thomas Jefferson's "Nature and . . . Nature's God" (U.S. Declaration of Independence), structural traces of universal transcendence after UN legislators wrote out the traditional underwriters of natural law, the extra-textual guarantors of inalienability and inherency. In the wake of World War II, the UDHR architects chose to think not "in terms of totality"[50] so much as in received *forms* of totality, even as they dispensed with the figures historically invoked to certify that totality: God and Nature; the sovereign and the patriarch. Contemporary human rights law, as Gayatri Chakravorty Spivak reminds us, necessarily begged the question of nature as the source of rights;[51] it also unnamed all the other symbolic functions of Jacques Lacan's Name-of-the-Father. The tautological structure of contemporary human rights law is the formal symptom of this metaphysical begging, but it is not a simple sign of the law's debility.

Tautology is the rhetorical and logical form that natural-law categories of inherency and inalienability take as names of capacities for something to be the same as itself, what George Puttenham identified in 1589 as the trope of "selfe saying."[52] The rhetorical form of self-evidence and imma-nence, tautology mystifies the foundation of its authority to assume the cultural positivity of a proverb: "Man is man," in the words of French philosopher and UNESCO consultant on the UDHR Jacques Maritain.[53] Tautology is the emphatic form of common sense, or the formal mani-festation of a hegemonic will to common sense. It marks a boundary of knowledge at "the periphery of one's [intellectual] culture."[54] This cul-tural inflection is important because tautology delimits the margins of a culturally situated logos, signaling the site where culture-bound knowl-edge confronts its own limits and turns back on itself to produce the most concise and chiastic formulation of constitutive common sense, of what "everyone" presumably already knows: human rights are the rights of human beings, inalienability is inalienable, a person is a person, "man [sic] is man [sic]." The tautological form of human rights law sustains an image of a self-substantiating, self-saying citizen-subject, but this "com-monsensical" formulation is not only culturally conditioned; it is consti-tutive, determining who is obviously included and "excluded from the benefits of human rights."[55] The corporate "everyone" encompassed in human rights discourse is, at least in part, incorporated by the degree to which these tautologies are, or come to be, compelling common sense, the consensual "sense that founds community."[56]

Paradoxically, perhaps, contemporary human rights law becomes more formally tautological the more it insists upon a teleology of human devel-opment. For example, the 1986 Declaration on the Right to Development formulates its developmental common sense as a perfect tautology. Its final preambular paragraph *confirms* "that the right to development is an inalien-able human right," anticipating article 1, which now *proclaims*, "The right to development is an inalienable human right." Beyond their internal tau-tologies (a right is a right), each of the preambular statements of recognition and confirmation has a corresponding statement in the body of the text that articulates the same content (often verbatim) in the declarative mode. These two speech acts—the constative that confirms and the declarative that enacts—interact to imbue the hermetic legal tautologies with kinetic energy and a temporal dimension that initiates a sort of teleology-in-tautology. This tautological-teleological configuration is perhaps most dramatic when the declaration first recognizes and then declares, "therefore," that "[t]he human person is the central subject of development and should be the active participant and beneficiary of the right to development."[57]

The legal documents inscribe their moment of enunciation in the transitive space between preamble and text, in a "therefore" that marks the rhetorical turn where the constative becomes performative. The "therefore" of human rights law, to paraphrase Frank Kermode on the novel, inaugurates "an accepted freedom" through its tropological "magic."[58] Therefore, the human person is declared to be the central subject of development that the human being was presupposed to be by both prior right and the natural disposition of the human personality. The infusion of temporality into the human rights tautologies changes their aspect from natural to positive, from expositive to narrative. The tautological structure of this teleology animates natural law's categories of inherency and inalienability as projects of cultural development by which nature is to become a kind of second nature, and the human person is to become, and to be recognized as, the freely and fully developed and dignified international human rights person. The *Bildungsroman* generally makes legible this esoteric, impossible plot structure of human rights subjectivation.

THE NARRATIVE TIME AND SPACE OF HUMAN RIGHTS

In making the human personality and recognition of its dignity matters of cultivation, the transition narrative of human rights situates the very human capable of bearing rights and duties as their product, in the mode of a subject yet to come, a subject not yet fully capable of recognizing the inherent dignity of the human personality or itself as a person before human rights law. Defending the UDHR in *Foreign Affairs* while its eventual adoption was still in doubt, Eleanor Roosevelt—chair of the UN drafting committee—eloquently summarized this improbable figurative temporality: "If the Declaration is accepted by the Assembly, it will mean that all the nations accepting hope that the day will come when these rights are considered inherent rights belonging to every human being."[59] Roosevelt reconciled the seemingly incongruous time frames of human rights by animating the natural-law category of inherency as an inherency-in-becoming that anticipates a day when human rights law's common sense will have become and been confirmed as universal common sense, when formal tautologies will have become in practice and effect redundantly tautological, when the human person will have become positively the human person that she or he ostensibly already is by natural right. This narrative aspirationalism anticipates a future-anterior perspective from which a projected inalienability of human rights will have been recognized and confirmed as inalienable, an imaginary perspective from which the "project of becoming a person"—a project, as Drucilla Cornell notes, "that can never be fulfilled, once and for all"—may be viewed as the consummation of free and full human personality development.[60]

The tautological-teleological complex of inherency-in-becoming articulates the impossibly anticipatory and retrospective (proleptic and analeptic) temporality of the story of modern citizen-subjectivation shared by human rights and the *Bildungsroman*. These cooperative idealist discourses are tendentially reformist and normative, sketching the narrative terms by which the individual might recognize and confirm itself in the socio-political structures of democratic citizenship so that *man* and *citizen* might co-designate the human person without the need for violence. This temporal contortion is conventionalized in a common transformation of the narrative grammar of first-person *Bildungsromane*, in which the novel concludes where it began after bringing the past into conjunction with the present and the earlier protagonist self into correspondence with a later narrator self, producing the *Bildungsheld* as the narrator-protagonist (citizen-subject) of its own *Bildungsroman*.[61] The elder narrator acts as a guarantor, like the Society of the Tower, of the younger protagonist's enfranchisement. This narratorial agency bends teleological linear development into a reflexive structure of narrative self-sponsorship that repairs the initial diagetic split between protagonist (man) and narrator (citizen).

Becoming what one already is by right is a serviceable abstract for the plot of human personality development projected in human rights law and the idealist *Bildungsroman*, which gives novelistic form to the affirmative rights claim—the assertion of a right that must be made to be activated. A "constative declaration," the rights claim transacts the rhetorically obvious "in order to make," in Thomas Keenan's felicitous phrase, "what's already so manifest manifest."[62] A rights claim requires a subject who is prepositioned to assert rights who will, in principle, only have acquired such capacity through the act of claiming. The demarginalizing *Bildungsroman* makes such a claim for inclusion in the human rights franchise, plotting the teleology of development as the narrative expression of tautological obviousness—becoming what one is by right—in which a narrator (among the already incorporated) publishes the story of the development of a protagonist's autobio*graphical* consciousness capable of recounting the acquisition of the capacities, habits, and dispositions necessary to narrate the story of their acquisition after the fact and to plot it from the position of the incorporated citizen-subject as the consummation of personal will. Few *Bildungsromane* depict the ideal, but even those that ironize its generic promise by narrating the frustration of incorporation make rights claims, generally affirming the egalitarian imaginary of rights while dramatizing the discrepancy between their universalist rhetoric and their real differential dispensation. Narrated from "a split situation of being at once authorized and deauthorized," this more ordinary use of the *Bildungsroman* by "one who is excluded from the universal, and yet belongs to it nevertheless," reconfigures the effective coverage of the socio-historical universal.[63]

Enlightenment theorists of human rights and *Bildung* elaborated their solutions to the perceived conflict between individual and state in the name of the universal *and* in the service of nationalization. Despite the egalitarian pretensions of the Rights of Man, post-revolutionary bourgeois France effectively nationalized those "imprescriptible and natural" rights as "uniquely [its] own, concerned with French values and culture," conscripting them to rationalize the *mission civilisatrice*, the universalization of French civilization.[64] Similarly, over the nineteenth century, *Bildung* and the *Bildungsroman* were retroactively enshrined as the unique national expressions of German values and culture, as "the German national genre" that was "not for export."[65] In the early nineteenth century, Wilhelm von Humboldt linked these two projects, characterizing the fruit of *Bildung* as "the idea of merely respecting a person as a human being" and the "sentiments of . . . human rights and duties."[66] However, Humboldt derived from this sentimental education of the human to its own dignity a responsibility of the freely and fully developed to transport "to the remotest parts of the earth . . . [*Bildung*'s] governing principle of universal humanity." Historically, what the Rights of Man and *Bildung* cultivated were not primarily universalist sensibilities about the inherent and inalienable equality of man but patriotic senses of national particularity, of what it means to be, and how to become, a French or German citizen. The complicity of modern(izing) *Bildung* and human rights with nationalism and colonialism belies the narrowness of the socio-historical universality that underpins the rights man's burden (to trope on Rudyard Kipling) described by Humboldt.

Modern human rights and theories of *Bildung* set the state-citizen bind as the ultimate horizon of universal human personality, but contemporary human rights and postcolonial *Bildungsromane* do not merely replicate their modern counterparts. In principle, they have a different compass, as Barbara Harlow emphasizes in her assertion that the UDHR "translated the standard literary paradigm of individual versus society . . . by mapping an identification of the individual within a *specifically international* construction of rights and responsibilities . . . recharting the trajectory and peripeties of the classical *Bildungsroman*."[67] Such a translation presses the nationalizing *Bildungsroman* into the service of an international order that is without formal administrative and social structures comparable to those of the nation-state. In a sense, the UN's reconditioning of these literary and legal genres of personality development attempts to internationalize the cultural nationalism that David Lloyd described, in the Irish context, as providing the surrogate "institutions that stood in for the political institutions yet to be, . . . forming citizens in anticipation of the founding of the state of which they were to be citizens."[68] However, legislated in a statist international order, the contemporary human rights regime has so far proved incapable of imagining a developmental narrative outside the Westphalian unities of nation-statism; the person must still be nationalized before it can conceivably be internationalized, patriated before being expatriated.

International human rights is a notoriously feeble legal regime. That it has proved historically insufficient as law to procure its effective universal recognition is partly a consequence of the residual nationalism and narrow universalism comprehended by the legal and literary forms that the UN conscripted to realize an international community of freely and fully developed persons; it is also partly because the traditional "guarantor of the completeness of the law" has been symbolically deposed.[69] Human rights' cultural common sense is underwritten by little more than its begged tautological form; juridical authority to substantiate law's tautologies arrives only as a retrofitting of its conventions. For example, instruments of petition and enforcement, when provided at all, are appended as "optional protocols";[70] thus, states may ratify legal conventions without extending to their citizens the right to lay claim to those rights. The recent establishment of the International Criminal Court represents a similarly belated attempt to retrofit human rights with the sanction to execute its weak positivized natural law. If these efforts cannot rename the transcendental father, they intend to revive his sovereign function, to give international law the force of law.

SUSPICIOUS VEHICLES: THE *WUTHERING HEIGHTS* PRINCIPLE

In contrast to the infirmity of the legal apparatus, cultural forms like the novel have cooperated with human rights to naturalize their common sense, to give law the Gramscian force of culture. The *Bildungsroman* has been doing some of the socio-cultural work that human rights law cannot do for itself to extend its incorporative franchise and to make its tautologies compelling, acting—if rarely so dramatically as *Robinson Crusoe* did for the UDHR—as a kind of cultural surrogate for the missing warrant and executive sanction of human rights law and supplying (in content and form) a certain symbolic legitimacy for the law's tautologies. As one of the primary carriers of human rights culture, the novel of demarginalization, more than any other genre, is said to perform what it thematizes, imagined to effect in the reader the modernizing process of personality development that it narrates for the protagonist. Since at least the Atlantic movement for the abolition of the slave trade, the *Bildungsroman* and human rights discourse have been part of the freight of globalization as the West has prosecuted it through colonialism, (neo-)imperialisms, international humanitarianism, and multinational consumer capitalism.[71] Their complicity can materialize uncannily. For instance, in his narrative sociology of the Rwandan genocide, Philip Gourevitch recounts a conversation with a man who identifies himself only as a pygmy.[72] After a cursory reference to *Great Expectations*, Gourevitch's interlocutor expounds his *Wuthering Heights* "principle," a "theory" apparently derived from reading Brontë's novel, that "all humanity is one": "The concept is *Homo sapiens*. . . . It is the only hope."[73]

The human rights claimant's citation of *Bildungsromane* has a generic analogue in the contemporary *Bildungsroman*, in *mise en abyme* scenes of reading in which we read of the *Bildungsheld*'s reading of other *Bildungsromane*. These scenes construct reading genealogies that situate reader-protagonists in an international imaginary, an intertextual order of *Bildungsromane*. For example, along with the revolutionary theory of Frantz Fanon, Che Guevara, Régis Debray, and pan-Arabic Baathists, Saudi novelist Turki al-Hamad's Hisham (in *Adama*) reads classic European *Bildungsromane* but is particularly affected by the novels of Charles Dickens and Maxim Gorky's *Mother*. The Zimbabwean author Tsitsi Dangarembga's Tambu (in *Nervous Conditions*) responds to, and is ultimately deluded by, the novels of the Brontës, Louisa May Alcott, and Enid Blyton; the Nigerian 'Biyi Bandele-Thomas's Rayo (in *The Sympathetic Undertaker*) measures himself against Camara Laye's *The Dark Child*, itself modeled, according to Laye, on Gustave Flaubert's *Sentimental Education*.[74] The Guatemalan Arturo Arias's Máximo (in *After the Bombs*) mixes stories of humankind's emergence from the *Popol Vuh* with his idolization of Flaubert and Thomas Mann. The Martiniquan Joseph Zobel's José (in *Black Shack Alley*) syncretizes plantation oral forms with lycée prescriptions of French classics and extracurricular reading of René Maran's *Batouala* and Claude McKay's *Banjo*.

This topos of contemporary *Bildungsromane* images a geocultural and geopolitical alternative to the Westphalian model of national citizenship as the ultimate expression of human sociality and personality. What emerges from this reading practice is not merely a transnational matrix of postcolonial *Bildungsromane* whose contemporary protagonists read classical *Bildungsromane* (which, along with the Jamesonian "national allegory," is how the western literary industry generally markets the phenomenon). More important, the imaginary topography of an inchoate international literary public sphere begins to take shape. These books function, for authors and protagonists alike, as what I call *clefs à roman*, generic keys to the lettered city that come with an almost obligatory novel about an individual's attempts to gain access to a public sphere.[75] As it did in Jürgen Habermas's account of the rise of the democratic public sphere in modern Europe,[76] the *Bildungsroman* remains the primary enabling fiction for and privileged genre of incorporation into an international "reading public"[77] that is emerging, we like to think, in advance of administrative institutions and social relations which such a sphere ordinarily serves, foreshadowing the contours of, and terms of participation in, a projective international order still to come.

The public sphere provides more than the ultimate setting of *Bildungsromane*; it is also the location of their publication, circulation, and consumption—activities that on a global scale remain differentially inflected by north-south power relations that belie the cosmopolitan reading public's egalitarian self-image as "a world of free and equal access in which literary recognition is available to all writers."[78] As human rights claims, many contemporary "Third World" *Bildungsromane*, like many of their nineteenth-century European counterparts, make legible the inequities of this egalitarian imaginary. That is, these novels reveal some of the exclusions and disparities enacted when the *Bildungsroman* is itself canonized as the compulsory genre of incorporation into an international community of readers and rights holders and when its ideal of human rights personality development is projected as the exclusive paradigm of human sociality. Consequentially, some of the not-yet-hegemonic norms of universal human rights begin to become internationally legible in the appropriations and transformations of the *Bildungsroman*'s normative generic conventions. These *Bildungsromane* demonstrate not the "universal application and full triumph" of human rights[79] but the hegemony of their emancipatory discourse and the contemporary condition of their still-unfulfilled promise, the current location where "the[ir] tradition of what has not yet become" now stands.[80] In this regard, the racialist lesson that Gourevitch's "pygmy" draws from his reading of British *Bildungsromane* should be cautionary; he concludes—perhaps for reasons not unlike "dark-skinned" Heathcliff's[81]— that his opportunities for free and full personality development, and thus for his incorporation as a human rights person, depend upon marrying a "white woman," since "[o]nly [she] can understand my universal principle of *Homo sapiens*."[82]

Human rights are a culture and a legal regime, as much matters of literature as of legislation. Given the continued systemic disparities between the enfranchised and the unincorporated, we should approach both hegemonic international human rights and the normative *Bildungsroman* as necessary but suspicious vehicles, not so much because they naturalize a monadic individualism (which, as I have suggested, is more sociable than most critiques admit) as because of the historically narrow generic universalism and the residual nationalism of the forms they conscript to project a new international citizen-subjectivity. This is the formal gambit of both contemporary human rights and a still largely NATO-centric "world literature" that eagerly consumes and canonizes—to the likely exclusion of alternative generic forms and constructions of human rights—narratives of the historically marginalized when they come in the familiar national dress of the *Bildungsroman*, narratives that intensify the dominant enabling fictions that human rights and the *Bildungsroman* are intrinsically universal and fundamentally egalitarian. Recognizing the mutual complicities of human rights and the *Bildungsroman*—and their historical cooperation in naturalizing the terms of both incorporation *and* disenfranchisement—means also recognizing that our reading acts have implications not only for the imagination but also for the legislation of an international community constituted on human rights. That is, the texts we read, and how we read, teach, and write about them impact (however unpredictably) the possibility that the projection of a world in which "recognition of the inherent dignity and of the equal and inalienable rights of all members of the human family" might become legible, articulable, and perhaps even commonsensical.

NOTES

1. Ian Watt, *The Rise of the Novel: Studies in Defoe, Richardson, and Fielding* (Berkeley: University of California Press, 1957), 92.
2. United Nations, *Third Session, Proceedings of the Third Social and Humanitarian Committee* (New York: United Nations, 1948), 658, my emphasis.
3. At the urging of female delegates, most notably from Denmark, India, and Pakistan, "his personality" was to be replaced with the gender-neutral "human personality," as it appears elsewhere in the declaration; through some bureaucratic oversight, the revision was never implemented. See United Nations *Third Session*, 659, and Johannes Morsink, *The Universal Declaration of Human Rights: Origins, Drafting, and Intent.* Pennsylvania Studies in Human Rights (Philadelphia: University of Pennsylvania Press, 1999), 116–29; 241–52. Early drafts of Article 29 used the term "state" instead of "community," which, throughout the UDHR, signifies a range of "group units," from the family, society, and nation to the state. M. Glen Johnson, "A Magna Carta for Mankind: Writing the Universal Declaration of Human Rights" in *The Universal Declaration of Human Rights: A History of Its Creation and Implementation, 1948–1998*, ed. UNESCO (Paris: UNESCO Publishing, 1998), 19–75.
4. United Nations, *Third Session*, 659.
5. United Nations, *Third Session*, 659–660.
6. Erich Auerbach, *Mimesis: The Representation of Reality in Western Literature*, 1946, trans. Willard Trask (Garden City, NY: Doubleday, 1957), 58–59.
7. For Auerbach, it is precisely a *Bildungsroman*, Stendhal's *The Red and the Black* (1830), which epitomizes this formal development.
8. Edward W. Said, *Culture and Imperialism* (New York: Knopf, 1993), 69, 71.
9. Rita Felski, *Beyond Feminist Aesthetics: Feminist Literature and Social Change* (Cambridge, MA: Harvard University Press, 1989), 168.
10. Ernesto Laclau and Chantal Mouffe, *Hegemony and Socialist Strategy: Towards a Radical Democratic Politics* (London: Verso, 1985), 159–160.
11. Laclau and Mouffe, *Hegemony and Socialist Strategy*, 154.
12. Article 13, *International Covenant on Economic, Social, and Cultural Rights.* G.A. res. 2200A (XXI), 21 U.N.GAOR Supp. (No. 16) at 49, U.N. Doc. A/6316 (1966), 993 U.N.T.S. 3, entered into force Jan 3, 1976. <http://www1.umn.edu/humanrts/instree/b2esc.htm>.

    Although the "sense of [the human personality's] dignity" as a goal of sentimental education is ambiguous in English, it is explicit in the other official language versions.

13. Upendra Baxi maintains this important distinction between modern human rights, grounded in natural law and the Anglo-European eighteenth century, and contemporary human rights, whose codification began with mid-twentieth-century international treaties. Arguing that contemporary human rights developed through interactions between the "West" and the "non-West," not least in anti-imperial struggles, Baxi also corrects the myopic genealogy that takes the European revolutions as their singular source. Upendra Baxi, *The Future of Human Rights* (New Delhi: Oxford University Press, 2002), 101–102.

14. Roberto Schwarz, *Misplaced Ideas: Essays on Brazilian Culture*, trans. John Gledson, ed. James Dunkerley, Jean Franco, and John King (London: Verso, 1992), 53.

15. Watt, *The Rise of the Novel*, 19.

16. Northrop Frye, *Anatomy of Criticism* (Princeton, NJ: Princeton University Press, 1957), 308.

17. Robert E. Scholes and Robert Kellogg, *The Nature of Narrative* (New York: Oxford University Press, 1966), 236, my emphasis.

18. M. M. Bakhtin, "The *Bildungsroman* and Its Significance in the History of Realism (toward a Historical Typology of the Novel)," trans. Vern W. McGee, in *Speech Genres and Other Late Essays*, University of Texas Press Slavic Series, No. 8, ed. Caryl Emerson and Michael Holquist (Austin: University of Texas Press, 1986), 22.

19. Chakrabarty, *Provincializing Europe*, 34.

20. Chakrabarty, *Provincializing Europe*, 37. Chakrabarty suggests that the hegemony of this narrative pattern occludes alternative, subaltern "constructions of self and community [that], while documentable, will never enjoy the privilege of providing the meta-narratives or teleologies . . . of our histories" (37).

21. See Benedict Anderson, *Imagined Communities: Reflections on the Origin and Spread of Nationalism*, 1983, Revised ed. (London: Verson, 2006).

22. Wilhelm Dilthey, Rudolf A. Makkreel, and Frithjof Rodi, *Selected Works, Vol. 5: Poetry and Experience*, 1910 (Princeton, NJ: Princeton University Press, 1985), 336.

23. Franco Moretti, *The Way of the World: The Bildungsroman in European Culture*, 1987, trans. Albert Sbragia (London: Verso, 2000), 64.

24. For similar arguments in the eighteenth century, see Susan L. Cocalis, "The Transformation of Bildung from an Image to an Ideal," in *Monatshefte: Fur Deutschen Unterricht, Deutsche Sprache und Literatur* 70, no. 4 (1978): 399–414.

25. Preamble, *Universal Declaration of Human Rights*, G.A. res. 217A (III), U.N. Doc A/810 at 71 (1948).

26. Moretti, *The Way of the World*, 229–245.

27. For discussions of various philosophers' inflections of *Bildung*, see Pheng Cheah, *Spectral Nationality: Passages of Freedom from Kant to Postcolonial Literatures of Liberation* (New York: Columbia University Press, 2003); Todd Curtis Kontje, *The German Bildungsroman: History of a National Genre* (Columbia, SC: Camden House, 1993); David Lloyd, "Arnold, Ferguson, Schiller: Aesthetic Culture and the Politics of Aesthetics," in *Cultural Critique* 2 (Winter 1985–1986): 137–169; Marc Redfield, *Phantom Formations: Aesthetic Ideology and the Bildungsroman* (Ithaca, NY: Cornell University Press, 1996); and John H. Smith, *The Spirit and Its Letter: Traces of Rhetoric in Hegel's Philosophy of Bildung* (Ithaca, NY: Cornell University Press, 1988).

28. Fredric Jameson, "Third-World Literature in the Era of Multinational Capitalism," in *Social Text* 15, no. 3 (1986): 69.

29. Fredric Jameson, "On Literary and Cultural Import-Substitution in the Third World: The Case of the Testimonio," in *The Real Thing: Testimonial Discourse and Latin America*, ed. Georg M. Gugelberger (Durham, NC: Duke University Press, 1996), 172. In the question period of his keynote address to the American Comparative Literature Association (2004), Arjun Appadurai suggested that Jameson's "national allegory" was perhaps formulated too early. We could, however, conclude from the classical theories of *Bildung* that his reading prescription was too late or that it took too narrow a view of the "Third World" as its singular subject.

30. Marianne Hirsch, "The Novel of Formation as Genre: Between Great Expectations and Lost Illusions," in *Genre* XII, no. 3 (1979): 300. Ellen Morgan appears to have been the first to note this phenomenon, whose identitarian coverage critics have steadily expanded (Ellen Morgan, "Human Becoming: Form and Focus in the Neo-Feminist Novel" in *Images of Women in Fiction: Feminist Perspectives*, ed. Susan Koppelman Cornillon (Bowling Green, OH: Bowling Green University Popular Press, 1972), 185; Bonnie Hoover Braendlin, "*Bildung* in Ethnic Women Writers," in *Denver Quarterly* 17, no. 4 (1983): 75; Elizabeth Abel, Marianne Hirsch, and Elizabeth Langland, "Introduction," in *The Voyage In: Fictions of Female Development*, ed. Elizabeth Abel, Marianne Hirsch, and Elizabeth Langland (Hanover, NH: University Press of New England, 1983), 3–19.

31. Leigh Gilmore, *The Limits of Autobiography: Trauma and Testimony* (Ithaca, NY: Cornell University Press, 2001), 2.

32. Kay Schaffer and Sidonie Smith, *Human Rights and Narrated Lives: The Ethics of Recognition* (New York: Palgrave, 2004), 13.

33. Abel, Hirsch, and Langland, "Introduction," 13.

34. Georg Lukács, *Goethe and His Age*, 1947, trans. Robert Anchor (London: Merlin Press, 1968), 51. Because Germany was excluded from UN membership after World War II, German was not a drafting language for the UDHR. Nonetheless, Lukács' phrasing, written in the 1930s, corresponds almost verbatim to the declaration's later German translation. Lukács may be drawing upon Marx's prophesied "higher form of society, a society in which the full and free development of every individual forms the ruling principle." Karl Marx, *Capital: A Critique of Political Economy*, 1867, trans. Ben Fowkes (New York: Vintage, 1977), I: 739.

35. Johann Wolfgang von Goethe, *Wilhelm Meister's Apprenticeship and Travels*, 1824, trans. Thomas Carlyle (London: Chapman & Hill, 1894), 8; vol. 2, bk. 5, ch. 3.

36. Georg Lukács, *The Theory of the Novel: A Historico-Philosophical Essay on the Forms of Great Epic Literature*, 1920, trans. Anna Bostock (Cambridge, MA: MIT Press, 1971), 134.

37. Goethe, *Wilhelm Meister's Apprenticeship*, vol. 2, bk. 8, ch. 1, 193.

38. Charles Taylor, *The Ethics of Authenticity* (Cambridge, MA: Harvard University Press, 1992), 77.

39. Michael Minden, "The Place of Inheritance in the Bildungsroman: Agathon, Wilhelm Meister's Lehrjahre, and Der Nachsommer," in *Reflection and Action: Essays on the Bildungsroman*, ed. James Hardin (Columbia: University of South Carolina Press, 1991), 274.

40. Étienne Balibar, "Citizen Subject," trans. James B. Swenson Jr., in *Who Comes after the Subject?* ed. Jean-Luc Nancy (New York: Routledge, 1991), 46.

41. Hannah Arendt, *The Origins of Totalitarianism*, 1951 (New York: Harcourt Brace and Company, 1973), 267–302.

42. On the role of shame in human rights activism, see Thomas Keenan, "Mobilizing Shame," *South Atlantic Quarterly* 103, nos. 2/3 (2004): 435–49 and Robert F. Drinan, *The Mobilization of Shame: A World View of Human Rights* (New Haven, CT: Yale University Press, 2001).

43. Stanley Cohen and Bruna Seu, "Knowing Enough Not to Feel Too Much: Emotional Thinking about Human Rights Appeals," in *Truth Claims: Representation and Human Rights*, ed. Mark Philip Bradley and Patrice Petro (New Brunswick, NJ: Rutgers University Press, 2002), 188.

44. Wendy Brown, "Suffering the Paradoxes of Rights," in *Left Legalism/Left Critique*, ed. Wendy Brown and Janet E. Halley (Durham, NC: Duke University Press, 2002), 432.

45. Giorgio Agamben, *Homo Sacer: Sovereign Power and Bare Life*, 1995, trans. Daniel Heller-Roazen, ed. David E. Wellbery (Stanford, CA: Stanford University Press, 1998), 52.

46. Jack Donnelly, *Universal Human Rights in Theory and Practice* (Ithaca, NY: Cornell University Press, 1989), 9.

47. John P. Humphrey, "The Magna Carta of Mankind," in *Human Rights*, ed. Peter Davies (New York: Routledge, 1988), 31.

48. I examine this temporalization of dignity in more detail in "A Question of Narration: The Voice in International Human Rights Law," *Human Rights Quarterly* 19, no. 2 (1997): 406–430.

49. Cited in Susan Maslan, "The Anti-Human: Man and Citizen before the Declaration of the Rights of Man and of the Citizen," *South Atlantic Quarterly* 103, no. 2/3 (2004): 358.

50. Lukács, *The Theory of the Novel*, 56.

51. Gayatri Chakravorty Spivak, "Righting Wrongs," in *Human Rights, Human Wrongs: Oxford Amnesty Lectures 2001*, ed. Nicholas Owen (Oxford: Oxford University Press, 2003), 189.

52. George Puttenham, *The Arte of English Poesie, 1859*, ed. R. C. Alston (Menston: Scholar, 1968), 213.

53. Jacques Maritain, *The Rights of Man and Natural Law*, trans. Doris C. Anson (New York: Scribner's Sons, 1943), 63.

54. Walter O. Weyrauch, "On Definitions, Tautologies, and Ethnocentrism in Regard to Universal Human Rights," in *Human Rights*, ed. Ervin H. Pollack (Buffalo, NY: Jay Stewart Publications, 1971), 199.

55. Charlotte Bunch, "Transforming Human Rights from a Feminist Perspective," in *Women's Rights, Human Rights: International Feminist Perspectives*, ed. Julie Peters and Andrea Wolper (New York: Routledge, 1995), 12. In addition to Bunch's seminal critique of the gender bias of human rights law ("Women's Rights as Human Rights: Toward a Re-Vision of Human Rights," *Human Rights Quarterly* 12 (1990): 486–498, see Adamantia Pollis and Peter Schwab, "Human Rights: A Western Construct with Limited Applicability," *Human Rights: Cultural and Ideological Perspectives*, eds. Adamantia Pollis and Peter Schwab (New York: Praeger, 1979), 1–18; Makau Mutua, *Human Rights: A Political and Cultural Critique* (Philadelphia: University of Pennsylvania Press, 2002) on the Euro-centrism of the law's normative image of the "individual."

56. This formulation of "common sense" comes from Hans Georg Gadamer's discussion of *Bildung* through Shaftesbury and Vico in *Truth and Method*, trans. Garrett Barden and John Cumming (New York: Seabury Press, 1975), 21. However, my sense of common sense is both more functionalist and affective, akin to Gramsci's ideological notion and Laclau and Mouffe's insistence that common sense is the hegemonic result of antagonistic, democratic struggles that are necessarily political in character.

57. *Declaration on the Right to Development,* GA/RES/41/128 Preamble, art. 2.
58. Frank Kermode, *The Sense of an Ending* (New York: Oxford University Press, 1966), 135.
59. Eleanor Roosevelt, "The Promise of Human Rights," *Foreign Affairs* 26 (1948): 473.
60. Drucilla Cornell, *Just Cause: Freedom, Identity, and Rights* (Lanham, MD: Rowman & Littlefield Publishers, 2000), 18–19. See also Cornell, "Bodily Integrity and the Right to Abortion," in *Identities, Politics, and Rights,* ed. Austin Sarat and Thomas R. Kearns (Ann Arbor: University of Michigan Press, 1995), 21–84.
61. In strict narratological terms, the teleological line of development is proper to the *fabula* and is emplotted tautologically in the *sjuzet.* Here is a short list of contemporary novels that offer formal refinements (and complications) to this generic structure of *Great Expectations*: Dangarembga, *Nervous Conditions*; Laferrière, *Dining with the Dictator*; al-Hamad, *Adama*; Edgell, *Beka Lamb*; Roy, *The God of Small Things*; Dow, *Juggling Truths*; Hope, *A Separate Development*; Beti, *Mission to Kala*; Bandele-Thomas, *The Sympathetic Undertaker and Other Dreams*; Gunesekera, *Reef*; Markandaya, *Nectar in a Sieve*; Bénabou, *To Write on Tamara?*; Vargas Llosa, *The Storyteller*; Parra, *Mama Blanca's Memoirs.*
62. Thomas Keenan, *Fables of Responsibility: Aberrations and Predicaments in Ethics and Politics* (Stanford, CA: Stanford University Press, 1997), 39–41.
63. Judith Butler, "Universality in Culture," in *Comparative Political Culture in the Age of Globalization: An Introductory Anthology,* ed. Hwa Yol Jung (Lanham, MD: Lexington Books, 2002), 360.
64. Rita Maran, *Torture: The Role of Ideology in the French- Algerian War* (New York: Praeger, 1989), 142.
65. On the *Bildungsroman* German national genre, see Todd Curtis Kontje, *The German* Bildungsroman: *History of a National Genre* (Columbia, SC: Camden House, 1994); W. Witte, "Alien Corn—The 'Bildungsroman': Not for Export?" *German Life and Letters* 33.1 (1979): 87–96; see also Klaus Vondung, "Unity through *Bildung*: A German Dream of Perfection," *Independent Journal of Philosophy* 5/6 (1988): 47–55, and Jeffrey L. Sammons, "The Mystery of the Missing *Bildungsroman*; or, What Happened to Wilhelm Meister's Legacy?" *Genre: Forms of Discourse and Culture* 14, no. 2 (1981): 229–246.
66. Wilhelm von Humboldt, *Linguistic Variability and Intellectual Development,* 1836, trans. Frithjof A. Raven (Philadelphia: University of Pennsylvania Press, 1971), 13. All recent translations of this passage into English share the phrase "human rights," and although it is a retrojective translation of Humboldt's eighteenth-century German, it does capture his sentiment. See Humboldt's *Humanist without Portfolio: An Anthology of the Writings of Wilhelm Von Humboldt,* trans. Marianne Cowan (Detroit, MI: Wayne State University Press, 1963), 267, and *Über die Verschiedenheit Des Menschlichen Sprachbaues Und Ihren Einfluß Auf Die Geistige Entwicklung Des Menschengeschlechts* (Darmstadt: Claassen & Roether, 1949), 28.
67. Barbara Harlow, *Barred: Women, Writing, and Political Detention* (Hanover, NH: University Press of New England, 1992), 252–3, my emphasis.
68. David Lloyd, *Anomalous States: Irish Writing and the Post-Colonial Moment* (Dublin: The Lilliput Press, 1993), 69.
69. Costas Douzinas, "Human Rights, Humanism and Desire," *Angelaki* 6, no. 3 (2001): 202.
70. For instance, the 1979 Convention on the Elimination of Discrimination Against Women was retrofitted in 1999 with an "optional protocol" that came into force a year later. The International Covenant on Civil and Political Rights (1966) has two optional protocols; the second (1989), aimed at

abolishing the death penalty, has not yet entered into force. The Convention Against Torture (1984) has a justiciable option (2002) that also has not yet come into force.

71. On the role of human rights in pre-twentieth-century "globalization," see Paul Gordon Lauren, *The Evolution of International Human Rights: Visions Seen* (Philadelphia: University of Pennsylvania Press, 1998).

72. Gourevitch's text was a source for the film *Hotel Rwanda*, which mobilized the *Bildungsroman* formula within a Hollywood idiom to merchandize the story of how genocide might have been avoided by affective self-identification with multinational tourism capital.

73. Philip Gourevitch, *We Wish to Inform You That Tomorrow We Will Be Killed with Our Families: Stories from Rwanda* (New York: Farrar Straus and Giroux, 1998), 6–9.

74. Laye's comments cited in Adele King, *Rereading Camara Laye* (Lincoln: University of Nebraska Press, 2002), 52.

75. Joseph Slaughter, "*Clef à Roman*: Some Uses of Human Rights and the *Bildungsroman*," *Politics and Culture* 4, no. 3 (2003). http://aspen.conncoll.edu/politicsandculture/page.cfm?key=244.

76. Jürgen Habermas, *The Structural Transformation of the Public Sphere: An Inquiry into a Category of Bourgeois Society*, 1962, trans. Thomas Burger and Frederick Lawrence, (Cambridge, MA: MIT Press, 1989; 1991), 12–13, 72.

77. Habermas, *Structural Transformation*, 85.

78. Pascale Casanova, *The World Republic of Letters*, 1999, trans. M. B. DeBevoise (Cambridge, MA: Harvard University Press, 2004), 43.

79. Costas Douzinas, *The End of Human Rights*, 2.

80. Ernst Bloch, *Natural Law and Human Dignity*, 1961, trans. Dennis J. Schmidt, ed. Thomas McCarthy (Cambridge, MA: MIT Press, 1986), 172.

81. Emily Brontë and William M. Sale, Jr., *Wuthering Heights: An Authoritative Text, with Essays in Criticism*, 2nd ed. (New York: Norton, 1972), 15.

82. Gourevitch, *We Wish to Inform You*, 6.

3 Top-Down, Bottom-Up, Horizontally

Resignifying the Universal in Human Rights Discourse

Domna C. Stanton

The past fifteen years have witnessed a dramatic return of universalism.[1] In contrast to Chinua Achebe's call in 1975 to see the term, "universalism," "banned altogether from discussions of African literature," because of its synonymity to "the narrow, self-serving parochialism of Europe,"[2] this recent turn means a rejection of postmodernism's own rejection of an Enlightenment master narrative, and its own privileging of the micro narratives of the local, most famously defined in Lyotard's *The Postmodern Condition*.[3] For the local (and, by extension, the particular and the relative),[4] in their traditional binary opposition to the universal, have come to be viewed as abstract, idealized notions that deny their own internal (and constitutive) plurality, the competing claims that exist within any concrete situation at any point in time. Bruce Robbins, for instance, has questioned the nostalgic associations of the local with uniqueness, presence, immediate experience and accessible subjectivity,[5] and he has criticized binary thinking for its rigid division of the universal from the particular. Going further, Ernesto Laclau has inveighed against particularism as confining, ultimately self-defeating, because it does not allow for a notion outside of the self or a movement toward those with different aspirations, thus blocking the possibility of a politics of transformation.[6] In so many words, the local (often identified with a politics of identity) has itself been cast as narrow, self-serving, and parochial. Already in the 1980s, some postcolonial critics, such as Satya Mohanty, had foregrounded key limitations of the fixation on the local, and its correlative, cultural relativism: foreclosing dialogue, relational possibilities, and the potential for learning and for change; avoiding the challenge of competing claims of rationality; and as a result, promoting political apathy.[7] In light of such criticism, Amanda Anderson heralded in 1998 the potential of a "new universalism [that] focuses on those ideals and practices that propel individuals and groups beyond the confines of restricted or circumscribed identities."[8]

However, just what defines this "new universal," how "new" it effectively is or, more important, can become remains a contested issue. For "universalism" has so many sedimented meanings and is so deeply rooted in the historical and present dynamics of power/knowledge that it is, as

Edward Said observed, "very difficult to construct *another* universality alongside this one."[9] And yet, in a latter-day version of the problem that Derrida tried to overcome with the notion of "under erasure" (*sous rature*),[10] it is, arguably, impossible to do without the term "universalism" or "the universal," even though it is always already permeated by layers of meaning and by regulatory norms, and thus that the best—or only—alternative is to subject it to critique and to attempt to resignify it through ongoing contest, even though its promise and significance, as Judith Butler noted, remain unclear.[11]

Not surprisingly, there seems to be greater unanimity as to what this new universalism should not be: classical, ancient, static;[12] immutable, eternal, essentialist;[13] in a word, Hegelian (in its "singular" or "abstract" form).[14] The proliferation of adjectives, which has marked attempts to define the new universal, in opposition to simple, absolute unity,[15] foregrounds the historical, contingent, concrete, contextual,[16] above all, the multiple and plural. These proposed terms, which represent tropes in poststructuralist thought, would seem to be, from a traditional perspective, the universal's antithesis. They are designed to permeate the universal with constitutive particularity, but in so doing, they turn the new universalism into a catachresis (rhetorically, a misuse of terms that constructs a paradox).[17] Thus, for Alessandro Ferrara, the "establishment of a credible form of universalism . . . a new 'concrete universalism'" will have to incorporate "the contextuality of knowledge" and "a genuine acceptance of . . . pluralism."[18]

And yet, the resignification of the universal as a productive catachrestic figure does not resolve issues of contest among concrete, plural, particular claims and how to adjudicate them. As Linda G. M. Zirilli emphasizes in her review essay of Ernesto Laclau's *Emancipations* (1996), which she entitles, "This Universalism Which Is Not One," after Luce Irigaray's *This Sex Which Isn't One* (1977), plurality will not be something to overcome in constructing the universal as the site of multiple significations and standpoints made up of particulars—fragile, shifting, incomplete.[19] But when Laclau insists on the equivalence of particulars and promotes mediation among competing particulars, it is difficult to see how intersubjective agreement can ever be reached, even tentatively. Further, as Zirilli suggests, without a recognition of power differentials, some particulars will be more central in constructing the new universal than others, which will thereby be relegated to the periphery or margins; the new universal can well turn out to be more of the same.[20]

More than any other contemporary theorist, Butler has grappled since 1995 with the imperative of the universal's transformation and re-articulation.[21] According to her antifoundationalist definition,[22] the universal has shifted meanings over time and in different places—what is particular in one place can be universal in another. The universal is not simply and fundamentally culturally variable, then, but its significance comes from the cultural conditions of its articulations, indeed, it is not possible to speak the universal outside of those articulations.[23] Thus, Butler examines past and present definitions of the universal for their particular exclusions, arguing, in a move that is analogous to her discussion of the abject in *Bodies that Matter*, that what is excluded from the universal is precisely what constitutes it, and that these exclusions must first be exposed.[24] At the same time, the excluded engage in challenges to the universal, in struggles to be included, even advocate for their own identificatory concept to dominate. This ongoing process, which Butler terms universalization, serves to re-articulate the universal, and has the capacity, she claims, not to domesticate differences within.[25] Such a contest (or negotiation) is permanently open-ended, for Butler, since there is no way of knowing or anticipating what the universal will include in the future; an ultimate form of universalism is thus never achievable or realizable.[26]

Leaving aside for the moment, the possible work that such a conception of the universal can achieve, I want to consider its significance for the human rights regime at present and in the future. The universalism of human rights was decried as Euro-centric, and impervious to cultural particularity, even before the passage of the Universal Declaration of Human Rights (hereafter, UDHR) in 1948. "How can the proposed Declaration be applicable to all human beings?" asked the American Anthropological Association in its 1947 statement on human rights, "how can the proposed Declaration . . . not be a statement of rights conceived only in terms of the values prevalent in the countries of Western Europe and America?"[27] More recently, of course, in the wake of the postmodern turn, the values of Enlightenment humanism, which provided the philosophical underpinnings of human rights declarations, covenants, conventions, protocols, and charters,[28] have been widely criticized for their blind spots. As Tzvetan Todorov has noted, humanists saw themselves as universalists, when in truth their horizon ended at the edges of Europe; their universalism was ethnocentrism's mask.[29] The occidentocentrism of the UDHR, more broadly, of the human rights regime has been denounced in anti-imperialist, postcolonial, and progressive interventions aimed at instituting discursive and other political practices that do not "speak for others," as Linda Alcoff put it,[30] but speak "with them" in particular, concrete, local ways.

If the difficulty of overcoming an imperialist "speaking for others" should not be underestimated, as Gayatri Spivak has shown,[31] the rejection of universalism in the name of cultural particularity is neither easy nor necessarily emancipatory. In recent years, western and non-western critics have emphasized the abuse of the local as an alibi for human rights violations perpetrated with dictatorial impunity; or as Michael Ignatieff put it somewhat hyperbolically, "relativism is the invariable alibi of tyranny."[32] All too often, Bonny Ibhawoh argues, dictators have rejected interventions ("interference") from human rights non-governmental organizations (hereafter NGOs) by brandishing the alibi of their cultural rights and their national sovereignty.[33] Analogously, the legitimate insistence, in many emerging societies, that economic development should be weighed as heavily, or even more heavily, than human rights has been compromised by claims that the suppression or denial of those rights is a necessary condition for development, although in our globalized world, development overwhelmingly benefits multinational corporations or national elites, rather than the local populations who do the dangerous labor.[34] Louis Henkin thus asks: "how much industry is built by massacre, torture, and detention, by unfair trials and other injustice, by abuse of minorities, by denials of freedoms of conscience, by suppression of political association and expression?"[35]

Without ignoring these various critiques, which are part and parcel of the contest surrounding the universal, the broad critical project to articulate "a new universal" makes it imperative to examine the nature—and extent—of human rights universalism, and the degree to which it is, always already was, or has become—precisely through ongoing contest—plurally inflected by concrete and contingent claims. In the following pages, I consider some aspects of these issues, by looking first, "top down," at the semantic usage of the "universal" and the purview of the "human" in human rights documents, such as the UDHR, as well as the proliferation of documents in this regime over the past sixty years. I then look briefly at the structure of the human rights regime, including its top/down and/or bottom/up regionalism, national institutions and transnational non-profit organizations (NGOs), which are part of global civil society. And last, I grapple with the problematics of mediation in the contest among particulars to re-articulate the universal, whether by a process that Butler terms "cultural translation" or a bottom-up process I call generalizability. So doing, I aim to highlight the meanings, the important work, but also the necessary vigilance in all efforts to re-articulate the universalism of human rights discourse, a process without end.

ON THE "UNIVERSAL" AND THE "HUMAN" IN HUMAN RIGHTS DOCUMENTS

The language of universalism rarely appears in human rights declarations, and where it does, its meaning in context seems circumscribed. To be sure, the preamble of the UDHR affirms "the promotion of universal respect and observance of human rights and fundamental freedoms" and the goal to "secure their universal and effective recognition and observance"[36]; or, in a more specific instance, it states that "the will of the people shall be expressed . . . by universal and equal suffrage" (*TFHRD*, 8, art. 21). In all these cases, however, the term does not mean a "necessary *a priori*," as an Aristotelian or a Platonic universal would, nor does it have the strong sense of "the whole universe," but rather something like a synonym for "wholesale" or "comprehensive."[37]

In addition to the circumscribed purview of "the universal," the human rights regime, since 1948, has been marked by a steady proliferation of documents, both in response to new historical, political, economic, and cultural conditions and in multiple efforts to compensate for, amend, or even contradict earlier formulations. Thus, for instance, the International Convention on the Elimination of all Forms of Racial Discrimination (entered into force in 1969), while referencing as its ground the articles of the UDHR, pointedly highlights the need for a new convention, beyond the United Nations Declaration on the Granting of Independence to Colonial Countries and Peoples (1960), because of widespread "alarm . . . by manifestations of racial discrimination still in evidence in some areas of the world and by governmental policies based on racial superiority or hatred, such as policies of *apartheid*, segregation or separation."[38] Similarly, the convention on the Elimination of all Forms of Discrimination against Women (CEDAW, 1979) begins by expressing its concern that "despite . . . various instruments," such as the UDHR and other resolutions and declarations, "extensive discrimination against women continues to exist" (*TFHRD*, 48).

More broadly than these particular documentary instances, the human rights regime has expanded beyond the first generation of civil and political rights, which dealt essentially with liberty, to a second generation of affirmative or positive rights, focused on equality and defined most notably by economic, social, and cultural rights, including the right to food, housing, work and to an adequate standard of living and health. Outlined in the International Covenant on Economic, Social, and Cultural rights (entered into force in 1976),[39] the dimensions and methodology of these affirmative rights are still the subject of considerable contest today.[40] More recently, a third generation of group and collective rights (or rights of solidarity) has emerged,[41] partially, I would argue, in response to the problematic focus on individual rights in earlier documents, such as the UDHR.[42] These group rights, which include the right to economic and social development and to sovereignty over natural resources, have been promoted by "the Third World," in contrast to first-generation rights, thought to reflect the interests of the West, and second-generation rights, those of the East.[43] In 1999, for instance, nation-states began to ratify the Protection of the Rights of all Migrant Workers and Members of their Families; and in 2007, the United Nations approved a declaration on the rights of indigenous peoples.

This ongoing production of new texts to affirm rights that new contextual conditions make apparent and that require address undermines the notion of a fixed, timeless, eternal universalism in this regime, even from the outset. The foundational 1948 UDHR inscribes its own historical situatedness as a concrete response to Nazi Germany: its self-justificative preamble evokes the World War II "disregard and contempt for human rights [that] have resulted in barbarous acts which have outraged the conscience of mankind" (*TFHRD*, 6). The UDHR can be read as an international attempt to reorder the normative structure of postwar international relations, and to give individuals agency to disobey the state's legal but immoral orders.[44] If this and other documents empower the individual, they also make states, indeed only member states of the United Nations, the signatories and the subjects, the addressees and actors of the human rights regime. The preamble of the UDHR openly aims for observance only "among the peoples of Members States themselves and among the peoples of territories under their jurisdiction" (*TFHRD*, 6), a 1948 reference to colonial subjects. As a result, the International Covenant on Civil and Political Rights (ratified in 1966) formulates political rights for citizens, not for humans universally. This specification, which is grounded in the dominant notion after 1948 of "freedom from" the trampling on human rights by the state, simultaneously exposes one of the major weaknesses of the entire regime: the state is the ultimate determinant of rights within its territory. Almost every convention in the regime contains the caveat that exists in the Covenant on Civil and Political Rights: that "in time of public emergency . . . the States Parties to the present Covenant may take measures derogating from their obligations under the present Covenant to the extent strictly required by the exigencies of the situation" (*TFHRD*, 18). This derogation is also stipulated when the covenant does not accord with the law of the state in force at the time of the commission of the crime, even when that law contravenes the articles of the UDHR, such as freedom from capital punishment (*TFHRD*, 12–4, 18–9, 21–2).[45] This caveat, which was undoubtedly the price for gaining signatories to the document, has, of course, been sorely abused by states— two recent instances are the Darfur genocides in the Sudan and the flagrant flouting of the Geneva conventions in the United States after 9/11.[46]

As a result, a movement has emerged to limit the state's impunity and thus its sovereignty (as well as to articulate the instances that demand external intervention), known as "the responsibility to protect" (R2P). The report of the International Commission on Intervention and State Sovereignty, under the leadership of Gareth Evans and Mohamed Sahnoun, underscores the primary responsibility of sovereign states to protect their own citizens from genocide, war crimes, crimes against humanity, and other massive human rights violations, including starvation, ethnic cleansing, and rape, and it articulates a normative (legal and ethical) basis for transferring that responsibility collectively to the international community when states fail to fulfill it.[47]

The goals of R2P—to minimize the power of sovereign nations, notably through humanitarian interventions or then through criminal prosecutions at the International Criminal Court of the perpetrators of gross violations, including heads of state,[48] as well as to expand their responsibilities to populations within their borders—aim to redress omissions and more fundamental exclusions in the human rights regime, such as the rights of stateless people living within a national territory. As Hannah Arendt argued in the *Origins of Totalitarianism* (1951), the human right to have rights proved not to exist for the stateless during the holocaust.[49] And it still does not properly exist within the human rights regime sixty years later. Conventions on refugees (for instance, Convention Relating to the Status of Refugees and Protocol Relating to the Status of Refugees [entered into force in 1954 and 1967, respectively]) do not begin to include and to protect adequately non-state actors or minority populations, such as gypsies.[50]

The UDHR may deploy circumlocutions for "the universal," such as "all members of the human family, "the human person," "all human beings," "all peoples and all nations," and most frequent by far, "everyone/no one,"[51] but in point of fact, the human rights regime is constituted by its inclusions, and more important, its exclusions. Since universalism in human rights discourse has everything to do with the definition of the "human," a term rarely examined and denaturalized in human rights discourse, "it is an ongoing task of human rights," says Butler rightly, "to reconceive the human [in human rights] when it finds that its putative universality does not have universal reach."[52]

While the conventions, declarations, and charters that have made up this regime since 1948 have expanded and thus arguably redefined the "human," it is nonetheless critical to expose the constitutive exclusions of "the human" that narrow the purview of any notion of "the universal." As Luce Irigaray has argued, perhaps with excessive unambiguity, the UDHR "may be a moving document, but from the very first article, I, a woman, no longer feel 'human' . . . I cannot feel that this 'universal' charter includes me. . . . "[It] means nothing in terms of my everyday reality as a woman," she continues, pointing to the various articles whose substance and goals have not been realized—"I am not 'born free and equal in dignity and rights' [to 'men'],"" and similarly, "I" do not have the right to freedom of movement, do not have equal access to public service, and my body does not have equal treatment to that given a man's.[53] And yet, what Irigaray condemns as "egalitarian slogans . . . [that] simply promote a totalitarian ideology" (*thinking the difference*, ix–xi) could also be viewed as part of the aspirational, possibly unrealizable goals of the human rights regime that only contestatory political work can strive to change, as CEDAW and other efforts on behalf of the excluded do, in the process of subjecting the human to redefinition. To claim specific rights for women and other others is, as Butler recognizes, to admit "the human's" constitutive outside and in a productive sense to destroy the universal.[54] To be sure, as she observes, the very fact that there exists a "women's human rights" or a "gay and lesbian human rights" movement means that these humans have been excluded from the normative understanding of the "human," as have peoples of color and of certain ethnic origins in the colonialist and racist understanding of universalism, which provided, as Butler puts it, "the frame by which the human was constituted."[55] What she terms the "spectrally human," "the inhuman, the beyond the human, the less than human" is perhaps most radically exemplified today by "jihadists" and "terrorists," as their treatment by U.S. military and intelligence institutions, special forces, and subcontractors have horrifically confirmed in the torture memos, the visual record of their treatment, and the bits of information about the black holes of non-humanity in which they were cast and that now are coming to light.[56] For moments of heightened conflict and violence test a state's commitment to a "universal" inclusion of human beings, and can become the catalyst for expanding "the human." As Butler writes in *Precarious Life*, "Whether or not we continue to enforce a universal conception of human rights at moments of outrage and incomprehension, precisely when we think that others have taken themselves out of the human community as we know it, is a test of our very humanity."[57]

THE MULTI-FACETED STRUCTURE
OF THE HUMAN RIGHTS REGIME

The agonistic process of expanding and resignifying the "human," as well as the ongoing proliferation of documents that begin to compensate for and to speak the omissions/commissions of earlier texts are part and parcel of the human rights regime. This dynamic structure is further pluralized by constituent sub-structures, such as the system of regional and national organizations as well as transnational and local groups and networks that make up global civil society.

Although it is difficult to define the regional, to establish meaningful divisions, and, even more, to organize nation states into collaborative and powerful alliances,[58] regional rights organizations began to develop in the 1950s soon after the passing of the UDHR. The European convention for the Protection of Human Rights entered into force in 1953, others later, such as the African Charter on People's and Human Rights in 1986 and the Cairo Declaration on Human Rights in Islam signed in 1990.[59] Regional organizations initially confronted resistance within the United Nations over what was perceived to be a breakaway movement that would undermine the universality of human rights.[60] Since then, regional organizations have achieved different levels of activism and of effective collaboration, but because of their self-interests,[61] they can—at least their states' representatives can—hypothetically articulate their plural differences and so provide ongoing contest to a dominant discourse within the human rights regime. It could be argued that regional organizations have foregrounded values and institutions that have inflected the global regime. Thus, the African Union has emphasized distinctive norms of duties and responsibilities to the community as much as rights,[62] and these duties are now embedded within human rights instruments; the European Union and the Inter-American system have each produced an effective supranational court that, in the first case, has taken on—and thus put into more visible circulation—such contested issues as blasphemy and gay rights and, in the second, has created a powerful Commission on Human Rights. Spivak describes a crosshatching of regional organizations in the global south that consist not only of the Association of South East Asian Nations and the South Asian Association for Regional Cooperation, but also of emerging groupings within them, such as West Asia or Eurasia. These can "produce something other than nation-statism tied by national sovereignty, to check post–cold war Euro–U.S.'s perennial dream of universalism," she argues, a "critical regionalism" that would go "under and over nationalisms but kee[p] the abstract structures of something like a state that allows for constitutional redress . . . in the interest of a public that cannot act for itself."[63]

In an effort to construct a productive division of labor between the regional and the global dimensions of the human rights regime, a 1980 Commission to Study the Organization of Peace recommended that "the global [human rights] instrument would contain the minimum normative standard, whereas the regional instrument might go further, add further rights, refine some rights and take into account special differences within the region and between one region and another."[64] This significant function of the supplement(al) can deflect radical particularisms among which no communication is possible, on the one hand, and on the other, it should help combat assimilation to a pre-existing, purportedly "universal" norm. Such supra-national organizations, engaged in a "critical regionalism," can expose instances where a human rights utterance does not have the same meaning in situ, and where conflicting positions emerge, it can catalyze a fruitful contest of understandings.

Despite the fact—or, more likely, because—the nation-state has been viewed as the source of violations of human rights, since 1993 the United Nations has established national human rights institutions (NHRIs). Now numbering over 100, NHRIs were formed, says Anne Smith, in nation-states either making the transition from conflict (such as North Ireland, Latvia, South Africa, the Philippines) or trying to consolidate and underpin other human rights protections (e.g., Australia, Canada, and France) or, then, under pressure to respond to allegations of abuses (e.g., Cameroon, Nigeria, Togo, and Mexico). NHRIs are governed in principle, if not in actuality, by the Paris Principles,[65] which include the mandate to monitor the state's violations of human rights, advise competent national bodies on specific violations or on legislation's compliance with international human rights instruments,[66] educate and inform the population, from which it is to receive and investigate complaints, and create relations with regional and international organizations. Key to the effectiveness of an NHRI, Smith shows, is pluralism in its composition (reflecting differences of religion, language, socioeconomics, ethnicity, gender, sexual orientation, and disability), independence from the government (adequate finances and powers to initiate investigations and to compel witnesses to testify),[67] and accountability to the population of the nation-state. NHRIs occupy "a unique space," Smith concludes, but the difficulties of negotiating independence *and* accountability can be overwhelming for many of these institutions,[68] which in some instances may represent nothing more than a propaganda machine for governments in power.

In the human rights regime, NHRIs are situated—often uncomfortably—between national governments and civil society, among which, most notably, are NGOs. A contested term that has catalyzed a multitude of definitions and emphases, civil society is generally held to be a space that is neither governmental (official) nor commercial.[69] However, its exponential growth in recent decades,[70] enhanced by the reach of global media, tele-communications industries, and the advent of the internet also means that civil society cannot be neatly separated from the commercial: since NGOs and the non-profit sector in general are a major international economic force for employment and income, they are of necessity contaminated or inflected by economic imperatives.[71] Moreover, the idea(l) in the 1990s that NGOs and new social movements would help to construct an alternative social and world order, even replace the state in service provision and social care, has been contested by anti-globalization movements, even before the global downturn in economies.

Still, NGOs (can) remain a powerful counter-force and a complement to the nation-state, and to the human rights regime through their concrete activities at transnational, national, and local levels, where they can further the work of—and build coalitions with—groups on the ground. For at bottom, human rights are the praxis of activists around the world, who often bear witness to gross human rights violations.[72] To be sure, Human Rights Watch, Amnesty International, Oxfam, Lawyers for Human Rights, and a host of other western-based NGOs are often accused of perpetrating their own brand of western imperialism at one level and, at another, of capriciously focusing on a particular human rights problem in a particular locality, only to pick up and go to the next hot spot, failing to do essential advocacy work to support the development of local activisms. The difficult balancing act of staying in one place or shifting resources to another site of violation, with which all human rights organizations struggle, should not efface the multiple ways in which NGOs help local groups further their own concrete priorities and goals—for example, the plight of homosexuals in Jamaica, water free of toxic poisons in Latin America, honor killings in Jordan—and assist their efforts to become visible in—eventually, to contest, perhaps transform— "universal" human rights. Like national and regional human rights associations, NGOs and civil society organizations constitute a third space between the local and the global, a plural mediating position between the particular and the universal that does what Bruce Robbins calls "translocal connecting" (Robbins, 196), and further pluralizes the human rights regime.

CONCEPTUALIZING NEGOTIATION HORIZONTALLY AND BOTTOM UP: CULTURAL TRANSLATION AND THE GENERALIZABLE

The dynamic structure of the pluralistic human rights regime does not eliminate—but on the contrary, highlights—the problematics of negotiating differences among particular claims anchored in localities and, moreover, of ensuring that adjudicated claims (always already impregnated with aspects of globality) enter a space where they can pressure—and help to resignify—the universal.

To describe this process, Butler has advanced the principle of cultural translation, which she takes from Homi Bhabha, to articulate the "necessarily difficult task of forging a universal consensus from various locations of culture," the "difficult practice of translation among the various languages in which universality makes its varied and contending appearances."[73] This concept, which I extend here to the problem of negotiation at every level of the human rights regime, predicates the idea that different, contested meanings must not represent, in Butler's words, "the simple entry of the deauthorized into the authorized, whereby . . . the latter domain simply makes room for what it has unwittingly failed to accommodate."[74] This, then, is not assimilation to an existing norm, or "incorporation [of] alienness into an established lexicon," Butler explains, but rather, a labor "in which the terms made to stand for one another are transformed in the process," an "unanticipated transformation that establishe[s] the universal as that which is yet to be achieved."[75] There are inescapable risks in this project, as Butler recognizes: translation can "work in full complicity with the logic of colonial expansion [and become] . . . the instrument through which dominant values are transposed into the language of the subordinated, and the subordinated run the risk of coming to know and understand them as token of their 'liberation'"[76]; similarly, translation can become the "imposition of a universal claim on a culture that resists it, or . . . those who defend the universal will domesticate the challenge posed by alterity by invoking that very cultural claim as an example of its own nascent universality, one which confirms that such a universality is already achieved."[77] Such concerns implicitly acknowledge, but perhaps do not sufficiently highlight, the radical differences in power (economic, political, military, cultural and sexual) between the "dominant" and the "subordinated," for, in Butler's analysis, this process seems to move top down, rather than horizontally, as the concept of translation suggests.[78] Even more important, Butler follows Bhabha to cast translation predominantly as a movement between/among languages, a linguistic model that does not elaborate what the "cultural" encompasses.[79] And, as Mora Lloyd points out, Butler nowhere underscores, as Bhabha and Walter Benjamin do, what always remains "untranslatable" between two languages, and thus what cannot be transformed by a translational encounter. In Bhabha's example, the migrant experience, operating between cultures, "dramatizes the activity of culture's untranslatability," puts into jeopardy the possibility of achieving a shared language, indeed does not relieve conflict nor the agonistic attempt to "exclude the other."[80]

Butler exemplifies the conceptual and, more difficult by far, the practical and political difficulties of negotiating cultural and other differences in the contest of meanings to expand and transform the universal in the human rights regime. As with definitions of the new universal itself, it is easier to say what the concept of negotiation—and its process—must reject: the

76 Domna C. Stanton

idea(l) of consensus, based on an enlightenment top-down model. There is a shared view among many writers on "the new universal" that the process of transaction cannot be achieved through a neo-Kantian notion of communicative reason, predicated on reciprocity and equality. This Habermasian vision of consensus, which Lyotard frontally attacks in *The Postmodern Condition* and which Butler dubs prelapsarian,[81] does not only lack sensitivity to context, diversity, and multiplicity but also denies differences of power/knowledge among human subjects who come to the "public space"—if they are allowed within it to speak—even the existence of an ongoing agon for conceptual domination.

From yet another perspective, Clifford Geertz rejects the possibility of consensus in any methodology for ascertaining what is universal or local, constant or variable. Observing that "the notion of a *consensus gentium* (a consensus of all mankind) . . . was present in the Enlightenment and probably has been present in some form or another in all ages and climes," Geertz deems a consensus approach a failure because substantive core elements are invariably outweighed by particularities.[82] "Generalizations about man as man [sic] are not to be discovered through a Baconian search for cultural universals, a kind of public-opinion polling of the world's people in search of a *consensus gentium* that does not in fact exist," he states; the only generalization that can be made is that "[man] is a most various animal" and that this essential variousness is best garnered through the study of particular details in the system of human relations.[83]

While he stresses the lack of opposition between general and circumstantial understanding, Geertz still highlights the importance of drawing "general propositions out of particular phenomena," and he maintains that this "road to the general . . . lies through a concern with the particular, the circumstantial, the concrete."[84] Such a conceptual and methodological road can be productively (albeit heuristically) applied to the problematics of transaction and negotiation in the human rights regime, in my view, providing a bottom up approach that seems critical for the resignification of the universal. But rather than "the general," I prefer the notion of "the generalizable," in an attempt to delineate a process without end—generalizabilization—for forging commonalities through a contest of meanings, rather than achieving a product, a generalization.[85]

This concept bears some similarity to M. G. Singer's "generalization argument," even though he alleges it holds for all moral judgments, and thus makes it normative, too "universal" for my argument.[86] And yet, Singer's schema valorizes cultural diversity, "the empirically ascertained fact that there are a great many different and even conflicting rules and practices prevailing at different times and in different places," while it also rejects "the theory that moral ideas . . . reflect the 'standpoint' of some particular society and only 'hold for' that society."[87] His generalization argument does not "require any uniformity of practices in different cultures . . . what is right in Pomerania need not be right in Polynesia, or among the Dobuans, or in Rome. What is puzzling is that it should ever have been supposed that it should."[88] According to Singer's analysis, human subject A is right in doing X and subject B would be right in doing the same "if there is a relevant similarity in their . . . circumstances"—an argument that makes space for contextual particularity and difference. Although it may be difficult to determine the precise nature of the "relevant" and the exact moment when similarity emerges in the circumstances of human agents, Singer's emphasis on context and on what he calls "the condition of restricted universality" seems potentially useful for imagining an intersubjective process that negotiates between the particular and the universal in the human rights regime.[89]

The concept of the generalizable is an attempt to think through nonviolent negotiations and transactions of differences and contests, and to shift the focus from a top-down (e.g., from the "universal" in the UDHR) to a bottom-up approach, rooted in various, concrete localities, but not bound or limited by them, and moving potentially in every wider circles of agreement and commonality. In the pragmatic terms that John Dewey spells out for achieving "the general," in what he calls the continuum of judgment, a proposition proceeds from singulars to other singulars and is proved (or reconfirmed) by a sufficient number of particular cases; but all the while, singulars demonstratively refer back to those singulars; then—and here Dewey borrows from John Stuart Mill's account of generalization—propositions proceed from observed to unobserved cases by "a generalizing propensity," which may turn out to be unwarranted and thus would need to be rejected.[90] This movement involves "processes of comparison which extract elements that are *common* to many cases and drop out those that differ," in an effort to control over-extensive inference. Through this process, says Dewey, there must be "existential material . . . selectively discriminated and related (ordered) so that it functions as the ground for warranted inferential conclusions."[91]

In trying to translate this structure of logical judgment into the terms of the human rights regime, I aim to emphasize singular, particular contestations and transactions that must occur at every step of the way: from local NGOs to the national NHRI to critical regional organizations, on to cross-national social networks and new social movements in global civil society, and then throughout the proliferated set of documents, conventions and charters—all of which make up the complex, dynamic structure of the human rights regime. This contingent process, in which unwarranted generalizations, based on inferences, will need to be rejected, would involve a critical, vigilant comparativism focused on gauging what has been excluded or not spoken in the universal statements of this regime, but also, concurrently, on any emergent generalizable issues and claims that need to be inscribed into human rights discourse, and thereby, expand and transform it. A process that must be open-ended, generalizabilization can produce provisional universalizing statements, propositions that must, of course, be subject to constant re-examination and revision over time to forge and to sustain intersubjective agreements.

I am pointing to a problem here, not a solution. I am outlining a possible approach to counteract the conceptual and political predominance of the global and the universal in human rights discourse, to put a concept into circulation, to see whether it can take, take off, as part of what Anne Phillips calls "a politics of greater generality and alliance."[92] The goal of a concept such as the generalizable is to find a transactional way to make ever widening connections, something like the concept that Charles Sanders Pierce deployed through the metaphor of the cable to describe the work of philosophy. He writes: we should "trust rather to the multiplicity and variety of . . . arguments than to the conclusiveness of any one. Its reasoning should not form a chain which is no stronger than its weakest link, but a cable whose fibers may be ever so slender, provided they are sufficiently numerous and intimately connected."[93]

That "the new universal" does not—and cannot—resolve the problematics of transaction or negotiation between (the false binaries of) the local and the global, the universal and the particular does not diminish the value of the multiple efforts to elaborate the notion in recent years, for this project has denaturalized universalism and reached beyond the romance of the local to search for generalizabilizations and, in the process, to forge alliances for change and to effect transformations within the human rights regime. As a body of work, these efforts outline "a critical universalism," and they replicate the move that Spivak once advocated for essentialism: a "strategic use of positivist [universalism] in a scrupulously visible political interest."[94]

Of necessity, this project must abandon a totalizing representation of the universal in the human rights regime and recognize its dynamic, plural, historically more expansive and more inclusive structure. And from their various privileged locations, those (we) who write and work on this "critical" universalism also need to remember the *political* work that "universalism" has achieved and continues to perform. As Baxi reminds us, most decolonized nations asserted the universality of rights in their struggle for self-determination against imperial powers;[95] thus in the 1990s, blacks and "coloreds," excluded from South Africa's definition of rights holders, enlisted human rights universalism to make claims for their own emancipation and inclusion in "the human." For South Asia and for indigenous peoples in general, as Spivak acknowledges, United Nations "universalistic" declarations that recognize rights to self-determination constitute "an excellent tool for political maneuvering."[96] This holds true as well for women, gays, lesbians, and other others, Butler emphasizes: "although many feminist have come to the conclusion that the universal is always a cover for certain epistemological imperialism, insensitive to cultural texture and difference, the rhetorical power of claiming universality for rights of sexual autonomy and related rights of sexual orientation within the international human rights domain appears indisputable."[97]

The praxis of critical human rights—in the last analysis, all critical practices—demand both a commitment to what might be and a self-conscious vigilance about what is and what has been naturalized so thoroughly we think it must always be. Aspirations to possibilities of becoming do not mean belief in some future perfect. The work of contest and resignification knows no human end. And that is as it should be, since the stakes are enormous for determining who is "the human," what our local, our general, and our universal rights are, and thus what we make of the world.

NOTES

1. Naomi Schor claimed that universalism marked its "return" in Ernesto Laclau's talk at a conference, cosponsored by *October* and the Collège International de Philosophie, on November 16, 1991, and held at the Graduate Center of the City University of New York; the papers became a special issue of *October*. See Laclau, "Universalism, Particularism and the Question of Identity," *October* 61 (1992): 83–90; Schor, "French Feminism is a Universalism," *differences: a journal of feminist cultural studies* 7, no.1 (1995): 28–29. As Amanda Anderson notes in "Cosmopolitanism, Universalism and the Divided Legacies of Modernity," "One of the more remarkable developments in contemporary cultural criticism has been the surge of interest in the idea and history of universalism" (*Cosmopolitics: Thinking and Feeling Beyond the Nation*, ed. Pheng Cheah and Bruce Robbins [Minneapolis: University of Minnesota Press, 1998], 265).
2. Chinua Achebe, *Morning Yet on Creation Day*, cited in Neil Lazarus et al., "The Necessity of Universalism," *differences: a journal of feminist cultural studies* 7, no.1 (1995): 89.
3. Jean Lyotard, *The Postmodern Condition*, trans. G. Bennington and B. Massumi (Minneapolis: University of Minnesota Press, 1984); see also in this work, the Epilogue, "Answering the Question: What Is Postmodernism," trans. Régis Durand, 71–82.
4. I do not deny differences among the particular, the relative, and the local on the one hand, postcolonialism and postmodernism on the other; I lump them here provisionally to signal an important trend.
5. Bruce Robbins, *Secular Vocations: Intellectuals, Professionalism, Culture* (New York: Verso, 1993), 188. Analogously, Tracy Higgins has warned against essentializing the local: "Anti-Essentialism, Relativism and Human Rights," in *Harvard Women's Law Journal* 89 (1996): 89–126.
6. Laclau, "Universalism," 87. Upendra Baxi has labeled the discourse of relativism "deeply diversionary." *The Future of Human Rights* (Oxford: Oxford University Press, 2002) 96, 101.
7. Satya Mohanty, "Epilogue: Colonial Legacies, Multicultural Futures: Relativism, Objectivity and the Challenge of Otherness," *Colonialism and the Postcolonial Condition*, special issue of *PMLA* 110, no.1 (1995): 108–118.
8. Anderson, "Cosmopolitanism," 266. See also Anne Phillips's insistence that "We cannot . . . do without some notion of stretching outside of ourselves . . . some imaginative—and more importantly, some practical—movement towards linking up with those who have seemed different. This remnant of the old pretensions is perhaps best described as an aspiration or an impulse towards universality: a recognition of the partial, and potentially confining,

nature of all our different and specific identities." "Universal Pretensions to Political Thought," in *Destabilizing Theory: Contemporary Feminist Debates*, ed. Michèle Barrett and Anne Phillips (Stanford, CA: Stanford University Press, 1992), 27.

9. Edward W. Said, "Nationalism, Human Rights and Interpretation," in *On Human Rights: The Oxford Amnesty Lectures, 1993*, ed. Stephen Shute and Susan Hurley (New York: Basic Books, 1994), 198.

10. Jacques Derrida never presented a systematic analysis of the concept, but it is first discussed in *Of Grammatology*, trans. Gayatri Chakravorty Spivak (Baltimore: Johns Hopkins University Press, 1976), 23. See Spivak's comments in her Preface, lxxx.

11. Judith Butler, "Restaging the Universal: Hegemony and the Limits of Formalism," in *Contingency, Universality, Hegemony* (New York: Verso, 2000), 38.

12. Linda M. G. Zirilli, "This Universalism Which Is Not One," *Diacritics* 28, no. 2 (1998): 2; Laclau, "Universalism," 84, 89; Anderson, "Cosmopolitanism," 282.

13. See Schor, "French Feminism Is a Universalism," 24, 29, 33.

14. On the different types of universality in Hegel, see Etienne Balibar, "Ambiguous Universality," *differences: a journal of feminist cultural studies* 7, no.1 (1995): 48; Butler, "Restaging the Universal," 4ff, 14ff; Baxi, *The Future of Human Rights*, 93–94; Luce Irigaray, *Sexes et parentés* (Paris: Editions de Minuit, 1987) and *J'aime à toi: Esquisse d'une félicité en histoire* (Paris: Grasset, 1992).

15. Balibar, "Ambiguous Universality," 72.

16. See Etienne Balibar, *Masses, Classes, Ideas; Studies on Politics and Philosophy Before and After Marx* (New York: Routledge, 1994), 48; Laclau, "Universalism," 88.

17. On the overlapping, interpenetrating nature of the particular and the universal and the impossibility of drawing a line between them, see Clifford Geertz, "The Impact of the Concept of Culture on the Concept of Man," in *The Interpretation of Cultures: Selected Essays* (New York: Basic Books, 1973), 36; Laclau, *Emancipation(s)* (London: Verso, 1996); Judith Butler, "Competing Universalities" in Judith Butler, Ernesto Laclau and Slavoj Zizek, *Contingency, Universality, Hegemony* (New York: Verso, 2000), 166–167.

18. Alessandro Ferrara, "Universalisms: Procedural, Contextualist and Prudential," *Philosophy and Social Criticism* 14, no. 3/4 (1996): 243ff. On the multiple or plural in the universal, see Laclau, "Universalism," 84 and Balibar, "Ambiguous Universality," 72. However, as Butler cautions, pluralism can reinstall homogeneity after a little complexity is admitted into its fold; see Butler and Gayatri Chakravorty Spivak, *Who Sings the Nation State?* (New York: Seagull Books, 2007), 62.

19. Zirilli, "This Universalism Which Is Not One," 7–8, 10–11, 15–16.

20. Zirilli, "This Universalism Which Is Not One," 6–8, 11. As Zirilli also asks: "does the particular in Laclau overflow, is it overcome, divested of its particularity or transformed?" "This Universalism Which Is Not One," 15.

21. Butler, "Universality in Culture," in *For Love of Country: Debating the Limits of Patriotism; Martha Nussbaum with Respondents*, ed. Joshua Cohen (Boston: Beacon Press, 1996), 48, 51.

22. Butler, in Seyla Benhabib et al., *Feminist Contentions: A Philosophical Exchange* (New York: Routledge, 1995), 41; *Undoing Gender* (New York: Routledge, 2004), 190–1.

23. Butler, "Universality in Culture," 50; Butler, "Restaging the Universal," 33, 41; Butler, in Benhabib et al., *Feminist Contentions*, 129–30.

24. Butler, "Restaging the Universal," 39–41, Butler, "Universality in Culture," 48–9; and Butler, *Bodies that Matter: On the Discursive Limits of "Sex"* (New York: Routledge, 1993), xi, 3, 16.
25. Butler, "Universality in Culture," 48–50; Butler, "Competing Universalities," 164, 168.
26. Butler, *Feminist Contentions*, 40–1, 130–1; Butler, "Universality in Culture," 46–9; Butler, *Undoing Gender* (New York: Routledge, 2004), 189–191.
27. Quoted in Henry J. Steiner and Philip Alston, eds., *International Human Rights in Context* (New York: Oxford University Press, 2006), 372. The American Anthropological Society later recognized the "universal," cross-cultural relevance of human rights. However, the notion of human rights as "a western construct" has continued to be upheld, by, among others, Adamantia Pollis and Peter Schwab, eds., "Human Rights: A Western Construct with Limited Applicability," in *Human Rights: Cultural and Ideological Perspectives*, ed. Adamantia Pollis and Peter Schwab (New York: Praeger, 1979), 1–18.
28. I am not taking a position here on the occidentrism of human rights. Some have argued that all societies, western and non-western, have a concept of human dignity, which is often seen as the fundamental basis for the assertion of human rights. Others have claimed that duties are as important as rights; still others that development is more important for emerging nation states than rights.
29. Tzvetan Todorov, *On Human Diversity: Nationalism, Racism and Exoticism in French Thought* (Cambridge, MA: Harvard University Press, 1933), 66.
30. Linda Alcoff, "The Problem of Speaking for Others," *Cultural Critique* 20 (1991): 5–32.
31. Spivak, "Can the Subaltern Speak," in *Marxism and the Study of Culture*, ed. Cary Nelson and Lawrence Grossberg (Urbana: University of Illinois Press, 1988), 271–312.
32. Michael Ignatieff, *Human Rights as Politics and Idolatry* (Princeton, NJ: Princeton University Press, 2001), 74–76.
33. Bonny Ibhawoh, "Restraining Universalism: Africanist Perspectives on Cultural Relativism in Human Rights," in *Human Rights, The Rule of Law and Development in Africa*, ed. Paul Tiyambe Zelera and Philip J. McConnaughay (Philadelphia: University of Pennsylvania Press, 2004), 21–39, 257–59.
34. For a critical assessment of the imbrication of global capital in the human rights regime, see Pheng Cheah, "Posit(ion)ing Human Rights in the Current Global Conjuncture" and "'Bringing into the Home a Stranger far more Foreign': Human Rights and the Global Trade in Domestic Labor," in *Inhuman Conditions: On Cosmopolitan and Human Rights* (Cambridge, MA: Harvard University Press, 2000), 145–229.
35. Louis Henkin, *The Rights of Man Today* (Boulder, CO: Westview Press, 1978), 130. The importance of development is noted in the UDHR (articles 26:2 and 29:1), and especially in the African Charter on Human and People's Rights (adopted in 1981, entered into force, 1986): "Convinced that it is henceforth essential to pay a particular attention to the right to development and that civil and political rights cannot be dissociated from economic, social and cultural rights in their conception as well as universally. . . ." *Twenty-Five Human Rights Documents (TFHRD)* (New York: Center for the Study of Human Rights, Columbia University, 1994), preamble, 121.
36. The same phrase appears in the International Covenant on Economic, Social and Cultural rights, *TFHRD*, 10.

37. Today some writers believe that "universal" basically means "global" (Igna-tieff, *Human Rights*, 71) or simply, international. See Fernando Teson, "International Human Rights and Cultural Relativism," *Virginia Journal of International Law* 25, no.4 (1985): 869–898.
38. *TFHRD*, preamble, 39.
39. In keeping with the pattern of later documents that compensated for fail-ures and omissions in earlier documents, the International Covenant on Eco-nomic, Social and Cultural Rights takes up rights already articulated in the UDHR.
40. Some commentators have categorized these as desirable, aspirational goals, but not rights—since they cannot be pursued within the dominant meth-odology for prosecuting violations of human rights: being able to identify the violation clearly, targeting the violator and articulating a remedy. On the board of Human Rights Watch (HRW) on which I served, there were tensions between the proponents of economic, social, and cultural rights (ESCR) and those who felt that pursuing these rights would compromise the organization's stature and authority—whence the efforts of emeritus board member, Stephen L. Kass, to apply the traditional HRW methodology to climate change and poverty, in "Integrated Justice," *Transnational Law & Contemporary Problems* 18 (2009): 115–38. Another approach could exam-ine a state's allocation of resources to ensure that ESCR are not ignored, and that the needs of particular populations, such as women or the indigenous, receive proportional allocation. In my view, the interconnections of ESCR and "traditional" human rights are undeniable: a society cannot ensure human rights without ESCR.
41. Briefly covered in the International Covenant on Civil and Political Rights, these collective rights have not as yet been incorporated into any legally binding human rights equivalent to those first two generations of rights. See *TFHRD*, 10–16.
42. I say "in response," because one of the notable divisions between western and non-western conceptions of rights is the emphasis on duties to the com-munity as opposed to the rights of the individual. See note 62, below.
43. However, Amartya Sen insists that claims for "Asian values" usually come from authoritarian governments and deny diversity within Asia, including a belief in personal freedom. See *Development as Freedom* (New York: Anchor Books, 2000).
44. The contest among individuals and nations in the production of this doc-ument, mainly drafted by John Peters Humphrey (Canada), René Cas-sin (France), P. C. Chang (China), Charles Malik (Lebanon), and Eleanor Roosevelt, has often been ignored. The Soviet bloc, South Africa, and Saudi Arabia abstained from signing the UDHR.
45. See the Second Optional Protocol Aiming at the Abolition of the Death Pen-alty, *TFHRD*, 33–35.
46. The apparent weakness of the regime in exempting states from complying with human rights laws may also be a strength when human rights—and international—law promote respect for cultural identities, local traditions, and customs of peoples. Thus, in the Declaration on Principles of Interna-tional Law Concerning Friendly Relations and Cooperation among States in Accordance with the Charter of the United Nations (1970), "every state has an inalienable right to choose its political, economic, social and cultural sys-tems without interference in any form by another State." See Teson, "Inter-national Human Rights and Cultural Relativism," 873, n. 21.
47. Gareth J. Evans and Mohamed Sahnoun, eds., *The Responsibility to Pro-tect: Report of the International Commission on Intervention and State*

Sovereignty (Ottawa: International Development Research Center, 2001). See also the companion volume, written by Thomas Weiss, Gareth J. Evans, and Don Hubert, *The Responsibility to Protect: Research, Bibliography, Background (R2P)* (Ottawa: International Development Research Center, 2001). The impetus for *R2P* is the problematic international responses to the crises in Somalia, Bosnia, Rwanda, and Kosovo in the 1990s. *R2P* aims to move away from the right to intervene to a primary emphasis on the responsibility of sovereign states to protect their citizens, though once again, the focus is on citizens and not all human beings in the territory of the state. For a critique of *R2P* as a form of imperialism that would allow powerful states to further their own interests, see Walden Bello, "Humanitarian Intervention: The Evolution of a Dangerous Doctrine," in *Focus on the Global South*, FocusWeb.org (posted January 19, 2006). In 2006, The United Nations Security Council approved a resolution that reaffirmed the relevant paragraphs (138 and 139) describing *R2P* in the 2005 World Summit Outcome Document, accessed November 9, 2010, http://daccess-dds-ny.un.org/doc/UNDOC/GEN/N05/487/60/PDF/N0548760.pdf.

48. On the International Criminal Court, se Richard Goldstone, *International Judicial Institutions* (New York: Routledge, 2009).
49. Hannah Arendt, "The Decline of the Nation State and the End of the Rights of Man," in *The Origins of Totalitarianism* (New York: Harcourt Brace, World, 1968), 147–82. On Arendt and the production of the stateless, see Butler and Spivak, *Who Sings*, 44–50. In 1951, and in the aftermath of the holocaust, Arendt could not imagine that rights were enforceable outside of the nation and thus the rights of citizens; indeed, her conception of the nation limited her notion of the stateless.
50. To be sure, there are some references to non-state actors in the UDHR: articles 23 and 26. On the rights of the stateless now being more openly addressed, see David Weissbrodt and Clay Collins, "The Human Rights of Stateless Persons," *Human Rights Quarterly* 28, no.1 (2006): 24–76; Linda Kerber, "The Stateless as the Citizen's Other: A View from the United States," in *Migrations and Mobilities: Citizenship, Borders and Gender*, ed. Seyla Benhabib and Judith Resnik (New York: New York University Press, 2009), 76–213. And yet, at the end of 2010, the Roma have been expelled from France by order of President Nicolas Sarkozy.
51. *TFHRD*, 6.E.g. Art 2: "Everyone is entitled to all rights and freedoms set forth in this Declaration without distinction of any kind, such as race, color, sex, language, religion, political or other opinion, national or social origin, property, birth or other status"; Art 5: "No one shall be subjected to torture or to cruel, inhuman or degrading treatment or punishment."
52. Judith Butler, *Precarious Life: The Powers of Mourning and Violence* (New York: Verso, 2004), 91.
53. Luce Irigaray, *thinking the difference: for a peaceful revolution*, trans. Karin Montin (New York: Routledge, 1994), ix–xi. Irigaray cites articles of the UDHR, but her text manifests no awareness of her own class, educational and situational privileges in comparison to the condition of most women in the world.
54. Butler, *Undoing Gender*, 190–191.
55. Butler, *Undoing Gender*, 38, 13, 38; Butler, *Precarious Life*, 90.
56. Butler, *Precarious Life*, 91; *Undoing Gender*, 30. See the essays in the section, "Who Is the Human in Human Rights," in the special issue of *PMLA*, "The Humanities in Human Rights; Critique, Language, Politics," ed. Judith Butler and Domna C. Stanton, 121, no. 5 (October 2006): 1526–1557.
57. Butler, *Precarious Life*, 89–90.

84   *Domna C. Stanton*

58. See Steiner and Alston, *International Human Rights in Concert*, 782ff, including the Report on the Regional Promotion and Protection of Human Rights.
59. In 2000, Muslim member nations of the Organization of the Islamic Conference officially supported the Cairo Declaration on Human Rights in Islam, which states that people have "freedom and right to a dignified life in accordance with the Islamic Shari'ah." See David Littman, "Universal Human Rights and Human Rights in Islam," *Midstream* (1999), http://www.dhimmi.org/Islam. html. Organisation of the Islamic Conference, http://www.oic-oci.org/. *Report and Resolutions on Political, Muslim Minorities and Communities, Legal and Information Affairs*, http://www.oic-oci.org/english/conf/fm/27/27th-fm-political(3).HTM. In 1995, states from the former Soviet Union adopted a Commonwealth of Independent States Convention on Human Rights in Minsk, but its relevance has been checkmated by efforts to crack down on dissidents, casting them since 9/11, in Russia for instance, as terrorists. There is no pan-Asian regional system because of the heterogeneity of states, but there are regional instruments. The African Union, established in 2002, to succeed the Organization of African Unity, consists of 53 African states. Some sub-regional organizations are devoted to economic integration or development, such as the Economic Community of West African States, made up of 15 nations and founded in 1975.
60. See Steiner and Alston, *International Human Rights in Concert*, 748–785, 799ff. However, since 1977, the UN General Assembly has adopted annually a resolution calling upon relevant regions to act, even though to date, the United Nations Charter is silent as to human rights cooperation at the regional level (780).
61. As the case of the Darfur genocide in the Sudan suggests emblematically, the African union has resisted external interventions by states or by non-governmental organizations, and seems reluctant to infringe the sovereign rights of another state in the region, even if it means tolerating another genocide on African soil. Given the authoritarian nature of many neocolonial African regimes, nations in the region may fear they would be next on the list for an armed intervention by UN forces.
62. See e.g., the articles of the African Charter on Human and People's Rights specifically devoted to duties: chapter 2, articles 27, 29 (*TFHRD*, 123).
63. Butler and Spivak, *Who Sings*, 83, 91–2, 94. However, Spivak does not specify the exact contours of this "critical" project.
64. See Steiner and Alston, *International Human Rights in Concert*, 784.
65. See the Paris Principles, *National Institutions for the Promotion and Protection of Human Rights*, adopted 4 March 1994, U.N. Doc. A/Res/48/134 (1994), http://www.nhri.net/pdf/HRCres1994.pdf.
66. Some NHRIs have a quasi-judicial power.
67. The Office of the United Nations High Commissioner for Human Rights Handbook provides guidance on establishing and strengthening the independence of the NHRIs (see Professional Training Series no 54, 1995).
68. Anne Smith, "The Unique Position of National Human Rights Institutions: A Mixed Blessing?" *Human Rights Quarterly* 28 (2006): 928–44. Smith's balanced approach differs from the "top down" approach and the unconvincing conclusions of Thomas Risse and Kathryn Sikkink's "The Socialization of International Human Rights Norms into Domestic Practices: Introduction," in *The Power of Human Rights: International Norms and Domestic Change*, ed. Thomas Risse, Stephen C. Ropp, and Kathryn Sikkink (Cambridge: Cambridge University Press, 1999).
69. In "What is Civil Society," the London School of Economics Centre for Civil Society offers this working definition: "Civil society refers to the

arena of uncoerced collective action around shared interests, purposes, and values. In theory, its institutional forms are distinct from those of the state, family, and market, though in practice, the boundaries between state, civil society, family, and market are often complex, blurred and negotiated. Civil societies are often populated by organizations such as registered charities, development nongovernmental organizations, community groups, women's organizations, faith-based organizations, professional associations, trade unions, self-help groups, social movements, business associations, coalitions and advocacy groups," http://www.lse.ac.uk/collections/CCS/what_is_civil_society.htm (accessed October 10, 2006). Differences in emphasis in various definitions of civil society involve the degree to which a particular factor is uppermost, such as a commitment to the redistribution of power in society. See also Mary Kaldor, *Global Civil Society: An Answer to War* (London: Polity, 2003).
70. To give a sense of the dimensions of civil society organizations (CSOs): the United Nations Department of Economic and Social Affairs has established relationships with over 12,000; there are almost 1,000 Indigenous Peoples organizations listed as CSOs as well—a level of growth that has generated a backlash; see for instance NGOWATCH, created by the American Enterprise Institute and the Federalist Society. Lester M. Salamon, S. Wojciech Sokolowski and Associates (*Global Civil Society: Dimensions of the Nonprofit Sector* II [Bloomfield, CT: Kumarian Press, 2004]), document the size and financing of nonprofit organizations or civil society in thirty-six countries.
71. Donors in the United States, for instance, are typically tax-exempt organizations, often derived from—and connected to—multinational corporations (e.g., the Ford and Gates foundations).
72. In doing critical analysis, it is easy to forget (perhaps because of the danger of romanticization) the risks that human rights workers take, venturing into dangerous sites to document violations and atrocities. As a member of the board of Human Rights Watch for ten years, I encountered extraordinarily brave individuals ("monitors"), four of whom are honored annually, though many a year, an empty chair signals that the monitor is in prison. I recall the Turkish journalist who, once out of prison, fought widespread state censorship by proliferating the publications of celebrated authors; the African doctor, trained in western psychiatry, who also used tribal customs to help reintegrate child soldiers into civil society; the woman raped in Bosnia who, in the midst of war and despite the harrassment of the police and of "peacekeepers," created a safe place for raped and battered women; or the human rights worker in Uzbekistan, who wore/bore a veil and carried someone's baby into Andijan to document the massacre that had taken place there in May 2005.
73. Butler, "Universality in Culture," 49 and Homi K. Bhabha, *The Location of Culture* (New York: Routledge, 1994), 226–229. Bhabha, in turn, takes the concept of cultural translation from Walter Benjamin's work on the translator in *Illuminations*. In "Restaging the Universal," Butler also ascribes the notion to Spivak, specifically her essay, "Can the Subaltern Speak?" (36).
74. Butler, "Universality in Culture,"50.
75. Butler, "Universality in Culture," 50; *Undoing Gender*, 38.
76. Butler, "Restaging the Universal," 35.
77. Butler, "Universality in Culture," 51–2.
78. Surprisingly, for someone influenced by Michel Foucault, Butler does not speak of power/knowledge, but rather, in passing, of differential "strengths" in "Universality in Culture": whether a claim to universality by women or gays, for instance, "is preposterous, provocative, or efficacious depends

on the collective strength with which it is asserted, the institutional condition of its assertion and reception, and the unpredictable political forces at work" (46).

79. Compare Butler's predominant linguistic emphasis with her (occasional) usage of the "cultural" in "Restaging the Universal," 35.

80. Moya Lloyd, *Judith Butler: From Norms to Politics* (Malden, MA: Polity Press, 2007), 151; See Bhabha, *The Location of Culture*, 224, 227–28.

81. Lyotard, *The Postmodern Condition*, 65–6, 72–3; Butler, "Universality," 49. For other critiques of Habermas's "procedural universalism," see Ferrara's "Universalisms," 245–51, and Anderson, "Cosmopolitanism," 279.

82. Clifford Geertz, "The Impact of the Concept of Culture on the Concept of Man," 38–40; on his theory of "control mechanisms" for studying complexes of concrete behavior patterns, see 44–45.

83. Geertz, "The Impact of the Concept of Culture on the Concept of Man," 40.

84. Geertz, "The Impact of the Concept of Culture on the Concept of Man," 51–3.

85. Robbins points to a similar idea when he speaks of cosmopolitanism as making room for "moments of generalizing . . . without offering license for uninhibited universalizing" (*Secular Vocations*, 196).

86. Marcus George Singer, *Generalization in Ethics* (New York: Alfred A. Knopf, 1961), 31.

87. Singer, *Generalization in Ethics*, 328, 75. Singer insists, and I obviously part company with him here, that he holds to fundamental, and apparently, invariant principles, despite the variety of existing rules and practices (329).

88. Singer, *Generalization in Ethics*, 328–329.

89. Singer, *Generalization in Ethics*, 14–15, 68.

90. John Dewey, *Logic: The Theory of Inquiry* (New York: Irvington Publishers, 1982), 257.

91. Dewey, *Logic: The Theory of Inquiry*, 260, 269–270.

92. Anne Phillips, "Universal Pretensions," 27.

93. Charles Hartshorne and Paul Weiss, *The Collected Papers of Charles Sanders Pierce* (Cambridge, MA: Harvard University Press, 1932–1935), 5:265; for Pierce's remarks on the general, see 5:101 and 5:152.

94. See Butler, *Feminist Contentions*, 129; Spivak, *In Other Worlds: Essays in Cultural Politics* (New York: Methuen, 1987), 205.

95. Upendra Baxi, *Mambrino's Helmet?: Human Rights for a Changing World* (Delhi: Hjar-Amand, 1994), 5.

96. Spivak, "Righting Wrongs," *Freedom and Interpretation: Amnesty Lectures in Human Rights* (Oxford: Oxford University Press, 1993), 196. See also, Pheng Cheah, *Inhuman Conditions*, 172; Etienne Balibar, "Ambiguous Universality," 61–62.

97. Butler, *Undoing Gender*, 182.

4 The Social Imaginary as a Problematic for Human Rights

Meili Steele

The goal of my chapter is to propose a new problematic for reasoning about human rights, a problematic that gives the social imaginary and literature a prominent place in normative reasoning. The idea of the social imaginary has been widely discussed in literary, historical, sociological, and political scholarship for some time; however, the imaginary has been studied largely as the *object* of investigation rather than the *subject* of normative reasoning, which is how I will develop it.[1] In order to understand the significance of this problematic, we need to look quickly at how literary theory's relationship to political philosophy has kept this conception of the imaginary out of view.

Literary studies of ethics, politics and rights have been dominated by different strains of poststructuralism that criticize many of the premises of the liberal social contract theory, the theory that underwrites human rights for mainstream political philosophy.[2] Literary theorists and critics have aimed to show that liberalism's conceptions of subjectivity, justice, history, and power fail to articulate the complex textual and social processes by which societies oppress and occlude difference.[3]

Even though I can hardly survey these rich contributions, I want to highlight two problems with how critiques in the social constructivist version of poststructuralism are executed. The social constructivist or "constitutive" strain of poststructuralism shows that the object of investigation is not an entity that stands independently of the discourses used to describe it but is in fact constituted by them. Edward Said's pioneering works, *Orientalism* and *Culture and Imperialism*, are examples of this approach. While Said is certainly offering a powerful critique of liberal imperialism, he makes two similar moves. He objectifies and unmasks the history of culture as an unreliable guide to ethical and political norms; he then appeals to Kantian moral universalism and justice that can be separated from their damaged historical instantiations that he examined. This is what liberals such as Jack Donnelly and John Rawls do, as we will see momentarily. What liberals and constructivists share is a hostility toward the normative potential of texts.

In this chapter, I will be drawing on Taylor to develop a dual conception of the social imaginary. First, it is part of a transcendental philosophy of language that understands normative concepts as woven into holistic webs of beliefs and social practices into which we are thrown, not as principles that stand above historical shapes. This dimension is the logically prior hermeneutic background to any constructivist operation or normative procedure. Taylor combines this philosophical conception with a historiographical conception that goes beyond the history of ideas to "what enables, through making sense of, the practices of a society. . . . [Thus,] the notion of moral order goes beyond some proposed schedule of norms that ought to govern our mutual relations and/or political life. . . . The image of order carries a definition not only of what is right, but of the context in which makes sense to strive for and hope to realize the right."[4] This conception transforms the opposition between historical objects and principled subjects by showing how principles are inevitably constituted by imaginaries, imaginaries that receive important articulation through literature. I will speak of the social imaginary in the singular when I am using it in the transcendental sense and use the term "historical social imaginaries" when I am talking about particular historical cultural locations.

This chapter proceeds in three sections. In the first, I will sketch briefly the tension between normative and constitutive approaches to rights in order to set up my contribution. In the next section, I will develop my problematic of the social imaginary and its alternative portrait of public reasoning about rights. In the third section, I discuss an example of such reasoning through a reading of the work of Ralph Ellison.

NORMATIVE AND SOCIAL CONSTRUCTIVISM: ELIDING THE SOCIAL IMAGINARY

The best way to see the importance of this conception of the social imaginary is to bring out how both the contract tradition and social constructivist theory occlude it. The hallmark of contractual normativity is what political philosophers call "normative constructivism." This approach uses procedures, such as Habermas's universal presuppositions of communicative action or Rawls's original position, to separate the production of moral/political concepts from the languages of everyday life.[5] In this way, the principles of rights are protected from the ambiguities of history, language, and interpretation. Social constructivism, on the other hand, examines normative and epistemological principles from the outside as part of the ideological web of meanings developed in particular communities. Social constructivism does not just show how language invents the objects to which it purportedly refers—"orientalism," the "nation"; it also shows how norms that are often taken to be independent external standards do not "regulate" subjects from the outside but constitute them from the inside.[6] I will begin with the normative approach, focusing on Habermas, and then look at the social constructivist position.

Habermas's constructivist device is the idea of the presuppositions of communicative action. The priority of the communicative use of language is the key to Habermas's philosophical project because it enables him to claim that communicative discourse is fundamental and liberating from the constraints of any ideological formation. Communicative reason does not "tell actors what they ought to do"[7] but instead what presuppositions must inform their dialogues. The theory of communicative action thus reconciles rights and popular sovereignty, reason and will, because "human rights institutionalize the communicative conditions for a reasonable political will-formation."[8] These ideal conditions are then turned into dialogical procedures, which serve as tests for the outcome of the rational and legitimate exchange. The procedures embody the norms that assure the legitimacy of the content. In this way, Habermas keeps his regulative ideals apart from any particular social imaginaries that structure the phenomenology of everyday life.

For Habermas, public reasoning about rights thus should be carried out in a normative language that swings free of the semantic context of the imaginary: "Participants must know that this kind of public controversy has to be carried out in the light of publicly acceptable reasons, independently of any philosophy of history or Weltanschauung."[9] Thus, Habermas is committed to the problematic of the isolated normative utterance in which the same reasons reappear. Disagreements, in Habermas's view, can only be over the application and best interpretation of "the same constitutional rights and principles." This view ignores the ways that arguments often proceed by lengthy semantic contextualization, in which the speakers revise the assumptions of the existing imaginary, as we will see in some examples momentarily. Habermas tries to negotiate the historicity of historical meanings by isolating a "moral learning process" from history, so that societies move from substantive, communal worldviews to universal, egalitarian procedures.[10] Hence, there are many routes to the recognition of these idealizations, and we do not need to be concerned with giving an account of the diverse linguistic self-understandings of the historical actors but only the formal properties of the normative problematic that assure universality and consensus about rights.

Social constructivist theorists show that the principles of human rights cannot be divorced from the substantive assumptions and narratives that they claim to stand above and evaluate. Joseph Slaughter nicely sums up the assumptions of this approach: "[L]aw and literature are discursive regimes that constitute and regulate, imagine and test, kinds of subjects, subjectivities, and social formations; . . . they are 'machines for producing [and governing] subjectivity' and social relations."[11] The constitutive thesis adopts a third-person stance toward law and literature—what legal theorists often call an "external approach"—that unmasks the ways that supposedly neutral procedures and assumptions, in fact, have much broader commitments—in the case of Slaughter's project, for instance, that human rights theorizing is linked to the *Bildungsroman* genre.[12] However, constitutive theorists do not typically go on to propose new ways of public reasoning about the historical and normative dimensions of rights. Constitutive or constructive approaches are deliberately unspecified since they eschew the evaluative and referential vocabularies in which such commitments could be made.

Both normative philosophers and constitutive theorists ignore the normative potential of historical imaginaries. For their views, these imaginaries that structure everyday common sense are ideological lures to be exposed rather than the possibilities to be reworked. This common suspicion of the languages of daily life has led some theorists to combine the two approaches—a constructivist approach to the meanings of everyday life with a normative constructivism. Conflicted historical meanings and languages are objectified and discredited as obfuscatory and ideologically damaged, so that our only guidance comes from counterfactual moral ideals and the idea of dialogue as such.

What both sides leave out is the way that imaginaries create modes of being, thinking, and agency. The imaginary is not just an impediment to negative liberty but a resource for positive liberty. There can be no quick move from the objectification and critique of the social imaginary to the ahistorical idealization of moral concepts. Such a move impoverishes both the moral and historical sides of the issues. The result is an inadequate portrait of the stakes and dynamics of public reasoning about rights.

THE SOCIAL IMAGINARY AS TRANSCENDENTAL AND HISTORICAL PROJECT

To introduce my problematic, I will draw on the work of Charles Taylor since he takes on the transcendental and the historical dimensions of human rights projects in a productive way.[13] What differentiates Taylor's position from those of Habermas and social constructivists is how he understands the relationship of the subject to the social imaginary in both a philosophical and historical sense, and this understanding makes possible a new conception of reasoning about rights. He begins with a transcendental argument since his challenge to modern self-understandings is global, not local, and he offers an alternative account of normativity, history, and the imaginary. Taylor's concern is to leverage a certain account of the subject's relationship to the historical imaginary that can provide a perspicuous description of the strains of modernity that he wants to advocate as well as those he urges us to repudiate.

The critique of contemporary approaches to human rights emerges from his broad attack on modernity's disengaged conceptions of reason, both theoretical and practical, and he seeks to rule them out as possible points of departure. Normative proceduralism and social constructivism—along with atomism, positivism, and naturalism—misunderstand the proper ontological and historical understanding of the subject's relationship to the social imaginary and its historicity. Modernity's "pervasive bewitchment" is that we can live without evaluative frameworks.[14] We do not choose to commit to evaluative frameworks; rather, evaluative frameworks are logically prior to choice and reflection. Taylor is not advocating community, as many commentators claim. Rather, he is articulating the inescapable commitments of historical linguistic beings through transcendental argument and the shapes of the social imaginary that subtend the debates about modernity. Modernity's misdescription of the subject's being in the world has led to a specious isolation of moral philosophy, history, and literature. We cannot reason about rights through procedures; rather, rights are embedded in western historical identity in ways that must be articulated if we are to reason about them.

But if history is so important, then why transcendental argument? Why not take an historical stance such as Foucault's or Quentin Skinner's, in which transcendental conditions are the objects under investigation rather than something linked to both the subject and object of investigation?[15] Don't transcendental arguments seem to make a dangerously ethnocentric move in which one's own cultural assumptions are generalized as the necessary assumptions of all cultures, including one's own past? What about the simple anthropological point that Taylor's assumptions about such ideas as "the self" are western and not universal? Isn't this precisely the problem of Heidegger's transcendental anthropology in *Being and Time*, in which the diverse historical practices of the west disappear behind the anguish of modernity that has lost touch with Being?

Taylor argues that transcendental investigation produces just the opposite effect—if we do it properly. In seeking the transcendental background that subtends first-order speech, Taylor does not aim to give Habermas's rules of validity but to present the presuppositions and the field of historical possibilities that stand behind our individual sentences. Moreover, the philosophical historian cannot, like the social constructivist, ignore the horizon of the present and simply objectify the past and the present. Instead, one must develop a language of perspicuous contrast for discussing the past and the present, and this requires investigating the inescapable frameworks. If we enter a debate only with our position and those of others arrayed as individual positions, we miss points of similarity and difference that appear when we articulate backgrounds to our positions and the horizons of the possible that surround our individuated philosophical stances. When we see our present position as a possible outcome of a constellation of conditions that underpin it, then we have opened our own resources of debate.[16] In sum, this transcendental argument is what opens the way for bringing history into normative reasoning.

We need transcendental arguments to distinguish between historically effective forms of the imaginary (i.e., ones that enjoyed wide acceptance, such as the atomistic view of the subject) from the historian's philosophical and historical understandings. For example, in *Sources*, Taylor reads Locke critically from the point of view of his transcendental argument: "Locke tried to maintain that even the ideas in our minds which have general import are themselves particulars. The deep muddle has its source in the entire 'building block' theory of thinking."[17] In *Modern Social Imaginaries*, by contrast, Taylor is less interested in assessing Lockean notions than he is in examining the historical effectiveness of the moral image developed by Locke and Grotius, its impact on generating the forms of modernity that we know as the public sphere, popular sovereignty, etc.[18] The history that emerges in this account is not an empirical history of events but an interpretive study of the historical conditions of certain possibilities. The problematic of the social imaginary combines a philosophical account of meaning with a historiographical technique, so that force of objectifying historical accounts never evaporates the space of subjective interrogation. Spelling out these two dimensions will widen the argumentative space of discussion, so that we are not forced to choose between liberal normativism and neo-Foucauldian forms of negative liberty.

Taylor directs one line of his argument at Habermasian assumptions about language and the normativity of rights that evaporate the social imaginary into universal presuppositions and shared meaning as such. For Taylor, we should abandon the search for universalized moral rules that can stand "outside the perspective in the dispute . . . [for] there cannot be such considerations."[19] Instead, we reason by seeking "to articulate a framework . . . , to try to spell out what is it that we presuppose when we make judgment that a certain form of life is truly worthwhile, or place our dignity in a certain achievement."[20] In his view, Habermas, like Rawls, is surreptitiously appealing to the good and hence misdescribes claims.[21] The significance of procedures depends on the background imaginary it attempts to disown. Reasoning about rights does not require an upfront thinning out of our commitments but giving them a richer context synchronically and diachronically.

In order to bring out the background, we need to go beyond the explicit concepts of a culture to engage the more primordial semantic landscape of the social imaginary, the practices, languages, and images that give norms in their contexts of realization. This historical work is placed in the philosophical context of Taylor's transcendental argument that establishes the priority of the imaginary to the isolated normative or referential proposition.

In other words, there are no brute facts or values, nor are there singular statements of position. The articulation of a particular position on, say, the nature of autonomy or secularism depends upon large-scale assumptions about language, subjectivity, and historicity as well as specific historical arguments. Such historical reconstruction will involve not only developing the lines of argument that led to the current position but also making intelligible the discarded strands.

In opposing the universality of principles to the infinite particularity of context, philosophers of practical reason run together two ideas of context—empirical context, which is infinitely variable, and semantic context or social imaginary, which is not. The shapes of public imagination are not universal, but they are historically generalizable constituents of the public mind. Thus, when citizens confront an innovative situation or text, they are not simply applying principles or recognizing that norms and reality are constructed but recontextualizing beliefs, concepts, and images—that is, reasoning through the social imaginary. Literature, particularly the novel, argues through a speculative reworking of ideas and images that are not circumscribed the way that philosophical thought experiments are.

This is not to say literature is necessarily innovative, insightful, or politically useful. My point is that reading literature through the problematic of the imaginary enables us to see how normative arguments can work in richer ways than isolating the content of a principle and then applying it. Human rights cannot be contained within normative ideals that swing free from politics. Instead, rights are inevitably packaged in imaginaries that demand historical, philosophical, and literary understanding. Literature reveals the overlapping moral and epistemological commitments of diverse interlocutors, which can help political reasoning to avoid backing away from actual differences into differences per se.

Imaginaries do not work through regulative ideals but transitional arguments that urge us to shift the way we understand packages of ideas, images, and principles. To be sure, transitional arguments do not call everything into question at once; they depend on shared meaning in order to leverage new understandings. Transitional arguments are not necessarily historically accurate or without considerable ideological baggage. My claim is about the shape of argument, not its content.

This conception of transition includes genealogical accounts of loss as well as accounts of gain over the past. A genealogical approach is one way of bringing out a hitherto unrecognized loss, and it works through a process of articulation rather than explanation (e.g., Foucault's exposure of the losses in the transition from premodern to modern). Genealogists do not seek to discredit an historical interpretation by pointing to causal forces that make the interpretive claim irrelevant; rather, they seek to discredit the evaluative ontological frameworks through which a particular historical account is rendered. Genealogical or constructivist readings are then options of arguing through the social imaginary and they appear within a larger framework that displays its historical and transcendental assumptions and justifications.

ELLISON, *BROWN V. BOARD OF EDUCATION,* AND THE SOCIAL IMAGINARY

I will use the model of reasoning developed in the last section to show how the work of Ralph Ellison argues through the social imaginary to enrich our understanding of human rights. I will start by defining the two traditions of reasoning about rights that emerge from *Brown v. Board of Education* in order to situate Ellison's argument and then look at the broader human rights context. The two major traditions that frame *Brown*'s legacy are the anticlassification (or antidiscrimination) approach and the antisubordination approach. These two modes of reading continue the split that we found between the normative approach to meaning and society (what legal theorists call the "internal" approach) in which principles are articulated and the "external" approaches of social sciences or of Foucauldian gene-alogies.[22] Ellison takes a different route. He does not assume that we have an adequate language for making either normative claims or the referential claims, opting instead to explore how normative and referential questions emerge from the medium of the social imaginary. My reading will look at how Ellison's texts argue with the social imaginaries of his time in ways that offer lessons for the present, thus illustrating both the transcendental and historical dimensions of the social imaginary. Moreover, rather than simply exposing the debilitating structures of the imaginary in genealogi-cal fashion, he also argues for the superiority of his languages. Although Ellison never specifically engages the *Brown* opinion, he addresses all of the relevant issues in both his fiction and his essays. I will first define these two frameworks and then look at Ellison.

In the antidiscrimination reading, which is the dominant paradigm in the American legal tradition and public culture, *Brown* represents the prin-ciple that the law should be colorblind. The American legal tradition is rich in metaphors for how this thought experiment is to be carried out, from Rawls's original position to the image of the orchestra audition behind a screen.[23] The metaphor of blindness captures nicely western modernity's misguided urge to achieve normative clarity by blocking out the histori-cal background that makes such thought experiments intelligible. These antidiscrimination norms regulate "the process through which a scarce opportunity is allowed or a burden imposed on an individual and seeks to regulate the criteria that might be used in that process."[24]

The antisubordination thesis, on the other hand, argues that the *Plessey v. Ferguson* doctrine of "separate but equal" was part of a larger pattern of racial subordination, a pattern that the antidiscrimination thesis system-atically occludes.[25] The antisubordination principle condemns "practices [that] create or perpetuate the subordination of the group of which the individual excluded or rejected is a member."[26] Antisubordination read-ings look beyond the intentions and self-understandings of the law to its effects (e.g., damage to black school children in *Brown*). If subordinating effects are shown, then the law can be held to violate equal protection and remedies for historical inequalities can be proposed (e.g., desegregation or, later, affirmative action). Antisubordination thus pursues equality as a sub-stantive rather than procedural end.

Antisubordination theorists claim that looking through the single lens of classification helps, as Jack Balkin says, "to freeze the cumulative black disadvantages in place."[27] Thus, "it encourages people to explain persistent black inequality as the result of private choices, cultural differences, or black inferiority rather than at least partially as the result of facially neutral legal policies that help preserve social stratification."[28]

Even though the antisubordination reading is an important supplement to the omissions of anticlassification approaches, both occlude what, for Ellison, is the crucial impediment to the realization of human rights and popular sovereignty at his time: the deliberative medium through which a society articulates itself. Ellison rejects the oscillation between external and internal approaches, between facts and norms, by attacking the languages of referentiality and normativity simultaneously.

I will begin with Ellison's critical review of Gunnar Myrdal's *American Dilemma*. This work was cited by Chief Justice Earl Warren in *Brown* to document the damage that school segregation did to African American children. Although Myrdal's sociological study brings out many significant features of the American racial landscape, Ellison objected to his assumptions that "Negroes [were] simply the creation of white men" and that "Negro culture and personality [were] the product of a 'social pathology.'"[29] Ellison acknowledges that "Negro" culture has some undesirable features, but he insists that "there is much of great value and richness, which because it has been secreted by living has made their lives more meaningful."[30] African Americans have thus "helped to create themselves out of what they found around them."[31] Moreover, this culture is not in the narrow service of identity politics, for "in Negro culture there is much of value for America as a whole."[32]

These two misreadings led Myrdal to assume that "it is to the advantage of American Negroes as a group to become assimilated into American culture, to acquire the traits held in esteem by the dominant white Americans."[33] The antisubordination thesis, as articulated by *Brown* at the time, and the anticlassification thesis both assumed that African American culture has been so damaged by racism that it is only a prison-house of internalized oppression, while the dominant culture has emerged unscathed. For Ellison, neither white nor black culture can be affirmed in an unqualified way. Both have been severely damaged and need to be critically worked through: "What is needed in our country is not an exchange of pathologies but a change in the basis of society. This is a job which both Negroes and whites must perform together."[34] No thought experiment of blindness can provide satisfactory critical distance, and no collection of data can document the damage done to all Americans. Both depend on a language that can ask questions, understand history in the proper way, a language that, in Ellison's view, was not available. Antisubordination remedies, such as integration or affirmative action, do not address these questions directly.

This evasion becomes clearer when we look at the limits of legal reasoning from the perspective of transitional justice and its institutions, such as truth commissions. In these contexts, the establishment of a shared understanding of the past with appropriate normative and referential languages is immediately on the table. The context of truth commissions has helped scholars from different fields examine how American political, legal, and social institutions continually failed to address their own imaginary.[35] My reading of Ellison aims to show how the problematic of the social imaginary can bring out these issues that surface only in transitional justice venues and make them part of the everyday framework of reasoning about rights.

To assess the complex ways that race is woven into the existing imaginaries of both black and white Americans requires a genealogical treatment: "This unwillingness to resolve the conflict in keeping with his democratic ideals has compelled the American, figuratively, to force the Negro down in the deeper level of his consciousness, into the inner world."[36] One of the effects of this inarticulate conflict is the unacknowledged presence of race in every facet of what white culture understands as "white": "It is practically impossible for the white American to think of sex, of economics, his children, womenfolk, or of sweeping sociopolitical changes, without summoning into consciousness fear-flecked images of black men."[37]

These features of the imaginary have been argued into place not just by legal and historical texts and practices but also by popular arts such as film. Ellison was aware of the argumentative power of film, and he analyzed some of this in his discussion of *Birth of a Nation*.[38] This film is not simply a narrative account of the nation. It is a *Bildungsroman* of the nation and white male subjectivity. We are not just told a story with names and dates, causes, and effects, but given an education about how we should understand ourselves as citizens. The real subject of the film is the spectator who views the action through the eyes of white male subjectivity. This citizen is educated and empowered through this reading of American history. He is the kind of subject who writes the majority opinion in *Plessey*. At the same time, the film develops black stereotypes and makes them part of an argument for Jim Crow: "The anti-Negro images of Hollywood films . . . constitute justifications for all these acts, legal, emotional, economic and political which we label Jim Crow."[39] Criticizing the naturalized reality of *Birth of Nation* through appeals to principle could not do the critical work that Ellison wanted. To thematize and counter these powerful imaginaries requires more than a principle of discrimination or subordination; it requires a new language that can reveal the American nightmare and work toward a new imaginary.

This collective inarticulacy was not just limited to such obvious forms of racism. Ellison contested similar misreadings by thinkers from the Left as well, such as Irving Howe and Richard Wright, who also ignored the agency of African Americans and the worth of their culture. What is important for my argument here are not the details of the debate but Ellison's thematization of the social imaginary and his understanding of the novel as a mode of argument. The novel provides ways to take on the dominant configurations of the social imaginary of his time—whether they emerged in fiction, history, political discourse, newspaper columns, films etc. The unit of argument cannot be the empirical or normative proposition but the vocabularies of the social imaginary: "All novels of a given historical moment form an argument over the nature of reality and are, to an extent, criticisms of each other."[40] Hence, for Ellison, "art is social action itself."[41] The novel argues with its historical predecessors so that truth, not just meaning, is part of public political deliberation. This truth appears not simply as an appeal to the world but by an historical argument against or with its predecessor's language, the interpretive medium common to history, literature, and law. Ellison addresses directly language's political ambiguity and its ontological power to imprison and empower: "If the word has the potency to revive and make us free, it has also the power to blind, imprison, and destroy. . . . The essence of the word is its ambivalence."[42]

Ellison agrees with Habermas that human rights depend on popular sovereignty; however, instead of connecting them formally, Ellison reworks and theorizes the medium of deliberation. In the Introduction to *Invisible Man*, he announces his concern with the conditions of self-governance, conditions that cannot be thematized only in the liberal language of rights, for democracy: "is not only a collection of individuals . . . but a collectivity of politically astute citizens who, by virtue of our vaunted system of universal education and our freedom of opportunity, would be prepared to govern."[43] But if, as Habermas says, "popular sovereignty . . . resides in 'subjectless' forms of communication and discourse circulating through forums and legislative bodies," we need to understand the powers and constraints of these forms with a richer problematic than regulative ideals, one that that addresses the capacity to imagine the relationship of individual to popular sovereign.[44]

Ellison articulates our inescapable embedding in the languages of "strong evaluation," to use Taylor's term, that partially constitute our experience rather than merely describing it. Rather, it is that "certain modes of experience are not possible without certain self-descriptions."[45] What is at stake here is not the phenomenology of an individual subject, but an argumentative space in the inherited discourse of a culture that is inhabited and affirmed by the speaker: "The meanings and norms implicit in [. . .] practices are not just in the minds of the actors but are out there in the practices themselves."[46] Ellison wants to thematize the different argument spaces in the American social imaginary so that he can rework these languages.[47]

The Prologue to *Invisible Man* announces the text's challenges to the received public languages. In the opening scene, the narrating subject of the present—that is, the subject who has already been through the entire story that is about to be told—confronts the reader with an allegory of recognition. In this fable, the protagonist attacks someone who does not see him. The narrator comments: "Something in this man's thick head had sprung out and beaten him within an inch of his life."[48] This allegory initiates a drama of recognition, not just within the work but between text and reader. The text deliberately disorients the reader, through its confusing style and multiple allusions—the slave narrative, *Notes from Underground*, *The Divine Comedy*, and blues traditions. These allusions alert the reader that he/she should not expect a typical account of the horrors of "black experience." This is a warning that readers will simply repeat the misrecognition, commit a hermeneutic mugging of the text, if they are not prepared to give up the assumption of a shared linguistic world, which means giving up their self-understanding and going through a linguistic apprenticeship. Getting to the point where he could write the Prologue has required transformation and loss for the narrator and the reader should expect a similar wrenching.

The Invisible Man takes the entire novel to learn that he is "an invisible man."[49] Ellison brings out many of the dominant patterns of the languages of his time (e.g., the discourses of Booker T. Washington, Marcus Garvey, and the American Left) and then has his protagonist inhabit and work through them, not just for himself but for the reader. Ellison describes the way he first evokes and then transforms these patterns: "I could not violate the reader's sense of reality, his sense of the way things were done, at least on the surface. My task would be to give him the surface and then try to take him into the internalities, take him below the level of racial structuring."[50] Ellison did not seek to represent historical events or people but to draw out the structures of the imaginary that make available the world of reference: "I didn't want to describe an existing Socialist or Communist or Marxist political group, primarily because it would have allowed the reader to escape confronting certain political patterns, patterns which still exist."[51] The past cannot be simply put behind us "because it is within us. But we *do* modify the past as we live our own lives."[52] Ellison does not take a constructivist approach that simply exposes negative languages and makes normative evaluations of these facts; rather, he argues for a new language of reference and evaluation that can make possible positive, not just negative liberty. In striving to make available a new language of being together in a democratic public, the narrator must not address readers as they are but as they could be: "Who knows," says the narrator at the end of the novel, "but that, on lower frequencies I speak *for* you."[53]

The novel shows how rights depend on the normative and referential shapes of imaginaries and how making claims means engaging these languages of public life through novelistic argument rather than by appealing to sociological facts and moral principle. Trying to take shortcuts around the imaginaries through the objectifications of social science, the counterfactuals of normative theory, or the self-consciousness of social contructivism will not work.

Thus, Ellison's democratic project interrogates the historical media which articulate subjects and institutions, the tissues of being that connect and fragment subjects. Ellison is forever turning back on language, memory, and history as he moves through the world. Ellison portrays language as an ambiguous protean medium that articulates pain, triumph, love, and failure, a medium that connects and isolates us, enables and deprives, that shapes in a way that opens and forecloses the possibilities of the world.

CONCLUSION: FROM MORAL MINIMUMS
TO CONTESTED PACKAGES OF BELIEF

The argument of this essay is that reasoning about rights and self-governance through the social imaginary opens resources of public debate that have been blocked by modernity's disengaged epistemological and moral reasoning. But doesn't moving from individually contested concepts to contested packages of beliefs simply multiply the difficulties of reaching an effective political consensus on human rights, particularly across cultures? I want to check this impulse to minimalism as the first move when confronted with disagreement. First, the imaginaries are already at work in the stripped down debates. "Moral minimalists" usually have large unspoken agendas, agendas that are difficult to thematize when all we have are principles. Second, the focus on principles has meant that histories of human rights ignore—through various means—the rich historical imaginaries that surrounded the philosophical/juridical accounts. We saw some of these in Habermas, but they are particularly characteristic of the historiography of human rights.[54] National and international historical imaginaries are important resources for cross-cultural discussion. Instead of scaling back in the face of disagreement, we need a theory that permits us to move through social imaginaries with interpretive agility that can address various types of interrogation—transcendental, normative, empirical, causal, etc. In other words, the problematic of the social imaginary will not only offer us more to argue about but more to argue with. Scaling back is always an option but beginning with more rather than less gives interlocutors greater intuitive access to arguments and more ways to initiate questioning, ways that will include literature and history and not just religion and philosophy. Arguing through the social imaginary also means that we are not asserting self-evident rights that serve as historical and philosophical foundations but accepting the risk that public reasoning about rights may demand changes in who we are and who we think we've been.

NOTES

1. See, for example, Benedict Anderson's *Imagined Communities: Reflections on the Origin and Spread of Nationalism* (London: Verso, 1991).
2. See Jack Donnelly's *Universal Human Rights In Theory and Practice*, 2nd ed. (Ithaca, NY: Cornell University Press, 2003), especially 35, for a typical reading of the tight connection between political liberalism and the philosophy of human rights.

3. To speak very broadly, there have been Derridean and Foucauldian lines of poststructuralist critique. I will address the Foucauldian line in this chapter and have discussed both lines in *Hiding from History: Politics and Public Imagination* (Ithaca, NY: Cornell University Press, 2005), chapter 2.

4. Charles Taylor, *Modern Social Imaginaries* (Durham, NC: Duke University Press, 2004), 2, 8–9.

5. Rawls says that the original position is designed to remove what "sets men at odds and allows them to be guided by their prejudices." John Rawls, *A Theory of Justice* (Cambridge, MA: Harvard University Press, 1971), 15.

6. Austin Sarat summarizes this view, "The constitutive view suggests that law shapes society from the inside out by providing the principle categories in terms of which social life is made to seem largely natural, moral, cohesive" ("Toward Something New or Maybe Something Not So New: Is There Room for Legal Scholarship in Law Schools," *Yale Journal of Law and Humanities* 12 (2000): 134).

7. Jürgen Habermas, *Between Facts and Norms: Contributions to a Discourse Theory of Law and Democracy,* translated by William Rehg (Cambridge, MA: MIT Press, 1996), 4.

8. Jürgen Habermas, "On Legitimation Through Human Rights," in *Global Justice and Transnational Politics*, ed. Pablo De Greiff and Ciaran Cronin (Cambridge, MA: MIT Press, 2002), 201.

9. Jürgen Habermas, *Truth and Justification*, trans. Barbara Fultner (Cambridge, MA: MIT Press, 2003), 49. Rawls rejects Habermas's approach and proposes an overlapping political consensus on norms from a variety of different moral, religious or philosophical positions. Donnelly endorses Rawls's view in *Universal Human Rights*, 40–43.

10. See Habermas, *Truth and Justification* 262–3 and Donnelly, *Universal Human Rights*, 58.

11. Joseph Slaughter, *Human Rights, Inc.: The World Novel, Narrative Form, and International Law* (New York: Fordham University Press, 2007), 8.

12. For example, the deliberations surrounding the Universal Declaration of Human Rights, as Joseph Slaughter points out, drew on the unacknowledged imaginary of the *Bildungsroman*.

13. In the opening section of *Sources of the Self* (Cambridge, MA: Harvard University Press, 1989), Taylor makes a transcendental argument for the imaginary, and in *Modern Social Imaginaries*, he explores the historiographical fruitfulness of the notion.

14. Taylor, *Sources of the Self*, 27.

15. Foucault says, "I try to historicize to the utmost in order to leave as little space as possible to the transcendental." Michel Foucault, *Foucault Live: Interviews 1966–84*, trans. John Johnston, ed. Sylvère Lotringer (New York: Semiotext(e), 1989), 79.

16. Taylor, *Sources of the Self*, 40.

17. Taylor, *Sources of the Self*, 167.

18. This study of the historical effectiveness of concepts in generating an imaginary parallels Foucault, who, for instance, wants to show that the idea of the individual is not a normative philosophical presupposition but a historical artifact (imaginary). "Individuality is neither the real atomistic basis of society [i.e., liberalism] nor an ideological illusion of liberal economics [i.e., Marxism], but an effective artifact of a very long and complicated historical process" (Michel Foucault, *Discipline and Punish*, trans. Alan Sheridan [New York: Vintage, 1977; 1995], 194).

19. Taylor, *Sources of the Self*, 73.

20. Taylor, *Sources of the Self*, 26.

21. Taylor, *Sources of the Self*, 89.
22. See Neil MacCormick, *Legal Reasoning and Legal Theory* (New York: Oxford University Press, 1978), 275–292.
23. Post says, "The image of the orchestra audition distills the logic of American antidiscrimination law" (*Prejudicial Appearances* (Durham, NC: Duke University Press, 2001), 19. And this is: "the dominant conception [antidiscrimination] expresses a moral vision that is internal to the law, while the sociological account represents an external account of the operation of law" (Post, *Prejudicial Appearances*, 20).
24. Owen Fiss, "Another Equality," *Issues in Legal Scholarship, The Origins and Fate of Antisubordination Theory*, Article 20 (2004), 1, http://www/.bepress.com/ils/1552/art20.
25. In terms of human rights, antisubordination can be understood as the "right to self-determination," which is articulated in Article I of the International Covenant on Economic, Social and Cultural Rights and in Article I of the International Covenant on Civil and Political Rights.
26. Fiss, "Another Equality," 2–3.
27. Jack Balkin, *What Brown v. Board of Education Should Have Said* (New York: New York University Press, 2001), 13.
28. Balkin, *What Brown v. Board of Education Should Have Said*, 13.
29. Ralph Ellison, *The Collected Essays of Ralph Ellison*, ed. John Callahan (New York: Modern Library, 1995), 339.
30. Ellison, *Essays*, 340.
31. Ellison, *Essays*, 339.
32. Ellison, *Essays*, 340.
33. Ellison, *Essays*, 340.
34. Ellison, *Essays*, 340.
35. Robert Meister has looked at the history of race in the United States in the wider context provided by transitional justice in "Forgiving and Forgetting: Lincoln and the Politics of National Recovery," *Human Rights in Political Transitions: Gettysburg to Bosnia*, ed. Carla Hesse and Robert Post (New York: Zone Books, 1999), 135–76.
36. Ellison, *Essays*, 149.
37. Ellison, *Essays*, 149.
38. Ellison, *Essays*, 304.
39. Ellison, *Essays*, 305
40. Ellison, *Essays*, 165.
41. Ellison, *Essays*, 91.
42. Ellison, *Essays*, 81.
43. Ralph Ellison, "Introduction," *Invisible Man* (New York: Vintage, 1981), xxi.
44. Habermas, *Between Facts and Norms*, 136.
45. Charles Taylor, *Language and Human Agency* (Cambridge: Cambridge University Press, , 37.
46. Charles Taylor, *Philosophy and the Human Sciences* (Cambridge: Cambridge University Press, 1985) 36.
47. Taylor emphasizes the long-term development "of the forms of social imaginary that have underpinned the rise of western modernity" (*Modern Social Imaginaries*, 2) and speaks of literature in his historical exposition, while I emphasize the role of the imaginary in public deliberations in the present.
48. Ellison, *Invisible Man*, 5.
49. Ellison, *Invisible Man*, 5.
50. Ellison, *Essays*, 532.
51. Ellison, *Essays*, 538.

52. Ellison, *Essays*, 413.
53. Ellison, *Invisible Man*, 568.
54. Isolating the normative concepts of rights creates problems for historians of human rights as well. See Samuel Moyn's critique of Lynn Hunt's *Inventing Human Rights*, in which he says that Hunt often treats "'human rights' as a body of ideas somehow insulated from history" (*The Nation*, http://www. thenation.com/doc/20070416/moyn. April 6, 2007 and his *The Last Utopia* [Cambridge, MA: Harvard University Press, 2010]).

5 Intimations of What Was to Come

Edwidge Danticat's *The Farming of Bones* and the Indivisibility of Human Rights[1]

Elizabeth Swanson Goldberg

Critical reception of *The Farming of Bones* (1998), Edwidge Danticat's novel chronicling the 1937 massacre of Haitian workers in the Dominican Republic, has emphasized its status as witness literature, a reclamation of collective memory of the experiences of those most often excluded from official historical accounts: women, people of color, and the poor. Jana Braziel describes Danticat's larger literary project as an attempt to rectify "historical amnesia, [the] deep unwillingness to face and confront the inflicted wounds of the past"[2] that marks the history of the Americas in general, and Danticat herself has described the writing *The Farming of Bones* as an act of "remembrance."[3] I included the novel in my own work on witness literature, examining Danticat's structural innovations in constructing a narrative able to capture survivor voices and the traumatic time characteristic of genocide.[4]

To date, witness literature has been defined in terms of the civil and political rights given priority in western rights discourse after the split of the 1948 Universal Declaration of Human Rights (UDHR) into the separate binding enforcement protocols, the Covenant on Civil and Political Rights and Covenant on Economic, Social, and Cultural Rights (1966). In other words, what witness literature typically witnesses is harm done to bodies and/or restrictions of personal, civic, and religious freedoms, the paradigmatic case on both counts being the Nazi holocaust and particularly the experience of Jewish people during the World War II era. Less prominent in this genre—if addressed at all, at least in generic or theoretical terms—is the act of witnessing chronic violations of social, economic, and cultural rights. As interdisciplinary work in human rights and literature gains momentum, it is critical to expand theories of literary witness from their focus upon civil and political rights violations to include so-called "aspirational" economic, social, and cultural rights.

In this chapter, I want to build upon readings of *The Farming of Bones* as a novel of witness to genocide in order to make a broader claim for the novel as truly postcolonial in its sweep. In other words, it bears witness to far more than the massacre of Haitians in the Dominican Republic between

October 2 and 8, 1937, foregrounding as well the structural connection between the acute violence of genocide and the sustained violence of poverty, oppression, and the colonial legacy—a connection often obscured, if not disavowed, in global human rights discourse. A deeper reading of the novel's system of image, metaphor, and character reveals important meditations upon the deeply contested history of the Saint Domingue/ Haitian Revolution and its legacies; the neocolonial history of Haiti that began before Saint Domingue had officially become Ayiti in 1804; and the imbrications of economic, social, and cultural rights with political and civil rights at the historical moment directly preceding their first construction as indivisible, and then their interminable tearing asunder in justiciable international law.

SOCIAL, ECONOMIC, AND CULTURAL RIGHTS

Historians of the contemporary western human rights movement commonly trace its origin to Franklin D. Roosevelt's 1941 State of the Union address, known as the Four Freedoms speech, in which he articulated two basic "positive rights" (freedom *of* speech and religion") and two "negative rights" (freedom *from* want and fear).[5] Roosevelt laid the foundation for contemporary economic rights in his statement regarding freedom from want, which, he noted, "translated into world terms, means economic understandings which will secure to every nation a healthy peace-time life for its inhabitants everywhere in the world." (The idea of translating freedom from want from its origin in the experience of the individual person to what Roosevelt calls the "world terms" of the nation is important, and we shall return to it below.) Economic rights were then addressed in the UN Charter; were defined broadly in UDHR Article 22: "Everyone, as a member of society, has the right to social security and is entitled to realization, through national effort and international co-operation and in accordance with the organization and resources of each State, of the economic, social and cultural rights indispensable for his [sic] dignity and the free development of his personality;" and were delineated more specifically in UDHR Article 25 (1): "Everyone has the right to a standard of living adequate for the health and well-being of himself and of his family, including food, clothing, housing, medical care and necessary social services, and the right to security in the event of unemployment, sickness, disability, widowhood, old age or other lack of livelihood in circumstances beyond his control." Of course, the period of time stretching from Roosevelt's Four Freedoms address to the drafting of the UDHR in 1948 is, in historical retrospect, exceptional in the remarkable clarity of its "good war" fought against an indisputable evil (fascism) that had produced "barbarous acts that outraged the conscience of mankind"[6]— specifically, the Nazi death camps and gas chambers. The powers-that-were in 1945–1948 arguably were united in the ideal of a cooperative, harmonious, prosperous, and humane world in a way that they had not been before and would not be again, even as they glossed the inconsistencies of their own discriminations, colonizations, imperialisms, and brutalities, and even as the uneasy alliance of the USSR and the U.S. began to creep toward the monstrous stalemate that became the cold war. The slam of cold war fear and antagonism into the revolutionary energies of anti-colonial movements in Africa and Asia meant that the pursuit of freedom by colonized peoples, with its logical vision of wealth redistribution, was interpreted through the tunnel vision of (Soviet) alignment. This mis-understanding, in turn, led to the many overt and clandestine interventions—from Congo to Korea; from Angola to Afghanistan—that have marked U.S. foreign policy since 1945. The same ideological clash ultimately informed the separation of the UDHR in 1966 into the two Covenants that have left economic, social, and cultural rights comparatively unrealized.[7]

Since 1966, human rights advocates have worried about the loss of the claim to "indivisibility" of rights resulting not only from the split of the UDHR into its two Covenants, but also from the disproportionate attention given to civil and political rights in global human rights policy and practice. Further, human rights work simply cannot get out from under the paradox of a human rights regime emanating from "the sole super-power" leading a global capitalist system that depends upon an exploitable underclass, imbalanced trade relations, and the over-accumulation of individual wealth and property. Whatever gains the human rights movement has made can be countered, if not undone, by the production of a normalized condition of global impoverishment that rapidly expands, even (especially?) in the context of economic development and aid policies.[8] Thus, to consider the massacre of Haitians in the borderlands of the Dominican Republic in 1937, at the start of World War II and just prior to the consolidation of both contemporary global human rights discourse and global capitalism, provides a useful perspective upon these concerns. Undertaking that study through the lens of a literary representation rather than solely through historical accounts enables the imaginative depth perception necessary to the "creative remembrance" of Caribbean history, fractured by the genocide of indigenous Americans, the Atlantic slave trade, American plantation system, and centuries of political struggle and economic exploitation. Turning to this notion of "creative remembrance," I rely in this chapter upon theories of American history as an ongoing process of discovery, discernment, retelling, and rejection of dominant western historical paradigms by such Caribbean thinkers as Edouard Glissant, Martin Munro, and Antonio Benitez-Rojo.

(NOT) A SINGULAR HISTORY

Broadening literary critical response to *The Farming of Bones* from its tight focus upon the events of 1937 to the full range of Haiti's post-colonial history makes sense in terms of the body of literature on Haiti from historical and political disciplines, which reveals that many of the same structures, institutions, identity formations, and problems in evidence during the eras of plantation slavery and of revolution remain in the contemporary context. Historical and political literature on Haiti also offers a critique of the common construction of Haitian history as "exceptional" in this regard. The subject of much discussion and debate, Haiti also has been put to many uses—symbolic, rhetorical, material, and political—since its national birth in 1804, as Paul Farmer has persuasively shown.[9] Its status as exceptional in fact is arguably based upon the ways in which its history is at once extraordinary and representative; extreme and tragically commonplace. *The First Black Republic in the Americas! The Nation of Slaves that Defeated Napoleon's Armies! The Synonym for Freedom and Emancipation! The fulfillment of the Enlightenment promise of freedom for all!* Or, alternatively/simultaneously: *The Poorest Country in the Western Hemisphere! The Land That Breeds Dictators More Brutal than its Slavers! A Black Country Unable to Govern Itself! Prototype for Troubled Independent Post-Colonial Nations in the Americas, Africa, and Asia!* As Nick Nesbitt has argued, "Two of the processes that came to distinguish the twentieth century were invented in Haiti: decolonization and neocolonialism."[10] In other words, triumphant liberation was followed by an almost immediate collapse into a newly defined state of imbalance and domination.

A study of literature about the Saint-Domingue revolution, its heroes and its legacies, reveals that the meanings of that revolution are still very much contested. I would like to investigate the ways in which Danticat embeds this ambivalence—rejecting simplistic binary notions of triumph or failure—in the metaphorical structure of her novel. Danticat sets out the complex structure of her image system on the first page of the novel, in a tender gesture from Sebastien Onius, a cane cutter who later is killed in the massacre, to his lover, and the novel's protagonist, Amabelle: "'Look at you,' he says, taking my face into one of his spacious bowl-shaped hands, where the palms have lost their life-lines to the machetes that cut the cane. 'You are glowing like a Christmas lantern, even with this skin that is the color of driftwood ashes in the rain.'"[11] This passage contains three recurring images that will structure the novel's themes and its historical commentary: the palms whose life-lines have been rubbed away by work; the Christmas lantern; and ashes from burned wood.

Let us begin with the Christmas lantern, for it evokes most directly the Haitian revolution and its philosophical and political relation to the Enlightenment and the struggle for democracy in the western world. This first reference to the Christmas lantern symbolizes Sebastien's perception of Amabelle's singular beauty, of the individuation soon to be denied in the erasure that is genocide. The symbol builds later in the novel into a reference to the Citadel, the fortress built by the last of Haiti's "trinity" of founding fathers, Henri Christophe. It is no accident that the character Amabelle, a survivor of genocide perpetrated in the Dominican Republic as the result of long historical conflict between the two nations sharing the small island of Hispaniola, hails from the northern city of Cap Haitien, specifically in the shadow of The Citadel, its great monument to Haiti's independence, for The Citadel is an exemplary symbol of the ambivalence with which Haitian history is received, interpreted, and lived. On the one hand, it has been constructed as the indulgence of a "megalomaniac" king who was not only hungry for power but was also cruel to the black peasants who had so recently been liberated from slavery, forcing them to labor on his palace (Sans Souci) and fortress until the day of his death. On the other hand, a recent essay by Frederick Mangonés offers an alternative perspective upon this monument, along with a forceful rejection of what he considers the egregiously west-centric perspective of Christophe as megalomaniacal king: "The Citadel is the symbol of the will of the people not only to free themselves from the chains of slavery, but to keep, at any price, that painfully earned liberty."[12] Mangones further identifies the Citadel as "an important Lieu de Memoire [site of collective memory] for the *Haitian people and the black people*, symbolic of the 'right to dignity for every human being.'"[13]

Mangonés's differentiation between "the Haitian people" and "the black people" is significant, evoking the problematics of race and color that have marked Haiti's history and politics since its inception, and that also informed the genocide of Haitian people in the border regions of the Dominican Republic in 1937. It also evokes Haiti's historical status as liberatory, aspirational symbol for the black diaspora created in the transatlantic slave trade. While the three iconic heroes of the Haitian Revolution—Toussaint L'Ouverture, Jean-Jacques Dessalines, and Henri Christophe—were all born slaves, Henri Christophe was said to be of mixed European and African descent. By 1791, upon the outbreak of the slave revolt that would end with the creation of the self-governed French colony Saint-Domingue in 1801, and then of Haiti in 1804, the *gens de couleur*, the mixed race elite, were already gathering the force that would inform their domination of the political and economic structures of Haiti for centuries to come, and that have structured relations with the Dominican Republic as well.

In her work on Haiti's early Constitutions (1801; 1805; 1806; and 1807), Julia Gaffield shows how the ideas of national and racial identity were re-imagined by Toussaint, Dessalines, and then Christophe. Article 3 of Toussaint's 1801 Saint-Domingue Constitution articulated that "All men born here live and die free and *French*" (emphasis added). While Toussaint is known for establishing the self-governing colony of Saint-Domingue and abolishing slavery, Dessalines is credited with establishing a specifically *black* identity in his 1805 Constitution for the newly independent state of Haiti by limiting citizenship rights of property ownership to black citizens: "Article twelve states that, 'no whiteman [sic] of whatever nation he may be, shall put his foot on this territory with the title of master or proprietor, neither shall he in future acquire any property therein.'"[14] Dessalines, credited as the Father of Noirisme, or Negritude, was murdered by political enemies who were, not surprisingly, *gens de couleur*. It was not until Christophe's Constitution, written for the northern region of Haiti which he ruled as self-proclaimed Emperor, that all citizens were defined as Haitian, and a national identity independent from colonial and racialized identities was imagined.

Danticat's emphasis upon Christophe from among the three leaders, then, is meaningful for two reasons. First, in terms of the imagined community of the nation, Christophe is the first truly *nationalist Haitian* leader, although the fact that he ruled only in the north reveals the schisms in Haitian national identity and politics that would come to structure Haitian history for the next two centuries. Second, had Danticat chosen to highlight the figure of Toussaint L'Ouverture, the message would have been much less ambiguous, and much of the nuanced signification of her symbolic structure lost. Toussaint's revolutionary, heroic mythology is entrenched in a way that Christophe's and Dessalines's are not; indeed, Edouard Glissant has called Toussaint's unique iconic status in Caribbean history and letters a "complexe de Toussaint," described by Charles Forsdick as a means by which "Caribbean DOMs [Départements d'Outre Mer] compensate for their history of (perceived) lack, loss and failure by turning to the example of Haiti."[15] This iconicity is increased by the proliferation of major literary works about Toussaint, written by such postcolonial luminaries as Aimé Césaire, Rene Depestre, Glissant, and C. L. R. James (all of which Danticat would have evoked had she conjured Toussaint as the primary focus of her narrative symbolism) and prompting Forsdick's observation that "Toussaint L'Ouverture is one of the federating figures of the francophone Atlantic: in this sphere the trans-Caribbean and transatlantic resonances of his character have granted him a privileged status perhaps only rivaled in scope and impact by a much later activist and theorist such as Frantz Fanon."[16] Evoking Toussaint more substantially in the symbolic scheme of the novel arguably would have set up too strong an opposition between the triumph of the revolution and the promise of freedom in the first black republic in the western hemisphere, on the one hand, and, on the other, what Nesbitt has called the "pessimism" of postcolonial Haitian history: "a succession of despotic regimes, systematic economic underdevelopment, and terrifying social injustice."[17] Setting Christophe and the monuments he left behind as the foil to Amabelle's experience of genocide more profoundly emphasizes the ambiguous legacy of the Saint-Domingue revolution itself, and of the earliest manifestations of nationalism in postcolonial Haiti.

Examining the function of Christophe's monuments in Danticat's novelistic treatment of the 1937 massacre alongside Dominican writer Julia Alvarez's 1995 novel of Rafael Trujillo's dictatorship, *In the Time of the Butterflies*, Kelli Lyon Johnson notes that Haiti and the Dominican Republic differ significantly in their relation to monuments and commemoration: "Danticat and Alvarez come from two very different traditions of commemoration: the official silence of commemoration in Haiti contrasts with the cacophony of the Dominican Republic, in which the truth of the *trujillato* must be distinguished amid too many stories, memories, monuments, markers, and rituals."[18] While Johnson wryly notes that Trujillo won a place in the Guinness Book of World Records "as the leader who built the most statues of himself,"[19] she argues that "there is little evidence that the people of Haiti locate their national identity within physical institutions such as universities, museums, historical markers or monuments in the same way that Trujillo invested these sites with meaning and history."[20] Johnson builds this argument upon the work of historian Franklin Knight, who argued that at the time of independence, "Haiti was confronted with a hard choice: independence or general well-being. [. . .] The Haitians opted for independence, which meant nothing short of the total physical destruction of every institutional form which made plantation life possible."[21]

Here we have one of the many reductive historical constructions that historiographers such as Glissant have shown to be fallacious. As many other historians, including C. L. R. James in his seminal work *The Black Jacobins* (1963) have shown, the early Haitian leaders *did* "opt for independence," and *did* seek to protect that independence at nearly any cost, but that choice certainly did *not* mean the destruction of the institutional forms of plantation life. Indeed, the complex truth returns us to Nick Nesbitt's formulation of the near-simultaneity of decolonization and neocolonialism, for Toussaint, Dessalines, and Christophe all sought to build upon Saint Domingue's acknowledged status as the world's most profitable colony as a means to ensure its independence.[22] For these leaders, that meant shoring up Haiti's place in the global mercantilist economy by continuing the system of plantation labor and participation in the sugar industry; it also meant strengthening the military culture of the island in such a way that the military and economic systems became mutually reinforcing. As historians have shown, the French were determined to reclaim Saint-Domingue (and indeed, the island of Hispaniola as a whole, which also meant defeating the British and Spanish in the race for territorial control), and, for better or for worse, Haiti's early leaders could not put themselves to the task of realizing the triumphant potential of prosperity and cultural development after emancipation and independence with the specter of Napoleon's armies just off the coastline. In addition, the European powers were terrified by the possibility that the Haitian slave revolts and revolution would spread to other Caribbean territories (in much the same way that the U.S. later feared the spread of Communism in its "backyard" and reviled Castro's Cuba as the source of the germ). As a result, these powers did everything possible to isolate Haiti economically through trade restrictions and the institution of reparations to be paid to France for the loss of income it suffered upon the destruction of its plantation economy. As Nesbitt argues, at the time of its independence "Haiti was immediately quarantined and pauperized in the forced dysfunction of a postcolonial state undermined and hamstrung by the terrified slave-holding powers that then controlled the globe."[23] Christopher Miller outlines the economically disastrous conditions of emancipation: "Haiti is required to pay [the] ruinous sum [150 million francs of 'indemnity'] in order to end French schemes of reinvasion and re-enslavement."[24]

Considering Danticat's evocation of Haiti's revolutionary history through the recurring metaphor of the Citadel, then, the monument serves both its commonsense purpose as reminder of Haiti's nationalist triumph and military might—particularly in contrast to President Stenio Vincent's criminal passivity during and after the massacre of Haitians in the Dominican Republic in 1937—but also evokes the complexity of a history which is, to borrow from Toni Morrison, "both/and" rather than "either/or." In this regard, the Citadel is neither the symbol of postcolonial Haitian leaders' cruelty and megalomania in forcing its construction by conscripted Haitian laborers, echoing the slave system that the Saint Domingue revolution had fought so hard to undo, nor is it the sign of a glorious Haitian nationalism—it is both at once. Perhaps most importantly, the Citadel evokes the eternal threat of re-colonization, inasmuch as it was both a fortress and a lookout, situated high in the hills in order to give an early alarm should Napoleon's ships be spotted on the horizon. Such watchfuless has become a staple of postcolonial Haitian life, inasmuch as it has endured the presence of U.S. warships in its waters starting in 1850, multiple U.S. interventions to "recover debt and restore order," and most recently, two U.S.-sponsored coups removing populist, democratically elected President Jean-Bertrande Aristide from office. The object lessons regarding postcolonial history and discourses of freedom and human rights inscribed in Danticat's novel are partly to be had, then, by fully engaging the ambivalence and overdetermination of the Citadel's symbolic value, which she skillfully allows to emerge in her narrative.

After its first evocation by Sebastien, we next encounter the image of the Citadel in one of the sequences of memory and indirect discourse set off in bold type-face in the first and last sections of the novel, as Amabelle describes the Christmas lanterns made of paper in the hills beneath the citadel. In this passage, Amabelle describes the paper lanterns made by her father, which took the shape of many monuments to Haiti's revolutionary past—La Place Toussaint L'ouverture, or General Toussaint's "feather-capped hat," or the citadel itself, "which takes twelve months of secret work."[25] Significantly, this sequence directly follows a highly symbolic racist act committed by General Pico, Dominican landowner, rising star of Trujillo's military, and head of the family for which Amabelle is a servant. In this plot point, Pico smashes an imported tea set in which his wife had served a group of Haitians, one of whom is Kongo, the father of the man whom Pico struck and killed in his car. Like Kongo, Joel had been a Haitian cane cutter; he is also, in the nominal scheme of the novel, the son of Africa, literally, as Kongo (referring to the ancient African

kingdom) was also a term used to refer to black slaves during the plantation era. The careless murder of this "son of Africa," and then the act of
racial and national hatred implied in Pico's destruction of the European
tea set soiled by the touch of those people of African descent, foreshad-
ows the massacre of Haitians which is just then gathering steam under
General Pico's leadership. The construction of Haitian lives as without
value in Trujillo's racist-nationalist scheme is followed immediately in the
narrative by Amabelle's memory of the glowing lanterns in the landscape
guarded by the Citadel, evoking a sense of nationalist history, tradition,
and both national and familial safety.

The mythical narrative of the founding fathers is evoked again in the
urgent testimonials of survivors who have safely crossed back into Haiti,
one of whom proclaims: "In those times we had respect. When Dessalines,
Toussaint, Henry, when those men walked the earth, we were a strong
nation. Those men would go to war to defend our blood."[26] Indeed, these
leaders did fight to the death for the emancipation and independence of
Haiti, even if it meant conscripting Haitians in the process, and denying
true emancipation to the peasant class who envisioned a small agricultural
existence, but who were forced back onto the plantation in order to support
the new nation-state in the brutal mercantilist economy still dominated by
the slave trade and plantation system.

This mixed legacy of strength and destruction resonates in Sebastien's
description of Amabelle in the image that begins the novel, her face that
glows "like a Christmas lantern, *even with this skin that is the color of
driftwood ashes in the rain.*"[27] These ashes signal another aspect of Haiti's revolutionary history: the decision to destroy oneself rather than to be
enslaved again. This is both the personal history of Henri Christophe, who
took his own life rather than succumbing to death at the hands of his enemies, but who vowed to "rise again from the ashes," but also the history of
the Saint-Domingue revolution, in which a desperate slash-and-burn military strategy was employed. In a letter during the war with the French in
1802, Toussaint admonished Dessalines:

> Do not forget, while waiting for the rainy season which will rid us of
> our foes, that we have no other resource than destruction and flames.
> Bear in mind that the soil bathed with our sweat must not furnish our
> enemies with the smallest aliment. Tear up the roads with shot; throw
> corpses and horses into all the fountains; burn and annihilate every-
> thing, in order that those who have come to reduce us to slavery may
> have before their eyes the image of that hell which they deserve.

Le Cap was indeed razed in the war with the French; its ashes, like those of
King Christophe himself, drifting aimlessly through history and the conceptions of Haitian nationalism and the racial identities of the inhabitants
of Saint Domingue that marked the next two hundred years, captured by

Danticat in the image of Amabelle's skin as "driftwood ashes in the rain," a melancholy image indeed.[28] The rebuilding of Le Cap with the fortresses and palaces by Christophe may have been an act of glorious defiance against the French, but by the time of the 1937 massacre of Haitians, the Citadel lay in ruins (it has since been restored as a World Historic Site by the United Nations Educational, Scientific and Cultural Organization [UNESCO]).

One piece of evidence used by Mangonés to support his claim regarding the status of The Citadel as a significant monument to positively charged Haitian nationalism is the fact that each year during the Easter season, thousands of Haitians visit the Citadel: "The daily register of the number of visitors kept by ISPAN (Haitian Institute for the Protection of National Heritage) since 1979 shows that on Holy Thursday the number of pilgrims reaches 5,000. They come from every part of the country and walk the long steep road up the mountain 2,000 feet above sea level to spend the day at the Citadel. This tradition is evidently an old one. The pilgrims whom we have asked admit not knowing the origins of this custom."[29] While Mangones hypothesizes that the tradition may have originated in family visits to Haitians working or garrisoned at the Citadel, it is interesting to think about what such a pilgrimage may have come to signify over time. Danticat's novel ends with two pilgrimages, both made by Amabelle—one is to the site of the massacre, to bear witness to the violation of civil and political rights, and one is to the Citadel, which I would argue is a witness to the violation of economic, social, and cultural rights implicated in and determinative of the massacre itself. On this occasion, we encounter the Citadel as a tourist destination in which Haitian guides tell the story of Henri Christophe, born a slave and died a king. Danticat's narrative structure reveals the indivisibility of rights lost in the construction of the two 1966 human rights Covenants by emphasizing that Amabelle's pilgrimage to the Citadel provide homage not only to a mythical hero such as Christophe, but also to the "nameless and faceless who vanish like smoke into the early morning air."[30] In the context of this narrative, then, the Citadel does signal the "right to dignity of every human being," as Mangonés argues: the right to one's name, one's story, the value and importance of one's individual life and experience, and one's dignified existence over time—all of which are lost in the blur of unindividuated humans who have fed the global capitalist machine since its emergence alongside discourses of freedom and enlightenment.

Sebastien Onius (whose experience arguably constitutes the central subject of the novel's witness, inasmuch as the narrative begins and ends with the declarative "His name is Sebastien Onius") bears a doubled status when considered through the lens of human rights discourse and practice: first a victim of economic, social, and cultural rights violations as an exploited cane worker, and then the victim of the ultimate civil and political rights violation, genocide. There is a direct causal link between the chronic violation of Sebastien Onius's economic, social, and cultural rights and his vulnerability to the political and civil rights violation of genocide, and Amabelle bears witness to this on her visit to the Citadel. The complex metaphorical system created by Danticat around the figure of the Citadel, then, evokes a full range of "positive" and "negative," or "active" and "passive," human rights, as well as the doubled post/colonial history for which Haiti has become sign and symbol throughout the world.

(NEO)COLONIAL CONTINUITY

As I have suggested elsewhere, Danticat's novel helps readers to perceive the indivisibility of rights violations by inscribing racism and the neocolonial will to power that precede genocide into the bodies of her characters such that they may be read as elemental, essential—simultaneously produced by and transcending history.[31] When labor pains set in for Senora Valencia, her servant Amabelle considers leaving momentarily to gather items to aid in the birth; however, she quickly reconsiders, noting that "[a]nything could happen in my absence, the worst of it being if a lady of her stature had to push that child out alone, like a field hand suddenly feeling her labor pains beneath a tent of cane."[32] Anxiety regarding the hazards of a woman birthing alone is directed away from more obvious physical dangers to the denigration of status that would link the wealthy Dominican Creole to the figure of the modern slave. The requirement of maintaining the (b)order distinguishing members of these races/classes/nations is etched into the most essential experience of childbirth, just as the unnamed modern slavery of the cane workers is evident in Sebastien's palms, which, as told in that paradigmatic line at the start of the novel, "have lost their life-lines to the machetes that cut the cane."[33] The mark that makes Sebastien's exploitation visible performs its metonymic work by rendering a textual aspect of his body invisible, his existential erasure implicated through this removal of one of the body's individuating signs. The symbolic loss of one's future, the sense of hope and suspense about the turns that future might take when one gazes at one's life line, is layered in this image over the material truth of palms whose surfaces have endured such blistering labor as to have been polished smooth. This, the novel insists, is the legacy of slavery and its repetition in modern neocolonial economies: the loss of individuation and hope, the terrible, glossed logic of sameness that structures slave labor in the new global economy. Such loss of individuation, the self determination which, as Makau Mutua has argued, constitutes the cross-cultural ground of all protected human rights and is the most glaring casualty of the new global economy, is also at the root of genocide.[34] This equation is concretized in the novel's title, "the farming of bones," translated from the Haitian Creole *travay te pou zo*, which is certainly the sadistically productive work of genocide, but also is the phrase used by workers to describe the labor of harvesting cane.

Danticat's decision to represent the genocide through the lens of the cane industry has been overlooked in literary reception of the novel. As Richard Lee Turits, eminent historian of Haitian–Dominican relations and of the 1937 massacre more specifically, points out, the targets of violence by the Dominican army and some civilians in the massacre ordered by President Trujillo on 2 October 1937 were not cane workers; instead, they were peasants, "mostly small farmers, many of whom had been born in the Dominican Republic (and thus were Dominican citizens according to the Dominican constitution) and some whose families had lived in the Dominican Republic for generations."[35] Turits's research counters dominant historiography on the subject and provides a foundation for a more nuanced reading of race and nation in the context of Haitian and Dominican histories. As he shows, much of the historical scholarship on the genocide describes that event as the result of an intense anti-Haitianism marked by a profound racism that constructed Dominicans as essentially European (Spanish) and Haitians as African, and that worried about Haitian immigration into the Dominican Republic. Indeed, there is some truth to this causal logic, evidenced in the speech given by Trujillo on October 2 that essentially launched the genocide:

> For some months, I have traveled and traversed the frontier in every sense of the word. I have seen, investigated, and inquired about the needs of the population. To the Dominicans who were complaining of the depredations by Haitians living among them, thefts of cattle, provisions, fruits, etc., and were thus prevented from enjoying in peace the products of their labor, I have responded, 'I will fix this.' And we have already begun to remedy the situation. Three hundred Haitians are now dead in Bánica. This remedy will continue."[36]

As Turits compellingly shows, however, the massacre was more the *cause* than the *effect* of anti-Haitianism, particularly in the border region where Haitians and Dominicans had maintained fluid bicultural and bilingual communities for decades: "What is so striking in the case of the Haitian massacre is that the Trujillo regime's anti-Haitian discourse was the product of rather than the precursor to state terror."[37] Turits shows that what was destroyed in the genocide, then, was not the Haitian community inside the Dominican Republic, nor the flow of Haitian workers into the Dominican sugar industry, but rather the fluid border community in the northern Dominican Republic. This community was destroyed in an effort to shore up a monolithic Dominican identity so as to consolidate Trujillo's political power. As Turits notes, "the violence in the Haitian massacre and the discourse within which it took place were themselves performances that helped constitute notions of inherent and transhistorical difference between Haitians and Dominicans."[38]

Crucially, Turits finds that there were *more* Haitian cane workers in the Dominican Republic *after* the massacre than before the massacre, indicating that the massacre was not meant to cleanse the Dominican Republic completely of its Haitian population. As he notes, "There was only one reported instance when the country's plantation workers were attacked during the massacre, in Bajabonico near Puerto Plata (western Cibao), in one of the few sugar plantations close to the northern frontier region. The rest of the country's over 20,000 Haitian sugar workers, most of whom resided in the eastern provinces near the cities of La Romana and San Pedro de Macoris, were not targeted."[39] In the process of writing *The Farming of Bones*, Danticat did a great deal of primary and secondary research about the 1937 massacre.[40] Why would she choose to represent what Turits clearly identifies as an exceptional case—the massacre of cane workers—in her novel, her "creative remembrance," of the genocide? One possible answer is that, in so doing, Danticat expands our understanding of the massacre itself, effectively situating it as an event within the larger history of the colonization of Hispaniola; the triangular trade; the revolution of Saint Domingue; and the postcolonial history of Haiti, which is a history of political fragmentation and economic exploitation. These histories are also the histories of the development of human rights discourse from the Enlightenment through their modern incarnations in the UDHR and beyond.

To take the analysis one step further is to link the representation of the exceptional case of the cane worker in the 1937 massacre to the economic history beginning to be made by Toussaint, and entrenched under Dessalines and, especially, Christophe, immediately after the Haitian revolution. For as Turits points out, while the 1937 massacre did not eliminate Haitians from the Dominican Republic, it did create a newly racialized class and labor system, what Turits calls "a severe new ethnic division of labor:" "After 1937, Haitians in the Dominican Republic were relegated almost exclusively, and in increasing numbers, to the role of plantation workers at the bottom rung of the labor market. The state and the sugar companies would consistently and flagrantly violate Haitians' human rights, subjecting them to slave-like material conditions with which they became associated."[41] If Turits is correct that the small-scale agricultural lives of Haitians sharing the border with Dominicans was wiped out by the massacre, and that the number of Haitians working on cane plantations *increased* after this point, then we see emerging the historic pattern by which subsistence farmers—who are poor but "free"—are transformed into (neo) slave labor. As Toussaint, Dessalines, and Christophe—all of whom engaged in forced conscription of peasant labor onto plantations with sugar, cotton, tobacco, and indigo crops in the post–revolutionary era—discovered, only violence could compel peasants with dreams of small-scale subsistence agricultural lives back onto the plantation after emancipation. In 1937, Trujillo's massacre acted as just such a violent catalyst.

Indeed, the novel is inhabited by references to the arc of Haitian history from the plantation era to the present, all of which are important to fully grasping the breadth of what the narrative *witnesses* in its generic relation to the form of witness literature. In short, the novel and its characters are haunted by what the vodun tradition would call a zombie figure: a revenant come to life again and again, occupying different forms; the undead dead. Neocolonialism: the capitalist present possessed by the powerful energy of slavery past.

In her recurrent dreams of the "sugar woman," Amabelle asks her why she has come: "'I told you before,' she says. 'I am the sugar woman. You, my eternity.'"[42] Although the novel is populated with maternal visions, this one is nightmarish: "Around her face, she wears a shiny silver muzzle, and on her neck there is a collar with a clasped lock dangling from it."[43] The sugar woman testifies that she is muzzled to keep her from eating the cane. The dreams signify Amabelle's relation to the history of slavery on the island of Hispaniola; specifically, Amabelle, whose parents were healers who helped with birth, illness, and death, and who herself was a member of the servant class, a large step up from the laboring class of cane workers she associates with through her lover Sebastien, is still haunted by the specter of slavery, as is the Haitian community more broadly. After the massacre, when Amabelle arrives with other survivors in the Dominican border town of Dajabon, just on the other side of the aptly named Massacre River from the safety of Haiti, they "try to mix, wanting to appear like confused visitors from the interior campos rather than the frightened maroons that we were."[44] Maroons, *marronage*: communities of ex-slaves, those who had escaped, who were, unlike these survivors, often on the offensive, launching resistance attacks on plantation property and owners. Escaped slaves, in 1937. And then, walking through her hometown city, Le Cap, Amabelle is greeted by the specter of—again—civil and political, and economic and social rights violations. She sees "people with deformities," and wonders whether they are survivors of the massacre; she walks out to the harbor to see men "with more than the weight of their bodies in sugar on their heads."[45] The wounds from these different systems and temporalities of rights violations blur, indistinguishable from one another. They are indivisible.

The images accumulate. In her important work on death and black subjectivity, Sharon Patricia Holland reads a variety of cultural texts to demonstrate the blurred boundary between life and death in a doubled context related to the African diaspora. While Holland locates the rich legacy of African spiritual understandings of death, diasporically exported and locally re-visioned, as central to a transcultural black ontology, she identifies this same equation of death and black subjectivity in the convergence of racial and economic violence in the modern and postmodern eras. In this regard, Holland admonishes literary and cultural critics to "attend to those who live in the space of death" and asserts that "[p]erhaps the most revolutionary intervention into conversations at the margins of race, gender, and sexuality is to let the dead—those already denied a sustainable subjectivity—speak from the place that is familiar to them."[46] Holland's naming of the massive "denial of sustainable *subjectivity*" is a crucial addition to human rights discourse that worries about how global economic imbalance limits and denies sustainable *lives*, fleshing out the fullness of human loss incurred in chronic social and economic deprivation.

While many discussions of the two major human rights covenants focus upon how to remedy the fact that "the failure of the international community to elaborate the content of economic, social, and cultural rights has perpetuated the notion that these rights are less essential to dignified personhood than civil or political rights" (in other words, how to integrate the two covenants as one indivisible set of rights), Danticat's novel invites us to think of how this failure is not simply one of equal attention and enforcement, but rather the inability to perceive the deep causal structure by which chronic violation of economic, social, and cultural rights creates the conditions for civil and political rights violations, including the extreme case of genocide.[47] Considering this causal structure substantiates perceptions of human rights talk from western governments simultaneously involved—via their dominant share of global institutions such as the World Trade Organization, the International Monetary Fund, and the World Bank—in negotiating the very conditions that perpetuate untenable economic imbalance as the most intensely cynical manifestations of neocolonialism. Further, the post-1989 decline of oppositional Marxist and anti-colonialist discourse has left us with the overwhelming hegemony of neoliberal capitalism, and without a coherent vision of systemic change that would enable the kind of radical redistribution of economic and social rights necessary to the project of a truly ethical vision of global human rights.

Even though Danticat's novel is historical in its telling of the 1937 genocide, it continues to resonate in the contemporary global context. The conditions Danticat dramatizes of the sugar industry in the Dominican Republic and the treatment of Haitian migrant workers continue. A headline in *The Christian Science Monitor* announces: "Haitian cane-cutters struggle; Little has changed in the sugar fields of in the Dominican Republic since the 1870s—including how workers fare,"[48] and as recently as spring 2005, "upwards of 3500 Haitians were expelled from the border town of Dajabon (the site of the 1937 massacre), after mobs made up of Dominican civilians and soldiers attacked them and burned their homes." The novel instructs us about the link between intractable racist economic exploitation and political violence, and it is no accident that the work of the machete harvesting cane leaves similar marks on the body—deep, visible scars; lost limbs—as the genocidal machete used in the massacre. *The Farming of Bones* identifies neocolonial capitalist economics as limit to the promise signified in the emergence of the first independent black republic in the western hemisphere, and in the full articulation of indivisible human rights in the United Nations Universal Declaration of Human Rights.

NOTES

1. I am grateful to the Babson College Faculty Research Fund, which provided generous support for this project, and especially to Susan Chern, for her assistance.
2. Jana Braziel, "Re-Membering Défilée: Dédée Bazile as Revolutionary *Lieu de Mémoire*," in *Small Axe* 18 (Sept. 2005): 72.
3. Mallay Charters, "Edwidge Danticat: A Bitter Legacy Revisited," *Publishers Weekly* 245, no. 33 (17 August 1998): 43.
4. Elizabeth Swanson Goldberg, *Beyond Terror: Gender, Narrative, Human Rights* (New Brunswick, NJ: Rutgers University Press, 2007), 159–164.
5. See, for instance, Jack Donnelly, *International Human Rights* (Boulder, CO: Westview Press, 2008); Louis Henken, "Human Rights: Ideology and Aspiration, Reality and Prospect," in *Realizing Human Rights: Moving from Inspiration to Impact*, ed. Samantha Power and Graham Allison (New York: Palgrave Macmillan, 2006), 3–39; and Johannes Morsink, *The Universal Declaration of Human Rights: Origins, Drafting, and Intent* (Philadelphia: University of Pennsylvania Press, 2000).
6. "Preamble," *Universal Declaration of Human Rights*, G.A. res. 217A (III), U.N. Doc A/810 at 71 (1948), http://www.unm.edu/humanrts/instree/bludhr.htm.
7. See Morsink, *Universal Declaration Of Human Rights*, for a seminal account of this process. See also Susan Koshy, "From Cold War to Trade War: Neocolonialism and Human Rights," *Social Text* 58 (1999): 1–32.
8. See, for instance, Arturo Escobar, *Encountering Development: The Making and Unmaking of the Third World* (Princeton, NJ: Princeton University Press, 1995); see also Amartya Sen, *Development as Freedom* (New York: Anchor Books, 2000). For incisive analysis of the expansion of poverty topographically, see Mike Davis, *Planet of Slums* (London: Verso, 2007).
9. Paul Farmer, *The Uses of Haiti* (Monroe, ME: Common Courage Press, 1994).
10. Nick Nesbitt, "The Idea of 1804," in *Yale French Studies* 107. *The Haiti Issue: 1804 and Nineteenth-Century French Studies* (2005): 6–38.
11. Danticat, *The Farming of Bones*, 1.
12. Frederik Mangonés, "The Citadel as Site of Haitian Memory," in *Callaloo* 15, no. 3 (Summer 1992): 857.
13. Mangonés, "Citadel," 861; emphasis added.
14. Julia Gaffield, "Complexities of Imagining Haiti: A Study of National Constitutions, 1801–1807," *Journal of Social History* 41, no. 1 (Fall 2007): 90.
15. Charles Forsdick, "Situating Haiti: On Some Early 19th Century Representations of Toussaint L'Ouverture," *International Journal of Francophone Studies* 10, no. 1/2 (2007): 19.
16. Forsdick, "Situating Haiti," 22.
17. Nick Nesbitt, "Troping Toussaint, Reading Revolution," *Research in African Literatures* 35, no. 2 (Summer 2004): 18.
18. Kelli Lyon Johnson, "Both Sides of the Massacre: Collective Memory and Narrative on Hispaniola," *Mosaic: A Journal for the Interdisciplinary Study of Literature* 36, no. 2 (June 2003): 78.
19. Johnson, "Both Sides of the Massacre," 76.
20. Johnson, "Both Sides of the Massacre," 79.
21. Qtd. in Johnson, "Both Sides of the Massacre," 79.
22. There seems to be consensus among historians about the status of Saint Domingue as the "most profitable" colony in the Americas until its revolution; although figures are at times unreliable, Robert Stein asserts, "All that can be said for certain is that Saint Domingue produced from two-thirds to three-quarters of all French West Indian sugar late in the Old Regime" (Robert Stein, "The French West Indian Sugar Business," in *Caribbean Slave*

Society and Economy, ed. Hilary Beckles and Verene Shepherd [New York: The New Press, 1993], 99), while C.L.R. James assert unequivocally that in 1789, "[Saint Domingue] was the most profitable colony the world had ever known." C. L. R. James, "French Capitalism and Caribbean Slavery," in *Caribbean Slave Society and Economy*, ed. Hilary Beckles and Verene Shepherd (New York: The New Press, 1993), 133.

23. Nesbitt, "The Idea of 1804," 8.

24. Charles Miller, "Forget Haiti: Baron Roger and the New Africa," *Yale French Studies* 107, *The Haiti Issue: 1804 and Nineteenth-Century French Studies* (2005): 44.

25. Danticat, *The Farming of Bones*, 116.

26. Danticat, *The Farming of Bones*, 212. This passage contains the narrative's only direct reference to the figure of Toussaint, when a survivor references one of his most famous quotations: "I'm one of those trees whose roots reach the bottom of the earth. They can cut down my branches, but they will never uproot the tree. The roots are too strong, and there are too many" (*The Farming of Bones*, 212).

27. Danticat, *The Farming of Bones*, 1; emphasis mine.

28. Danticat, *The Farming of Bones*, 1.

29. Mangonés, "Citadel," 860.

30. Danticat, *The Farming of Bones*, 282.

31. Goldberg, *Beyond Terror*, 159–164.

32. Danticat, *The Farming of Bones*, 7.

33. Danticat, *The Farming of Bones*, 1.

34. Makau Mutua, *Human Rights: A Political and Cultural Critique* (Philadelphia: University of Pennsylvania Press, 2002; 2008), 108. See also Jean Hatzfeld, *Machete Season: The Killers in Rwanda Speak*, trans. Linda Coverdale (New York: Farrar, Straus and Giroux, 2005), for a discussion of the way in which struggles over resources—most notably sheets of tin used for roofing in the Rwandan countryside—informed the 1994 genocide in Rwanda.

35. Richard Lee Turits, "A World Destroyed, A Nation Imposed: The 1937 Haitian Massacre in the Dominican Republic," *Hispanic American Historical Review* 82, no. 3 (August 2002): 590.

36. Qtd. in Turits, "A World Destroyed," 613.

37. Turits, "A World Destroyed," 628.

38. Turits, "A World Destroyed," 618.

39. Turits, "A World Destroyed," 626.

40. See, for instance, David Barsamian, "Edwidge Danticat Interview," in *The Progressive* (October 2003) <http://www.progressive.org/mag_intvdanticat> and Eleanor Wachtel, "A Conversation with Edwidge Danticat," *Brick* 65 (Fall 2000): 106–119.

41. Turits, "A World Destroyed," 634.

42. Danticat, *The Farming of Bones*, 133.

43. Danticat, *The Farming of Bones*, 133.

44. Danticat, *The Farming of Bones*, 189.

45. Danticat, *The Farming of Bones*, 243.

46. Sharon Patricia Holland, *Raising the Dead: Readings on Death and (Black) Subjectivity* (Durham, NC: Duke University Press, 2000), 4.

47. Chisanga Puta-Chekwe and Nora Flood, "From Division to Integration: Economic, Social, and Cultural Rights as Basic Human Rights," in *Giving Meaning to Economic Social and Cultural Rights*, ed. Isfahan Merali and Valerie Oosterveld (Philadelphia: University of Pennsylvania Press, 2001), 41.

48. Danna Harman, "Haitian Cane-Cutters Struggle," *The Christian Science Monitor*, 1 February 2006: 13

6   Paradoxes of Neoliberalism and Human Rights

Greg A. Mullins

Marcelino Freire, in his short story "Volte outro dia" [Come Another Day], captures a snapshot of the present moment of human rights. Rights talk, in the late twentieth and early twenty-first centuries, is everywhere. However, the classic liberal understanding that the citizen is the holder of rights against the state is under pressure; the category of "citizen" is increasingly supplanted by the category of "consumer." Freire underscores the ironies that follow upon this substitution. In this story a typical middle-class single man answers his door to find a homeless person asking for food. The middle-class man protests that his kitchen is empty, that he has no money on hand, that he is struggling to make ends meet and cannot help. We might find his protestation more plausible if the story didn't end with the arrival of the pizza deliveryman. We are offered this interior monologue as the man refuses beneficence: "Tantas ruas, casas, cabeças, por que logo a minha? Eu tenho direitos. O Governo conserte suas negligências. O Governo que se ocupe" [So many streets, houses, homeowners—so why me? I have rights. The government needs to fix its failures. It's the government's business"].[1]

What precisely is the "right" this citizen claims? A right not to be reminded of poverty? A right to eat pizza and watch television without knocks on the door? One would look in vain in Brazilian or international law for such a "right," which is framed as a "right to consume." Ironically, the protagonist's specious claim on rights rhetorically obscures the genuine social and economic rights of the homeless man to shelter and food.

The anthropologist James Holston offers us another helpful snapshot of our contemporary moment. In his book *Insurgent Citizenship* Holston draws to our attention the use of human rights language in an unexpected corner of Brazilian social and political life: in communiqués from the leading drug cartels in Rio de Janeiro and São Paulo. For example, in congressional testimony the leader of the principle drug cartel in São Paulo declared: "I am a person who fights for his rights. I have read the Penal Code and the Law of Penal Procedures, and I know that I am violated in all of my rights. . . . So, [I ask you], where is the state? . . . In this context, what is society for me?"[2] How are we to understand this claim on human rights? Is it a legitimate appeal for the rights codified in Brazilian law and international human rights law, including the right to due process, freedom from police brutality, and humane prison conditions? Or is it a belligerent accusation that the state has rendered itself illegitimate and its laws irrelevant through the violence of its policing systems? Do human rights indeed belong to all human beings? Or do human rights belong only to those who are socially and politically positioned to own them?

The use of rights talk by drug cartels that openly practice barbaric cruelty as a business strategy is ironic to be sure—and is a complex rather than a simple irony. One could say that human rights are rendered meaningless when they are claimed by political actors one disagrees with. However, I argue that the meaning making of human rights discourse is unmasked at such a moment. That is to say, meaning is made precisely through irony and paradox—not only in Freire's short story "Volte outro dia" and in Marcola's congressional testimony, but also in and through the very idea of human rights.

Many commentators have noted the systemic paradoxes of human rights. Costas Douzinas goes so far as to say that "Human Rights have 'only paradoxes to offer'; their energy comes from their aporetic nature."[3] His more specific observation is that "[h]uman rights are internally fissured: they are used as the defense of the individual against a state power built in the image of an individual with absolute rights."[4] A variation of this paradox might also be stated this way: if human beings have universal and inalienable rights, why do human beings need to be protected from the state, and more pointedly, why must they be protected *by* the very state they are being protected *from*? Agamben, following Arendt, clarifies the relation of the rights holder to the state, and demystifies the claim that human rights precede the rise of states: "Rights are attributed to man (or originate in him) solely to the extent that man is the immediately vanishing ground (who must never come to light as such) of the citizen."[5]

With origins in the Enlightenment and framed through liberal theory, human rights also bear a paradoxical relationship to capitalism and imperialism. The rhetoric of human liberty accompanies both capitalism and human rights, but capitalism facilitates an unequal production and distribution of wealth (and hence of political power); social inequality in turn leads to significant human rights crises in political participation, as well as other human rights concerns. Economic liberalism, in other words, may well undermine rather than undergird political and civil liberties. Similarly, western imperialism claims ideological legitimacy as a liberal project descended from the Enlightenment—standing in apparent contradiction to liberal notions of democracy, liberty and political self-determination. Human rights and "humanitarianism" are extensions of political power within imperial frameworks that claim to critique imperialism, but that may well end up reinforcing it.

Perhaps the most frequently lamented paradox of human rights is that violations of them are not infrequently carried out in the name of protecting them. States will curtail the right to free speech and political participation in order to protect the right to property or public security. The right to privacy, to marry a partner of one's choice or have access to reproductive health technologies will be curtailed in order to protect the right of a wider social group to cultural or religious traditions that constrain gender roles and reproductive choices. Human rights, in other words, do not resolve conflicts but rather provide a framework and vocabulary within which competing political claims can be made.

Furthermore, when one pursues politics through the language of human rights, one also funnels those conflicts through a structure of paradox. Wendy Brown notes that "[u]nlike contradictions, which can be exploited, or mystification, which can be exposed, or disavowal, which can be forced into confrontation with itself, or even despair, which can be negated, the politics of paradox is very difficult to negotiate."[6] In venturing that negotiation, I propose that paradox does not necessarily impede human rights, but actually gives them form, shape, and purpose.

The above examples of human rights paradoxes are illustrative rather than exhaustive; to the list I will add just one more in order to focus attention on our contemporary moment, which is profoundly shaped by the pressures of neoliberalism. Over the past thirty years, neoliberal economic policies have gained ascendance in international economic policy (at the International Monetary Fund, World Bank, World Trade Organization, G-8, etc). A central feature of neoliberal orthodoxy is a retreat of the state in favor of markets. During these same three decades, human rights frameworks, projects, and activism have proliferated rapidly in disparate local contexts and via interlocking global networks.

Yet human rights depend, both in theory and practice, on strong states. Whether the human rights in question are categorized as civil, political, social, economic, or cultural; whether they are conceived as individual or collective rights; whether the impetus to protect them arises from the state or from civil society, it is the state's responsibility to guarantee human rights. And a state must be strong if it is to stand up to powerful economic, social, or political actors (often actors within the state itself) who violate human rights.

Why, then, the rapid rise of rights talk during precisely the period when the state is supposedly taking a back seat to markets? Doesn't human rights activism in the age of neoliberalism amount to putting more and more eggs in a shrinking basket?

I would argue that the Brazilian state leverages anxiety arising from the urban crisis to strengthen its hand even as it cedes authority to markets. But I won't argue that the paradox is a false one, or that stricter analysis can make it fade away. More is to be gained by appreciating the extent to which human rights (both as theory and as politics) are so enmeshed with paradoxes as to be constituted not in spite of but precisely through them. As we will see, the neoliberal project bestows upon human rights a particularly vexed relationship between security and insecurity, and between the public and private spheres. These vexations operate in both the examples that open this chapter—the short story "Volte outro dia" and Marcola's congressional testimony. Below, I trace them in greater detail in additional texts by Marcelino Freire and also in the fiction of Amilcar Bettega Barbosa and Luiz Ruffato.

In this chapter I argue that the structural contradictions of irony and paradox appear not only in human rights, but also and tellingly in fictional accounts of Brazil's urban crisis. A study of the contradictions and counterintuitive logics of human rights under neoliberalism draws us strongly to analyze human rights through literature, for reading literature requires us to attend to the narrative and rhetorical structures that produce meaning via paradox, irony, ambiguity, ambivalence, and so forth.[7] Thinking in and through literary modes of representation may at least help us produce and sustain conceptual models of paradox that allow us to understand how and why human rights function as they do. Moreover, the mutual affinity for paradox that literature shares with human rights may well gesture toward a deeper structural connection between them.

In pursuit of these questions, I focus here on contemporary urban Brazilian fiction written in the thick of neoliberal economic policies under the presidencies of Itamar Franco and Fernando Henrique Cardoso. Although narrow, this focus is not random. If the relation between neoliberalism and human rights is poorly understood, that deficiency arises in part from a readiness to overly generalize analysis of both neoliberalism and human rights. The case of Brazil invites a context-specific analysis out of which we can better understand general trends. The focus in this chapter trains our attention on the intersection of a number of crucial axes: the lines of ideological continuity between liberal human rights and neoliberal market reforms; the violence of Brazil's urban crisis; and the transformation of the human rights activism in Brazil from pro-democracy agitation against military dictatorship to a critique of inequality in the 1980s, 1990s, and beyond. This case study may illuminate patterns that are shared in other national contexts; at the very least, it can start a conversation about the relations between neoliberalism and human rights that literary fiction helps make visible.

At first glance, casual observers might not think of Marcelino Freire's *Angu de sangue* (2000), Luiz Ruffato's *Eles eram muitos cavalos* (2001) or Amilcar Bettega Barbosa's *Os lados do círculo* (2004) as human rights stories.[8] To be sure, all contain episodes of crime, violence, and desperation—but these are among the great themes of literature broadly, and it isn't immediately apparent that they need to be understood in relation to human rights. However, I argue that these literary works help us analyze the puzzle of human rights in neoliberal Brazil in ways that other forms of cultural production leave wanting. As a cultural form of the middle class, novels and short stories focus our attention on middle class experience—in this case, on the shock of the middle class as it confronts endemic urban violence and persistent social inequality. Moreover, literary fiction is read in a largely "private" relationship of reader to book; fiction can generate wider public conversation and even social action, but its energies coalesce mainly in the intensely interior act of reading. Through form (and in these cases, also through content) fiction lends itself to a critical inquiry into the functions and modalities of "private" and "public" life. Most importantly, however, fiction structures meaning through metaphor, irony, and paradox.

Bettega Barbosa's short stories, collected in *Os lados do círculo* [The Sides of the Circle], steep us in irony and paradox. Circles spiral throughout these stories; by following them, forward movement bends on itself only to be renewed by repeating its old paths. Does a circle have one side or an infinite number of sides? It is a bounded figure that figures contradictory meanings of boundedness. In the prologue, a number of characters gather to scrutinize the patterns of random objects juxtaposed haphazardly on a beach. As shapes assume a pattern "um novo sentido se descortinava, um sentido particular e individual mas que ainda assim . . . comunicava, ainda assim alcançava o outro lado" [a new meaning was revealed, a particular and individual meaning which nonetheless . . . communicated, nonetheless reached the other side].[9] Just as meaning and knowledge appear to consolidate in a form capable of joining isolated persons in a collective experience, we see one of the characters "no outro lado . . . inventando um jogo novo" [on the other side . . . inventing a new game].[10] This image sets the stage for the entire collection of stories—and for our present exploration of the meanings of human rights—for a moment of clarity leads to a new circle of uncertainty, instability, and searching.

Amongst the many circles he traces, those in the story "Círculo vicioso" [Vicious Circle] are especially pernicious. In this story a Brazilian journalist named Roberto travels to Buenos Aires in Argentina and Colonia del Sacramento in Uruguay to research the period of military dictatorships in the Southern Cone. Brazilian readers would understand this story within the context of the wide arc of Brazilian history—not only the period of military dictatorship in Brazil from 1964 to 1985, but also a longer history of brutal governance. As a colony of Portugal from 1500 to 1822 and as an independent empire from 1822 to 1889, Brazil suffered under an extensive system of slavery; Brazil's contemporary race and class inequalities date from this time. Four hundred years of authoritarian rule and social inequality left Brazil ill prepared for experiments in liberal democracy in the twentieth century. From 1930 to 1945 the populist dictator Getulio Vargas seized power, and from 1964 to 1985 the politically conservative armed forces ruled the country. During both periods, the state security apparatus perpetrated atrocious human rights violations, including torture, assassination, "disappearance," persecution of dissidents and suspected dissidents, suspension of political rights, and censorship. The brutality and concentrated power of hardliners within Brazil's military governments of the 1960s and 1970s established the iconography and vocabulary through which the phrase "human rights violations" continues to be interpreted in Brazil today.

In the 1970s and 1980s Uruguay and Argentina were also governed by repressive military governments, and in Bettega Barbosa's "Círculo vicioso" the journalist journeys southward to research human rights violations across the region. This journey also takes him into the deeper history of colonial struggle for control over the River Plate and its hinterlands. In Buenos Aires Roberto meets a historian of the same period, Claudia, and a romance and marriage ensue. In Colonia del Sacramento he seeks information about the murder of an Argentine woman—a professor who initiated a lawsuit for damages suffered by her family during the dictatorship. As if falling through a crack in time, he discovers information not about her, but about la Monja, the ghost of a young woman of angelic beauty who, in a barbaric war between Portugal and Spain in 1706, was driven mad when her infant child was taken from her and she was imprisoned with lepers and lunatics. At night, the voice of la Monja calls him, "o lamento de uma mulher, clamando que a tirassem dali" [the lament of a woman, calling him to take her away from there].[11] As the romance between Roberto and Claudia deepens, and as they come closer to unveiling state secrets of crimes committed under military government, they are also drawn deeper into history, and into the ghostly legacies of colonial wars, rapes, and tortures. A Uruguayan explains the curse of la Monja: "su dolor continuaría vivo en nosotros" [her suffering continues to live in us], cursing us to live in an "eterno palco para la violencia y la arbitrariedad" [eternal box of violence and arbitrariness].[12]

Claudia and Roberto find themselves trapped in this box. Their research leads them to secrets of state violence via the colonial past; for Roberto, the murder of the Argentine professor "voltava sempre e cada vez mais vivo à sua cabeça e à sua imaginação, como se estivesse preso a um carrossel de tempo, come se a morte de tal professora tivesse a idade e o peso de todas as outras mortes" [returned repeatedly and each time more alive to his thoughts and his imagination, as if captured in a carousel of time, as if the death of that professor contained the age and weight of all the other deaths] (30). Circling in this carousel of time, Claudia suffers the curse of la Monja and repeats the fate of the Argentine. The record of state-sponsored violence from the past is obscured rather than recovered, with yet another murder and additional mysteries for the twenty-first century. As a meditation on human rights in the contemporary moment, "Círculo vicioso" suggests our need to escape the past that entraps us, but our inability to break through its walls. Boxed in by memory and forgetfulness, by evidence and mystery, a security apparatus surrounds us on all sides—and produces state security precisely by violating the security (and the lives) of its citizens.

Security and, for that matter, insecurity, are the hinges that connect the human rights struggles waged in Brazil from 1964–1985 with those waged since 1985. Today, the leading security concern in Brazil's major cities is public safety from the violence of the trade in illicit drugs: not only do drug lords rule their empires brutally, and not only do rivals feud over territory, but also organized crime carries on a bloody battle with the police. Additional violence accompanies other types of crime, and crime is deeply rooted in Brazil's entrenched poverty and social inequality. The police respond to violence with violence; policing methods in Brazil are based almost exclusively on military models of strong arm force.[13] Indeed, the homicide rate in Brazil is analogous to that of a country facing low-grade civil war, with 45,000 or more Brazilians murdered each year.[14] A high number of police officers are killed each year in this "war" (52 were killed on duty in Rio de Janeiro in 2004), but many more people are killed by the police (for example, in Rio de Janeiro in 2003, 1,195 persons).[15] Approximately 10 percent of the homicides committed in Rio de Janeiro and São Paulo in the late 1990s were committed by police officers, and 5 percent of the male population were victims of police extortion.[16] As a result, the leading human rights concerns in Brazil today focus on police and prison abuses: extrajudicial executions, brutal beatings, massacres (including of bystanders), lack of accountability, corruption (and collusion with organized crime), and prisons that offer both inhumane treatment and havens from which crime bosses direct their empires.[17] Militaristic policing has a long history in Brazil, stretching back to the colonial period; however, the military dictatorship offers a very particular legacy: methods of torture and extrajudicial execution. One of the hinges between the security apparatus during the dictatorship and today is the disregard for the human rights of criminal suspects or convicts, and an institutional culture that respects brutality.

Another hinge is structural: the military dictatorship prepared the way for Brazil's contemporary political economy.[18] It isn't as though the military generals instituted neoliberalism *avant le lettre*; their own macroeconomic policies fostered nationalism, protectionism, and strategic state intervention in economic life. Through most of the twentieth century, macroeconomic policy in Brazil included direct state investments and direct or indirect state control over a wide range of capitalist and labor activities. Military governments in the 1960s and 1970s pursued direct government investment and ownership of firms, and import-substitution policies that restricted foreign competition with local manufacturers.

With this economic history as backdrop, one can easily see why the neoliberal reforms promoted in the 1990s marked such a shift for Brazil. These reforms included several hallmarks of neoliberalism; those are helpfully outlined in David Harvey's succinct definition:

> Neoliberalism is in the first instance a theory of political economic practices that proposes that human well-being can best be advanced by liberating individual entrepreneurial freedoms and skills within

an institutional framework characterized by strong private property rights, free markets, and free trade. The role of the state is to create and preserve an institutional framework appropriate to such practices. The state has to guarantee, for example, the quality and integrity of money. It must also set up those military, defense, police, and legal structures and functions required to secure private property rights and to guarantee, by force if need be, the proper functioning of markets. Furthermore, if markets do not exist (in areas such as land, water, education, health care, social security, or environmental pollution) then they must be created, by state action if necessary. But beyond these tasks the state should not venture.[19]

In practice, in the case of Brazil, neoliberal economic policies are most closely associated with the presidencies of Itamar Franco and especially of Fernando Henrique Cardoso in the last decade of the twentieth century and the very early years of the twenty-first century. With reference to Harvey's definition, Franco and most especially Cardoso did indeed wish to liberate entrepreneurial energies, but even more importantly they wished to attract foreign capital investment to Brazil. In addition, they wished to diminish direct state investment in enterprises and to roll back government spending in general. All these efforts were linked to an overarching strategy to end hyperinflation and create a stable Brazilian currency.[20] Having ensured (in David Harvey's words) the "quality and integrity of money," the newly neoliberal Brazilian state pursued two additional aims that Harvey succinctly outlines in his definition of neoliberalism. These aims can be captured in the key words "private/privatization" and "security."

If the intelligibility of "security," "public good," and "privatization" seems strained in the context of human rights struggles in neoliberal Brazil, this is because these terms are contested by competing social and political actors, and because their meaning is produced in and through contradictions. Brazil is emblematic of states that embrace human rights discourse as a measure of democratization, but that leverage "security" concerns to successfully manage the reformist energies of human rights. In Brazil's case, the state security apparatus established under the military governments has been redeployed under elected governments—rhetorically, if not effectively, turning from "political crimes" of liberal and radical dissidence to "organized crime" and "street crime," particularly in Brazil's major cities. As it turns out, the paradoxes of "security/insecurity" and "public/private" are also especially apparent in Brazilian fiction of the early twenty-first century.

Neoliberalism arrived in Brazil at a particular phase in the effort to develop democracy through elected government. The rise of neoliberalism coincides with the global expansion of human rights talk; both democracy and human rights gain momentum in Brazil through a critique of the military dictatorship and of social inequality. At the end of the twentieth and beginning of the twenty-first century, the convergence of neoliberalism and democratization in Brazil affects human rights in these ways: (1) the number and kinds of people making rights claims expands dramatically, as poor and working people demand the state serve their needs and not merely the needs of the elite; (2) consumer society flourishes, and "the consumer" increasingly supplants "the citizen" as the figure through which one enters public life; and (3) entry into public life is further renovated as the boundary between "public" and "private" is redrawn. The very meaning and coherence of "public" and "private" is renegotiated by multiple and contradictory struggles over "security" and "insecurity." For human rights, these related but conflicting pressures increase the number of human rights claimants and the political legitimacy of their claims, while at the same time citizenship as such is increasingly sidelined by consumerism. Moreover, violence unleashed by street crime, organized crime, and the police increases the ferocity of human rights violations during precisely the moment when human rights talk gains greater rhetorical force.

The paradoxes that permeate this confluence of pressures surface in the fiction of Ruffato, Bettega Barbosa, and Freire. The latter opens *Angu de sangue* with a story entitled "Muribeca" in which the narrator mines garbage for a living. It is a good business, she claims, for "lixo dá lucro . . . lixo tem valor" [trash yields profit . . . trash has value].[21] She has found everything she needs in the garbage, including her daughter's wedding dress and the wedding ring—removed from the hand of a corpse. While the middle class and the elite avert their gaze from garbage, she finds in it the rich material of consumer society that would otherwise be inaccessible to the unemployed. She mocks the efforts of social reformers who wish to remove the trash hunters from the garbage heaps. "Tenho fé em Deus, com a ajuda de Deus, eles nunca vão tirar a gente deste lixo. . . . deste paraíso" [I have faith in God, with the help of God, they will never take us away from this trash. . . . from this paradise].[22]

Amilcar Bettega Barbosa pushes a similar critique deeper in his story "Verão" [Summer]. This story also features fetid urban garbage, and it is the garbage that both separates and unites the poor and the middle class; trash is the point of transaction between two worlds. In this story, an arrogant and overly entitled middle class man is brutally murdered after his luxury pickup truck kills a dog belonging to the leader of a gang of street kids. Everything this man values and stands for—prosperity, a luxurious home, status, wealth, a pending marriage to a beautiful young fiancée—wreaks its violence on the street kids through the man's arrogance, and they return violence by mutilating his corpse. The story ends by shifting focus to his grieving fiancée. Her friends encourage her to let go of her sorrow and live for the future. In a deeply ironic moment, one friend tells her "Você tem o direito de ser feliz" [You have the right to be happy].[23] This "right" seems to arise from nowhere, and to disappear as easily, in a narrative in which the materiality of consumer society provides an empty substitute for happiness, and in which no structure exists to guarantee rights.

Urban violence cuts across both time and space. Bettega Barbosa's "Círculo vicioso" reminds us of the legacies of centuries of political violence; his "Verão" suggests that grief extends the pain of loss from the past into our future. This same story charts a geography of violence in urban space: it extends from the public street where the dog and then the man are brutally murdered into the "private" space of his family and friends in mourning.

In the dominant narrative of urban violence, the home is a place of peace and refuge, and the street is the place of danger. These boundaries are, however, permeable, and Marcelino Freire stages that permeability in the title story of his collection, "Angu de sangue." The story begins on the street with the line, "Quando o bandido entrou em meu carro, eu pensava em Elisa" [When the thief entered my car, I was thinking of Elisa].[24] Elisa is the narrator's wife or girlfriend, with whom he has had an argument, and about whom he obsesses in an interior monologue as the assailant presses his demands for money. The sudden intimacy of violent aggression, especially as it is felt in the interior of the car, resonates as a counterpart to the passionate intimacy the narrator feels for his beloved: "Ele só quer o meu dinheiro, Elisa. Você é quem me ama. Não sou rico, mas sou dono do seu coração" ["He only wants my money, Elisa. You're the one who loves me. I'm not rich, but I'm the owner of your heart"].[25] The language of riches, of poverty, of ownership, of debt describes both the relationship the narrator has with the thief, and the relationship he has with his lover. These various slippages of signification lead toward an inversion of our expectations when the narrator brings the thief to his home on the pretense of handing him money, and we learn that the narrator has murdered his lover. The violence originated in the domestic space, and the narrator has enticed—even seduced—the thief to enter that domestic space where he becomes implicated in both theft and murder. Not only does the narrator's sanity dissolve in this story, but also coherence dissolves in the dominant narratives of love, domesticity, security, and violence in the city.

As readers assemble meaning from the narratives Freire, Ruffato, and Bettega Barbosa offer, we muddle through apparent contradictions, inconsistencies, and counterintuitive logics. At those moments when the language of human rights rises to the surface of their stories, its vocabularies are ironic, displaced, or inconsistent; more commonly, the language of human rights animates their stories covertly rather than overtly. Freire, Ruffato, and Bettega Barbosa write fiction during the years of Brazil's experiment with neoliberalism, and their texts underscore the pressure placed on the coherence of two related dichotomies that have in the past generated meaningful social and spatial divisions in Brazilian cities: "security/insecurity" and "public/private." As the coherence of these divisions dissolve in fictional narratives, we as readers are left with paradoxes to ponder: a world turned inside out, in which trash is value, waste is the glue that holds a society together, violence is a norm, the intimacy of love and of violence is confused, domestic trauma is on the street and street violence is in the home.

These paradoxes are not invented through fiction but are rather explored and exposed through it; they are produced by the contradictory pressures of neoliberalism, and the related contradictions of human rights.

Neoliberalism in Brazil and the return to elected government expanded the language of rights and the number and types of people who claim human rights. It is still unclear whether those claimants will be able to make use of rights language to fundamentally restructure the ailments that lead to rights violations. The proliferation of rights language in Brazil in the wake of two decades of military dictatorship does indeed offer a politics of aspiration for a better future. But it does not offer a solution to the contradictions and inconsistencies that surface in the narratives written by Freire, Ruffato, and Bettega Barbosa. Far from offering a solution to paradox, the human rights project is riddled with contradictions and is produced as paradox. As urban violence continues in Brazil alongside the expansion of consumer society and privatization, the volume of claims made on human rights continues to increase. In yet another paradox, the more abuse suffered, the greater the need and the demand for human rights.

NOTES

1. Marcelino Freire, *Angu de sangue*, 2nd ed. (São Paulo: Ateliê Editorial, 2005), 41.
2. Marcola, leader of the PCC (Primeiro Comando da Capital), as quoted in James Holston, *Insurgent Citizenship: Disjunctions of Democracy and Modernity in Brazil* (Princeton: Princeton University Press, 2008), 307. Holston suggests that Marcola's congressional testimony registers not so much an opportunistic deployment of rights language but rather the extent to which the self-evident merits of rights language have penetrated Brazilian social and political life. His study concerns legal struggles to establish land titles in a working class neighborhood of greater São Paulo.
3. Costas Douzinas, *The End of Human Rights: Critical Legal Thought at the Turn of the Century* (Oxford: Hart Publishing, 2000), 21.
4. Douzinas, *The End of Human Rights*, 20. For Douzinas's more expansive critique of human rights paradoxes, see *Human Rights and Empire: The Political Philosophy of Cosmopolitanism* (New York: Routledge-Cavendish, 2007).
5. Giorgio Agamben, *Homo Sacer: Sovereign Power and Bare Life*, trans. Daniel Heller-Roazen, Stanford, CA: Stanford University Press, 1998), 128.
6. Wendy Brown, "Suffering the Paradoxes of Rights," in *Left Legalism/Left Critique*, ed. Wendy Brown and Janet Halley (Durham, NC: Duke University Press, 2002), 432.
7. Joseph R. Slaughter makes this point brilliantly in *Human Rights, Inc.: The World Novel, Narrative Form, and International Law* (New York: Fordham University Press, 2007). For his analysis of paradox in particular, see pages 12–14.
8. None of the three books has been translated into English; all translations offered here are mine. *Angu de sangue* is particularly resistant to tidy

translation: "Cornmeal Mush of Blood" loses the play on the Latin root "angu" (to squeeze, strangle) that becomes "angustia" (painful tightness, anguish). *Eles eram muitos cavalos* translates as "They were many horses" but gains its force through the poem to which it alludes: Cecília Meireles's "Do Cavalos da Inconfidência." *Os lados do círculo* translates as "The Sides of the Circle."

9. Amilcar Bettega Barbosa, *Os lados do círculo* (São Paulo: Companhia das Letras, 2004), 18.
10. Bettega Barbosa, *Os lados*, 18.
11. Bettega Barbosa, *Os lados*, 32.
12. Bettega Barbosa, *Os lados*, 33. The Uruguayan speaks in Spanish.
13. See Mercedes S. Hinton, *The State on the Street: Police and Politics in Argentina and Brazil* (Boulder, CO: Lynne Rienner, 2006) and Anthony W. Pereira, "Public Security, Private Interests, and Police Reform," in *Democratic Brazil Revisited*, ed. Peter R. Kingstone, and Timothy J. Power (Pittsburgh: University of Pittsburgh Press, 2008), 185–208.
14. Pereira, "Public Security," 188.
15. Amnesty International, "'They Come in Shooting': Policing Socially Excluded Communities" (London: Amnesty International), 24, 37. http://www.amnesty.org/en/library/info/AMR19/025/2005
16. Leandro Piquet Carneiro, "Democratic Consolidation and Civil Rights: Brazil in Comparative Perspective," in *Brazil Since 1985: Economy, Polity and Society*, ed. Maria D'Alva Kinzo and James Dunkerley (London: Institute of Latin American Studies, 2003), 242.
17. Human rights activists work on the wide range of civil, political, social, economic, and environmental rights in Brazil; in this regard abuses perpetrated by the police are only one of many active human rights concerns. However, as registered by coverage in the news media, and as highlighted by high-profile interventions by the United Nations, social inequality, prison abuse, and police abuses headline the human rights challenges Brazil faces in the early twenty-first century.
18. See Idelber Avelar, *The Untimely Present: Postdictatorial Latin American Fiction and the Task of Mourning* (Durham, NC: Duke University Press, 1999).
19. David Harvey, *A Brief History of Neoliberalism* (Oxford: Oxford University Press, 2005), 2.
20. Impressive as this list may be, Brazil is hardly a model of a neoliberal state; for such a model one could look to the free market orthodoxy that Paul Bremer, in his role as administrator of the Coalition Provisional Authority, attempted to organize for Iraq (see Naomi Klein, *The Shock Doctrine: The Rise of Disaster Capitalism* (New York: Metropolitan Books/ Henry Holy, 2007)). In Brazil, the ideological advocacy for free markets has not been so strident as in the U.S., where retreating from historical promises to support social welfare has been painted as an advance for human liberty. Brazil retains significant public obligations to social security, public health, and education; its constitution requires state control over the oil industry; and Brazil's recent economic boom has been fueled in part by state poverty reduction programs. Moreover, the election of President Luiz Ignácio Lula da Silva in 2002 arguably marks a rejection of neoliberalism (although Lula has maintained the tight monetary policies that are a hallmark of neoliberal orthodoxy). Stable currency, favorable investment climates, relatively free markets, and relatively free trade have characterized part of Brazil's economic policy during the last two decades, but especially under Lula these

neoliberal policies were balanced with a willingness to manipulate the levers of state power to advance the welfare of ordinary people (rather than merely to advance the welfare of markets).

21. Freire, *Angu du sangue*, 24.
22. Freire, *Angu du sangue*, 25.
23. Bettega Barbosa, *Os lados do círculo*, 76.
24. Freire, *Angu de sangue*, 69.
25. Freire, *Angu de sangue*, 69.

Part II

Questions of Narration, Representation, and Evidence

7 Reading the Living Archives
The Witness of Literary Art

Carolyn Forché

The letter arrived on a series of plain postcards in Joseph Brodsky's penciled cursive, mailed separately from his newly imposed exile in Ann Arbor, Michigan, very near the township of my childhood. They contained his advice to the young poet I once was, who had been brash enough to send her youthful efforts to him. *You should consider including in your poems more of your own, well, philosophy*, he wrote, and on another card: *It is also a pity that you do not read Russian, but I think you should try to read Anna Akhmatova.*

It was, I believe, a year earlier, in the autumn of 1972, that I had read excerpts from the transcript of Brodsky's trial in the former Soviet Union, condemning him to forced labor. When asked on what authority he pronounced himself a poet, he had answered that the vocation came "from God."[1] Silence followed, further interrogation, and finally the sentencing of Brodsky to a labor camp. I couldn't yet find Brodsky's poems, but in search of Akhmatova's, I found a translation by Stanley Kunitz and Max Hayward in the stacks of the Library of Congress, where, that winter, I was employed to do research for a medical foundation. And so, kneeling on the floor in the space between the piled shelves I read:

> *In the terrible tears of the Yezhov terror I spent seventeen months waiting in line outside the prison in Leningrad. One day somebody in the crowd identified me. Standing behind me was a woman, with lips blue from the cold, who had, of course, never heard me called by name before. Now she started out of the torpor common to us all and asked me in a whisper (everyone whispered there):*
> *"Can you describe this?"*
> *And I said, "I can."*
> *Then something like a smile passed fleetingly over what had once been her face.*[2]

Akhmatova referred to this passage as *Vmesto predisoviia* (*Instead of a Preface*), adding it as prologue to her great poem, "Requiem," written during the years of her son Lev Gumilev's imprisonment. The poem was her *podvig*—her spiritual accomplishment—of remembering injustice and suffering, as experienced within herself and as collectively borne. Her son had been detained before, but on 10 March 1938 he was again arrested, and served seventeen months for the crime of being the son of two poets (his father, Nikolai Gumilev, had been executed in 1921). Lev's own death sentence was commuted to exile when those who had sentenced him were themselves purged and shot.

Anna's friend, Lidiya Chukovskaya, remembers her subsisting on black bread and tea. According to the research of Amanda Haight,

> She was extremely thin and frequently ill. She would get up from bed to go and stand, sometimes in freezing weather, in the long lines of people waiting outside the prisons, hoping against hope to be able to see her son or at least pass over a parcel. . . . The poems of "Requiem," composed at this time, were learnt by heart by Lidiya Chukovskaya, Nadezhda Mandelstam, and several other friends who did not know who else was preserving them. Sometimes Akhmatova showed them a poem on a piece of paper which she burnt as soon as she was sure it had been committed to memory. . . . In a time when a poem on a scrap of paper could mean a death sentence, to continue to write, to commit one's work to faithful friends who were prepared to learn poems by heart and thus preserve them, was only possible if one was convinced of the absolute importance and necessity of poetry.[3]

As I was still in my early twenties, and educated in the United States, I hadn't thought of poetry in these terms. I had not yet experienced war or life under military dictatorship, and had not yet, therefore, imagined the impress of extremity upon the poetic imagination, nor conceived of our infinite obligation each to all others: to stand with them in the hour of need, abject and destitute, in supplication and without calling for response. If it were so—if *de-scription* were possible, of world and its sufferings, then the response would be the smile on the woman whose lips were *blue with cold*, or rather something resembling this, passing over what had once been the face of the *other*. Akhmatova's "Requiem" meditates upon on the fate of Russia in her torment, marking the stages of suffering as one would visit the stations of Christ's passion. She wrote in the register of the cry of a woman who had become all women. In the poem's progression, Akhmatova takes leave of herself, becoming vigilant beyond all wakefulness. By turns she accepts and disowns her pain, becomes fearless, survives, forsakes the tribute of remembrance, and consigns her monument to the prison wall where she kept vigil with the others.

I was as yet unaware that *most* of the prominent twentieth-century poets beyond the English-speaking countries (and even some within them) had endured such experiences during their lives, and those blessed to survive the extremity of war, military occupation, dictatorship, imprisonment, torture, forced exile, and harsh forms of censorship wrote their poetry not *after* such experiences, but in their *aftermath*—in languages that had also *passed through*—languages that also continued to bear wounds, legible in the line-breaks, in constellations of imagery, in ruptures of utterance, in silences and fissures of written speech.

Aftermath became in this way a temporal debris field, where historical remains are strewn (*grand événements*, large events as well as those regarded as peripheral or lost), where that-which-happened remains present, including the consciousness in which such events arose and transpired. Insofar as the consciousness that produced the industrial genocide of the Shoah and subsequent genocides remains a human possibility, writing in the *aftermath*, with awareness of the debris field, is testamentary writing, a writing to be apprehended "in the light of conscience," as another Russian poet, Marina Tsvetayeva, wrote.[4] As such, it calls upon the reader, who is the *other* of this work, to be in turn marked by what such language makes present before her, what it holds open and begets in the reader, for witness *begets* witness.

In his *Ethics and Infinity,* Emmanuel Levinas writes: "*Le témoin témoigne de ce qu s'est dit par lui. Car il a dit 'Me voice!' devant autrui; et du fait que devant autrui il reconnait la responsabilité qui lui incombe, il se trouve avoir manifesté ce que le visage d'autrui a signifié pour lui. La gloire de l'Infini se révèle par ce qu'elle est capable de faire dans le témoin.*" [The witness witnesses to what is said by him (through him, or as him). For he has said "Here I am!" before the other one; and from the fact that before the one other he recognizes the responsibility incumbent upon him, he finds himself having manifested what the face of the other one has meant for him. The glory of the Infinite reveals itself by what it is capable of doing in the witness.][5]

This witness is a call to the *other* (perhaps in both senses, as the other within the poet, and the other whom the text addresses) to beget her as witness to what is held open in the writing, very much as in the face-to-face encounter of Martin Buber's *I/Thou,* later elaborated and extended by Levinas as

> an awakening that is neither reflection upon oneself nor universalization. An awakening signifying a responsibility for the other, the other who must be fed and clothed—my substitution for the other, my expiation for the suffering, and no doubt for the wrongdoing of the other. An expiation assigned to me without any possible avoidance, and by which my uniqueness as myself, instead of being alienated, is intensified by my irreplaceability.[6]

This awakening is also a reader's coming to awareness *before*—in both temporal and spatial senses—the *saying* of poetic text, which calls the reader to her irrevocable and inexhaustible responsibility for the other *as present* in the testamentary utterance. The text is lyric art, but a poetic work is at the same time a document, and the art that went into its making is at once a use of discourse. This discourse deals with objects that are also spoken in the newspapers, posters, memoirs and letters of every passing age—though in the case of poetry's strictly poetic expression these objects merely furnish a favorable occasion and serve as pretexts. It is of the essence of art to signify only between the lines—in the intervals of time, between times—like a footprint that would precede the step, or an echo preceding the sound of a voice.[7]

This voice is the saying of the witness, which is not a translation of experience into poetry, it is also itself experience. Philippe Lacoue-Labarthe, writing on the work of Celan, proposes "to call what [the poem] translates 'experience,' provided that we both understand the word in its strict sense—the Latin *ex-periri,* a crossing through danger—and especially that we avoid associating it with what is lived,' the stuff of anecdotes."[8] But according to Jacques Derrida, this poem, in its witnessing, arises out of experience that is not perceived as it occurs, is not registered in the first-person "precisely since it ruined this first person, reduced it to a ghost-like status, to being a 'me without me.'"[9] So the poem's witness is not a recounting, is not mimetic narrative, is not political confessionalism, "it is not simply an act of memory. It bears witness in the manner of an ethical or political act."[10]

The thought of the "poetry of witness," as a term of literary art, had not yet had its genesis in 1977, but as with all such terms, a genealogy can be traced through a convergence at once historical, philosophical, and personal. Soon after learning of Brodsky and Akhmatova, I began an epistolary friendship with the late Terrence Des Pres, author of *The Survivor: An Anatomy of Life in the Death Camps,* a scholarly study of survival in the face of industrial genocide and world death, which included a chapter on the will to bear witness experienced as a moral and spiritual imperative among survivors. My letter of thanks to him initiated a correspondence that would lead to a lifelong friendship. Des Pres had spent five years immersed in survivor literature: letters, journals, memoirs, novels, and poems written in the aftermath of the Shoah and the Soviet gulags. In the beginning, he told me, his research was tentative, as he was still imagining possibilities for a substantive monograph but after a few years, he experienced an epiphany regarding the enormity of his project, and what was at stake in addressing the literature of an event so "unimaginable" as to constitute a rupture of western history and thought. He knew, he said, that he would have to go forward with a book because there was no turning back. In a sense, the documents piled on his desk had taken up residence in his soul.

During one of our visits following the publication of *The Survivor,* I offered to read from the work of poets who endured sufferings that might seem tragically familiar to him. Des Pres was interested in poetry, having written his doctoral dissertation on Percy Bysshe Shelley—why not introduce him to Anna Akhmatova, Nazim Hikmet, Aleksander Wat, and Miguel Hernandez? The trunk of my car was filled with boxes of poetry in translation I hoped to share with students eager to know more about "world poetry." During the next days, Des Pres asked for poem after poem to be read to him, and the stories of the poets' lives recounted, and some time soon after, he decided that his next book would concern their work. During one of our many talks, we realized that poems could be read as a form of witness.

After spending the summer of 1977 in Mallorca translating a Salvadoran-born poet, I was invited to El Salvador, where I came to document human rights abuse, and my experiences there marked my second book of poems, *The Country Between Us,* which included poems both praised and vilified for purported "political" content. At the time the poems were written, El Salvador was not yet in the news; the country was "at peace," or rather, was suffering in the silence of misery endured.

In manuscript, *The Country Between Us* had been shelved for almost two years at the urging of well-meaning editors who believed that the poems were "too political" to publish in the United States, where they wouldn't be "well received." By the time the book did appear in print, through the intervention of Canadian poet and novelist Margaret Atwood, El Salvador was very much in the news, and so the book garnered the kind of attention almost never bestowed on a book of poems. I was invited to participate in discussions throughout the country on the subject of poetry and politics and the poet's relation to the State, discussions that were at once puzzling and disturbing to me. The commonplace that poetry doesn't "matter" in the United States was so often asserted then (as now) that one could be forgiven for wondering why such a marginal art should be so passionately policed as regards its content, much less the position of its practitioners with respect to their societies. The most often asked questions included these: What is the role of the poet? Does the poet have any responsibility to society? Why is political poetry almost always "bad"? And is there any place for politics in poetry?—as if Homer, whose work displeased Plato; Dante, himself a politician; and Milton, who served under Cromwell, had never written, nor the multitude of other poets in whose work we read evidence of the times in which they lived. The battle was joined between those who championed any poems proclaimed as political, and those who condemned all poetry with content that exceeded the bounds of private life. The term "political" seemed so variously applied as to become meaningless, and the realm of the private lyric was thus preserved at the expense of its vitality.

But there was a problem in restricting poetry to the interior compound of the "personal," and "insisting that individual experience is all that matters and there is no such thing as general suffering,"[11] or none that can be made visible in poetic art. Stephen Spender, in reviewing Nelly Sachs' book *O the Chimneys,* acknowledged this denial, and argued that

The conditions in which it is possible for writers to do their work—their writing, simply—always preclude their entering by their own experience into the centers of 'the destructive element.' Most writers gaze at the furnace through a fire-proofed window in a thick wall. Necessarily so, because they have to preserve the conditions in which their sensibility can act without becoming damaged; and to experience in its intensity the horrors of our time almost inevitably means being maimed or destroyed by it.[12]

What of those who had no "fire-proofed window"? Who found themselves within the inferno? While the solitude and tranquility thought to be the condition of literary production were absent for such poets, even in the aftermath of their survival, and while perhaps "being maimed or destroyed" is in some sense "inevitable," writers have survived and written despite all that happened, and against all odds. They have created exemplary literary art with language that itself passed through catastrophe. "The fundamental task of the critic," writes holocaust scholar Lawrence Langer, "is not to ask whether it should or can be done, since it already has been, but to evaluate *how* it has been done, judge its effectiveness, and analyze its implications for literature and for society."[13] What does it mean to regard literary art as a site of witness? To read poems as evidence rather than representation? What new "ethical" forensics is demanded in such reading? These questions preoccupied me, intellectually at first, but later more viscerally and in the depths of my being; something had happened, along the way, to the poet I had been.

It is now my sense that a rupture occurred in my work and myself in those years and thereafter. If asked, for example, *when* I returned from El Salvador, I have given the date: March 16, 1980, the week before the assassination of Monsignor Oscar Romero; but after thirty years, I now understand that I never returned, that the woman who traveled to El Salvador, the young poet she had been, did not come back. The woman who *did* return wrote, in those years, seven poems marked by the El Salvador *risky crossing*, and also an essay, published in the summer of 1981 in which the returning poet states: "It is my feeling that the twentieth century human condition demands a poetry of witness."[14]

Two years later, with the publication of Czeslaw Milosz's monograph, *The Witness of Poetry,* and the phrase entered the lexicon of literary terms, but was regarded at the time, skeptically by some, as a euphemism for "political poetry," or a "political poetry" by other means. "Witness" would come to refer, much of the time, to the person of the poet, much as it refers to a man or woman testifying under oath in a court of law. "Poets of witness" were thought to be writing documentary literature, or poetic reportage, in the mode of political confessionalism.

As compelling as many such "witness" poems are, "poetry of witness" originated in a very different constellation of thought, in which it was not regarded as constitutive of a poet's identity, or prescribing a new *littera-ture engagée*. "Poetry of witness," as a term descending from the litera-ture of the Shoah and complicated by philosophical, religious, linguistic, and psychoanalytic understandings of *witness*, remains to be set forth. In my sense of this term, it is a mode of reading rather than of writing, of a reader's encounter with the literature of that-which-happened, and its mode is evidentiary rather than representational. The poem inscribes the *risky crossing*, marked by that which happened, bearing the legible trace of extremity, at the same time enacting the rupture of the first-person, and hence voicing its *ghost-like status,* marking as it was marked, incising the wound in its inception and henceforth holding it open to the reader's encounter. Such utterance is as much evidence of what happened as the spatter of spilled blood.

This *essai* [15] is my attempt to re-enter the province of literary witness as an evidentiary mode beyond *mimesis,* as a textual encounter in the manner of an ethical act.

When asked by the editors at W. W. Norton & Co. to define "poetry of witness" in 1989, and at a loss to articulate a non-reductive response, I offered the story of Miklos Radnóti, foremost Hungarian poet of his generation, who, in 1944, was sent to do forced labor in what would become and what now once was Yugoslavia. In the labor camp, the poet Radnóti was able to procure a notebook, into which he inscribed his last ten poems, as well as a message in Hungarian, Croatian, German, French and English: "*contains the poems of the Hungarian poet Miklos Radnóti . . . to Mr. Gyula Ortutay, Budapest University lecturer . . . Thank you in advance.*"[16]

When it was clear that they would be defeated, the Germans decided to evacuate the camp and return the workers to Hungary. Radnóti, assuming that the first column would be the safest, volunteered for the march and recorded it in his poetry. Of more than two thousand men on this forced winter march, twenty-two survived, among them the poet Radnóti. Once in Hungary, the soldiers in charge, unable to find hospi-tal rooms for these prisoners, took Radnóti and twenty-one others to a clearing in the forest and executed them. However, the story does not end—as millions of such stories ended—with execution and the ano-nymity of a mass grave. After the war was over, Radnóti's body was among those found and exhumed near the village of Abda. His wife, Fanni Radnóti, identified him. In the pockets of his coat there was a small notebook, in which he had written his final poems. The notebook was opened and its pages were dried in the sun.

Among the poems in *Bori notesz* (Bor Notebook) were the *Razglednici* (postal cards) written during his imprisonment, which survived not only the poet's death, but also their burial with him for twenty months. Radnóti's story is simply an extreme version of the stories of many of twentieth-cen-tury poets. His poems were among those I selected for the volume *Against*

Forgetting: Twentieth Century Poetry of Witness (W. W. Norton & Co., 1993), an anthology of the work of one hundred forty-five poets, in English and in translation from thirty languages, who had passed through severe forms of collectively borne suffering during the last century, beginning with the Armenian genocide and ending at Tiananmen Square. It includes Miguel Hernandez, a poet sentenced to death in the aftermath of the Spanish Civil War, who lived to endure thirty years imprisonment under the harshest conditions before succumbing to tuberculosis; the great Russian poet Osip Mandelstam, who most probably died at Vtoraya Rechka, a transit camp near Vladivostok—his body was never recovered; the French Resistance poet Robert Desnos, who died of typhus in Terezin camp while whispering his last poems to a young medical student; Anna Swir (Świrszczyńska), who worked as a nurse in a makeshift hospital during the sixty-three-day Warsaw Uprising, an experience that silenced her for decades; Ilse Aichinger, who hid from the Nazis in Vienna; Gertrude Kolmar, sentenced to forced labor in Berlin and presumed to have died at Auschwitz; Primo Levi, survivor of Buno-Monowitz; Tadeusz Borowski, who survived Auschwitz and Dachau; Dan Pagis, interned in a camp in Ukraine; Paul Celan, sentenced to forced labor in Romania; Tudor Arghezi, who survived the concentration camp at Tirgu-Jiu; Aleksander Wat, arrested and jailed in Warsaw, then sent to prisons in Poland and the Soviet Union; Dylan Thomas and H.D. who survived the London blitz; the Guatemalan poet Otto Rene Castillo, who joined opposition forces against the dictatorship, was captured, tortured and immolated; Nazim Hikmet, politically imprisoned in Turkey for more than half of his adult life. These and other of the one hundred and forty-four anthologized poets would have been joined by another one hundred thirty, had I been accepted to publish multiple volumes or to print the book on onion-skin paper, of the kind Anna Akhmatova might have used to write down parts of her "Requiem" for her friends before consigning them to a fire.

The body of thought that informs "the poetry of witness" suggests that language can itself be damaged. This idea of "damaged language" appears in George Steiner's *Language and Silence,* when he considered German

> a language being used to run hell, getting the habits of hell into its syntax. . . . Gradually, words lost their original meaning and acquired nightmarish definitions. . . . language was . . . called upon to enforce innumerable falsehoods. . . . But there comes a breaking point. Use a language to conceive, organize, and justify Belsen; use it to make out specifications for gas ovens; use it to de-humanize man during twelve years of calculated bestiality. Something will happen to it. . . . Something of the lies and sadism will settle in the marrow of the language. Imperceptibly at first, like the poisons of radiation sifting silently into the bone. . . . It will no longer perform, quite as well as it used to, its two principal functions: the conveyance of human order which

we call law, and the communication of the quick of the human spirit which we call grace.[17]

The thinking of damaged language is also interrogated by Primo Levi in his memoir *The Drowned and the Saved,* wherein he describes the damage done to German in the mouths of those giving orders. Such damage to language is not, however, regarded as always irreparable. In the words of Paul Celan in his speech at Bremen: "One thing remained attainable, close and unlost amidst all the losses: language. Language was not lost, in spite of all that happened. But it had to go through its own responselessness, go through horrible silences, go through the thousand darknesses of death-bringing speech."[18]

One reads in these poets an impulse to announce themselves, and appeal to be believed. Charlotte Delbo opens her sequence, "None of Us Will Return," with the words: *"Today, I am not sure that what I wrote is true. / I am certain it is truthful."*[19] Armenian poet Siamanto (Atom Yarjanian) writes, in the aftermath of the Adana massacre, *"This incomprehensible thing I'm telling you about, I saw it with my own eyes."* Siamanto also joined the many attempting to console the reader: *"Don't be afraid. I must tell you what I saw, so people will understand/ the crimes men do to men."*[20] Common in these texts is a writing of the will to bear witness. Here is Nobel laureate Wislawa Szymborska in her poem "Hunger Camp at Jasło": *"Write it. Write. In ordinary ink/ on ordinary paper: they were given no food,/ they all died of hunger. 'All. How many?/ It's a big meadow. How much grass/ for each one?" Write: I don't know./ History counts its skeletons in round numbers.*[21] Szymborska also joins the many who lament the arbitrariness of fate: *"You survived because you were the first./ You survived because you were the last./ Because alone. Because the others./ Because on the left. Because on the right./ Because it was raining. Because it was sunny./ Because a shadow fell.// Luckily there was a forest./ Luckily there were no trees."*[22] There are inventories of losses, such as appear in Anna Akhmatova's "Requiem": *Nothing I counted mine, out of my life,/ is mine to take://not my son's terrible eyes,/ not the elaborate stone flower/ of grief, not the day of the storm,/ nor the trial of the visiting hour,// not the dear coolness of his hands,/ not the lime trees' agitated shade,/ not the thin cricket-sound/ of consolation's parting word."*[23] The difficulties of forgetting and remembering are marked. In Vahan Tekeyan's poem "Forgetting" we read: *"Forgetting. Yes. I will forget it all./ One after the other. The roads I crossed./ The roads I did not. Everything that happened.// And everything that did not."*[24] And in Guillaume Apollinaire's "Shadow": *"Memories composing now a single memory/ As a hundred furs make only one coat/ As thousands of wounds make only one newspaper article."*[25] Of the sense of the self's fragmentation, we read in Angel Cuadra: *"The common man I might have been/ reproaches me now,/ blaming me for his ostracism/ his solitary shadow,/ his silent exile."*[26]

Early in the twentieth century, there is evidence of faith and prayer in poetry, and of belief in the sacred. Toward the middle of the century, there is a discernible shift toward alienation from the deity, exemplified by Paul Celan in his poem "There Was Earth Inside Them": *"They dug and they dug, so their day/ went by for them, their night. And they did not praise God,/ who, so they heard, wanted all this,/ who, so they heard, knew all this."*[27] The temporal sense seems altered. In Velimir Khlebnikov's "Suppose I make a timepiece of humanity" we read this:" *I tell you, the universe is a scratch/ of a match on the face of the calculus./ And my thoughts are a picklock at work/ on a door, and behind it someone is dying."*[28] Turning to Zbigniew Herbert, we find "The Wall":

> We are standing under the wall. Our
> youth has been taken off like a shirt from
> the condemned men. We wait. Before the
> fat bullet will sit down on the nape of the
> neck, ten, twenty years pass. The wall is
> high and strong. Behind the wall is a tree
> and a star. The tree pries at the wall with
> its roots. The star nibbles the stone like a
> mouse. In a hundred, two hundred years
> there will already be a small window.[29]

There are many other shared qualities, such as the experience of consciousness itself as fragmented and altered, and for the first time, soldier poets wrote of the extremity of the battlefield explicitly in terms of its horrors. Poetic language attempts a coming to terms with evil and its embodiments, and there are appeals for a shared sense of humanity and collective resistance. There are many poems of address: to war as figural, to death and evil, memory and hunger as figural, and of course to the world to come, such as we find in Robert Desnos's "Epitaph": *"I lived in these times and I've been dead/ A thousand years [. . .] You who are living, what have you done with these treasures? / Do you regret the time of my struggle? / Have you raised your crops for a common harvest? / Have you made my town a richer place?"*[30] Horse Bienek joins this chorus in "Resistance": *"We speak loudly but no one understands us./ But we are not surprised/ For we are speaking the language/ That will be spoken tomorrow."*[31]

In conditions of extremity (war, suffering, struggle), the witness is *in relation*, and cannot remove him or herself. Relation is proximity, and this closeness subjects the witness to the possibility of being wounded. No special protection can be sought and no outcome intended. The witness who writes out of extremity writes his or her wound, as if such writing were making an incision. Consciousness itself is cut open. The self is fragmented, and the vessel of the self breaks into shards. The narrative also breaks. At the site of the wound, language breaks, interrogates itself, becomes tentative, kaleidoscopic. The form of this language bears the trace of extremity, and may be comprised of fragments: questions, aphorisms, broken passages of lyric prose or poetry, quotations, dialogue, brief and lucid passages that may or may not resemble what previously had been written.

The word "extremity" (*extremus*) is the superlative correlative of the word "exterior" (*exterus*), suggesting "utmost," "exceedingly great" and also "outermost," "farthest," implying intense suffering and even world-death; a suffering without knowledge of its own end. Ethical reading of such works does not inhere in assessing their truth value or efficacy as "representation," but rather in recognizing their evidentiary nature: here language is a life-form, marked by human experience, and is also itself material evidence that continues to mark human consciousness. The *aftermath* is a region of the devastated consciousness—of barbarism and the human capacity for cruelty and complicity with evil. In this *aftermath*, we are able to read, in the scarred landscape of battlefields, bomb craters and unreconstructed ruins, in oral and written testimony and in literary art, the mark or trace of extremity. The poem bears the wound in its language: in unexpected and at times broken rhythms, hesitancies, ruptured narratives, temporal distortions, polyphony, and in its silences, synaesthesias and resistances to poetic norms. The passage through extremity leaves a mark which remains legible in a poetry no longer conceived as an expressive "servant of thought in the Idealist tradition," but rather as "the very bursting forth of thought dialogically coming out of itself."[32]

In the work of witness, of writing out of extremity, the poem does not become a means to an extra-literary end: the poet, according to Levinas, "is excluded from the facile, humanistic hope that by writing, or 'creating,' he would transform his dark experience into greater consciousness. On the contrary: dismissed, excluded from what is written—unable even to be present by virtue of the non-presence of his very death—he has to renounce all conceivable relations of a self (either living or dying) to the poem which henceforth belongs to the other."[33] Des Pres would not have relinquished the "humanistic hope" of transformation, but Maurice Blanchot's reading of the poet's renunciation, of the poem as address to the other to whom it henceforth belonged, corresponds radiantly for me to formulations in the ethics of Levinas, and also the thought of Jacques Derrida (after his ethical turn). "This will be about bearing witness," Derrida writes in an essay on Paul Celan, "*Poétique et politique du témoinage*,"

> And about poetics as bearing witness. . . . A poem can 'bear witness' to a poetics. It can promise it, it can be a response to it, as to a testamentary promise. Indeed it must, it cannot not do so. But not with the idea of applying a previously existing art of writing or of referring to one as to a charter written somewhere else, or of obeying its laws like a transcendent authority, but rather by itself promising, in the act of its event, the foundation of a poetics.[34]

The poem would be a singularity, marked in its date, "that, in the reference that carries it beyond itself toward the other or toward the world, opens the verbal body to things other than itself."[35] What the poem lays open, to the other, is an unending address, a call to the other, that manifests that-which-happened. In the thought of "witness," I have proposed that we read language as *evidentiary* rather than as representational and explore the ways in which language becomes, itself, evidence.

Witness has been variously interrogated: in holocaust studies, it is the logic of survival, of witness, or of testimony. In critical legal studies, the logic of the evidentiary. In linguistics, the logic of the indexical (Peirce), or of the metonymic (Jakobson), or of the diachronic (Saussure). In historical studies, the logic of the fragment, the archive, or the living monument (Hilberg). In philosophy, it shows as the logic of the trace (Levinas), of repetition (Kierkegaard), of the legible (Benjamin), of the anamnetic (Plato). In psychoanalysis, it inheres in logic of the symptom (Freud), and throughout readings of tragedy and Hebraic Biblical scripture, it shows up as the logic of the prophetic. While many are accustomed to thinking of witness as the transmission of a knowledge that has come to us either through our senses or through inspiration, there is also the possibility of witness as a nonrepresentational, diachronic modality of thought.

Witness is neither martyrdom nor the saying of a juridical truth, but the owning of one's infinite responsibility for the *other one* (*l'autri*). It is not to be mistaken for politicized confessionalism. The confessional is the mode of the subjective, and the representational that of the objective, and it is necessary to move beyond both, and place ourselves *under* and *before* the other in an ethical relation that precedes ontology (Levinas). In the aftermath of Auschwitz, we begin with a heteronymous self and understand Descartes's subject/object construction as a two-century-old denial of the primacy of the *Other* and of relation. We abandon this denial to enter an intersubjective sphere of lived immediacy. In the poetry of witness, the poem makes present to us the experience of the *Other*, the poem *is* the experience, rather than a symbolic representation.

I began with Brodsky's postal cards to a young poet, and will end, after forty years, by sending his tutelary spirit, with gratitude, a return card: when we read the poem as witness, we are marked by it and become ourselves witnesses to what it has made present before us. Language incises the page, wounding it with testimonial presence, and the reader is marked by encounter with that presence. Witness begets witness. The text we read becomes a living archive.

NOTES

1. "The Trial of Joseph Brodsky," *The New York Times*, October 1, 1972.
2. Anna Akhmatova, *Poems of Akhmatova*, selected, trans. and intro. Stanley Kunitz with Max Hayward (New York: Houghton Mifflin, [1967] 1973), 99.

3. Amanda Haight, *Anna Akhmatova: A Poetic Pilgrimage* (Oxford: Oxford University Press, 1976), 224.
4. Marina Tsvetaeva, *Art in the Light of Conscience: Eight Essays on Poetry* (London: Bloodaxe Books, 2010), 224.
5. Emmanuel Levinas, *Ethique et infini: Dialogues avec Philippe Nemo* (Paris: Fayard, 1982), 115–16. Translation by author.
6. Emmanuel Levinas, *Proper Names*, trans. Michael B. Smith (Stanford, CA: Stanford University Press, 1996), 7.
7. Levinas, *Proper Names*, 7.
8. "Two Poems by Paul Celan" in Philippe Lacoue-Labarthe, *Poetry As Experience*, trans. Andrea Tarnowski (Stanford, CA: Stanford University Press, 1999), 18.
9. Quoted in Peter Baker, ed., *Onward: Contemporary Poetry & Poetics* (New York: Peter Lang, 1996), 353.
10. Jacques Derrida, "Beyond: Giving for the Taking, Teaching, and Learning to Give, Death*" ["Au-delà: donner à prendre, apprendre à donner—la mort"], in *The Gift of Death*, trans. David Wills (Chicago and London: University of Chicago Press, 1995), 35.
11. George Steiner, *Language and Silence* (London: Faber and Faber, Ltd., 1958), 122–123.
12. Stephen Spender, "Catastrophe and Redemption: O the Chimneys. By Nelly Sachs," *The New York Times Sunday Book Review*, October 1967, 5, 34.
13. Lawrence Langer, *The Holocaust and the Literary Imagination* (New Haven, CT: Yale University Press, 1975), 1.
14. Carolyn Forché, "El Salvador: An Aide Memoir," *American Poetry Review* (July–Aug. 1981): 3–7.
15. *essai: attempt* in Montaigne's sense.
16. Miklos Radnóti, *Under Gemini: A Prose Memoir and Selected Poetry*, trans. Kenneth McRobbie, Zita McRobbie, and Jascha Kessler (Athens, OH: Ohio University Press, 1985), 7.
17. George Steiner, *Language and Silence: Essays on Language, Literature, and the Inhuman* (London: Faber and Faber, 1958), 122–124.
18. Paul Celan, Speech at Bremen (1958), quoted in David Weiss, ed., *In the Act: Essays on the Poetry of Hayden Carruth* (Geneva, NY: Hobart and Williams Smith Colleges Press, 1990), 56.
19. Charlotte Delbo, *Auschwitz and After*, trans. Rosette C. Lamont (New Haven, CT: Yale University Press, 1995), 1.
20. Siamanto, "The Dance," trans. Peter Balakian and Nevart Yaghlian, in Carolyn Forché, *Against Forgetting: Twentieth-Century Poetry of Witness* (New York: W. W. Norton, 1993), 57, 58.
21. Wislawa Szymborska, "Hunger Camp at Jasło," trans. Grazyna Drabik and Austin Flint, in Forché, *Against Forgetting*, 459.
22. Szymborska, "Any Case," trans. Grazyna Drabik and Sharon Olds, in Forché, *Against Forgetting*, 458.
23. Anna Akhmatova, "Requiem," trans. Stanley Kunitz and Max Hayward, in Forché, *Against Forgetting*, 106.
24. Vahan Tekeyan, "Forgetting," trans. Diana Der Hovanessian and Marzbed Margossian, in Forché, *Against Forgetting*, 59.
25. Guillaume Apollinaire, "Shadow," trans. Anne Hyde Greet, in Forché, *Against Forgetting*, 67.
26. Angel Cuadra, "In Brief," trans. Catherine Rodríguez-Nieto, in Forché, *Against Forgetting*, 593.
27. Paul Celan, "There Was Earth Inside Them, and They Dug," trans. Michael Hamburger, in Forché, *Against Forgetting*, 382.

28. Velimir Khlebnikov, "Suppose I Make a Timepiece of Humanity," trans. Paul Schmidt, in Forché, *Against Forgetting*, 101.
29. Zbigniew Herbert, "The Wall," trans. John Carpenter and Bogdana Carpenter, in Forché, *Against Forgetting*, 464.
30. *The Selected Poems of Robert Desnos*, trans. Carolyn Forché and William Kulik, ed. William Kulik (New York: The Ecco Press, 1991), 176.
31. Horst Bienek, "Resistance," trans. Matthew Mead, in Forché, *Against Forgetting*, 471.
32. From Michael B. Smith, translator's introduction, *Outside the Subject* by Emmanuel Levinas (Stanford, CA: Stanford University Press, 1994), xxi.
33. Maurice Blanchot, *The Writing of the Disaster*, trans. Ann Smock (Lincoln: University of Nebraska Press, 1995), 135.
34. Jacques Derrida, "Poetics and Politics of Witnessing," in *Sovereignties in Question,* ed. Thomas Dutoit and Outi Pasanen (New York: Fordham University Press, 2005), 65–66.
35. Derrida, "Poetics and Politics of Witnessing," 66.

8 Narrating Human Rights and the Limits of Magic Realism in Salman Rushdie's *Shalimar the Clown*

Elizabeth S. Anker

Salman Rushdie's career affords a fertile opportunity to chart the multiple intersections between literature and human rights. Rushdie's fiction has consistently investigated the troubled status of human rights, whether through *Midnight's Children*'s (1981) treatment of the Bangladesh Liberation War, *Shame*'s (1983) indictment of the corruption afflicting the postcolonial nation-state, or *The Satanic Verses*'s (1988) exploration of postcolonial migrancy in the western metropolis. Indeed, the "Rushdie affair" following the publication of *The Satanic Verses* (1988) itself crystallizes debates over freedom of speech, which many define as a core human right.[1]

However, questions of human rights have received relatively scant attention within Rushdie criticism. We might venture two interrelated explanations for this neglect. First, Rushdie scholarship has generally privileged his fiction's formal and aesthetic properties by reading them to exemplify postmodernism, magical realism, and/or Bakhtinian heteroglossia. Such interpretive frameworks emphasize how Rushdie destabilizes or decenters authoritative accounts of history, politics, and truth—or, broadly speaking, expectations underlying liberal humanism in general. As Linda Hutcheon concludes, *Midnight's Children* "undermine[s] the ideological assumptions behind what has been accepted as universal and transhistorical in our culture: the humanist notion of Man as a coherent and continuous subject."[2] At once, other prevailing strains in Rushdie criticism foreground what *Midnight's Children* self-reflexively calls its own "inflated macrocosmic activity," or its commentary on the anatomy of abstract political constructs often defined as formative of global modernity—such as "nationalism," "democracy," and "secularism"[3]—and the ambivalent postcolonial relationship to them. Together, these dominant hermeneutics have functioned to discount the aesthetic features and implications of Rushdie's many representations of violated human rights.

Yet, in key respects, this oversight is not accidental. As critics have observed, Rushdie's fiction generally enlists irony, satire, and postmodern play rather than aspiring to mimetic realism or sincerity—which is to say that the generic and stylistic conventions of his writing might seem to divert attention from its depictions of abuses of human rights. Likewise, through encyclopedic summations of historical events, Rushdie subordinates the ordinary particularities of singular characters' lives to more epic, totalizing conflicts. As such, his writing has been seen to mute the affective fabric of his characters' encounters with suffering and loss, diminishing the magnitude of such experiences. As Michael Gorra observes: "[B]oth the fantasy and the rhetorical extravagance of *Midnight's Children* can numb its readers to anything but its own exhilaration. However entrancing—indeed, precisely because it is entrancing—Rushdie's style distances one from the horrors it describes, making his description of them not only bearable but even enjoyable."[4] If Rushdie's fiction indeed precludes emotional investment in its characters, we must ask whether it yields only tenuous purchase for theorizing literature's bearing on human rights, in particular both the representational stakes of trauma and the "ethics of recognition" that predetermine the veracity of human rights claims.[5]

Shalimar the Clown, however, strikingly diverges from much of Rushdie's preceding fiction to conspicuously contend with innumerable human rights crises, which centrally propel its narrative. *Shalimar* recounts nearly every type of horror afflicting the twentieth century—a humanitarian crisis in Kashmir, torture, rape, genocide, the death penalty, and a spate of other atrocities. Along the way, *Shalimar* meditates on dilemmas that beset human rights reportage by staging multiple failures of recognition, which it largely attributes to the deceptive, malleable nature of human rights talk. Even as *Shalimar* thus decries challenges confronted in the literary portrayal of human rights abuses, it simultaneously points to injuries that resist symbolization as well as bear perilous consequences when encountered in narrative form. Its stance toward human rights witnessing is, in turn, internally divided: while the narrative fixates on the scene and truth effects of atrocity, it enacts cautionary tales about the hazards of that very preoccupation, in effect problematizing its own ambitions. Additionally, *Shalimar* reveals how the surviving tropes of imperialist discourse color many accounts of human rights abuse, insofar as impenetrability and incomprehension become projected onto the underlying suffering.

Because much of *Shalimar* conducts a type of paean to human rights norms, its politics are often strident, another way in which it exhibits a degree of transparency unusual for Rushdie's fiction. This unprecedented gravitation toward mimetic realism reflects a re-evaluation of the aesthetic codes that have customarily informed Rushdie's corpus. Although *Shalimar*'s characters undergo fantastical visions and possess superhuman propensities, *Shalimar* refuses to celebrate those faculties, instead holding them accountable for engendering crime, vengeance, and hostility. *Shalimar* ultimately opposes fantasy and experimentation to social justice, impugning magic realism as an aesthetic. This departure further probes *why* matters of human rights have remained relatively submerged within Rushdie scholarship, despite their thematic prominence in his novels. Is there something about the postmodern suspicion of meaning and truth that has distracted readers from Rushdie's portraits of human suffering? Has

Rushdie's reliance on parody downplayed and apologized for human cruelty and wrong, much as Gorra alleges? And if *Shalimar* exposes the liabilities of magic realism, does it censure that aesthetic for deflecting attention from questions of justice and ethics?

Even as outrage at human rights abuse fuels the narrative of *Shalimar*, the novel offers an overwhelmingly bleak forecast for international social justice. While its overt political commentary bemoans general shortcomings that compromise human rights, the narrative connects U.S. foreign policy, which often masquerades as a defense of human rights, to the rise of global terror. Most prominently, the misadventures of its titular character Shalimar mine this relationship between proliferating human rights violations and the burgeoning of international terror. After being cuckolded by his wife Boonyi, Shalimar embarks on a career as an international terrorist, which begins in a Pakistani training camp administered by Islamic fundamentalists. Whereas Shalimar's motives derive from personal revenge, the novel largely attributes global terrorism to American neglect and malfeasance.[6] Indeed, the other of the novel's two protagonists, Shalimar's rival and nemesis Max Ophuls, is fictionally attributed with some of the most glaring misdeeds in recent U.S. diplomacy. While young Jewish Max is a renegade and heroic opponent of Nazism during World War II, he is converted into an agent of the most nefarious U.S. covert operations. Through Shalimar's vantage in the training camp, readers are informed that Afghan freedom fighters, less than subtly or accurately named "Talib the Afghan" and the "Muj," received their guns in transactions coordinated by Max himself.[7] Likewise, when a range of classified information becomes public after Max's death, his daughter India learns that he was a spy in many of the world's "hot zones," betraying him to have been "the occult servant of American geopolitical interest."[8] Through Max, Rushdie conspicuously castigates the U.S. for its exploitation of the postcolonial world, although we should note that this condemnation is premised on an often simplifying distortion of the historical record, such as when he erroneously conflates the Taliban with the Mujahideen.

Similarly, American domestic policy is depicted as routinely abusive of human rights. The novel's concluding chapter correlates a seemingly random death row execution with the Rodney King riots:

> Everywhere was a mirror of everywhere else. Executions, police brutality, explosions, riots: Los Angeles was beginning to look like wartime Strasbourg; like Kashmir. . . . The jury returned its verdict in the trial of the four officers accused of the beating of Rodney King in the San Fernando Valley Foothill Police Division, a beating so savage that the amateur videotape of it looked, to many people, like something from Tiananmen Square or Soweto. When the King jury found the policemen not guilty, the city exploded, giving its verdict on the verdict by setting itself on fire, like a suicide bomber.[9]

Aligning American racism with the holocaust, apartheid, and the Tiananmen Square massacre, Rushdie's narrative sweepingly elides a variety of state-sanctioned brutalities in a manner representative of other passages in the novel. Indicting the racism of the American jury system, the narrative parrots the very media frenzy that it condemns. In doing so, *Shalimar* both highlights the hypocrisy of America's self-proclaimed status as global humanitarian champion and reveals why that fantasy depends on exoticist stories of distant human rights abuse that "reinforce American claims to the moral high ground"[10]—although that very critique is one this essay levies against *Shalimar* and its own commitment to human rights.[11]

Beyond arraigning American exceptionalism, *Shalimar* evinces deep skepticism about legal process and the ease with which appeals to law can legitimate wrongdoing. Colonel Kachhwaha, the Indian military commander stationed at the Kashmiri Line of Control, recurrently invokes legalisms to cloak malfeasance. After being spurned by Shalimar's wife, Kachhwaha retaliates against her entire Kashmiri village, evading censure for his retributive acts by dexterously exploiting the law to license military aggression. Knowing that the friction in Kashmir is "unpopular," he stipulates, "unpopularity was illegal. The legal position was that the Indian military presence in Kashmir had the support of the population."[12] Here, Kachhwaha maneuvers the law to contravene truth, both obscuring and condoning underlying acts of persecution. The novel describes the Indian government's suspension of the rule of law in Kashmir by the "introduction of President's Rule" (reminiscent of the State of Emergency in *Midnight's Children*) in similar terms, as "immunizing all government agents" against the commission of particular crimes, including "destruction of private property, torture, rape and murder." Likewise, denominating Kashmir a "disturbed area" warrants long-term detention and torture as means to police mere speech acts as well as to define all confessions so elicited as "voluntary."[13] Overall, the narrative thus reproves how appeals to law can mask human rights violations while short-circuiting the moral deliberation of those charged with its enforcement. For Kachhwaha's soldiers, reliance on the façade of legality co-opts other faculties of judgment, removing individual aversion toward behaviors that would otherwise be reprehensible.

Kachhwaha's ability to manipulate legality additionally brings to mind debates about whether governance according to the rule of law alone is sufficient to instill other norms tied to democracy within a society. Despite widespread evidence to the contrary, the international legal community frequently assumes that juridico-political institutions modeled on "western," or European, democracy provide a natural antidote to wider sociopolitical ills and inequities.[14] As Talal Asad argues, the human rights community expects a precise convergence between a society's respect for the rule of law and its realization of more comprehensive liberal humanist values. In light of such presumptions, for Asad "*the rule called law* in effect usurps the entire universe of moral discourse," an assessment that certainly applies to Kachhwaha's machinations.[15] Moreover, a blanket faith in the salvific properties of European structures of law risks obscuring how under colonization legal codes were finessed by administrators to entrench class and racial disparities, which for many theorists still taints postcolonial legal infrastructures. As Abdullah A. An-Na'im thus asserts, "[i]t is unrealistic to expect the postcolonial state to effectively protect human rights when it is the product of colonial rule that is by definition the negation of these rights."[16] Within such a framework, Kachhwaha simply perpetuates a long history of law's complicity with unjust and exploitative practices within Indian legal culture.

Despite its dim prognosis for human rights, *Shalimar* gains momentum from its recurrent attempts to memorialize human rights violations, and the atrocity at the crux of its recuperative project arises within Kashmir. As the narrative recounts this tragedy, its aesthetic ratifies theorizations of trauma that insist on trauma's fundamentally incommunicable, destabilizing features. However, it is not merely that human rights abuses defy symbolization; rather, the representational barriers posed by trauma correspond with ethical casualties that stem from imaginatively confronting extreme brutality. *Shalimar* suggests that the psyche erects natural, productive obstacles to its ability to grasp egregious abuses of human rights, especially without some form of mediation, and these resistances yield their own independent, quasi-ethical merit.

When *Shalimar*'s narrative does eventually relate the devastation of Kashmir, it presents not one but multiple versions of the events, none of which exhaustively or straightforwardly contains them. Rather, the narrative approaches the atrocity through the juxtaposition of three competing descriptive idioms, each of which attempts but fails to adequately reckon with the human rights abuses at issue. First, Kachhwaha filters them through the depersonalized, aloof genre of a military briefing. The Indian military dispatches enumerate with objective dispassion the conspicuously unnamed villages that come "under crackdown."[17] Erasing their particularity through labels such as "Village Z," filled with the dehumanized populations of "terrorist youth, C" and "women G, H, and I,"[18] the reports suppress their victims' individuality, discount the violated lives, and thereby anesthetize their readers against guilt or self-scrutiny.[19] As Kachhwaha concludes after surveying the reports: "[t]hese were strategic and tactical matters and should not be discussed emotionally."[20] Much as Kachhwaha's response demonstrates, calculatingly remote, bureaucratic language enables him to evade moral compunction as well as the magnitude of his crimes. Such abstraction endemic to law is consequently shown to silence registers of judgment that bear directly on ethics and justice, even while the military records are cleansed of concrete "evidence" that would be relevant to future fact-finding or humanitarian missions.

The villagers of Pachigam, Shalimar and Boonyi's village, instead hear of the increasingly proximate violence through the obstructionist idiom of BBC reportage. Boonyi's father ironically remains glued to the radio awaiting the distant broadcasts, wherein certain hyperbolic words recur— "loot, plunder, arson, mayhem, murder, exodus"—with the most enigmatic phrase being "ethnic cleansing."[21] This inflammatory terminology inspires panic and thereafter a massive refugee aid crisis. The catch phrases of human rights alarmism mobilized by the western media simultaneously estrange the villagers from their immediate predicaments and spawn an emergency in excess of the original circumstances. In effect, the narrative arraigns the sensationalized disposition of human rights rhetoric and the way, like military language, it eclipses the lives it claims authority over. It thereby denounces a number of characteristics of human rights discourse: although the western media must ratify postcolonial crisis to endow it with international legitimacy, it does so by casting postcoloniality in strikingly neo-imperialist terms, vis-à-vis displays of remote savagery that end up circularly validating western beneficence and cultural superiority. Overall, the BBC's coverage neither incites an international response to the pending menace nor renders it comprehensible for the people it embroils; rather, the media's imprimatur packages it as a spectacle for global consumption. *Shalimar* thus exposes how the discursive codes popularized through media reportage not only fail to represent but can further aggravate large-scale abuses of human rights.

Beyond how these different explanatory prisms falsify the underlying tragedy, the narrative performs its own incredulity. In two separate passages, it begins to document the atrocity only to interrupt that effort. Its first aborted attempt concerns the Kashmiri refugees who flee in response to the BBC reports of looming genocide. In this case, the narrative's feint of puzzlement decries the miscarriages of justice that escalate the crisis, as it catalogues a series of non-existent interventions, inadequate facilities, and insufficient state support for the refugees. Each form of governmental negligence is encased within an interrogatory, "why was that." The narrative's litany of grievances culminates by falling apart into unintelligibility: "why was that why was that why was that why was that why was that."[22] The numbers cited—"six hundred thousand Indian troops in Kashmir" and "three and a half lakhs of human beings"—similarly distance the emergency and intensify its unfathomability.[23] Whereas Kachhwaha's military reports deployed abstraction to dehumanize, here scope and volume obstruct understanding, while at once registering impediments to the assignment of blame. Since the narrative now condemns inaction, vast numerosity denotes the incapacity to locate discrete, identifiable wrongdoers, much as the inconclusive status of its queries marks the futility of remedy. By abandoning a propositional sentence structure, it accordingly relinquishes the possibility of positivistic truth, certainty, or closure.[24]

The narrative's second episode of staged incomprehension addresses the actual demolition of Pachigam, and it, too, is executed indirectly through a compendium of unresolved questions that attest to the foreclosure of reparation and recovery. However, these interrogatories seek not justification but instead the individual perpetrators of, and by extension agentive liability for, the crimes. The narrative implores as it inventories the offenses (from which are excerpted the middle and end of a much lengthier record):

> Who smashed that house? Who smashed *that* house? Who smashed *that* house? [. . .] Who killed the children? Who whipped the parents? Who raped that lazy-eyed woman? Who raped that grey-haired lazy-eyed woman as she screamed about snake vengeance? Who raped that woman again? Who raped that woman again? Who raped that dead woman? Who raped that dead woman again?[25]

Repeating the word "that," the narrative emphasizes the specificity of the victims while amplifying the horror of the underlying violence. Although pleading for heightened clarity and reckoning, it nevertheless subverts that aim, again marking the aesthetic limits posed by trauma. Censoring the villagers' names, it instead describes Firdaus, Shalimar's mother, as having a "lazy eye," and her rape and death consequently mimic a process of delayed, unwilling acknowledgment. The endeavor that overlays all of *Shalimar*—the desire to authenticate human rights violations in Kashmir—is in turn confounded at its very moment of realization.

Concluding its compendium of unresolved queries, the narrative self-reflexively analyzes its own strategies, justifying its oblique, circuitous disclosures:

> What happened that day in Pachigam need not be set down here in full detail, because brutality is brutality and excess is excess and that's all there is to it. There are things that must be looked at indirectly because they would blind you if you looked them in the face, like the fire of the sun. So, to repeat: there was no Pachigam anymore. Pachigam was destroyed. Imagine it for yourself.[26]

Chastening his readers, Rushdie implicates us in whatever ethical stakes ensue from *Shalimar*'s fraught enterprise.[27] *Shalimar* thus self-critically meditates upon the liabilities of its own subject matter, while ensnaring its readers in whatever dilemmas derive from its recuperative project. After depicting explicit scenes of violence, it assigns the ultimate interpretive burden back to the reader, leaving its audience with the onus to negotiate the appropriate scope of human rights witnessing.

In light of the foregoing, trauma theory might seem to offer a helpful framework for analyzing Rushdie's representations of human rights violations. Dori Laub explains that "[m]assive trauma precludes its registration; the observing and recording mechanisms of the human mind are temporary knocked out, malfunction. The victim's narrative—the very process of bearing witness to massive trauma—does indeed begin with someone who testifies to an absence, to an event that has not yet come into existence, in spite of the overwhelming and compelling nature of the reality of its occurrence."[28] For Shoshana Felman, holocaust testimony similarly induces a "radical *failure of representation*":

> What the testimony does not offer is, however, a completed statement, a totalizable account of those events. In the testimony, language is in process and in trial. It does not possess itself as a conclusion, as the contestation of a verdict or the self-transparency of knowledge.[29]

Much as for Laub and Felman, *Shalimar*'s glimpses of atrocity construe it as premised on both aesthetic and intellectual limits that attest to a hermeneutic as well as descriptive impasse or impossibility. By portraying genocide via a series of unanswered questions, the narrative tracks the psychic barriers that both impede trauma's complete comprehension and cause language to collapse in its face.

Yet, we must ask whether such conclusions about *Shalimar* drawn from trauma studies are so easy. Does not Rushdie's enactment of incredulity paradoxically also heighten and concentrate our fixation on the genocide (compounding the narrative's own preoccupation)? By withholding these horrific events until its conclusion, *Shalimar* cultivates anticipation for them, intensifying their sublime qualities. Indeed, *Shalimar* not only delays but progressively converges on atrocity as its narrative destination, arousing its readers' desires for the very brutality that it cautions against—and arguably attenuating its own disclaimers.

In the end, it is therefore hard not to interpret *Shalimar*'s portrayal of postcolonial violence as deeply exoticizing, raising the question of whether it constitutes another instantiation of what Graham Huggan calls "the postcolonial exotic." As Huggan argues, strategic self-exoticism is an inevitable component of the marketing of postcolonial literature, being indicative of "the spiraling commodification of cultural difference."[30] In *Shalimar*, Kashmir accordingly becomes a space of irrational acts and unspeakable fears, which are what render it alien to western comprehension. As such, *Shalimar* probes what happens when the generally benign exoticism Huggan diagnoses emanates from a figuration of postcoloniality in terms of a chronic legacy of violated human rights.

It goes without saying that exoticism invokes and perpetuates many of the classic tropologies of imperialist discourse. In *The Rhetoric of Empire*, David Spurr delineates various of its contemporary iterations, and, unsurprisingly, Rushdie's rendition of the fate of Kashmir harnesses many of those stereotypes. By insisting on its unfathomability, the narrative enacts a form of "negation"; the postcolonial world is cast as a space of "debasement," insofar as that violence is suggested to be endemic and depraved; and, finally, the dream-like aura that surrounds the genocide produces "insubstantialization," causing the non-western landscape to become "the backdrop of a baseless fabric against which is played the drama of the writer's self." Indeed, Rushdie constructs even pre-partition Kashmir vis-à-vis attributes that fulfill western fantasies of pre-civilizational innocence and harmony, thereby displaying "idealization" and "aestheticization."[31]

In sum, while *Shalimar* deplores the media's tendency both to abstract non-western events and to sensationalize suffering through crisis-driven language, its narrative resorts to almost identical representational tactics in depicting abuses of human rights. By exaggerating their resistance to comprehension and construing postcolonial violence as acute, it exhibits obstructionism similar to that for which Rushdie berates media reportage. This tension in the novel opens up certain risks of trauma studies as an analytic—risks that emerge in particular when the experiential features of trauma are projected onto the non-western world to configure it as trapped outside objective knowledge. *Shalimar* confronts us with the paradox that the very aesthetic features it consecrates as inherent to trauma when transposed onto non-western scenes of suffering hazard reinscribing classic expectations that underlie the colonialist gaze. Those presumptions, moreover, confirm self-congratulatory western fantasies that sanction humanitarian interventionism, revealing it to be a present-day version of the White Man's Burden. We must ask, then, whether Rushdie's exposé of the debacle in Kashmir functions akin to how James Dawes describes accounts of the Rwandan genocide: "The genocide functions almost like a mirror, allowing the observer to gaze upon himself, to see how he has acquired new depth and meaning by encountering tragedy, to see how he has proven himself."[32]

Whereas *Shalimar* defamiliarizes the genocide in order to capture its horror, the bulk of the narrative adopts a posture closer to realism. Rushdie's narrative ventures with earnestness and persistence to authenticate infringements of human rights, bemoaning representational hurdles to doing so. For one, its plot satirizes its own attempts to incite humanitarian concern for Kashmir by fictionally dramatizing pitfalls that beset public, in particular political, speech. Parodying its own consciousness-raising aims, Max Ophuls is depicted on two separate instances trying to incite outrage at the turmoil in Kashmir but meeting with indifferent, reluctant audiences. In the early, idealistic stages of Max's career when he serves in the late 1960s as U.S. Ambassador to India, Max strives to induce the two governments to intervene in the deteriorating situation, but he mistakenly deploys the rhetoric of "oppression" and the "oppressors," which, at the height of American involvement in Vietnam, conjures up damning resemblances between the two situations.[33] To deflect such parallels, the two countries are forced to strategically ignore the situation. Furthermore, Max's investment originates in the first place from Boonyi's amorous remarks, which in reality encode her resentment of Max within extended diatribes about the Indian military's ravaging of Kashmir.[34] The spy Max ironically fails to decrypt Boonyi's entreaties and pursues them at a political level. However, his outspoken defense of Kashmir coincides with the leaking of their affair, and the Indian government publicizes Max's behavior to applaud its own presence in the region. The narrative comments: "A Kashmiri girl ruined and destroyed by a powerful American gave the Indian government an opportunity to look like it would stand up and defend Kashmiris against marauders of all types."[35] While forfeiting Max's reputation, this diversionary spin on the scandal highlights the paternalism that infects even Max's superficially humanitarian desire to intercede on behalf of Kashmir.

Right before his death in the early 1990s, Max again endeavors to focus public attention on looming conflict in Kashmir. Max "on an impulse" appears on a trendy late-night talk show, but instead of engaging in the banter appropriate to that forum he unleashes, from the host's perspective, "a political diatribe on the so-called Kashmir issue."[36] Max at length "rant[s] about fanaticism and bombs," enumerating the many rights abuses inflicted upon Kashmir. Naturally, the talk show host stifles his passionate invective, and, fearing that Max's "killjoy news" will disrupt the humor of the viewing audience, he abbreviates Max's interview for the show's televised airing. Through this incident, *Shalimar* impugns the western media for both evading controversy and its impoverished discursive and explanatory reserves, which together lead to the dismissal of non-western lives.

Because Max is a self-transforming, exiled figure for the public artist, the novel invites its readers to interpret him as a proxy for Rushdie himself. To this end, his thwarted attempts at political advocacy reenact Rushdie's frustrations at the recurrently negative reception of his political speech.[37] Rushdie contributes to public debate with remarkable frequency, editorializing on everything from politics in Ireland and Kosovo, to Elian Gonzalez, to the Kansas ban on teaching evolution.[38] Yet his reactionary commentaries have met with significant criticism, having been castigated for being hyperbolic, inconsistent, and one-sided—much like the petitions of Max in *Shalimar.* [39] It is tempting, then, to read *Shalimar* as covertly undertaking the sorts of political speech that would inspire renewed cycles of Rushdie bashing were they not encased within and tempered by the fictional medium.

It is this yearning for the truth effects of frank political speech that engenders *Shalimar*'s conflicted posture toward magical realism. Magical realism is commonly defined as an "assault on the basic structures of rationalism and realism" and refusal of "assumption[s] of objective (hence universal) representation of natural and social realities."[40] It has been construed as "doom[ing] to obscurity . . . any attempt to relegate specific versions of reality to such categories as *true* or *false*, *high* or *low*."[41] Likewise, Maggie Ann Bowers cites the genre's "inherent transgressive and subversive qualities." [42] However, while *Shalimar* manifests properties of magic realism, it simultaneously counteracts those impulses. It does not celebrate transgression for the sake of sheer play; rather, it decries both excess and subversion by displaying their devastating consequences on its characters—most prominently, Shalimar the terrorist. Thus querying whether negation and falsehood represent viable means of ideological resistance, the narrative instead seeks to excavate suppressed truths in its pursuit of human rights and social justice. By recuperating historical and material realities—here again, the fate of Kashmir—that have been silenced and overlooked, it aspires to render them, while unverifiable, nonetheless incontrovertible, objective, and authentically "true."

This ambivalence toward magical realism in *Shalimar* is what furnishes much of its relevance to theorizing the relationship between human rights and literary form. Indeed, Rushdie's unprecedented realism in *Shalimar* prompts the question of whether human rights abuses demand heightened focus and narrative persistence for their literary depiction. If so, is magic realism predicated on a sportive luxury aesthetically at odds with volatile subject matter and the rendering of it compelling and morally imperative? By upsetting magical realism's codes, does *Shalimar* underscore how they pose obstacles to the assignation of blame and responsibility? In the end, *Shalimar*'s paramount commitments are not to aesthetic experimentation and play but to awakening social conscience, a project requiring persuasion and credibility. Unlike *Midnight's Children* and *The Satanic Verses*, texts that not only exhibit aesthetic innovation but also de-authorize dominant accounts of truth, *Shalimar* is oriented toward a strikingly divergent enterprise—that is, to confirming realities neglected by the western media. Because of this, its overriding goals appear relatively transparent and univocal compared to Rushdie's other novels, even as it forswears a certain aesthetic extravagance.

Along with magical realism, Rushdie's novels have also been interpreted in terms of Bakhtinian heteroglossia and dialogism, devices understood by some critics to overlap with those of magical realism.[43] Indeed, *Shalimar* contains a multiplicity of divergent, contradictory perspectives. However, it is not dialogic in the conventional sense of presenting opposing political or ideological viewpoints that contribute to mutually negating interpretations of truth. Rather, the competing perspectives it contains merely propose alternate takes on the same events, although without disputing their basic factuality. Here again, these disparate vantages coalesce around the tragedy of Kashmir. Max, the BBC, the villagers of Pachigam, Rushdie's narrator, and even Shalimar and Kachhawa all corroborate the existence of the atrocity. None controverts the events' sheer substance (although Kachhawa does applaud them); rather, they are in collective agreement over the basic effort to record and comprehend.[44]

Likewise, *Shalimar* does not relish the "carnivalesque" with the exuberance of other Rushdie novels. Philip Engblom has explained Bakhtinian carnival in Rushdie's fiction: "Carnival itself is characterized first and foremost by the suspension of all law, prohibitions, and restrictions that order 'normal' life. . . . Behavior, gesture, and discourse are thus freed to become eccentric and inappropriate in normal terms."[45] However, *Shalimar* does not revel in the flouting of tradition or the status quo. Rather, it despairs of the enormities that erupt after legality and prohibition cease to be salient or become replaced by deformed parodies of law, as exemplified in Shalimar's murderous oath to kill Boonyi and Kachhwaha's legal maneuverings. The central figure of carnival offered up by the novel is Shalimar "the Clown," a superhumanly inventive terrorist, whereas pre-partition Kashmir, although idealized, serves as a symbol for "normalcy," a state to which the narrative invariably longs to return.

Those elements of carnival and magic that do populate the novel, moreover, primarily induce ethical quandaries. Rushdie's characters endowed with heightened, fantastical sensibilities do not find them exhilarating or productive but instead revolt against them. For instance, Max's daughter India is vested with powers of foresight; however, she labels them her "hallucinatory curse" and yearns instead to "inhabit facts, not dreams."[46] Insofar as India strives to keep "the strangeness of her seeing under control,"[47] she disciplines her gifts, in stark contrast to *Midnight's Children*'s Saleem Sinai, who instead mythologizes and profits from his telepathic vision. For India, fantasy's incursions into reality are unnerving rather than colorful embellishments or opportunities for empowerment. Likewise, exorbitant memories generate deleterious consequences for Kachhwaha, who experiences the casualties "of excessive remembering."[48] Kachhwaha is unable to forget anything he has seen or heard, and even when he sleeps chaotic images besiege him, so as in his head "the accumulation [of memories] grew every day more oppressive." He surmises about "what the long-term effect of so much remembering might be" and whether "there might be moral consequences" to his oppressive recollections.[49] Beyond jumbling his perceptions, Kachhwaha's neurological agony inspires his ruthless militarization of Kashmir. The burden of near-encyclopedic memory—a syndrome inscribed on many of Rushdie's novels—unhinges Kachhwaha's senses, and with them his moral barometer.

Perhaps of greatest importance, Shalimar's trial for murdering Max can be read as an allegory demonstrating the perils of aesthetic chimera and play. During the eighteen months that Shalimar awaits his hearing in prison, India is determined to avenge the deaths of her father Max and mother Boonyi (whom Shalimar also brutally kills). She sends Shalimar volumes of letters that "torture" him, making his "life a living hell."[50] The letters plague Shalimar psychologically, causing nightmares in which he "complain[s] about a female demon."[51] Consequently, they come to the attention of his attorney, who spins their existence into a smoothly concocted defense that resonates especially well with the temper of the times. Coining a new "diagnostic tool," the attorney claims that Shalimar was hypnotized into committing murder and therefore should be absolved of legal responsibility.[52] The attorney revealingly terms Shalimar's defense the "'sorcerer's' or 'Manchurian' defense"—an apparent allusion to the "magic" of magical realism and its diversionary tactics.[53] When the prosecuting attorney counters with a more prosaic explanation—"the vengeful husband theory"—for the jury "the plainness of the truth was suffering by comparison with [the] paranoid scenario, which was so perfectly attuned to the mood of the moment."[54] Again critiquing the media, here for its enthrallment with terror, the exotic mystique of magic obscures not only the banality of Shalimar's revenge but also the valid political outrage underlying his crimes.[55] It ultimately distracts the jury from murkier calculations of social justice, almost trivializing the actual dilemmas posed by terrorism.

Although India testifies and disabuses the jury of their illusions, Shalimar's defense can be read as something of a self-appraisal by Rushdie. By invoking "sorcery" to excuse Shalimar's actions, the novel evinces the anxiety that fantasy can become a "sorcerer's defense" that will obfuscate pressing matters, much as the seductive aura of magic in Shalimar's trial renders the truth mundane. While India exposes it to be an alluring hoax, *Shalimar* forewarns that the explanatory prism of fantasy risks obstructing issues that demand a different kind of scrutiny. Its sublime appeal in Shalimar's trial works to sensationalize his calculated violence, rather than to force an unmediated encounter with its sheer brutality. In short, employing "magic" to condone human behavior—in particular the legacy of human rights abuses within which Shalimar's actions are implicated—co-opts questions of individual agency and responsibility, undermining the expectation that people morally deliberate and are accountable for their crimes. Along with the jury's seduction by the "sorcerer's defense," we might wonder whether Rushdie, then, coyly self-recriminates for his own historic investment in the tantalizingly diversions of magic realism.

Shalimar the Clown is a novel preoccupied with human rights violations as well as the scope and tenor of their memorialization. While this concern may be characteristic of Rushdie's fiction, *Shalimar* approaches its subject matter with heightened circumspection, although its treatment of human rights remains overridingly ambivalent. On the one hand, the narrative self-consciously despairs of its own inability to incite humanitarian action. But on the other, it implies that there are limits to the types of realities, especially those involving egregious suffering, which can find full, comprehensive narrative representation. Indeed, *Shalimar* repeatedly suggests that unmediated experience is sufficiently contested and vertiginous on its own terms, which the dissimulation of magic only compounds. In the thoughts of a Kashmiri villager who discovers Boonyi's murdered body, from which her head has been severed, "the putrescent, flyblown reality of the world possessed a horrific force far in excess of any dream."[56] This impetus to confront the unadorned "reality of the world" is precisely what seems to compel *Shalimar*'s narrative and also to render abuses of human rights a source of such profound and troubling urgency. In this respect, it marks both an important departure for Rushdie as well as an invitation for his critics to contemplate the investment in human rights throughout his corpus, an inquiry that might shed new light on the humanist leanings of even the most "postmodern" of postcolonial fiction.

NOTES

1. Joseph R. Slaughter, "Narration in International Human Rights Law," *Comparative Literature and Culture* 9, no. 1 (2007). For a discussion of the furor over *The Satanic Verses* see Pinaki Chakravorty, "The Rushdie Incident as Law-and-Literature Parable," *The Yale Law Journal* 1048 (June 1995).
2. Linda Hutcheon, *A Poetics of Postmodernism* (New York: Routledge, 1988), 177.
3. Salman Rushdie, *Midnight's Children* (New York: Penguin, 1981), 5. Timothy Brennan's scholarship is a notable exception to this trend in that Brennan explicitly links the "disease of nationalism" to failures of human rights. See *Salman Rushdie and the Third World* (New York: St. Martin, 1989).
4. Michael Gorra, "'This Angrezi in which I am forced to write': On the Language of *Midnight's Children*," in Booker, 200.
5. Judith Butler, *Precarious Life: The Powers of Mourning and Violence* (New York: Verso, 2004); Kim Schaffer and Sidonie Smith, *Human Rights and Narrated Lives: The Ethics of Recognition* (New York: Palgrave, 2004).
6. Salman Rushdie, *Shalimar the Clown* (New York: Random House, 2005), 268. This is a rather common device in fiction about terrorism. For just two recent examples that attribute the terrorist's motives to the experience of personal injury, see Viken Berberien's *The Cyclist* (New York: Simon & Schuster, 2003) and Yasmina Khadra's *The Attack* (New York: Doubleday, 2005).
7. Rushdie, *Shalimar the Clown*, 270–272.
8. Rushdie, *Shalimar the Clown*, 333.
9. Rushdie, *Shalimar the Clown*, 356.
10. Schaffer and Smith, *Human Rights and Narrated Lives*, 156.
11. Ian Balfour and Eduardo Cadava describe such a phenomenon, namely that "the line of complicity between those who commit and enable such violence and those who claim to intervene against it increasingly has been effaced." "The Claims of Human Rights: An Introduction," *South Atlantic Quarterly* 103, no. 2/3 (Spring/Summer 2004): 288.
12. Rushdie, *Shalimar the Clown*, 96.
13. Rushdie, *Shalimar the Clown*, 290–291.
14. This tendency leads human rights to pose a "kind of legal imperialism, in which Western ideas and institutions take on an unhealthy prominence." Austin Sarat and Thomas Kearns, "The Unsettled Status of Human Rights: An Introduction," in *Human Rights*, ed. Sarat and Kearns (Ann Arbor: University of Michigan Press, 2001), 5.
15. Talal Asad, *Formations of the Secular: Christianity, Islam, Modernity* (Palo Alto, CA: Stanford University Press, 2003), 138.
16. Abdullahi A. An-Na'im, "The Legal Protection of Rights in Africa: How to Do More with Less," in *Human Rights: Concepts, Contests, Contingencies*, ed. Austin Sarat and Thomas R. Kearns (Ann Arbor: University of Michigan Press, 2001), 98.
17. Rushdie, *Shalimar the Clown*, 292.
18. Rushdie, *Shalimar the Clown*, 292–293.
19. For a discussion of how discourse can be manipulated to permit atrocity, see Jonathan Glover, *Humanity: A Moral History of the Twentieth Century* (New Haven, CT: Yale University Press, 1999).
20. Rushdie, *Shalimar the Clown*, 294.
21. Rushdie, *Shalimar the Clown*, 270–272.
22. Rushdie, *Shalimar the Clown*, 297.

23. A "lakh" is a numerical unit widely used in India that denotes one hundred thousand.
24. James Dawes explains: "Justice suggests clarity, completion, and proportion: x has been compensated by y. But the point of much of this literature is that we are caught in a terrible double-bind: we must seek recompense even though we know there can never be any recompense." In James Dawes, *That the World May Know: Bearing Witness to Atrocity* (Cambridge, MA: Harvard University Press, 2007), 195.
25. Rushdie, *Shalimar the Clown*, 308.
26. Rushdie, *Shalimar the Clown*, 309.
27. In a similar gesture, Chilean playwright Ariel Dorfman concludes his play *Death and the Maiden* (New York: Penguin, 1991) by lowering a giant mirror before the stage, thereby forcing the audience to look at their own reflections.
28. Shoshana Felman and Dori Laub, M.D., *Testimony: Crises of Witnessing in Literature, Psychoanalysis, and History* (New York: Routledge, 1992), 57.
29. Felman and Laub, *Testimony*, 5, 197.
30. Graham Huggan, *The Postcolonial Exotic: Marketing the Margins* (New York and London: Routledge, 2001), 33.
31. David Spurr, *The Rhetoric of Empire: Colonial Discourse in Journalism, Travel Writing, and Imperial Administration* (Durham, NC: Duke University Press, 1993), 142.
32. Dawes, *That the World May Know*, 34.
33. Rushdie, *Shalimar the Clown*, 197–198.
34. Rushdie, *Shalimar the Clown*, 196.
35. Rushdie, *Shalimar the Clown*, 206.
36. Rushdie, *Shalimar the Clown*, 27.
37. Anurandha Disngwaney Needham explains that, "according to Rushdie, the writer functions as a natural rival of the politician; like the politician, he tries to make the world in his own image, competing for the same territory." See "The Politics of Post-Colonial Identity in Salman Rushdie," in *Reading Rushdie: Perspectives on the Fiction of Salman Rushdie*, ed. D. M. Fletcher (Amsterdam: Rodopi, 1994), 155.
38. See Salman Rushdie, *Imaginary Homelands* (New York: Penguin, 1982) and *Step Across this Line: Collected Nonfiction 1992–2002* (New York: Modern Library, 2003).
39. For example, Tariq Ali labeled Rushdie one of the "belligerati" apologizing for U.S. actions post-9/11.
40. Lois Parkinson Zamora and Wendy B. Faris, "Introduction: Daiquiri Birds and Flaubertian Parrot(ie)s," in *Magical Realism: Theory History Community*, ed. Zamora and Faris (Durham, NC: Duke University Press, 1995).
41. Roger Y. Clark, *Stranger Gods: Salman Rushdie's Other Worlds* (Montreal: McGill-Queen's, 2001), 20. Similarly, Wendy B. Faris understands the magical realist approach to "question received ideas about time, space, and identity." "Scheherazade's Children: Magical Realism and Postmodern Fiction," in Zamora and Faris, 173.
42. Zamora and Faris, eds., *Magical Realism* (New York: Routledge, 2004), 66.
43. See Stephen Slemon, "Magical Realism as Postcolonial Discourse," in Zamora and Faris, 410.
44. We should remember that Rushdie himself takes liberties within the historical record to bolster the novel's strident politics.

164   *Elizabeth S. Anker*

45. Philip Engblom, "A Multitude of Voices: Carnivalization and Dialogicality in the Novels of Salman Rushdie," in *Reading Rushdie: Perspectives of the Fiction of Salman Rushdie*, ed. D. M. Fletcher (Amsterdam: Rodopi, 1994), 296.
46. Rushdie, *Shalimar the Clown*, 12.
47. Rushdie, *Shalimar the Clown*, 5–6.
48. Rushdie, *Shalimar the Clown*, 122.
49. Rushdie, *Shalimar the Clown*, 97.
50. Rushdie, *Shalimar the Clown*, 373.
51. Rushdie, *Shalimar the Clown*, 374.
52. Rushdie, *Shalimar the Clown*, 382.
53. Rushdie, *Shalimar the Clown*, 384.
54. Rushdie, *Shalimar the Clown*, 384.
55. We must note that such "psychological diagnostics" often mask contemporary racism, as Gayatri Spivak argues with reference to terrorism. See "Terror: A Speech After 9–11," *boundary2* 31, no. 2 (Summer 2004): 91–92.
56. Rushdie, *Shalimar the Clown*, 366.

9 Complicities of Witnessing in Joe Sacco's *Palestine*

Wendy Kozol

In early January 2009, Israel denied international journalists access to Gaza during three weeks of missile attacks against the region. News correspondents wearing flak jackets instead stood on bluffs overlooking the desert landscape with Gaza in the distance as they reported on the escalating death toll among civilians and the rising scarcity of food and medical supplies. Far from the violence, it was not clear why they were wearing flak jackets other than to signify that they were putting themselves at risk in a war zone to bring this urgent human rights crisis to the world's attention.[1] With limited images of the devastation circulating outside of the Arab world, western news media's conventional reliance on the intrepid war correspondent as an intermediary figure between the viewer and victims of war became even more apparent. This distancing mechanism structures the figure of identification as the recognizable face of the "trustworthy" reporter rather than the subjects of the news story. Equally pressing, framing human rights violations through the perspective of the western observer, as Elizabeth Swanson Goldberg demonstrates, too readily positions the west, and especially the U.S., as saviors devoid of complicity in the economic, political, and social conditions that produce such violence.[2]

In the graphic narrative, *Palestine*, Joe Sacco takes up this framing mechanism in his trenchant critique of western media coverage of human rights crises.[3] The book employs close-ups, point of view shots, and other techniques familiar from documentary photography and film to represent imprisonment, torture, and violent death as well as the daily struggles of Palestinians under Israeli occupation during the first *intifada* (1987–1993). One remarkable episode, for instance, visualizes the memories of a Palestinian tortured in an Israeli prison. As the violence intensifies, each panel gets smaller and more claustrophobic, drawing the viewer into the man's experience. Yet, framing devices also remind the viewer that this memory is itself a doubly mediated representation by both the informant and the narrator. Elsewhere, Sacco foregrounds the careerist objectives of the reporter who will do almost anything for a story. Through such strategies, *Palestine*

addresses the ethical challenges embedded in reporters' search for documentary evidence of human rights violations.

Far from being distinct entities, the intertwining of human rights advocacy and mainstream news media has been crucial to public awareness about
humanitarian crises, or what Luc Boltanski refers to as "distant suffering."[4]
Human rights and media scholars have long debated whether television,
photojournalism, and other visual media have the potential to mobilize
empathy and action or if they simply produce spectacles that lack the critical insights necessary to foster political engagement. Many insist that the
experience of seeing individual suffering can motivate viewers to move
beyond personal or national self-interest to encourage political activism.
On the other side, social critics have long decried mainstream news reporting for its voyeurism and promotion of hegemonic politics.[5] Furthermore,
John Taylor argues that codes of respectability result in self-censorship by
mainstream media outlets that limit and distort the flow of information.[6]
The urgent need to publicize violent acts must be reconciled with the risks
of creating spectacles of suffering, especially since state-sanctioned violence
persists unabated, often in full public view, as in Darfur, Sudan, today.

Scholars often define witnessing as politically engaged practices distinct
from media portrayals characterized by a focus on violent spectacle. Such
claims presume that the spectator gazes passively at violence, whereas the
witness undertakes an ethical look that mobilizes the viewer's sense of
responsibility. Central to these concepts of witnessing is a faith in certain
acts of looking as ethically engaged and able to resist spectacularization.
Anne Cubilie, for instance, argues that spectatorship "may engage our
emotions, even our guilt, but . . . does not impel us toward intervention."
In contrast she defines witnessing as a "difficult and more active engagement . . . [that] works to (re)build structures of responsibility and ethics."[7]
If, however, witnessing is about engagement, and not passive viewing, what
kinds of representations enable action?

In order to address that question, we need to consider how visual practices
are structured by various factors of production, circulation, and reception.
As Boltanski asks, "on what conditions is the spectacle of distant suffering
brought to us by the media morally acceptable?"[8] How, in other words, do
commercial interests, institutional resources, historical discourses about the
Middle East, and the social locations of the reporter and the viewer shape
public perceptions of the Israel–Palestine conflict? While all these factors
are key to understanding how visual cultures mobilize different emotional
and political reactions, the methodological focus of this chapter centers
on representational strategies themselves to consider the formal elements
that structure the witnessing gaze. Through visual and narrative analysis
of *Palestine*, I explore the possibilities for ethical spectatorship, that is,
forms of representation that foreground the dialogic interactions between
ethical looking and the role of spectacle in transnational visual witnessing
of human rights crises.[9]

The point here is not to seek alternatives that may be devoid of voyeurism and thus offer a more truthful or transparent reportage (a rather impossible ideal) but instead to seek out representational forms that engage with the challenges of viewing human rights crises. Sacco confronts this problematic directly through his self-mockery of the intrepid western male reporter while also disrupting the "politics of pity" endemic to much media coverage.[10] Notably, complex representations of gender challenge Orientalist narratives that figure Muslim men as terrorists and veiled women as subjugated. In varied ways, *Palestine* provides a pedagogical model of ethical spectatorship that grapples with the urgent need to make human rights violations visible to international communities while recognizing how representations depend on gendered and racialized spectacles of violence for their commercial and humanitarian currency.

NEWS MEDIA AND HUMAN RIGHTS WITNESSING

Palestine follows the reporter's journey from Egypt to Jerusalem to the Occupied Territories as he collects information on the *intifada* for his "comic book."[11] Significantly, throughout the text Sacco depicts the narrator without eyes behind his black-framed eyeglasses to highlight his avatar's role as a voyeur. This visual reference to the media's myopic perspective on the Israel–Palestinian conflict persistently calls attention to the privileged perspective of the outside observer.

Complying with the "fair and balanced" model of mainstream news media, the reporter interviews American Jewish tourists, Israeli citizens and soldiers, Palestinians, and human rights workers with the aim of obtaining "authentic" firsthand accounts of the *intifada*. The Israeli occupation of the West Bank and Gaza after the 1967 war led, by the early 1980s, to increased resistance by Palestinian opposition groups and greater repression by the Israeli Defense Force (IDF). The *intifada* began as a series of civil disobedience actions ranging from the refusal to pay taxes to strikes by local merchants and street demonstrations. As the IDF attempted to control the opposition, stone throwing (a hallmark of this first *intifada*) and other street violence escalated along with injuries and deaths.[12] While providing space and voice to Israeli security concerns at the beginning and end of the book, most of *Palestine* takes place in the West Bank and Gaza. Palestinian translators take the reporter into homes, schools, and hospitals, where people tell him their stories of physical deprivation, destruction of property, economic struggle, and woefully inadequate conditions, as well as experiences of arrests, torture, and imprisonment. As bookends to these stories, Sacco interviews Israelis about their security concerns, and they display little recognition of conditions in the Occupied Territories.

Ethnographic details of life under Occupation repeatedly appear alongside the reporter's flippant comments about stories of suffering being "good for the comic."[13] Comic books have historically been associated with children's reading practices, and often dismissed as trivial or ephemeral. This emphasis on genre reminds the reader of the mediated nature of representations of suffering as well as the commercial spectacle of media reportage.[14] Since most viewers observe human rights violations from a distance, they remain dependent on the media for information. In this regard, witnesses to human rights violations are implicated in the problematic gaze of western reportage. How, then, to produce an ethical gaze? In attempting to address the challenge of witnessing the devastations of war, Kyo Maclear defines ethical vision as the "tension between the desire to 'know' something about the subject being represented . . . and recognition of the limits of that knowing."[15] She defines ethical vision as a "fraught process of understanding our complicity and responsibility to witness, to interpret, to act, towards the cessation of violence and oppression."[16] Maclear's compelling argument that ethics resides in the recognition of the limits of vision makes reference to complicity and responsibility in witnessing.

Building upon Maclear's insights, I argue that Sacco's critical gaze grapples with the ethical complexities of the news as a form of witnessing. Notably, *Palestine* engages directly with explicit demands for visibility prevalent in human rights discourse through the reporter's efforts to accumulate evidence. As the narrator says, "I'm there, spending consecutive Saturday mornings waiting for something else to happen . . . something dicier. . . . A comic needs some bangbang and I'm praying Ramallah will deliver."[17] Not unexpectedly, subsequent scenes of a protest fulfill the reporter's desire. Panels of varying sizes feature close-up shots of angry Palestinian faces and distance shots of soldiers from the IDF confronting crowds with semi-automatic weapons and batons.

Depicting human rights crises through the gaze of an intermediary western figure is a representational convention used in human rights literature, advocacy groups' appeals to contributors and, of course, Hollywood.[18] Films ranging from *The Year of Living Dangerously* to *The Killing Fields* feature sympathetic, mostly male, Americans who risk their lives to report on human rights crises resulting from state violence against its citizens. As Goldberg insightfully argues, "the reins of the story, which constitute its narrative point of view, are wrenched from the historic actors and handed to a privileged western observer/participant, resulting in the illusion that there is no story—no historic event—unless it is witnessed, shaped, and experienced by western agents."[19]

Writing the reporter into the narrative enables Sacco to confront the western rescue narrative that structures such forms of witnessing. Significantly, attention to identity, including citizenship, race, and gender renders the witnessing gaze a problematic and often exploitative one. Encounters with angry Palestinian youths, staying out after curfew, carrying contraband videos, or simply being mistaken for a Palestinian by Israeli soldiers, all create situations of danger for the reporter. In these scenes, he appears shivering, sweating, and/or trembling with fear. At one point, the reporter and Sameh, one of his translators, are out past curfew carrying a clandestine videotape of Israeli brutality. Sacco is visibly nervous as he says, "One could be mistaken for a Palestinian out here."[20] Mocking this "inadequate" masculine response to fear—not to mention the emphasis on the mobility provided by his passport—self-referentially critiques the gender, racial, and national privileges typically accorded the western war correspondent.

Unlike linear conventions of journalism, Sacco deftly utilizes graphic narrative strategies of varied actions and multiple text boxes on the same page. In an episode about a street protest, for instance, the first two pages show Israeli military arriving with tear gas and batons. The largest text box moves from the gutter in the upper right of the two-page spread toward the bottom left in a dramatic diagonal that gains in size as it reaches the border of the page. Other text boxes are scattered around the two pages with no clear narrative path. Here, the visual and textual movement in the scene recreates the emotional intensity of protestors clashing with soldiers or police. On the next page, close-ups of women's angry faces and text boxes with "screaming" words next to an Israeli soldier with a baton cutting through the middle of the composition intensify this chaotic energy. Shifts in pacing occur between panels with extensive text and pages with multiple scenes and/or points of view that have no apparent order. The lack of guidance forces the reader into an active engagement with the decision-making practices of reading. Hillary Chute argues that politically oriented graphic narratives confront the problematics of historical representation through disruptions and reconfigurations of narrative elements; "it is precisely in its insistent, affective, urgent visualizing of historical circumstance that comics aspires to ethical engagement."[21]

The news reporter's obsession with getting the story, rather than empathy for the suffering of his interviewees, expands Sacco's commentary on the media to include criticism of the commodity value of human rights photographs. Repeatedly, the narrator appears as a consuming tourist avidly collecting pictures of suffering. In an episode about the killing of two young boys by IDF soldiers, close-ups feature relatives' anguished faces, along with a grueling high angle shot of the two boys' dead and dying bodies. A text panel emphasizes the reporter's acquisitive desire when he says, "I'm a skeptic. Journalistically speaking, you gotta be a Doubting Thomas: you gotta make sure. It's good to get your finger in the wound. Your whole head would be better." Asking a photojournalist if he got the picture of the baby with the very large head whose mother when pregnant had become sick from tear gas, he comments, "Man, I wish I'd seen the soldiers firing tear gas . . . wish I'd seen that baby."[22] Here, *Palestine* addresses the ways in which western visual witnessing of human rights abuses is deeply imbricated in commercial imperatives for violent spectacles that structure contemporary news reportage.

Sacco's incisive critique of the media contains a deep ambivalence about the value of the media gaze. Palestinians in the book seek out the publicity provided by the reporter even as they recognize his more exploitative motives. Acknowledging the power of reportage to publicize human rights violations resonates with the stated objectives of other war correspondents and human rights activists who employ visual culture as part of their oppositional practices. James Natchway, for instance, makes this point forcefully in the 2002 documentary, *War Photographer*, when he states that he could not do his work without the compliance of the subjects who themselves recognize the importance of visual culture in gaining world attention to their situations.[23] *Palestine*, however, more directly confronts the vexed politics of visibility. For instance, a Gazan woman challenges the reporter's objectives after finishing a wrenching narrative about the deaths of two sons during a conflict between soldiers and civilians in Rafa. Through the translator Sameh, she asks the reporter "What good is it to talk with you? . . . She wants to know how talking to you is going to help her. We don't want money, she says, we want our land, our humanity."[24] The reporter's attempts to justify his presence sound unconvincing and trite, ultimately leaving these provocative questions unanswered. This is, however, no absolute condemnation since Sameh also translates that the woman has talked to many other reporters.

Ambivalence calls into question the binary opposition between passive spectactorship and witnessing as "active engagement" claimed by Cubilie and others. Instead, *Palestine* provides a form of ethical spectatorship that grapples with the irresolvable conundrum of visibility by depicting witnesses as spectators complicit with the violence. Unfortunately, Sacco does not explicitly address U.S. military, political, and economic support of Israel nor consider other regional and global factors contributing to this ongoing conflict. While he attends to media complicity, and by extension the viewer's, *Palestine* offers only a muted commentary on the role of citizenship in the witnessing gaze.

SEEING THE OCCUPATION

Sacco's focus on western media raises concerns about solipsism, since this clearly runs the danger of a relentless focus on the self. After all, even critique can be a way of reinvigorating western hegemony whereby the non-western other never gains subjectivity. One temptation, then, is to turn to the victims themselves who, presumably, can provide truthful accounts to counteract the western gaze. Yet, here too, we need to be cautious about desires to seek "better" or more authentic representations of human rights violations. Postcolonial and transnational feminist theorists have sought to navigate between the imperative to give voice to subaltern women's experiences and the problematics of essentialism. Rey Chow, for instance, warns against too quick a turn to the authentic survivor, the "passive victim on display."[25] She criticizes the use of "history" and "representation" as avenues to find the authentic other, arguing that such impulses continue to prioritize the colonial gaze by assuming a static and monolithic Third World figure. As Chow suggests, the search for the authentic subject may be more about "enriching ourselves precisely with what can be called the surplus value of the oppressed."[26]

Reliance on a native informant has long been the means by which westerners, from news reporters to anthropologists and feminists, have sought access to knowledge about the Third World.[27] A prominent news convention, for instance, relies on an individual or family as a metonym for collective suffering. In contrast, Sacco expands the ethnographic frame to include numerous voices and experiences, ranging from a despondent elderly street peddler to a young woman holding a baby while making racist pronouncements about Israelis. Unlikeable Palestinians, in particular, help to avoid romanticizing victimhood endemic to some documentary traditions. Significantly, though, individuals rarely appear on the page alone. Instead, Sacco conveys the scale of Palestinian struggles and resistance through interviews that almost always take place in collective settings, usually around a tea or coffee circle. Groups listening to a storyteller provide a visual equivalent of *testimonios* whereby speakers articulate collective experiences of trauma and resistance.[28] Moreover, Sacco hardly ever witnesses violence himself except for street protests; instead, storytellers recount their memories of arrests, abuse, and deaths. Multiple stories with shifting points of view jostle each other as does the emotional range from anger to grief to introspection.[29] In sharing narrative authority, Sacco both undercuts the privileged perspective of the observer and emphasizes the personal and collective nature of human rights struggles.

Along with interviews, *Palestine* includes lengthy historical explanations of Zionism, crippling economic practices by Israelis such as road closures and the destruction of olive trees, and other historical information reminiscent of voiceovers in documentary film. Mini–history lessons force the reader to a slow pace unexpected in a graphic novel. As Chute argues, the density of information in *Palestine*, along with the "disjunctive back-and-forth between looking and reading," slows down the rhythm of reading, producing what Edward Said calls Sacco's "power to detain."[30] At the same time, detailed handwritten texts "lend a subjective register to the narrative surface" to emphasize the mediated nature of the historical record.[31]

This "power to detain," coupled with varied depictions of Palestinians' experiences, fosters nuanced portraits of people living under Occupation. Rather than focus solely on victimization, Sacco's attention to gender identity and gender politics addresses how the interconnections of agency, resistance, regulation, and violence shape subjectivity. Perhaps expectedly, he depicts women most often either silently serving food or as mothers narrating stories about the violent deaths of their children. Alongside these images, though, women appear in public spaces claiming rights, confronting soldiers on the street, and struggling to maintain households. On the opening page of Chapter Three, for instance, Palestinian women and children march down the street during a protest. Viewed from a low angle, the women appear as if they are moving into the viewer's space. A low angle of view emphasizes, even distorts, their mouths, heads and feet, which seem overly large, strong and intimidating. In an interesting gender reversal, Sacco and his photographer friend, Saburo, appear small and insignificant in the background. Here, the visuals complicate textual explanations about the often-futile struggle of Palestinian protests by emphasizing these women's resistance and courage in confronting the IDF.

Women's fierce protection of their children and willingness to protest in public undermines the logic of Orientalism that presumes that Muslim women live in a premodern, oppressive, patriarchal society.[32] Palestinian feminists in the Occupied Territories made headway within resistance movements in the 1970s, but the *intifada*, as Frances Hasso demonstrates, was a turning point for feminist activism. "As mass-based and nonviolent popular resistance organizations were increasingly weakened by a repressive Israeli state, women and girls lost significant ground on the streets and in national agenda setting."[33] Despite positive depictions by journalists at the time, male political leaders provided little beyond verbal assurances that a future Palestinian state would give women equal suffrage and access to state resources.

Chapter Five confronts western misperceptions about Islamic women's rights and religious practices. In a four-page story on the Palestinian Federation of Women's Action Committees, for instance, feminist activists address the multiple challenges they face in working for women's rights within the context of a national resistance movement. In this episode, alternating panels contrast feminists in contemporary clothing in an office setting with scenes of women in traditional dress harvesting crops. Modernity and tradition are visualized side by side as activists talk about the challenges facing them. Rather than privilege modernity, an Islamic woman offers a feminist interpretation of Muslim doctrine on women's rights. Sacco, moreover, astutely represents Palestinian feminists' concerns about the danger of repeating anti-colonial histories in which male resistance leaders made promises to women activists, only to betray them in postcolonial governments.[34]

Increased repression by Israeli forces during the *intifada*, including school closures, curfews, and road closures, led to greater restrictions on Palestinian women's and girls' mobility. In the early 1990s, violence against women intensified as religious groups like Hamas attempted to impose a moral code to restrict women's political and social activities, efforts that sometimes led to physical violence and even murder. As the *intifada* continued, a "culture of modesty" increasingly took hold and by the early 1990s, Islamic leaders had initiated the *"hijab"* campaign in Gaza that aimed to impose the veil on all women in public.[35] This is a challenging subject to represent to American audiences with a long history of Orientalist assumptions about Islamic attitudes toward gender and sexuality.[36] Sacco wades into this difficult terrain, using the narrator as the foil for western assumptions, such as when he expresses surprise at the political astuteness of a veiled woman.[37] A discussion between Sacco and several Muslim women about the veil repositions the debate between modernity and tradition to one of competing secular and religious beliefs. Text panels discuss efforts by Hamas and other Islamic militant factions to impose the veil and the narrator's observation that he saw no women on the streets without one. At the same time, women tell him about their pride in wearing the *hijab* and their negative responses to western women's apparel. In one panel, a group of women all wear *hijabs*, yet each woman's clothing has different patterns that visually challenge western assumptions that veiling denies individuation. Again, the reporter's voice does not trump the women with a voice-over that asserts an authoritative perspective. Instead, whether framed as a contrast between tradition and modernity or religion and secularism, this chapter emphasizes Palestinian women's diverse subjectivities without denying the political forces pressuring women.

Complex portraits of Palestinian masculinity also challenge western understandings of the goals, desires, and political objectives of Palestinians. Pictures of young boys throwing rocks at soldiers certainly visualize popular notions of Arab masculinity, but alongside that more familiar view of the *intifada* are nuanced characterizations of other forms of masculinity.

Of all the figures that populate this book, Sameh, one of Sacco's translators and guides, is the most extensively rendered character. Notably his generosity toward Sacco and his concern for the suffering of other Palestinians contrasts with the reporter's rapacious consumption of misery. The tone and style shift noticeably in Chapters Seven and Eight about Gaza City, where Sameh lives.[38] The flippancy of the reporter's earlier commentary has lessened, and there are no more extensive written commentaries. Few words appear on each page that instead features scenes of poverty, decrepit housing, endless rain, and mud-filled streets. The emotional bleakness of these pages affectively resonates throughout this section. Significantly, Sameh's desire to become a teacher and his commitment to others underscore his humanness amidst and against the degradations and humiliations of the Occupation. His affective significance for the book is most notable in scenes where he translates painful interviews. At one point, Sacco turns from a woman describing the excruciating loss of a son to a close-up of Sameh with tears in his eyes.[39] Sameh's willingness to endure physical and emotional hardships to help the reporter challenges the victim/hero dichotomy of conventional masculinity often associated with conflict zones.

Chapter Eight contrasts this portrait of Sameh with two poignant episodes, Boys, and Boys II, about young men in Gaza who have limited options for schooling and work and instead seek ways to defy the occupying forces. Heroic masculinity here comes under scrutiny in a painful story about a boy who ends up in a wheelchair after being shot by the IDF. At first hailed as a hero, his insistence that the other boys still respect him echoes painfully in the last panel that depicts him isolated from his peers. Juxtaposing heroism with the quotidian conditions of living as a disabled person in an environment without material and psychological resources acutely highlights the crushing impact of life in a militarized zone. Rather than "icons of outrage,"[40] *Palestine* features the daily humiliations and struggles for people living under occupation to refute the image of inexplicable terrorism that dominates mainstream news reporting on the *intifada*.

Sacco's relentless focus on the depravations of the Occupation leads not to romanticizing the oppressed but to an exploration of the devastating impacts of oppression and subjugation. Toward the end of the book where the tone gets even bleaker, one of the last scenes demonstrates the efficacy of ethical spectatorship. A stunning visualization of the centrality of violence in the formation of Palestinian subjectivity occurs in an episode in which three Israeli soldiers stop a teenage boy in the street. While they stand underneath a shelter, they force the boy to remove his *keffiyah* and stand in the rain while they interrogate him. Gone is the earlier sarcasm as Sacco says, "if I'd guessed before I got here, and found with little astonishment once I'd arrived what can happen to someone who thinks he has all the power, what of this—what becomes of someone when he believes himself to have none?"[41] The by-now familiar visual strategy of close-ups and high angle perspectives positions the viewer's gaze from behind the dry head of the Israeli soldier looking down at the face of the young boy with rain beating down on him.

Subsequent panels visualize power and powerlessness through contrasting gazes. The top panel takes its perspective from behind the boy's head as he looks upward toward three soldiers who form a wall blocking the background. Most of the soldiers' heads are cut off in the framing of the picture so that only their tough, angry mouths are visible. The reporter comments that "the boy stood there and answered their questions, and what choice did he have." The middle picture then shifts perspective to look directly at his face with gritted teeth and one eye closed against the rain. Beyond such looming obstacles as the status of Jerusalem and the future of the settlements, the reporter comments, is the boy with few hopes for the future. The perspective of the final panel shifts back to that of one of the soldiers looking down on the boy, who now appears small and vulnerable. Shifting gazes destabilize a privileged subjectivity, instead visualizing how factors of citizenship, gender, and age shape the political experiences of people on both sides of this conflict. Importantly, the only person in this scene with a face is the boy. He may be powerless, but he does not lack agency for, as Sacco suggests, what he is thinking takes us into an unknown future. Through shifting perspectives, the gaze also draws the viewer into a complicit position of witnessing the boy's humiliation in a scene at the end of the book that offers no satisfying closure.

GAZING AT TORTURE

Nowhere is the tension between the human rights imperative for evidentiary images and the dangers of spectacle more apparent than in visual representations of torture. Rather than turn away from torture, or claim its unrepresentability, as Chute argues, Sacco uses graphic narrative to present the "traumatic side of history." Like other graphic artists such as Art Spigelman, Alison Bechdel, and Marjane Satrapi, he refuses the claim of "unspeakability or invisibility, instead registering its difficulty through inventive (and various) textual practice."[42] One of the most remarkable episodes in the book visually depicts the costs of withstanding sustained violence to the body. A twelve-page narrative features a Palestinian man named Ghassan who was jailed by the IDF and tortured for several weeks. The episode begins with quarter-page pictures of children running around Ghassan's living room and then his youngest daughter falling asleep on his lap. As he narrates his experience of arrest, imprisonment, and ever-intensifying torture, the panels shift temporally back to the events. Rectangular panels framed in black and reminiscent of a photographic contact sheet get smaller and smaller as the story of torture unfolds. The affective contrast between the living room and the torture cell as well as the visual framing of torture through ever-smaller panels locates the narrative as a memoryscape rather than a transcription.

Visibilities and invisibilities that structure public and private spaces here become locations of different brutalities. Beginning with a half-page picture of the IDF entering Ghassan's home in the middle of the night, followed by two quarter-page pictures of him blindfolded and handcuffed, the number of panels per page changes from six to nine to twelve to sixteen to twenty. This layout intensifies the sense of claustrophobia as Ghassan remembers the acute pain brought on by various abusive tactics. Human Rights Watch (HRW) claims that over 100,000 Palestinians were detained by the IDF between 1987 and 1993 and estimates that thousands were abused during interrogation. Sacco visualizes many of the IDF's interrogation tactics, as described by HRW, including rigid physical constraints that force prisoners into painful body positions; psychological pressure; food and sleep deprivation; the use of blindfolds and hoods; and physical beatings.[43]

Small panels that feature close-ups of Ghassan's cell encourage an intimate gaze at his tortured body. As he huddles in a corner, the gaze from above emphasizes his vulnerability. The hood over his face denying him a subjective perspective turns Ghassan into an object of suffering. At one point he starts to hallucinate that his daughter lies dead next to him on the urine-soaked floor. Framing and point of view distance the reporter and reader who are not in the cell, and who are not cold, sleep-deprived, or in pain. The visual perspective from a high angle along with the hood over his face means that many of the visualizations of torture are not from Ghassan's perspective. The imperative to "look" at human rights crimes that typically go on behind closed doors here confronts the voyeurism that structures this gaze. This spectacle of suffering does more, however, than provide another opportunity to stare at the faceless victim who has no visual subjectivity or agency. Instead, a dual point of view contrasts the reporter and viewer's gaze from above with Ghassan's own words told in first person.[44] Even the depiction of his hallucination speaks to his subjective desires that are socially specific, thereby refusing to put him in a universalizing category of victimization.

Sacco's complex form of ethical spectatorship calls to mind Dominick LaCapra's concept of empathetic unsettlement, which he defines as a form of witnessing that does not appropriate the experience of the other but rather, through the "radical ambivalence of clear-cut positions," attends to the "problem of the relation between the past and the present."[45] As La Capra explains, empathetic unsettlement "comes with respect for the other and the realization that the experience of the other is not one's own."[46] In *Palestine*, this refusal to claim the experience of another emerges through the dual perspective of Ghassan's narrative and Sacco's visuals, themselves both temporally removed from the actual events. Troubling viewers' desire to "know" the other, to be intimate with suffering by emphasizing processes of mediation produces a distancing effect in which viewers must recognize that we cannot know or take the other's place.

Rather than turn away from images of suffering because of the danger of dehumanization, Sacco confronts the necessity of visual representations of torture by reminding the reader of the politics of in/visibility. After Ghassan is finally released due to a lack of evidence, three smaller panels show him sequentially getting into a car in a crowded street, the car driving off, and then the car farther in the background of a crowded urban street. In the last half-page picture, the car can no longer be identified. This last panel elides Ghassan's horrific experiences as people walk about in this public setting intent upon their own concerns. Invisibility in this final scene recalls Sacco's opening comment for this chapter:

> Make no mistake, everywhere you go, not just in Marvel Comics, there's parallel universes. . . . Here? On the surface streets: traffic, couples in love, falafel-to-go, tourists in jogging suits, licking stamps for postcards. . . . And over the wall behind closed doors: other things— people strapped to chairs, sleep deprivation, the smell of piss . . . other things happening for "reasons of national security."[47]

Human rights advocates' calls for visibility seem warranted here in light of these "parallel universes," and yet by this point the reader has been made well aware of the risks of spectacularizing suffering.

HUMAN RIGHTS AND THE DILEMMA OF VISIBILITY

As I wrote this chapter at the end of January 2009, a temporary Israeli–Palestinian cease-fire has begun, but one image stood out to me among the many available pictures of death and destruction. A week into the Israeli offensive in Gaza, on 5 January 2009, various media outlets published a video and photo stills of Palestinian Wael Samouni collapsing in grief at the sight of his three very young children dead on the floor of the morgue.[48] They look like they are asleep except for the bandage wrapped around the middle child's head and the bloodstained clothing. This deeply disturbing image circulated internationally and provoked many calls for an end to this humanitarian disaster. Yet, it also raises questions about the ethics of exposing intense grief and suffering. Do news media have the necessary political and ethical tools to handle an image like this with the insight and care we would hope to have if the image depicted our loved ones?

Here, it might seem appropriate to argue that given the commercial imperatives structuring current news practices, it is difficult, if not impossible, to represent the effects of violence or trauma without turning victims into spectacles. I reject this argument for two reasons. First, there is a danger in not looking. Too often, looking away accompanies a refusal to acknowledge or to act upon knowledge about what is done to people in the name of the nation. Without such images, it seems hard to imagine what strategies would generate the ethical and political energies required to mobilize against human rights crimes. Second, visual news practices are proliferating in various arenas today and even within constraining commercial imperatives, photographers, videographers, filmmakers, and graphic artists have wide latitude to produce a range of visual imagery. Rather than turn away from trauma, Sacco's graphic narrative provides a visual and textual model for ethical witnessing that never loses sight of its own complicity. As *Palestine* demonstrates, transnational human rights witnessing must confront the politics of the gaze, not to find ready-made understandings but to recognize the ethical *and* spectacular interactions in visual acts of looking.

NOTES

1. Chris McGreal, "Ban on Foreign Journalists Skews Coverage of Conflict," *The Guardian,* January 10, 2009, http://www.guardian.co.uk/world/2009/jan/10/gaza-israel-reporters-foreign-journalists. Both *al-Jazeera* and *al-Arabiya* continued to broadcast from Gaza throughout the crisis, and western media did circulate some of that footage.
2. Elizabeth Swanson Goldberg, *Beyond Terror: Gender, Narrative, Human Rights* (New Brunswick, NJ: Rutgers University Press, 2007), esp. chaps. 1 and 2.
3. Joe Sacco, *Palestine* (Seattle: Fantagraphic Books, 2001). Originally published as nine issues of a comic book series beginning in 1993, it received the

American Book Award in 1996. The collection was reissued as a single book in 2001 with a foreword by Edward W. Said.

4. Luc Boltanski, *Distant Suffering: Morality, Media, and Politics*, trans. Graham Burchell (Cambridge: Cambridge University Press, 1999), 173–178.

5. For two recent perspectives on this debate, see David Campbell, "Horrific Blindness: Images of Death in Contemporary Media," *Journal for Cultural Research* 8, no. 1 (January 2004): 55–74; and Rosalind C. Morris, "Images of Untranslatability in the US War on Terror," *interventions* 6, no. 3 (2004): 401–423. Susan Sontag's last work, *Regarding the Pain of Others* (New York: Farrar, Straus and Giroux, 2003), also addresses this debate.

6. John Taylor, *Body Horror: Photojournalism, Catastrophe, and War* (New York: New York University Press, 1998).

7. Anne Cubilié, *Women Witnessing Terror: Testimony and the Cultural Politics of Human Rights* (New York: Fordham University Press, 2005), 218.

8. Boltanski, *Distant Suffering*, xv.

9. See Ariella Azoulay, *The Civil Contract of Photography*, trans. Rela Mazali and Ruvik Danieli (New York: Zone Books, 2008) who uses this term to address ethical viewing, although she does not explore the politics of spectacle in the ways I call for here.

10. See Boltanski, *Distant Suffering*, 3–19.

11. See Hillary Chute, "Comics as Literature? Reading Graphic Narrative," *PMLA: Publications of the Modern Language Association of America* 123, no. 2 (Sept. 2008).

12. Frances Susan Hasso, *Resistance, Repression, and Gender Politics in Occupied Palestine and Jordan* (Syracuse, NY: Syracuse University Press, 2005), 119; and Human Rights Watch, "Torture and Ill-Treatment: Israel's Interrogation of Palestinians from the Occupied Territories," June 1, 1994, http://www.hrw.org/legacy/reports/1994/israel/.

13. Sacco, *Palestine*, 217.

14. See also Edward Said, "Introduction: Homage to Joe Sacco," in Sacco, *Palestine*, i–ii.

15. Kyo Maclear, "The Limits of Vision: Hiroshima Mon Amour and the Subversion of Representation," in *Witness and Memory: The Discourse of Trauma*, eds. Ana Douglass and Thomas A. Vogler (New York: Routledge, 2003), 234.

16. Maclear, "Limits of Vision," 247.

17. Sacco, *Palestine*, 118.

18. See e.g., Patrice McDermott and Amy Farrell, "Claiming Afghan Women: The Challenge of Human Rights Discourse for Transnational Feminism," in *Just Advocacy: Women's Human Rights, Transnational Feminism, and the Politics of Representation*, ed. W. Hesford and W. Kozol (New Brunswick, NJ: Rutgers University Press, 2005), 33–55, for a critique of American feminists' use of this rescue narrative.

19. Goldberg, *Beyond Terror*, 32.

20. Sacco, *Palestine*, 212.

21. Chute, "Comics as Literature?" 457; see also Gillian Whitlock, "Autographics: the Seeing 'I' of the Comics," *Modern Fiction Studies* 52, no. 4 (Winter 2006), 968.

22. Sacco, *Palestine*, 77.

23. *War Photographer*, produced and directed by Christian Frei with James Natchway (New York: Christian Frei Film Productions, 2001).

24. Sacco, *Palestine*, 242.

25. Rey Chow, "Where Have All the Natives Gone?" in *Contemporary Postcolonial Theory: A Reader*, ed. Padmini Mongia (New York: St. Martin's Press, 1996), 123.

26. Chow, "Where Have All the Natives Gone?" 124.
27. For a critique of the native informant, see Shahnaz Khan, "Reconfiguring the Native Informant: Positionality in the Global Age," *Signs: Journal of Women in Culture & Society* 30, no. 4 (2005): 2017–2035.
28. John Beverley, *Testimonio: On the Politics of Truth* (Minneapolis: University of Minnesota Press, 2004).
29. Mary Layoun, "The Trans-, the Multi-, the Pluri-, and the Global: a Few Thoughts on Comparative and Relational Literacy," *Passages: A Journal of Transnational & Transcultural Studies* 1, no. 2 (1999), 182–188.
30. Said, "Introduction." Quoted in Chute, "Comics as Literature?" 460.
31. Chute, "Comics as Literature?" 457.
32. See Whitlock, "Autographics," for a related discussion of Marjane Satrapi's depictions of women in *The Complete Persepolis* as "human, and full of character and individuality even with the veil," 975.
33. Hasso, *Resistance, Repression, and Gender Politics*, 119.
34. Hasso, *Resistance, Repression, and Gender Politics*, xxv.
35. Hasso, *Resistance, Repression, and Gender Politics*, 124–126.
36. Despite the wide range of veiling practices, and their different political and social histories, the veil as the symbol of gender oppression pervades American media about the Middle East. See Annabelle Sreberny, "Unsuitable Coverage: The Media, the Veil, and Regimes of Representation," in *Global Currents: Media and Technology Now,* ed. Tasha G. Oren and Patrice Petro (New Brunswick, NJ: Rutgers University Press, 2004), 171–185.
37. Layoun, "The Trans-, the Multi-, the Pluri-, and the Global," 191–192.
38. Layoun, "The Trans-, the Multi-, the Pluri-, and the Global," esp. 183–185.
39. Layoun, "The Trans-, the Multi-, the Pluri-, and the Global," 194.
40. David D. Perlmutter, *Photojournalism and Foreign Policy: Icons of Outrage in International Crises* (Westport, CT: Praeger, 1998).
41. Sacco, *Palestine*, 283.
42. Chute, "Comics as Literature?" 459.
43. Human Rights Watch, "Torture and Ill-Treatment."
44. Layoun, "Trans-, the Multi-, the Pluri-, and the Global," 189.
45. Dominick LaCapra, *Writing History, Writing Trauma* (Baltimore: Johns Hopkins University Press, 2001), 20.
46. LaCapra, *Writing History*, 40.
47. Sacco, *Palestine*, 102.
48. See, e.g., Hazem Balousha and Rory McCarthy, "'As I ran I saw three of my children. All dead,'" *The Guardian*, January 6, 2009, http://www.guardian.co.uk/world/2009/jan/06/gaza-israel (downloaded Jan. 28, 2009).

10 Dark Chamber, Colonial Scene
Post-9/11 Torture and Representation

Stephanie Athey

"We hear from some quarters nothing but feigned outrage based on a false narrative. In my long experience in Washington, few matters have inspired so much contrived indignation and phony moralizing as the interrogation methods applied to a few captured terrorists."
—Former U.S. Vice-President Cheney, May 21, 2009

"Official accounts are not mere fictions or rhetorical flourishes. . . . These accounts have been offered and accepted long enough to be part of the moral fabric. A culture of denial is in place."
—Stanley Cohen, *States of Denial*

This chapter takes seriously the role of fiction in the public discourse on torture. Looking first at the imaginative nature of that discourse as it evolved in the US after September 2001, the chapter considers the highly provocative depiction of torture in fiction from the year 2004, one of the high-water marks in the public discussion owing to the release of photographs from Abu Ghraib prison in Iraq. Vyvyane Loh's *Breaking the Tongue*, a powerful and surprising contribution to that debate, situates the novel within a larger set of questions that have propelled the public discourse. The present chapter argues that whereas the relevance of fiction or literary studies seems to be radically demoted when it comes to contemporary debates on the problem and practice of torture, a turn to fiction can illuminate and redirect that discussion in necessary ways.

Perhaps one of the most startling things to note about the discourse on torture in the years since 9/11 is that it emerged in mid-September 2001, when dozens of US news analyses, commentaries, and feature stories began to assess the utility of torture in the newly declared "war on terror." These press pieces echoed, generated, and publicized what would become known as a "debate" on torture in legal reviews and academic publishing.

The timing was significant. *Speculative* news arguments for and against torture proliferated and achieved critical mass across 2001–2004 in places like the *New York Times*, *Washington Post*, *Wall Street Journal*, *Newsweek*, *Time*, *Atlantic*, and *New Yorker*, *before* the Abu Ghraib photos of 2004. During that same period, only seven *investigative* stories on actual detainee treatment appeared according to the *Columbia Journalism Review*.[1] Plainly put, hypothetical torture became a big news story, while actual torture went unreported. That is, the speculative press was busily defining torture publicly and imagining its uses well in advance of and alongside torture memos and interrogation protocols being drawn up quietly inside the Executive Branch.[2]

Even though little attention has been paid to the highly imaginative dimensions of this "torture debate" or the role of news media prior to 2004, torture on dramatic television and film and its reported influence on actual interrogation practice did become a subject of concern. The portrayal of torture and terror in Fox Television's series *24*, for instance, was the subject of a 2006 Heritage Foundation policy conference, was referenced prominently in the Republican presidential primary debates in 2007, and fueled myriad print and internet commentaries. Monitoring organization Human Rights First leveraged the attention to television in late 2007 with its "Prime Time Torture Project."

The attention to the symbolic construction of "torture" in the entertainment media has stood in striking contrast to attention paid the construction of "torture" in the news, a mode of representation with patterns and consequences of its own. As both governments and human rights workers know when confronting atrocities, the careful construction of a surrounding narrative is the key to meaning and consequence—legal, political, and moral. This is why historical and political counter-narratives and strategies for depicting violence and victims have long been a central concern for human rights campaigns and other cultural workers. As the Abu Ghraib photographs have shown, the meaning of images is volatile and contested. Photos do not "speak for themselves." Journalists, jurists, human rights organizations, and academic commentators of all sorts rush to offer caption, context, and narrative. In other words, representation itself and specifically representation in *language* is central to the perpetuation or elimination of torture on a grand scale.

Public discourse prepares for torture and is part of it, laying groundwork for practice, shaping the *meaning* of the experience and consequences for survivors, families, and societies. News, law reviews, Senate hearings, participant and survivor accounts all define and stage "torture" verbally as surely as do popular television and film.

Noting the imaginative zeal brought to bear on "torture" in the speculative press before 2004, it is important to see that the storytelling impulse has remained strong after that date when the broad and systematic nature of torture under the Bush administration began to be pursued more steadily in the press. Since leaving office, former Vice-President Dick Cheney has vociferously defended the Bush record. One speech accused those who condemn torture of "feigned outrage" and a "false narrative." He decried euphemisms in the Obama administration's national security rhetoric, only to counter with his own.[3] For his part, Obama has not shied from the term "torture," but he is working to free the term from its status as *crime*. Citing a desire to "look forward," the Obama Department of Justice has put forth "state secrets" claims to dismiss court cases despite emerging skepticism on the bench, and he has moved to shield additional visual evidence from public view, arguing it "would not add any additional benefit to our understanding of what was carried out in the past by a small number of individuals."[4]

In either administration's response to torture, there is more at stake than "mere fictions" of a shallowly political or rhetorical sort. Official denials are fictions deeply rooted in culture. Sociologist Stanley Cohen notes that official accounts meant to deny or redefine acts of atrocity are designed before the deed is done. Integral to the preparation and unfolding of an event, denials are drawn from a collective pool of "socially-approved vocabularies." These rationales not only help political actors prepare for an act. They also have the ring of credibility because they have been found to be socially acceptable before. To speak of the false narratives in our politics, as Mr. Cheney has done, is in fact to raise the stakes. One must grapple too with the cultural roots, communal functions, and storytelling traditions that fashion and transmit the tales we tell.[5]

THE DARK CHAMBER

Directly addressing the malignant political language of the apartheid state, Nobel-prize winning novelist J. M. Coetzee once put bluntly the problem at stake in imagining torture. His 1986 essay, "Into the Dark Chamber," describes the allure of the torture chamber, long hidden from view, wrapped in the secrets of the state. Imaginatively, the writer is drawn to what he or she is forbidden to look on. Yet, the writer must proceed with caution. Tales of "the dark chamber" can easily assist the state: the scene of torture can spread terror *or* overwhelm and paralyze the reader *or* infatuate the audience with the torturer's power. While the artist must bear witness to torture, "the true challenge," says Coetzee, "is how not to play the game by the rules of the state."[6] Representation, in other words, is a moral problem with political consequences.

The journalist, like the novelist, is also drawn to the dark chamber. In 2003, journalist Mark Bowden entered the speculative media debate on torture with a feature story in the *Atlantic Monthly*. It illustrates the compulsion to peer into the torture chamber and the kind of infatuation with power that Coetzee warns against. It struck a resonant chord. Other journalists speculating on torture referred to it frequently. It is no coincidence that this influential piece borrows techniques of fiction and constructs a "Heart of Darkness" journey of discovery.

To shed light on the question the media found so compelling, a lone feature writer sets forth across continents to explore the practice of torture, seeking out the torturer and his tools, the dark chamber itself. The writer/narrator exudes a calculated moral ambivalence but also a lyric intensity. The feature's obsession with special mastery, "dark arts" and "unthinkable choices" all signal a foregone conclusion: torture, what Bowden calls "intensive physical coercion," is a necessary evil at this special moment in history. Perhaps our very civilization depends upon it. His title captures the fascination and sense of inevitability: "The Dark Art of Interrogation: The Most Effective Way to Gather Intelligence and Thwart Terrorism Can also Be a Direct Route into Morally Repugnant Terrain."

Bowden's speculative piece works, as do many others in this vein, to illuminate the scene by shedding light on the torturers' fraught dilemmas, rather than on those who suffer or the social and political conditions that brought them there. In its Conradian quest and conclusion, "The Dark Art" gathers readers into a community ostensibly protected by torture, never subject to it. Bowden's feature proved influential among interrogators themselves. It was read as a type of underground guidebook by novice interrogators eager to refine their skills, according to US Army Specialist Tony Lagouranis, a man who admits he tortured prisoners in Mosul, Iraq.[7]

Given this impact, one thing seems clear. When it comes to confronting torture, although the novelist and journalist might share similar dilemmas, even aspects of technique, at least the journalist may be said to bend the structures of fiction to trace the pathways of fact—whatever one takes fact to be. Founded in "fact" and focused on the present, the journalist's craft is deemed relevant, urgent, while the novelist's is not. Writing in 2001 in the context of South American states, literary and cultural studies scholar Idelber Avelar sharpens the point. He asks whether the imaginative work of literature can have any role in confronting torture: "Testimony, accusation and empirical studies have told us all we need to know about the worldwide spread of torture. . . . Given all this, what do literature or philosophy, neither anchored in experience . . . still have to tell us about the phenomenon?"[8]

Remarkable, then, that novelists have not been silent or ceded the ground of relevance during this long, unfolding dialogue on the use of torture, though their contribution has gone unremarked. In 2004 alone, a point of intensive public debate owing to the release of the Abu Ghraib photos, several literary works by accomplished authors took up torture from aggressively historical, moral, and political standpoints, creating alternate angles of vision.

Consider the question of relevance against this striking contrast. News and public discussion since 2001 positioned torture as a "new" dilemma confronting the US, thereby disconnecting contemporary torture from its US history. Elements of that history have been visible in US practice since 2001, in immigrant round-ups, rendition relationships, and US detention centers around the world. Yet routinely and with few exceptions, public discussion has submerged that longer legacy and three clear lines of US descent: torture's use in lynching and internal racial repression, in US colonial wars

and counter-insurgency programs in cold war client states, and in policing contexts and prisons. These are precisely the legacies invoked by literary texts which appeared in 2004 or reached greatest circulation that
year: Edwidge Danticat's *Dew Breaker,* Ha Jin's *War Trash,* Vyvyane Loh's
Breaking the Tongue, Walter Mosley's *The Man in My Basement,* Alexandra Fuller's memoir *Scribbling the Cat,* and Coetzee's *Elizabeth Costello*
(2003). Based in the US, save Coetzee, the authors offer different diasporic
vantage points: Haitian American, Chinese American, Singaporean American, African American, Zimbabwean, and South African. They bring
historical and philosophical arguments on torture, complicity, and representation to a general audience. They examine torture as a tool that creates
and enforces racial and gender difference. They wrestle with contemporary
torture as a colonial legacy with a corporate future, what torture humanly
means for survivors, how it supports civilization, and how or if we may
reject it. All these problems deserve urgent exploration in the public debate.
It might seem telling that strategic repressions in the news debate return in
the form of fiction, but that would be to see the two discourses as separate
and opposed. This is far from the truth. Fiction is already woven deeply
into the public discourse and US torture policy.

Fictions do much more than animate the noirish origins of stock political
phrasing: "we have to work the dark side," "the gloves come off," "a brass-
knuckled quest for information."[9] Fictions shape the very ground of argument. For instance, the "ticking time bomb" scenario that for years now
has so dominated and structured the US public debate was first crystallized
then popularized in a French novel defending the military use of torture in
the war of Algerian independence. *Les Centurions,* by decorated soldier
and war correspondent Jean Lartéguy, was published in 1960. A feat of
pure invention, Lartéguy's torturer extracted the location of fifteen bombs
through one night of extended assault on a single prisoner. He not only protected a city from certain catastrophe, but his act re-imagined the causes
and consequences of colonial violence, and torture, in a way that stirred the
public. The book sold over 400,000 copies in France in two years and won
praise from both the military and the literary establishment.[10] Adapted as
Hollywood's *Lost Command* in 1966, the book is still recommended by
military readers for its lessons on counter-insurgency. These readers include
General David Petreaus, one-time commander of US ground forces in Iraq
and Afghanistan.[11] Though soundly debunked, torture apologists have long
hailed the success of France's widespread use of torture against the Algerian terrorists and citizens.[12] The novel's potent formulation of state torture
as a matter of ticking necessity, professional efficiency, and heroic drama
has exerted imaginative force over the structure of entertainment plots and
policy debates for decades.

The ubiquity of Lartéguy's scenario is no fluke. Think of the compression and crystallization of argument made possible in evocative fiction. He
combines this with a vivid revisionist historical imagining, producing a

masterwork of colonial nostalgia. These same principles converge in the Conradian *Heart of Darkness* narrative that structures Bowden's journalistic quest in "The Dark Art," and these elements combine and circulate in other forms we might consider folkloric. Consider: We know that torture policy itself did not spring from historical or practical evidence of torture's usefulness.[13] Instead, those policy choices, driven by many political, economic, and ideological factors, have been fueled as well by what we might call a resilient folklore of torture's success. Trade in such folklore was evident when the 1965 film *Battle of Algiers* was screened at the Pentagon in 2003 to stimulate discussion on Iraq.[14]

Folklore as well as protocol connect the Pentagon to personnel on the frontline. Interrogator Tony Lagouranis and others cite informal asides about torture during training and the braggadocio of veteran interrogators facing wide-eyed new initiates. They point as well to the formal slide presentations that greet new arrivals with racist imperial projections concerning Arab sexuality or phobias. At Abu Ghraib, these fantastical slide shows were distilled from Raphael Patai's 1973 *The Arab Mind*, an Orientalist analysis of "national character" itself derived from literary reference, anecdotal evidence, and the mists of colonial nostalgia. A common title on military and diplomatic reading lists, the book was reissued in 2001 with an introduction by the Director of Middle East Studies at the JFK Special Warfare Center and School at Fort Bragg.[15]

The folklore persists, supporting torture's necessity or efficacy in the face of evidence to the contrary. A belated 2006 report by the Intelligence Science Board examined all existing social and behavioral studies on effective interrogation. The report said flatly: "Virtually no research indicates accurate information can be produced from unwilling sources through torture or coercive techniques." Research and development in the field has gone in the wrong direction: "Ninety-nine percent of US research has been about how to achieve compliance not cooperation" from unwilling sources. More astonishingly, given that US torture has been promoted almost exclusively on the basis of anecdotes, the Intelligence Science Board report found that even "most personal and anecdotal accounts indicate that torture is not effective."[16]

If we fail to grasp the power of fantasy, fiction, or folklore supporting torture or framing the news debate, we do so at our peril. One could say with Idelber Avelar that "the torturer's great victory is to define the language in which the atrocity will be named" and, one might add, the narrative in which torture is cast.[17] In this respect novels—the foundry of narrative—have the capacity to intervene in the torture debate in ways that counter the folklore and offer new strategies and structures for reporting. As laboratories for language and narrative strategy, they can derail the political, historical, and emotional cliché, bypass cul-de-sacs of logic, and supplant alluring tales with new ones. Novels can make historical antecedents relevant and new arguments vivid with a graphic compression that amplifies their force and extends their reach. As importantly, they can identify and then unsettle reader fascinations and expectations. In doing so, they can forge new emotional, intellectual, and political investments.

Breaking the Tongue (2004), a first novel by Massachusetts writer Vyvyane Loh, shows the promise of fiction in this regard. The innovative aspects of Loh's fiction connect to problems in the current debate: to ways language and image arise as weapons in torture and to narrative strategies that might resist.

LANGUAGE, TORTURE, DISPLAY

Breaking the Tongue is about a young Eurasian boy being tortured in British colonial Singapore in 1942, the year the Japanese military handed the British a swift and surprising defeat. The defeat challenged notions of white and European supremacy that had long been cultivated among the native Chinese, Malay, Indians, and Thai of Singapore.

Claude Lim is seventeen; he is of Chinese descent. His Japanese torturers are exasperated to learn that to break him, they must speak to him in English. Claude speaks no Chinese. His torturers want the "truth" of his allegiance to the English language and the British. Claude learns the connection between torture, language, and narration immediately. Words can lie. If under torture, the overt resistance of silence breaks and becomes a chain of words, words might resist covertly. Tortured, Claude utters a signifying chain that tells the story of speech and of torture at the same time: "Mute"/"Mutilate"/"*mutatis mutandis*"/"covert mutiny."

As in this example, the scenes in the torture cell defy normal narrative coherence. They are filled with Claude's twisting etymologies and language games, not with blood and twisting flesh (though Loh depicts some of this). Instead of gore, we get strange meditations on language itself and the fictions Claude weaves, "All stories are corruptible," he says.[18]

With this warning, *Breaking the Tongue* alternates scenes of depicted torture with long "confessions" that do settle into a coherent, yet unreliable chronological narrative detailing Claude's upbringing in a hyper-Anglicized, Eurasian family and the fall of Singapore.

As these confessional sequences unfold, we learn that Claude's tormentors do not really want or need information about him or his female comrade, Ling-li. They have long since captured Ling-li; she is being humiliated and slowly killed in the next cell. Claude refuses to understand this until the book's end. But his imagination is drawn to the cell and its noises. Indeed, the events taking place in this mysterious cell are objects of building suspense. As Coetzee remarked eighteen years before *Breaking the Tongue*, we all—writer, reader, character—are fascinated and drawn to the dark chamber. And it is in that final revelation that the novel breaks new ground. Before arriving there, however, it is worth thinking how language, revelation, and display function in torture.

Language is central to classic understandings of what Elaine Scarry presumed to be the "basic structure" of torture. In *The Body in Pain*, for instance, Scarry focuses on what she views as the rhetorical structure of torture, in which the torturer works the subject's body in order to "break" speech itself, attempting to control the subject by dividing him or her from language, the self, the world. Not surprisingly, the role of language also arises in Mark Bowden's 2003 feature, "The Dark Art." Israeli master interrogator Michael Koubi says the interrogator's most important skill is "to know the prisoner's language. Language is at the root of all social connections . . . in secret societies like Hamas and Al Qaeda . . . [a] shared vocabulary or verbal shorthand helps to cement the group. 'I try to create the impression that I use his mother tongue even better than he does' says Koubi. . . . 'This embarrasses him very much.'" As the root of social connection, language can disarm, stimulating rapport or humiliation or working the finest of lines between the two. It can manipulate the subject's expectations surrounding language difference, power, and community as well.

Language can also dominate more crudely. For decades, human rights organizations reporting on the torture of Palestinians in Israeli detention have directed particular concern to the practice of compelling Palestinian prisoners to sign confessions written in Hebrew, a language few detainees understand. One organization found that these Hebrew confessions constitute the primary evidence against Palestinian detainees in Israeli military courts.[19]

Multilingual expertise is essential for intelligence-gathering or diplomacy. Yet expertise in language has been notoriously lacking in US interrogation efforts and detention centers. According to military interpreters and interrogators, inadequate communication routinely sabotaged rapport-based interrogation strategies, multiplied errors, and became one excuse to use coercion.[20] From within a national security paradigm, language difference is a key marker of adversarial boundaries, and "linguistic mediators [translators, interpreters] simultaneously become urgently necessary and irreparably suspect."[21] When bilingual ability bespeaks disloyalty, the cultural and linguistic competence urgently required is in itself a security risk. Three US soldiers, Arabic-speaking Muslims at Guantánamo, for instance, were arrested as spies with great fanfare in 2003; charges were later quietly dismissed.[22]

Scarry viewed the "basic structure" of torture as a rhetorical and physical exchange between two players. Widely influential, this view fails to account for the tense and competitive *group* dynamics at work.[23] So too, there has been little attention to the fact that torturers and subjects often speak *different* languages, that torture manipulates language difference, and that therefore linguistic violence in torture is of a different order. *Breaking the Tongue* is attuned specifically to this level of violence.

So too display of power is essential to terror. In his "Five Theses on Torture," Idelber Avelar notes that testimonials and human rights reporting demonstrate again and again that display and representation are fundamental components of torture: "The insistent sound of locks opening [announcing the arrival of the torturer] . . . or the exhibition [in sound or vision] of the tortured to their loved ones . . . : the modern technique of torture systematically includes, as a central element . . . its own double in the realm of signs. . . . What is proper to torture is the obscene exhibition . . . of its own power."[24] The 2007 International Committee of the Red Cross report on torture at US CIA black sites documents visual threats: the display during interrogation of a plastic collar previously used to slam the detainee into walls or of a small dark box in which the detainee had been forced to bend for hours at a time. So too, a photo of a battered co-detainee implied future torment.[25] The theatricality here points to multiple audiences. Scarry emphasizes the theater meant for those subjected to torture. Avelar steps beyond this with the "obscene exhibition of power." Photos are threats when circulated among detainees and trophies when circulated among their captors.

Yet strategic display asserts power more broadly still. The state tortures the few to control the many. The public exhibition, photography, and souvenirs that accompanied lynching "bees" in US history are an important reminder of the *community-building* as well as the terrorizing impulse at the heart of torture. The early now infamous images of orange-suited detainees—limbs bound, eyes goggled, ears muffed, kneeling in stress positions at Guantánamo—were deliberately released to the press and couched in terms of tough tactics against "the worst of the worst." The accompanying narrative forged twin communities. One, nebulously defined as "them," and projected as a target, the other, "us," enlisted to support terror.

Visual, auditory, tactile modes of representation and theatricality are central to the act of torture, as are the narratives that surround it. For this reason, Avelar, like Coetzee, is closely concerned with the representation of torture in *language*. How might one craft narratives that counter torture? How to display torture in prose? What sort of representations resist complicity in terror?[26]

Avelar reminds us that in the struggle against torture, narrative is particularly suspect. Survivors themselves may show a post-trauma resistance to language.[27] Some scholars have construed this radically as a problem of articulation. Indeed, the question of trauma's "unrepresentability" has itself become a trope.[28] Yet, no matter how partial or fragmentary the form of expression, many survivors do articulate their experiences in different forms for different purposes with varied effects. For this reason, other scholars hold that the inexpressibility that matters politically is not the inability to articulate, but rather society's inability to hear and understand. Torture functions to sever one from community; it forecloses common political space. To be marked by torture is to be marked off socially, encircled with doubt, denials, illusions. Words fail to register, to find political impact.[29]

In either case, survivors might be rightly suspicious of narrative for three reasons Avelar outlines. First, because narrative coherence and chronology all gesture toward meaning and order, betraying the disorder and nihilism of the subject's experience: "The worst insult to the experience of the victims—what Primo Levi called 'the obscenity of interpretation'—. . . [is] the rationalization and supposed comprehension of causes, experience and effects."[30]

Second, the demand that survivors *tell* reproduces the rhetorical situation of the interrogation room and mimes its power dynamic. It also falsely equates the act of *telling* with the *truth* of the experience. Žižek points to narrative as a symptom—not a resolution—in the therapeutic process for precisely this reason. Stories assemble confused experience into a fantasy of coherence covering over fundamental contradictions or conflicts.[31] Belief in the ultimate "truth" of confession is the same belief that justifies the torturer's craft.

Lastly, narration is suspect because it opens the unique experience of torture to simile and "*common* nouns."[32] In today's public discussion the simile normalizes violence. It might instead force us to question the norm. When a Red Cross report in 2004 found treatment at Guantánamo to be "tantamount to torture," some senators declared the conditions to be "no worse than those in American prisons."[33] Rather than spotlight violence in the American penal system, this comparison functioned to normalize and deflect. Marguerite Feitlowitz connects the public discourse of the Argentine regime to the argot of its torture camps, where elaborate verbal codes made words weapons. Familiar colloquial terms for painful techniques heightened the alienation and torment of the captive, as they increased sadistic satisfaction and granted enabling distance for the perpetrators and their masters. The US too has developed its own lexicon of terror: terms for public consumption—"enhanced interrogation," "torture lite," "rendition," "black site," "manipulative self-injurious behavior," "single-occupancy cell"—and the shorthand of the detention center: "the disco," "frequent flier," "reservation," "ghost," "Operation Sandman," "IRFing," "monstering."

Because language and narrative are suspect for these many reasons, Avelar argues that political and therapeutic confrontation with torture demand a collective and ongoing "war within language" over the naming of atrocity. The "permanent collective operation on language" he calls for is fought daily in our press, our political speech, and our fiction. Fiction, I would argue, has a major role in that discursive battle. George Orwell, after all, wrote powerful essays on the link between inhumane ideology and lying prose, but it was his novel on torture, *1984*, that fixed the concept of a war on language, and its stakes, most brilliantly and indelibly in the cultural imagination.

I would distill three observations on the representation of torture and bring them to bear on *Breaking the Tongue*. First, representation that refuses state torture must also refuse the idea that truth can or must be extorted under pressure. Confession is not truth; "intelligence" can be assembled by other means. Second, representation must presuppose the complicity of individuals, citizens, civil society, and democratic institutions in torture, refusing a false opposition between *civilization* and *torture*. Torture does not undermine or unmake the "civilized" world (in Scarry's terms), but rather is of a piece with that world and constitutes it. Third, the representation that does not perpetuate terror and trauma, or empower the torturer, or pay homage to his/her dilemmas is the representation that exposes the false "treachery" of narrative even as it fights for the *possibility* of narration. This means clearing a potential "place of witness," a space of possibility. This is ultimately a political space. There the act of adequate telling, accounting, accountability, might exist as a promise. This "so-called space of *narratibility*" must be "conquered" through the "war on language" Avelar calls for.

BREAKING THE TONGUE

Loh's *Breaking the Tongue* shows us what a resisting narrative, one that battles for a potential space of witness, might look like. As described, Claude's torture and his wayward narrations challenge the conflation of confession and truth early on. So too, the book underscores complicity of "domestic" life and colonial institutions in state torture. As the book shifts between Claude's torture at the hands of the Japanese and Claude's upbringing in the Anglicized Eurasian home, Loh deftly connects and compares the painful techniques of Japanese imperial domination with those of British imperial power preceding it. Finally, the book challenges the compulsion to seek understanding of torture in the particulars and practices of the "dark chamber."

The Lim home holds three generations, and deracination has been achieved and maintained there through the psychic and physical violence of empire over a long period of time. Loh dramatizes the relationship between state torture and the violence of the domestic realm with a figurine and a dream. Visiting the Ten Courts of Hell in a theme park, young Claude sees torture displayed. Miniature tableaux depict China's ten demon kings and the pain they inflict on disobedient mortals. One tableau depicts gross violence to the human tongue. Two men hold a third as his tongue is being severed. Claude experiences the figurine's severed tongue as an immediate, shocking, personal loss. Claude has had a recurring dream just like this: "It starts with the man being held down by others. A knife is produced. Sometimes a pair of scissors . . . from China. . . . Suddenly he is all the people in his dream at once. . . . he ululat[es] in pain as his tongue is . . .

severed, [finally] reduced to grunting and howling . . . he contorts his face . . . his whole being, in order to be understood." Waking in horror, Claude attempts to reassure himself by testing his English tongue, mouthing challenging "r" and "l" sounds: "reckless, palindrome, curtsey."[34]

Claude's dreams haunt him as he is tortured by the Japanese. They reflect an upbringing in which many have exerted their will on Claude's tongue to eradicate all signs of his Chinese-ness. Claude's English grammar, and above all his intonation and pronunciation have been policed closely and daily. The English-speaking Eurasian community must guard against any influence by Singapore's Thai, Malay, Tagalog, Hindi, and especially Chinese. Quite literally, the influence of these languages, suggested by the scissors from China in his dream, would cut him off from that English tongue and therefore his very self.

Perversely, Claude, in his Eurasian body, can never be good *enough* at English, his first and only language, a fact that induces shame daily, the kind of shame that is an important part of the suffering Israeli interrogator Michael Koubi carefully strives to produce in his prisoners. Loh is here reflecting a widespread concern of Singapore's colonial policy makers, educators, and parents of the 1930s and early 1940s. Empires have worked historically to manage populations—their movements, their labor, their consuming energies. This task, in one large dimension, is a linguistic one, conducted through language but also attentive to manipulating language difference. Regional English language newspapers, pamphlets, and magazines of that period routinely asserted the link between proper command and inflection of English and one's racial identity. That identity was extremely volatile in a region that had for many years encouraged white men to make mixed race unions to stabilize the colonial venture, and Anglicized mixed-race families like the Lims were not uncommon. English-educated, adhering to the same codes of dress, sentiment, and comportment as the upper-class English, maintaining "native" servants, cultivating English rose gardens or holding tea in the stifling tropics, they were neither English nor "local," and they held an ambiguous race and class status. Because there were also a great variety of "whites" who were ambiguously European—the poor, the Malaysian-born, the dangerously "native"—whiteness or racial essence could not be read simply in the skin. Language was an index to group. One's spoken English and lifestyle were critical markers.[35]

Through these scenes that torture the tongue—in the Haw Par theme park, in dreams, and in Claude's torture cell—Loh suggests torture undergirds the Chinese didactic tradition, the British colonial enterprise, and Japanese conquest. She establishes a continuity between the violence of the domestic realm and that of the state prison cell. She gestures beyond both to the colonial scene.

Yet it is in the torture cell that the novel purports to reach its climax. After the Japanese release him, Claude begins to study Chinese and comes to acknowledge Ling-li was tortured to death in the cell next to his. In an extraordinary vision, the deceased Ling-li calls him to return to the prison as witness. Bound and gagged, she demands he bear witness to each technique of her humiliation and murder so that history might take its proper foundation—on torture. "This is how our history starts and is transmitted, Claude. Witness and transmission of Story."[36]

Although the racialized, sexualized, and gendered dimensions of the scene have important implications, it is the more innovative dimension of this depiction that I wish to examine.[37] The novel draws readers suspensefully and voyeuristically to this ultimate revelation, although the novel invests the act of witness with great power and importance: "I will tell you, and you will witness it, but you will also tell me what I want to know— their faces, height, distinguishing features . . . to erase their anonymity."[38] Yet as Claude and Ling-li begin to narrate the torture in great detail, their language shifts from English into Chinese. The novel denotes this literally. English typescript changes to Chinese characters on the page; Chinese lettering stands without translation for several paragraphs. Only occasional English words interrupt the Chinese characters. Illegible to English readers who do not also read Chinese, the sequence both depicts and obscures the scene of torture. For most readers, the dark chamber is revealed and concealed at the same time.

THEORETICAL AND POLITICAL INTERVENTIONS

Many meanings emerge from the author's decision. In so doing, the novel brings us back to the public discourse of torture of which it is a part, the range of news debate, academic commentary, film, and television discussed at the start. Here, the subjects of torture working together *can* articulate or represent the experience in language, but, significantly, the English-only reader cannot read it. For the English-only reader, the scene holds out the *possibility* of understanding yet deliberately refuses it at the same time.

Second, the scene of torture can be narrated, but not in the language of the colonizers—be they British or Japanese. The novel presents a problem of recognition and reception *not* of traumatic memory or a survivor's resistance to language. This problem of comprehension is constituted by politics and power. The scene shows how language excludes, drawing communal and political boundaries. Further, although Chinese is privileged in this scene, the novel is clear because of this particular colonial context. Chinese is no less complicit in torture.

Indeed, rather than use language to normalize or lyricize torture, the book shows how torture works to estrange the language. The one Chinese character that Claude, and thus any English reader, learns to recognize in the course of the novel is *Ren, endurance*, a "made image" of Knife poised over Heart. That is, inscribed in the Chinese word for "endurance" is an image of torturer and victim.[39] All languages are contaminated for the purpose of witness.

Loh's proposed etymology for *Ren* as "knife over heart" is particularly fascinating. Dr. Inge Genefke, founder of RCT, the Danish research and rehabilitation center for torture survivors, says clients routinely present complaining of "shooting pains in the heart." Genefke notes these pains are "psychosomatic" but consistent among survivors from many regions. Loh's etymology not only touches on this experiential reality but also visibly inscribes torture with its consequence, the dailiness of suffering and endurance it produces. In this way the book self-consciously attempts a rethinking of the representation of torture—at the level of language as well as that of scene and narration.

Ultimately, *Breaking the Tongue* does expose the treacherous nature of narrative, and it does in the final pages open a potential *space of narratibility*—it envisions the possibility of witness, telling, and comprehension. Importantly, that space of narratibility is imagined as a political space. What I find critical here is that Loh does much more than depict a utopian space of witness and accountability. She creates that possibility and blocks it at the same time, potentially forcing the English-only reader into a reckoning with the role of language in colonial violence, and what is more, the ways the reader's own linguistic heritage may mark him or her as accomplice or beneficiary of that violence.

Perhaps most significantly, the novel warns us that the truth of torture will not be found in the workings of the torture chamber. After all, though the structure of the book lures us here, when we arrive, it complicates or refuses the knowledge or completion one might have hoped from such a viewing. Denied a clear view, we must ask why did we want to see that in the first place? And then, what does it mean to partially or selectively *deny* its depiction? In this way, the book foregrounds the moral and political dimensions of representation and the way torture's display is constituted and inflected by language. The book forces us to contemplate how language difference and power meet in torture and how the violence of empire supports torture and vice versa.

For Loh, "meaning" cannot be dragged out of the sufferer or the scene of suffering, instead it must be assembled from peripheral detail that turns out not to be peripheral at all—Loh's study of family, language, and the making of race under colonization where only control of the tongue can produce a good or loyal subject. If we are to find the "truth" of torture, we must seek it outside the dark chamber where Loh directs us, in the colonial scene and the institutions, values, and routines of self-discipline that normalize torture and make it systematic.

This argument arrived in 2004 on the heels of multiple books announcing a new American empire. As that year's photos from Abu Ghraib circulated widely, captivating and seeming to lay bare the scene, Loh's book suggested how narrow and partial a view of torture was really on display. The public discourse, in its repeated focus on the "inner workings of the torture chamber," purported to reckon with torture while diverting thought and argument from critical dimensions of the practice. These dimensions include the ideological and political context of torture, the social and legal conditions that precede it, the construction and denigration of a target group, the supply chain and profits, the multiple other less vividly sensational degradations and levels of violence, and the consequences for victims or survivors or families.

But the neglected dimensions are also historical. Given clear examples of torture as accomplice and tool of "civilizing" and "democratizing" efforts at home and abroad both past and present, the US public must also acknowledge torture as written deeply into legal and racial codes and policing practice.[40] A dual history begs examination: the long history of US torture and the long history of tolerance for it.[41]

Loh's work jarringly and effectively redesignates torture as a problem implicated in language, culture, and power—not matters of shallow political language but of colonial legacies and the deeper narratives that nations tell themselves. In this respect, her work reminds us that torture is protected by fantasies as much as by political ideologies and institutions. It demonstrates as well that novels might intervene in the torture debate in ways that counter the fantasies and unravel the folklore and fictions that sustain "debate" but block accountability for torture. Novels join the struggle against torture—and the "war on language" that struggle requires—with their own unique capacities and broad audiences. They unsettle old pathways of thought, de-naturalize political language, and forge new terms, new arguments, new strategies. They can highlight unconscious emotional, intellectual, and political investments and propose new ones. They may not always succeed, but they are part of a "collective operation," as Avelar has it. As Coetzee might say, the novel can explore what it might mean to represent torture "without playing the game by the rules of the state."

NOTES

1. Eric Umansky, "Failures of Imagination," *Columbia Journalism Review* (Sept. 2006). Sherry Ricchiardi identifies six: "Missed Signals," *American Journalism Review* (Aug.–Sept. 2004), http://findarticles.com/p/articles/mi_hb3138/is_4_26/ai_n29113376/?tag=content;col1. I gratefully acknowledge the translation assistance of Andy Nathan, as well as his careful reading and thoughtful comments on this chapter.
2. Stephanie Athey, "Torture Alibi and Archetype in US News and Law Since 2001," in *Culture, Trauma, and Conflict: Cultural Studies Perspectives on War*, ed. Nico Carpentier (Newcastle upon Tyne: Cambridge Scholars Press, 2007), 135–60; Athey, "The Terrorist We Torture: The Tale of Abdul Hakim Murad," in *On Torture*, ed. Thomas C. Hilde (Baltimore: Johns Hopkins University Press, 2008).
3. "Cheney's Speech on Bush Era Security Policies," Washington Wire, *Wall Street Journal*, May 21, 2009, http://blogs.wsj.com/washwire/2009/05/21/cheneys-speech-on-bush-era-security-policies.

4. Jeff Zeleny and Thom Shanker, "Obama Moves to Bar Release of Detainee Abuse Photos," *New York Times*, May 13, 2009; Liam Stack, "US Court Allows Rendition Lawsuit Against CIA Contractor," *Christian Science Monitor*, April 29, 2009, http://www.csmonitor.com/2009/0429/p99s01-duts.htm.
5. Stanley Cohen, *States of Denial: Knowing about Atrocities and Suffering* (Cambridge: Polity, 2001), 115.
6. J. M. Coetzee, "Into the Dark Chamber: The Novelist and South Africa," *New York Times Book Review*, January 12, 1986, 13.
7. Tony Lagouranis and Allen Mikaelian, *Fear Up Harsh: An Army Interrogator's Dark Journey Through Iraq* (New York: New American Library, 2007).
8. Idelber Avelar, "Five Theses on Torture," *Journal of Latin American Cultural Studies* 10, no.3 (2001): 255.
9. Phrases respectively: Vice-President Cheney on Meet the Press, September 16, 2001; Cofer Black, then head of the CIA Counterterrorist Center; Dana Priest and Barton Gellman, "US Decries Abuse but Defends Interrogations," *The Washington Post*, December 26, 2002, A1, 14, 15.
10. "The Red Berets," review of *The Centurions*, by Jean Lartéguy, *Time*, January 19, 1962, http://www.time.com/time/magazine/article/0,9171,895876-1,00.html.
11. Robert D. Kaplan, "Rereading Vietnam," *The Atlantic Monthly*, August 24, 2007, http://www.theatlantic.com/doc/200708u/kaplan-vietnam. See Darius Rejali's discussion of race and masculinity in "Torture Makes the Man," in *On Torture*, ed. Thomas C. Hilde (Baltimore: Johns Hopkins University Press, 2008).
12. Darius Rejali, *Torture and Democracy* (Princeton, NJ: Princeton University Press, 2007), 480–493.
13. Scott Shane and Mark Mazzetti, "In Adopting Harsh Tactics, No Look at Past Use," *The New York Times*, April 21, 2009.
14. Michael T. Kaufman, "What Does the Pentagon See in the 'Battle of Algiers'?" *The New York Times*, September 7, 2003, sec. 4, 3. He reports the screening was attended by forty officers and civilian experts.
15. Lagouranis and Mikaelian, *Fear Up Harsh*, 39, 50. Emram Qurush, "Misreading 'The Arab Mind: The Dubious Guidebook to Middle East Culture That Is on the Pentagon's Reading List,'" *The Boston Globe*, May 30 2004. http://www.boston.com/news/globe/ideas/articles/2004/05/30/misreading_the_arab_mind.
16. Intelligence Science Board, *Educing Information: Interrogation, Science and Art* (Washington, DC: National Defense Intelligence College, 2006). The ISB was chartered in 2002 as a scientific advisory group to the U.S. intelligence agencies.
17. Avelar, "Five Theses on Torture," 262.
18. Vyvyane Loh, *Breaking the Tongue* (New York: W. W. Norton, 2004), 56.
19. See United Against Torture Coalition, *Alternative Report for Consideration Regarding Israel's Fourth Periodic Report to the UN Committee Against Torture*, September 1, 2008, 9, http://www2.ohchr.org/english/bodies/cat/docs/ngos/UAT_Israel42_1.pdf; Defence for Children International, "Palestinian Child Prisoners," 2007, 19, http://www.dcipal.org/english/publ/research/2008/PCPReport.pdf; B'Tselem, *The Interrogation of Palestinians During the Intifada: Ill-Treatment, "Moderate Physical Pressure," or Torture?*, March 1991, 91, http://www.btselem.org/English/Publications/Summaries/199103_Torture.asp.
20. Chris Mackey (pseudonym) and Greg Miller, *Interrogator's War: Inside the Secret War Against Al Qaeda* (Boston: Little Brown, 2004); Erik Saar and Viveca Novak, *Inside the Wire: A Military Intelligence Soldier's Eyewitness Account of Life at Guantánamo* (New York: Penguin, 2005); and

Lagouranis and Mikaelian, *Fear Up Harsh* for Afghanistan, Guantánamo, and Iraq respectively.

21. Mary Louise Pratt, "Harm's Way: Language and the Contemporary Arts of War," *PMLA* 124, no. 5 (2009), 1526.
22. Chaplain James Yee, Airman Ahmad I. al-Halabi, and Ahmed F. Mehalba. See Neil Lewis and Thom Shanker, "As Chaplain's Spy Case Nears, Some Ask Why it Went so Far," *The New York Times*, January 4, 2004, http://www.nytimes.com/2004/01/04/us.
23. Elaine Scarry, *The Body in Pain: The Making and Unmaking of the World* (New York: Oxford University Press, 1985), 19–20. Spectators and co-participants and the group-based nature of the violence and its effects call any dualistic "basic structure" of torture into sharp question.
24. Avelar, "Five Theses on Torture," 257, 258.
25. International Committee of the Red Cross, *The ICRC Report on the Treatment of Fourteen "High Value Detainees" in CIA Custody*, February 2007, 17, http://www.nybooks.com/icrc-report.pdf.
26. Coetzee's classic novel, *Waiting for the Barbarians* (London; Secker and Warburg, 1980; New York: Penguin, 1982), takes up these questions via his "benevolent" colonial administrator.
27. Avelar, "Five Theses on Torture," 257.
28. Jill Bennett, *Empathic Vision: Affect, Trauma, and Contemporary Art* (Stanford, CA: Stanford University Press, 2005), 14; Avelar, "Five Theses on Torture," 262.
29. Rejali, *Torture and Democracy*, 31.
30. Avelar, "Five Theses on Torture," 260.
31. Avelar, "Five Theses on Torture," 261.
32. Avelar, "Five Theses on Torture," 257.
33. Neil A. Lewis, "Red Cross Finds Detainee Abuse in Guantánamo," *The New York Times*, November 30, 2004. http://www.nytimes.com/2004/11/30/politics/30gitmo.html?
34. Loh, *Breaking the Tongue*, 62, 63.
35. Ann Laura Stoler, *Carnal Knowledge and Imperial Power: Race and the Intimate in Colonial Rule* (Berkeley: University of California Press, 2002), 121, 129, 114. Stoler synthesizes primary documents on the Dutch Indies and European colonies in the region.
36. Loh, *Breaking the Tongue*, 398.
37. The novel's depiction of torture falls within a set of texts that envision the female subject of torture as the ultimate victim, the limit of representation. The device can reinforce the role of torture as a powerful tool by which to create and enforce race, gender, sexuality and domination. It also reinscribes long-standing gendered assumptions about language and reason (woman as inferiority, physicality, and hysterical unintelligibility), women's suffering and victimhood, political agency, and social status.
38. Loh, *Breaking the Tongue*, 398.
39. Loh, *Breaking the Tongue*, 49.
40. Colin Dayan, *The Story of Cruel and Unusual* (Cambridge, MA: MIT Press, 2007); Human Rights Clinic of Columbia Law School, *In The Shadows of The War on Terror: Persistent Police Brutality and Abuse in the United States. A Report Prepared for the United Nations Human Rights Committee on the Occasion of its Review of the United States of America's Second and Third Periodic Report to the Human Rights Committee*, New York, December 2007, http://www2.ohchr.org/english/bodies/cerd/docs/ngos/usa/USHRN15.pdf.; Darius Rejali, "Modern Torture as a Civic Marker: Solv-

ing a Global Anxiety with a New Political Technology," *Journal of Human Rights* 2, no. 2 (2003),153–171.

41. The Philippine and Vietnam Wars saw public debates on torture. Four major Congressional investigations into CIA torture between 1970 and 1988 roused little public interest or outcry. Alfred W. McCoy, *A Question of Torture: CIA Interrogation, from the Cold War to the War on Terror* (New York: Metropolitan Books, 2006), 208.

Part III

Rethinking the "Subject" of Human Rights

11 Human Rights as Violence and Enigma

Can Literature Really Be of Any Help with the Politics of Human Rights?

Nick Mansfield

In "Force of Law," his controversial paper on the relationship between violence and the law, Jacques Derrida argues that there is no law that does not have inscribed within it the possibility that one day it may need to be enforced, by violence if necessary.[1] Since the early modern period, there has always been an intimate if problematic relationship between law and violence, even when the aim has been to alienate the two from one another. Hobbes argued that the state of nature is violent simply because human beings are in proximity with one another without the regulation of sovereign authority. For Kant, the state of lawlessness was implicitly a state of violence, even if no violent acts take place.[2] According to these arguments, the possibility of violence is itself violence. Violence threatens law and must be resisted. The perimeter of law is violence, and at this perimeter, law must confront violence as its own limit. In order to do this, law must deploy a kind of counter-violence, distinguishing between criminal violence, which it traditionally has seen as the violence of nature enduring within the social, and the legitimate violence of organized society and its agents, which is deployed against natural violence. In this way, violence is inscribed in the heart of law as both an inevitable part of its operation and as its meaning. Over and above this, law is by definition universalizing. The violence that opposes law is to be annihilated. The most mundane example of this is that paradox that Derrida points out: in its daily operations, in the street, even the most benign and unambiguous law must be enforceable.

Human rights discourse comprises no less complicated a relationship with violence than does the law. The most significant documents in the history of the evolution of human rights—the *Déclaration des droits de l'Homme et du citoyen* and the *Universal Declaration of Human Rights (UDHR)*, for example—arose through violent conflict. In the latter case, the document represented the attempt at formulating the values for which the Second World War had ostensibly been fought, at least in hindsight. In fact, the very terms of the declaration constitute a direct response to the nature of that conflict (for example, the way in which the preamble of the

UDHR presents it as a reaction to "barbarous acts which have outraged the conscience of mankind" and Article Two's foregrounding of issues of race and color). The *Universal Declaration* would not be what it is if the Second World War had not been the kind of war it was. In other words—to misapply one of the ugliest platitudes of modern political history—war has been the midwife of human rights.

As with the law, the violence of human rights discourse goes further, however. This is because it is a discourse of universality and also of justice. Both of these require that human rights discourse anathematize alternatives. Arbitrary political prerogative, the silencing of dissenting voices, random or capricious tribunals, rape, torture, death squads, other forms of physical intimidation, and so on: all these and more must be reduced to zero as measures of the success and definitive indefeasibility of human rights logic. Justice itself is an asymptotic concept, something toward which our (democratic) politics must always orient us, but which it is impossible for us to realize fully. It will always require more of us than it is possible for us to deliver. Justice is by nature *excessive*. Our response to it is one of ambition and zeal, which overrides anything which might compromise or dilute justice. The commitment to the enlargement and purification of justice entangles it with an irresistible logic of necessary violence. We know that justice asks more of us than we are capable of giving. Similarly, the commitment to it in contemporary culture—from internet political activism, on the one hand, to tabloid journalism indignation at dishonest or unfair retail scams, on the other—is as visceral and intemperate as it is rational and intellectual. In short, justice is overwhelming. It is the thing of which we are in awe, yet to which we believe we can contribute. The intensity of our relationship with it gears us for violence. This may be a violence we are prepared to countenance. It is clearly one we routinely play down, as somehow lesser, purer, or more innocent than other less easily legitimized forms of violence. Like the violence of law and order administration, it may even be a violence greater than the violences which it opposes, or which it is designed to quell. Yet we excuse it routinely, and sometimes are negligent enough not even to notice it.

Human rights discourse, thus, is entangled with violence in two ways. Firstly it has been through violence that human rights discourse attained its signal moments of articulation. Secondly, a will-to-violence is entangled within the defining determination of human rights discourse to annihilate injustice and arbitrary power. If there is no law that does not at some point need to be enforceable, there is no human rights violation that does not call on us—or somebody, even *anybody*—to for god's sake do something (perhaps violent) about it. This problem does not undermine the authority of human rights discourse, but it does present it as necessarily problematic. This is more clear in the present, perhaps, than in any other epoch. We live in an era when human rights discourse is the most defensible and defended principle of political programmatics, even to the point of incontestability.

It has been at least the nominal justification for wars in Kosovo, Afghanistan, and Iraq, as well as the regular deployment of United Nations forces globally. It would be unwise to see these events as simply using human rights discourse as a cloak behind which imperial ambitions are played out. This unwillingness to take human rights wars on face value ends by reducing complex, even internally contradictory global political agendas to disabling platitude. It also ends by presenting too ideal an understanding of how human rights discourse can play out in the world. It is simply not possible for human rights to be advanced purely peacefully. Human rights have long been identified by political thinkers as problematic—for their symbiotic relationship with liberal individualism; their reduction to simple lists of absolute yet disconnected principles; and most importantly, for their compromising, even willingly and arrogantly blind, celebration of their Enlightenment (and thus imperial) inheritance. Human rights are always and everywhere a *problem*. In the present, especially since Kosovo and the formulation of the Blair doctrine, this is played out by their ambiguous relationship with war: wars are fought on behalf of human rights that reduce human rights in the war zone and at home, and that are vigorously opposed in the name of human rights. Human rights both subtend war and refuse it at one and the same time. This is an aporia which it is not easy to find a way through, and that both discourses which recommend and those which critique human rights prefer to ignore.

What can the role of literature be in this situation? Four main impulses motivate creative works that deal with human rights issues: they are the impulses to *remember*, to *reveal*, to *remind*, and to *resolve*. These four are not mutually exclusive and both overlap and condition one another. The first (to *remember)* involves the commemoration of historical events, such as the Rwandan genocide, the horrifying ordinariness of the bureaucracy that organized the Nazi holocaust, or the way in which modern national histories have been built on dispossession, slavery, and the inequitable application of the law. The aim here is to avert a forgetfulness that might make such appalling events disappear seamlessly into an unstudied history, or to commemorate things which, if not strongly remembered, might become prey to usually racially motivated revisionism.

The second impulse (to *reveal)* is to communicate to the world hitherto unknown atrocities, such as the existence and extent of the Gulag, the sadistic spasms of the Cultural Revolution, the details of the attempt to annihilate indigenous populations in settler colonies like Australia, or the recent events at Abu Ghraib prison in Iraq. The ambition here is to intervene spectacularly in contemporary politics. Such work relies on a logic of display, wherein the graphic exhibition of behavior without detailed and contextualizing analysis aims to appeal to a fundamental even visceral indignation. It is a politics, not of leadership or program, but of appeal to other people—politicians or voters, perhaps—to change and to cause change.

The third impulse (to *remind*) shifts from historical to more explicitly moral discourse. Here the aim is to shock us out of the complacencies in which we have been plunged in putatively democratic societies, either by the compromises we ourselves have made or the ones we routinely witness and condone. In our daily lives, we become impervious to the suffering of other people, over which a kind of bland and shallow amnesia settles. We are dimly aware that cruel and appalling things are going on in global political life, but because we are pre-occupied or cannot easily see a solution, we resign ourselves to the dissatisfactions of enduring comfort and the work we are told earns it for us. Properly managed creativity in the name of human rights can shock us by the intensity of our horror at what is happening around us, and how lazy we have been. How can we be the bystanders to such horror, especially if it seems bystanders and collaborators might not after all be so different from one another? We are reminded then of the intensity and purity of our feelings about abuse.

The fourth impulse (to *resolve)* grows from the third. The aim here is to turn the moral straightening experienced above either into some kind of activism or a general resolution that such things should not be allowed to happen again. Technically, this is the final goal of all work that deals with human rights issues: to make sure that abuse ends or is not repeated. The risk is that specific privileged case studies are de-historicized and then moralized in a way exploited by politicians with other agendas (the invasion of Iraq, for example) whose commitment to human rights is dubious or at best rhetorico-sentimental. The privileging of certain events at the expense of others (the Nazi holocaust over the slave trade; minority civil rights in democracies over the plight of asylum seekers or economic refugees) also risks the repetition of a colonial logic in which certain types of suffering (the torment of British prisoners by the Japanese) gain a meaning out of proportion with their ongoing historical significance (in contrast with, for example, the Indonesian occupation of Papua). In short, the affective intensity of the stage of resolution risks certain kinds of moralistic disproportion and exploitable enthusiasm.

What these four impulses have in common, what is problematic about them over and above the political complications I have already mentioned, and what connects them strongly with the liberal tradition in both literature and politics, is that they all rely on a logic of *the secret*, or at least of a kind of hidden depth. The impulse to *remember* restores to awareness events at risk of disappearing into the blur of over-abundant historical information or the quiet and remove of the increasing specialization of historical knowledge. The impulse to *reveal* relies explicitly upon the idea that certain historical events are unpublicized and thus unknown. The impulse to *remind* us of our commitment to human rights requires us to recover a purer more noble and intense feeling from behind our complacency, and the impulse to *resolve* also requires a commitment to values easily swamped by our other, likely pettier, entanglements.

The fundamental problem with the logic of the secret is that what is enduringly challenging and dangerous in the human rights issues that most tellingly confront us is not at all hidden. Our awareness of them is lived out every day. The nature of the impulse to remind and resolve that I have mentioned bear this out. Of course, as long as there are human rights abuses there will always be some need to reveal the hidden, publicize the ignored, and clarify the obscured. Unfortunately, it seems there will always be crimes that need to be revealed. However, I want to argue that we cannot continue to believe that the liberal drama of courageous investigation, climactic revelation, and bold accusation is the most relevant to our current global human rights situation. The key human rights problems we have to deal with involve the routine victimization of asylum seekers and economic refugees, the "collateral damages" of terroristic military campaigns, the pre-emptive targeting of minority groups deemed a threat to the social order, the opportunism of authoritarian and patriarchal ideological systems, and the ongoing harassment of enduringly and newly colonized populations. The sources of such victimization range from re-fundamentalizing religious groups attempting to find an alternative to global economic hegemonies, on the one hand, to the determination of the most powerful world coalitions—political and corporate—to overcome all resistance to such hegemonies, on the other. These abuses of freedom are not only not secret, they are proudly and publicly defended, often in the name of freedom itself. Freedom mutilates freedoms. Even those most committed to liberal freedom seem to be able to reconcile themselves to certain abuses of human rights. In short, there will continue to be episodes in which the secret needs to be revealed, yet the moral narcissism this may license risks occluding the most important and defining ways in which human rights issues currently play themselves out, in which violence is deployed to advance, protect, or enlarge human rights, or the most intransigent violations of human freedoms take place in the name of freedom. The logic of the secret is seductive to a liberal culture that values education, insight, judgment, the visibility of truth, and the accusing maverick. In fact, it conforms and forces politics to conform to this very model of agency. How politically useful a way of thinking is this, and what are the possible alternatives? I want to use Mario Perniola's work on the nature of the secret in an attempt to provide an alternative way of considering the relationship between the living political subject and the contemporary political situation of human rights.

To Perniola, the problem with the secret as an idea is that it is anti-intellectual. It demotes the analysis that alone would allow us to lay out the complexity of a political situation. It relies on the idea that the revelation of truth is sufficient and is enough to both trigger action and make clear what that action should be. He writes:

> What I find unsatisfactory and at bottom naïve in . . . the entire notion of the secret is precisely this conception of truth as something that at different times will just appear or disappear quite independently of

thought. The concept of the secret relies on the existence of a simple truth, the route to which may be long, complicated and tortuous; but once it is sighted, the secret is effaced. What I find unacceptable in the notion of the secret is that thinking is assigned a secondary and, in the final analysis, an inessential role. Each time that thinking is presented in terms of a police investigation, its dignity is assaulted, its primacy is compromised and any exit from the cultural framework of neo-obscurantism and neo-barbarism . . . is barred.[3]

The concept of the secret promotes the act of revelation, but discounts the need for rigorous analysis. It relies on an idea that the truth itself is unambiguous, and is not subject either to ambivalence or to difficulty. Judgment is to be quick and pragmatic, to the point where the revelation of truth is enough to encourage correct action. It is intolerant of the historical situation of the revealed truth other than as an obstacle to transparency. Yet it is this historical situation which determines the way in which political decisions are inflected and rationalized, and in which compromises are made. The result of too automatic a response is that human rights violations are complained of without an attempt to deal with the situation that has given rise to their being addressed, the very situation that will continue to allow the abuses to be rationalized and thus to endure.

To complain of the treatment of asylum seekers because it is racist, arbitrary, and cruel, for example (all of which is commonly true) will do little to revise policies which remain in the hands of national governments whose primary focus is the perpetuation of the economic advantages of their citizenry until they are many, many times greater than those of the poor. This is borne out by the fact that asylum seekers have been routinely discredited as economic refugees (ironically in nations which traditionally sentimentalize the fact that they were founded by earlier generations of economic refugees). In other words, abuses can be publicly and even proudly legitimated even in their cruelty and self-indulgence, and publicizing the plight of the victims will do little to solve the problem.

As an alternative to the logic of the secret, Perniola outlines the structure of what he calls the *enigma*. In contrast to the secret, in which the focus is on the simple revelation of hidden depths in an act deemed sufficient to provoke outrage and action, the logic of the enigma displays internal conditions that are enduringly problematic and must be investigated, worried, and developed by thought. In the enigma, "opposing forces do not succeed one another chronologically, but are held simultaneously present in the same object."[4] In contrast to the secret, in which revelation is the termination of intellectual work, the enigma opens up a necessary field of intense, energetic, and complex elaboration. It is not an "obstacle," or a "limit set on the quest for truth."[5] Indeed, it is only by recognizing the nature of truth as enigmatic that we can overcome the romance of the secret and deal with political situations in their dynamic and plural situatedness.

I want to propose that the contemporary politics of human rights is indeed enigmatic. As I have argued, human rights discourse both opposes and licenses violence, even war. Freedom compromises freedoms. This is a situation in which contradictory impulses subsist in one and the same formation, but in a strictly non-dialectical fashion. The intractability of many contemporary human rights issues arises not only because of the duplicity and cynicism of governments and corporations, or because of the callous indifference of democratic populations, or the endurance of pre-enlightened cultural formations. It is because the very thing that human rights are supposed to achieve is threatened by the violence deployed in its name. Countries which see their historical mission as both the modeling and export of freedom can only pursue their freedom, can only advance it, by means that inevitably involve the reduction of freedom both at home and abroad. It is often freedom that stands most tellingly in the way of freedom. Our human rights situation is enigmatic because of a set of paradoxical and intractable problems. Widespread awareness of human rights abuses and the proclaimed and sincere desire to deal with them does not necessarily lead to their mitigation because the world order run by affluent democracies is primarily committed to a certain organization of global power in which the availability of commodities must be maximized (no matter how much we abhor the conditions under which they were produced); the movement of populations must be controlled in order to preserve employment and social welfare rights for the citizens of wealthy countries alone (no matter how much the rich are appalled by global suffering); the disposability of energy must be absolutely uninterrupted (no matter the local politics that must make this possible and the environmental consequences we know we must minimize for our own survival); and the movement of capital must be absolutely uninhibited (no matter what the risk to ourselves and others of uncontrolled speculation); and so on and so on. All these flexibilities— which are seen to guarantee the lived experience of freedom in affluent societies—dream of liberalizing all world socialities by the establishment of the rule of law, the enfranchisement of all and the opening of cultures. This mission must be completed as quickly as possible, and the freedoms it achieves must be rigorously protected. The expansion and protection of freedom requires both a conquest and a policing, which when exercised in the name of liberality easily become unaccountable, even when clearly visible. No amount of investigation or revelation will unstitch this complex network of freedoms at the expense of freedom. The maximization of social and cultural liberality that has come to define whole transnational cultures requires the obstruction of the freedom that it seeks to exemplify. The problem of freedom lies at the heart of freedom itself, therefore. The extension of freedom costs freedom. This means that there is an impulse against freedom generated by the will-to-freedom itself. This problem is made more intense because the contradiction here goes also to the nature of human rights logic. Human rights discourse itself is inextricably entangled with a logic of overcoming and expansion that must at some point join, encourage, or rationalize violence, even war.

The problem that confronts us then when we consider the relationship between human rights and literature is that literary treatments of human rights usually require the reduction of human rights issues to a logic of the secret, yet our current human rights situation is one of *enigma*, in which human rights are played out as openly internally contradictory. Does literature have anything to offer at all as a way of dealing with this problem, or can it properly be dealt with only by philosophical, political, and historical writing? This question only gets asked because, through the twentieth century, literature was claimed to be the proper place for the elaboration and debate of key controversies in personal and also civic life. In the Leavisite and New Critical traditions, literature was itself democratic and thus the proper place for the discussion of issues central to the functioning of democracy. Neither as esoteric as specialist academic genres nor as predictable as popular culture, literature was seen as a domain both accessible enough to invite the participation of an imagined reflective general citizenry and subtle enough to deal with complex issues that required a nuanced treatment. It was the essence of the commons. It is unlikely that literature performed this function for the politics of national and international governmental institutions (as opposed to the politics of cultural and social identity and valuation) more than merely marginally, repeating and perhaps broadening awareness of some issues but not really pioneering ideas. It is even more unlikely that from the 1950s onwards it did any more in these domains than any other strand of creative work (popular or elite), despite claims made by influential theorists like Julia Kristeva about what only literature could offer.

Yet this does not mean that literature as just another strand of creative initiative cannot partake of broader aesthetic and para-aesthetic tendencies which may be of significant consequence. Indeed, I want to argue that one of the most telling ways in the past in which philosophy has addressed itself to the problematic nature of human rights has been by focusing on another aspect of the human rights enigma, the problem of liberal subjectivity, the deconstruction of which was pioneered by aesthetic, including literary, culture. To illustrate how the deconstruction of subjectivity reveals another enigma, I want to address the (undeclared) dispute between Giorgio Agamben and Emmanuel Levinas on the role of extra-political subjectivity in human rights issues. The problem with the identification of rights with individuality was raised by Marx, of course, who challenged the definition of rights as a kind of property. The arrogation of rights to the individual raises a series of problems: above all, it is a radically de-politicizing gesture. It locates rights in a private space that separates them from the public interchange of the political. Yet, the question is: does this doom individuality to a debilitating separation from political life, or is it in fact the thing that protects subjectivity from victimization?

Agamben discusses this issue in the context of his analysis of the separation of what he calls "bare life" from civic political identity. By making rights the natural and inevitable birthright of the individual, humanitarian doctrines, he argues, reinforce the idea that there is a kind of extra-social life separate from instituted political identities. The individual becomes separable from the civic identity developed in political life, and has a fundamentally natural truth inalienable from the simple fact of his or her basic biological existence. Yet, for Agamben, this separation of the bare biological life of the individual from her civic identity is the very separation by which various classes of human beings have been robbed of protections and become subject to arbitrary power—to the point of death in the concentration camp. To Agamben, then, the identification of human rights with the natural rights of the human being as born legitimates and facilitates the very abusive politics it claims to be fighting. Agamben writes:

> The separation between humanitarianism and politics that we are experiencing today is the extreme phase of the separation of the rights of man from the rights of the citizen. In the final analysis, however, humanitarian organisations . . . can only grasp human life in the figure of bare or sacred life, and therefore, despite themselves, maintain a secret solidarity with the very powers they ought to fight. . . . A humanitarianism separated from politics cannot fail to reproduce the isolation of sacred life at the basis of sovereignty, and the camp—which is to say, the pure space of exception—is the biopolitical paradigm that it cannot master.[6]

In other words, Agamben claims that human rights organizations may actually, paradoxically, be re-confirming the political arrangements that drive human rights abuse.

Emmanuel Levinas takes the opposite point of view to Agamben, arguing that it is only in a domain exempt from politics that what he calls "the rights of man" can be protected. He writes not only that "[T]he defense of the rights of man corresponds to a vocation *outside* the state" but that it requires "a vigilance totally different from political intelligence."[7] He goes on to claim that "the capacity to guarantee that extra-territoriality and that independence defines the liberal state."[8] In other words, it is in the liberal state's identification of a sphere separable from politics that the protection and advancement of human rights becomes possible. By re-imagining some extra-political space, this argument would seem to succumb to the very distinction—between civic identity and bare life—which Agamben would see as the source of the real problem, the logic whereby bodies become vulnerable to unaccountable, unmediated and ruthless administration. Yet, Levinas actually imagines this as the only way in which the "conjunction of politics and ethics is possible."[9]

Even in his endorsement of the liberal state, however, Levinas is not relying on an orthodox model of individual subjectivity. Indeed, he argues that the institution of justice, even in the name of an inalienable and unique individuality, risks reducing the person to something simply quantifiable "by submitting him or her (the unique, the incomparable) to comparison, to thought, to being placed on the famous scales of justice, and thus to calculation."[10] The alternative is, of course, to ground a thinking of rights in a model of a subjectivity emerging always already in relation to a prior otherness: "A freedom in fraternity, in which the responsibility of one-for-the-other is affirmed, and through which the rights of man manifest themselves *concretely* to consciousness as the rights of the other."[11] Only in overcoming the liberal model of the subject can the liberal rapprochement between politics and ethics be facilitated.

The notion of the individual presents an intractable problem for human rights discourse. The separation of subjectivity from politics may be the very thing that means subjects can be robbed of their civic protection, and thus exposed to abuse. On the other hand, the absolute and inflexible insistence on doctrines of individualism may at certain times in certain places be the only effective means to gain support for campaigns against torture, the exclusion of women, arbitrary justice, and so on. The situation of human rights organizations may in fact be the inverse of the one Agamben recognizes: the de-politicization of bare life may reinforce the logic of sovereignty; yet, the insistence that only a re-politicization can challenge biopolitics risks abolishing the fiction of the private, which, however deconstructible, may provide at times the only bulwark against the exposure of subjective life to the un-mediated political. Thus, in a paradox which Agamben will not entertain, the thing that exposes us to biopolitics may also in moments be the thing that protects us from it. I don't pretend to have a solution to this enigma. Indeed enigmas are not riddles: it is not of their nature simply to be "solved," as if we can somehow transcend the complexity and contradictions of our many lived political situations. This enigma will remain an issue that requires nuanced negotiation.

However, here philosophy re-proposes a problem dealt with extensively in the arts. The deconstruction of individualism that we see evidence of in the discussions of human rights here is part of a generalized problematization and reconsideration of subjectivity in modern and postmodern culture. Indeed, Perniola's own extensive work on aesthetics, for example on video art, has demonstrated lucidly that the simultaneous promotion and deconstruction of subjectivity is the defining theme of twentieth-century aesthetic practice. This reconsideration ranges from the complication of the unitary nature of perspective towards the pluralizations of expression and the objectification of both the abstract and the commodity in visual culture; the exploration of the possibilities of style in writing (from stream-of-consciousness's intensification of the subjective to the erasure of the individual voice in the *nouveau roman*, absurdism, and L=A=N=G=U=A=G=E P=O=E=T=R=Y); to the implicit deconstruction of individual subjectivity in montage to the widespread resonances between the trope of the unconscious and artistic practice. This is just to mention a few examples from a few specific locations. And, of course, this re-appraisal and indeed re-definition of individual subjectivity in cultural practice has fed into and in turn learned from the more systematic re-appraisal of the historicized subject in Freud, Heidegger, Derrida, Foucault, Lacan, Kristeva, and others. Human rights discourse as it progresses, then, is entangled in the experimentations of culture, from which it both learns and must also pressure, and for which it may provide an unacknowledged motivation. The radical reconsideration of subjectivity reveals liberal human rights discourse as irreducibly problematic. It is the most important relationship human rights discourse has with the aesthetic, and the literary in particular, far outweighing the role of those works which reiterate the same account of human rights abuse in terms of the exhibition of the secret. These latter may help publicize specific historical instances or current emergencies in human rights and galvanize those already committed. They risk ignoring, perhaps even in a high-handed manner, the problems which human rights discourse will have to negotiate if it is going to survive, what I have called above the enigmas of human rights.

The problematization of subjectivity has thus been a consistent theme in modern and postmodern literature, not least in novels dealing with political issues that have human rights ramifications. I want now briefly to contrast two novels which represent the different approaches to the representation of human rights I have outlined above: one a novel conforming to the orthodox literary logic of the secret, the second attempting to confront the problem of human rights as enigma. In J. M. Coetzee's *Waiting for the Barbarians*,[12] ethnically based political aggression on the part of a fictional Empire against adjoining "barbarians" is focused through the lens of the self-examination of a middle-aged frontier magistrate. Wrestling with his own implication and ineffectiveness in relation to this oppression, the magistrate crosses geographical and personal frontiers to reveal his own moral situation and nature, exploring challenges that risk violence and abjection. This narrative identifies political questions as, fundamentally, problems of self-revelation and redemption. It thus enacts the orthodox human rights logic of the secret: a person's un-noticed or at least unaddressed implication in a politics of oppression needs to be revealed and faced. What is at stake is the possible correct attunement of the self with political responsibility. This novel belongs to the twilight of an era of western narcissism where politics could be imagined as somehow a matter of conscience and correct (ideologically, morally, or spiritually "responsible") behavior, rather than as the achievement of satisfactory outcomes.

A contrasting example would be William T Vollmann's *Europe Central*.[13] Vollmann's very choice of the controversial and enigmatic Dmitri Shostakovich as his key focus presents the individual subject as a site of radical impossibility in the face of political violation. Paralyzed in an aporetic space between collaboration and dissent, Shostakovich is emblematic of the complex situation of contemporary subjectivity in the face of the politics of human rights: as we have seen in the unresolvable argument between Agamben and Levinas, subjectivity is torn between being excluded from politics, on the one hand, and being totally saturated with political meaning, on the other. The former may make it vulnerable to biopolitical administration, but it might also imagine some fictional space of exemption from total socialization. The latter may mean it is included in the polis, while at the same time requiring of it certain types of rigorous and transparent self-identity. Vollmann's Shostakovich never resolves these enigmas. He is never—or not quite—the abject collaborator with Stalinist terror, nor—at least not fully—the heroic martyr for the truisms of liberal freedom. Yet the vast canvas of European violence which Vollmann presents never proposes that individual self-correction or redemption is the main issue. Subjectivity is not meaningful on its own terms in its own space, as it is for Coetzee. Instead, it is sucked up into the larger politics of atrocity in which history has bigger fish to fry than whether an individual is, or can be held, responsible.

The challenge has been then to find a way in which literature can address the enigma of human rights. As Vollmann's novel shows, this can only be done in a literary form capable of presenting abstract theoretical issues in their incommensurate relationships with unfolding global political situations, which will always be larger than them, and of which they will never simply be the focus. In *Europe Central,* a range of mutually incommensurate discourses are collocated—discourses of historical problematization, conceptual dislocation, and aesthetic innovation as well as subjective experimentation—in a way that brings them into a productive but unresolvable clash with one another. Yet, importantly, this clash does not allow the homogenization of a writerly or readerly consciousness that licenses an ironic neutralization. The very subject matter of the novel precludes this. The enigma distinguishes itself from an aesthetic tradition in which the collocation of incommensurabilities is too easily read as irony or paradox. The easy quietism of a recourse to irony has done much to simultaneously elevate and neutralize art, at one and the same time rendering it a source of cultural capital, while risking its becoming historically inconsequential. If literature is to deal with the political enigmas that confront us, it must resist irony as both a creative principle and a reading strategy, as Vollmann's work does. In this way, it belongs to a long-standing literary trajectory in modernist fiction that has pioneered a complex elaboration of incommensurate discourses: from *Moby Dick* through works as different as *Gravity's Rainbow* and Carlos Fuentes's *Terra Nostra* to David Foster Wallace's *Infinite Jest* and to Vollmann's work. The lynchpin text here remains *Ulysses,* a work in which experimentation with the relationship between subjectivity and representation, the lived intensity of historical time, the fragmentation of political meaning, and the risks of aesthetic innovation all collide in a way that—despite all efforts—still remains unresolvable and irreducible to the tame aesthetic monumentalism which so many institutions have tried to induce in it. In the same way that literary culture has been crucial in the revaluation of subjectivity, it can in an enigmatic novel like *Europe Central* invent new ways of re-calibrating the discourses of historical, political, and subjective meaning. It is in the busy and intense convergence of these discourses that some means of understanding how we might work and live with our enigmas can arise.

Human rights discourse is beset with innumerable problems, most famously the cultural relativity of the Enlightenment values that explain human rights and their involvement in the worst kinds of imperialism. We have identified above other key problems with human rights discourses, most tellingly their relationship with violence: human rights discourses may encourage or license the very violence and warfare they should reduce. Following Perniola, we argued that conceiving of human rights in terms of the secret does little more than repeat well-worn and comforting platitudes that do nothing to address the problem. Only by a radical reconsideration of subjectivity, sociality, politics, and history can these problems be addressed. The reconsideration of subjectivity is both an enigma for human rights and the most defining theme of modern, postmodern, and now contemporary cultural practice, whether or not it is linked explicitly to human rights. We have seen how critiques and reinventions of human rights in the hands of Agamben and Levinas have relied on a re-thinking of subjectivity, and are thus linked to the broader aesthetic reconsideration of the self. Both Agamben and Levinas are attempting to deal with the enigma of human rights: to Agamben, the doctrine of human individuality on which human rights discourse depends is the very thing that separates bare life from civic and political identity, thus licensing biopolitical intervention. To Levinas, in modern political contexts "the rights of man are compromised by the very practices for which they supplied the motivation."[14] The reconsideration of the politics of subjectivity on which each of these thinkers embarks attempts to address the very enigmatic, self-contradicting problem of human rights, what has made us identify it as an enigma in Perniola's terms. In sum, by revealing or exhibiting the secrets of human rights abuse, literature publicizes and advances already established human rights values, but only by insisting that they are absolute and incontestable. Yet, human rights discourses remain historically problematic, and perhaps even a threat to themselves, even arguably constituting the very logic that does the most to undermine their own achievement. To deal with this problem, human rights must be dealt with as an enigma, and new ways of representing it must be found. In literature, this kind of deconstruction is already long underway. Literature's most valuable contribution to human rights discourse comes, therefore, from domains where human rights may not be mentioned or even recognized as an issue, by finding new ways to represent the enigmas we are living.

214 *Nick Mansfield*

NOTES

1. Jacques Derrida, "Force of Law: The 'Mystical Foundation of Authority'," in *Acts of Religion*, ed. Gil Anidjar (New York and London: Routledge), 228–98.
2. Immanuel Kant, *Perpetual Peace*, ed. Lewis White Beck (Indianapolis: Liberal Arts Press, 1957).
3. Mario Perniola, *Enigmas: The Egyptian Moment in Society and Art*, trans. Christopher Woodall (London: Verso, 1995), 4.
4. Perniola, *Enigmas*, 17.
5. Perniola, *Enigmas*, 15.
6. Giorgio Agamben, *Homo Sacer: Sovereign Power and Bare Life*, 1995, trans. Daniel Heller-Roazen (Stanford, CA: Stanford University Press, 1998), 133–134.
7. Emmanuel Levinas, *Time and the Other and Additional Essays*, trans. Richard A. Cohen (Pittsburgh: Duquesne University Press, 1987), 123.
8. Levinas, *Time and the Other and Additional Essays*, 123.
9. Levinas, *Time and the Other and Additional Essays*, 123.
10. Levinas, *Time and the Other and Additional Essays*, 122.
11. Levinas, *Time and the Other and Additional Essays*, 125.
12. J. M. Coetzee, *Waiting for the Barbarians* (London: Secker & Warburg; New York: Penguin, 1980).
13. William T. Vollmann, *Europe Central* (New York: Penguin, 2005).
14. Levinas, *Time and the Other and Additional Essays*, 121.

12 Imagining Women as Human

Hephzibah Roskelly

When Catherine MacKinnon asked *Are Women Human?* in her 2006 collection, it wasn't just a rhetorical question. The question expressed real puzzlement at what MacKinnon saw as a looming and continuing gap between the two terms—woman and human—in legal and human rights language. Human rights might be connected to women's rights, but as MacKinnon's question implies, the link cannot be taken for granted. MacKinnon contends that global gender inequality continues as long as human rights initiatives and international law do not spell out abuses of women as human rights issues. As she pointedly declares, "One is less than human when one's violations do not violate human rights.[1] Charlotte Bunch's question echoes MacKinnon's when she asks why so many "degrading life experiences of women [have] not been understood as human rights issues?"[2] Human rights discourse has been based primarily on "men's fears, men's experiences," Bunch asserts, while women's abuses have been ignored in human rights documents or dismissed as cultural or "natural" difference. It appears that *woman,* then, cannot yet be a "name for a way of being human," in Richard Rorty's phrase.[3]

In *Who Sings the Nation State?*, Gayatri Spivak and Judith Butler begin to answer the question they pose with an illustration of the politics of nationhood and of access to rights in the story of Spanish-speaking residents in California who sang the US National Anthem in Spanish at a public event. As they sang, people claimed not just the song but their right to the rights symbolized by the song. As Butler and Spivak point out, the exercise both calls for the right and exposes the difference between calling for and having it: "We have to understand the public exercise as enacting the freedom it posits and positing what is not there yet."[4] The gap between the fact of equality and the demand for it is expressed in the singing.

This chapter examines an exercise of the kind Spivak and Butler describe, a way to "sing" the claims of women as humans and thus show the need for human rights discourse that makes those claims explicit. It investigates the remaking of a literary genre that might offer possibilities for linking women's rights and human rights in productive ways. Using literature to teach

lessons is nothing new; it is as old as literature itself. The literary text creates symbolic dimensions of everyday life that invite readers to draw connections to lived experience; to locate differences and make them familiar;
to interpret fairly and with empathy. But if it's an old game, this employment of literature in the service of culture whether for change or stasis, it's
one that has remained elastic enough to be serviceable in our postmodern
climate. Postcolonial theory often uses the literature of postcolonial states
to ground and deepen its theories of literacy, development, and human
rights. The recognition of literature's rhetorical intentions and effects is
clear in the work of literary theorists from many ideological frameworks,
from Wayne Booth to Mikhail Bakhtin, from Raymond Williams to Toni
Morrison, who see that the power of a particular narrative can mirror the
power of a cultural narrative.

The ability of literature to provoke action or belief is one reason that
Joseph Slaughter makes one powerful genre of literature, the *Bildungsroman* or coming-of-age tale, the centerpiece of his critique of human rights
discourse. *Human Rights, Inc.* describes the recent history of international
human rights beginning with the United Nations' Universal Declaration
of Human Rights (UDHR) written in 1948 by UN delegates, who hoped
to address the horrific human rights violations of World War II by stating
those rights unequivocally. It began: "All human beings are born free and
equal in dignity and rights" (UDHR Article 1). To help describe its ideals
and assertions, and also, as Slaughter shows, to help writers from a variety
of nations and agendas collaborate, the declaration made both direct and
implicit use of the narrative and the literary, at several points referring to
one of the most famous of *Bildungsromane, Robinson Crusoe*, as proof of
its contentions about humanity and citizenship. The famous story of the
progress toward maturity of the young Crusoe on his desert island as an
Everyman whose success was assured if he followed the right paths helped
writers to frame their ideas about what human rights included and how
those rights were exercised and given full range. Like *Crusoe*, the UDHR
was premised on the idea that the universality of human rights and human
experience made conclusions inevitable. Slaughter quotes UDHR framer
and French philosopher, Jacques Maritain, who claims that human rights
are inherent and deducible *"from the simple fact that man is man."*[5]

The classic *Bildungsroman*, of which *Robinson Crusoe* (1745) is an early
example, tells a story whose conclusions are foregone specifically because
man is man: the young hero begins arrogantly or naively indifferent to his
society or responsibility, learns difficult life lessons that challenge his mistaken, often impetuous, moves and finally make him a better, more successful member of his community. The universality of the plot for both novels
and for the many that followed (including the seminal *Bildung Wilhelm
Meister's Apprenticeship* by Wolfgang Goethe [1795]) in the nineteenth
and twentieth centuries and the subsequent, partially dependent universality of human rights discourse make both "suspicious," as Slaughter argues,

for their generic universalism proceeds from a western bias and a "residual nationalism" that dictates both.[6] Human rights, Slaughter insists, is not only about the laws and declarations a group makes; it is about the symbols it depends on for its definitions. Human rights, he says, is therefore "a question of both literacy and legislation, as much matters of literature as of law."[7] The symbol of the *Bildungsroman* and the narrative of human development it proposes both compels and limits human rights initiatives.

The problem of literature and law in human rights discourse looms large for women. If males who do not fit the rubric assigned to *human* are ignored and abused, women in all class, economic, and political situations have been omitted consistently from the discourse of community and nation. Jacqueline Pitanguy, Director of Citizenship Studies, Information, Action (CEPIA) and one of the participants in the Global Tribunal on Violations of Women's Human Rights in Vienna in 1993, puts it in no uncertain terms: "If there is one intriguing pattern that seems to cut across centuries and different civilizations, it is that a woman is always less entitled to rights than a man. This is so in spite of inequalities of social class, race, ethnicity, religion, and culture that permeate societies and affect both men and women."[8] As the Vienna Tribunal, the Beijing Women's Conference, and a host of other campaigns for international women's rights assert, women in every part of the world need to be heard in order to make the claim to what seems commonsensical but is not: that women's rights are human rights.

There are no women in Daniel Defoe's *Robinson Crusoe*; in fact, there are hardly any people at all, which is the point of this coming-of-age story. Cast adrift on an almost uninhabited island far from the community he has scorned, Crusoe learns to become a fully developed human by recognizing in his isolation his duties to the community. As one writer of the UDHR put it, referring to Crusoe's tale, "Everyone has duties to the community in which alone the full and free development of his personality is possible."[9] The troubling contradictions the UDHR writers examined—whether personhood develops individually or socially, and which is more important— resolved themselves with the introduction of *Crusoe*. "Surprising though it may be that the ludicrous Robinson Crusoe acted as a serious literary surrogate for those controversies," Slaughter writes, "even more surprising is the efficiency with which the novel's invocation dispatched the perpetually nagging problematics of man and society by supplying an iconic literary shorthand for entire canons of intricate theoretical arguments."[10] Despite differences among committee members, *Crusoe* was broad enough in its rendering to become "proof" of the ideal in personality development.[11]

This reliance of the framers of the UDHR on Robinson Crusoe as a *proof* of individual and social effects on human development suggests how powerful the novel, and especially the *Bildungsroman*, is and how much human rights and the *Bildungsroman* became mutually ratifying. *Robinson Crusoe* became a touchstone for the writers and first readers of the UDHR precisely because it wasn't an intricate theoretical argument, but a story, a compelling narrative that described how a human was tested and grew in wisdom from the experience. The term "human" meant something different for each delegate: "the person the delegates imagined when they discussed human personality was not always (or ever) the same thing—each of them had some other person in mind."[12] And the differences meant that personhood and the law could be in conflict, could limit the free and full development of some. The person the UDHR document projects is, like the discussion of *Robinson Crusoe* that led to compromise in the document, "not quite 'natural man' and not quite 'positive man'—a creature fully interpellated by society, its institutions and its laws."[13] But he is a man.

One reason the writers of the UDHR were able to come to compromise around the issue of personhood by referring to the literary *Bildungsroman* of *Robinson Crusoe* is, as Slaughter suggests, an imaginative construction that creates and sustains a community by showing how individual and society merge by tests that guide the individual toward community, or state, interests. These include an understanding of the individual attributes the state holds dear: enterprise, conformity, and the civic virtue that guarantees citizenship. The *Bildungsroman* becomes more than a story; it is "the name of a trope, a figurative idea that turns the concrete individual into an instantiation of humanity's totality."[14] Because the values this trope represents are western Enlightenment values, and the *Bildungsroman* itself is a western Enlightenment creation, the tradition ignores the differences presented by individuals whose path toward adulthood and community diverge from the *Bildung* and from the values of the western nation-state. It is for this reason that Slaughter is critical of the human rights discourse embodied first in the UDHR and carried out in declarations and mandates from a host of nations since then. Those declarations are implicitly or explicitly based on the contentions about individual and nation that leave out many parts of the world, that in effect ignore the human rights of many because those individuals don't meet the requirements of citizenship or even the simple tautology of humanness. Yet readers in both First World and emerging nation-states recognize the story of the *Bildungsroman* and its symbolism and participate in it, implicitly aligning themselves with the narrow definitions of humanness presented through the trope of the *Bildungsroman*.

Slaughter gives great power to the audience, who must recognize itself as the "implicated reader" who colludes to produce the generic forms of socially acceptable human variation: "Our reading acts have implications not only for the imagination but the legislation of an international human rights community."[15] By extending the trope of the *Bildungsroman* into lived experience across the globe so seamlessly, readers, it seems, imagine too well.

Benedict Anderson agrees that readers' imaginations have consequences for the community. Readers create community by imagining it in the nation: "It is *imagined* because the members of even the smallest nation never know most of their fellow members, or even hear of them, yet in the minds of each lives the image of their communion."[16] Anderson's historical analysis of the emergence of nationalism suggests that it emerges from the *need* to imagine communion and continuity, needs once met by the religious and the dynastic registers of social life. It succeeded because of that need: "Nothing perhaps more precipitated this search, nor made it more fruitful, than print capitalism, which made it possible for rapidly growing numbers of people to think about themselves, and to relate themselves to others, in profoundly new ways."[17] Fictional narrative in the form of newspapers (which create narratives and communities through the stories they tell) and novels become deeply a part of this imagining of nationhood: "Fiction seeps quietly and continuously into reality, creating that remarkable confidence of community in anonymity which is the hallmark of modern nations."[18]

Anderson's contention that the fictional community "seeps quietly" into reality is seconded by critiques of the work of many First World feminists, whose arguments, critics maintain, often imply an anonymous, equal, ultimately unearned, notion of community like the one Anderson describes. It is clearly crucial to honor the variety of class, economic, and cultural situations occupied by women and the multiplicity of actions they perform within those contexts in order for community to be embodied rather than anonymous. Despite the challenges presented by such multiplicity, indeed perhaps because of them, the abuses against women worldwide, in all their difference and all their similarity, must be made overtly part of human rights discourse. To do so demands that the variety of experiences that shape women's lives across the globe be accounted for. Rather than the "suspicious" plot that imagines a universal developmental path toward full humanity, new plots that re-imagine relationships between what is individual and social, that re-see the connections between the private and the public, and that understand the implication of the global in the local are needed. These narratives, as they proliferate and juxtapose themselves, provide global culture with new ways of imagining women as some of the humans whose rights are asserted in documents like the UDHR. In finding and considering those narratives and in affirming those connections, human rights' advocates begin to put women into their discourses.[19]

If literature provokes the imagination in ways that promote the creation of community among strangers, as Anderson says, and if the literature used to make that community is limiting to the ability to imagine others, as Slaughter argues, it would seem obvious that a new kind of *Bildungsroman* might be called for, one that would present alternative possibilities for growth and development of human consciousness and thus new ways to imagine the growth and development of community and national awareness. Slaughter even describes a few of these kinds of narratives in postcolonial fiction that trace the subaltern's growth in contradistinction to the colonial past he has inherited.[20] But, as he admits, contemporary first-person *Bildungsromane* "tend to be novels of disillusionment, in which the promises of developmentism and self-determination are revealed to be empty, or at least exaggerated."²¹ They thus carry less of the trope of developmental success than the traditional coming of age tale does. Can western readers remain distant from these disillusioned stories? Can emerging nation-states read into them new ways of imagining community? The problem of human and women's rights is fundamentally a problem of the imagination, and of finding a way to imagine new possibilities for growth as well as despair or ironic disillusionment. What is needed perhaps are more stories that clear alternative paths for their readers, not just stories that critique, however trenchantly, old ones.

The American philosopher Susanne Langer notes that if thinkers are to imagine new solutions to problems, "we must get us a whole world of new questions."²² The *Bildungsromane,* the stories of development of individual and cultural consciousness I discuss here, do suggest new answers perhaps, but more importantly, they ask the new questions that arise with women as writers and main characters. As they demonstrate, the progress-toward-development plot of the classic *Bildungsroman* alters with the recognition of the difference difference makes. From their gendered positions, the main characters ask questions that challenge the received ideas about culture as they are presented by male writers and characters in the traditional *Bildungsroman* plot, "sing" their claims within culture and nation. From their gendered positions, the writers of these plots pose new questions for readers, as they ask about growth and resistance. Readers become "implicated," as Slaughter describes, in helping to pose these questions and considering alternative responses that lay outside the traditional tropes of progress and human development. These new stories give readers new ways to imagine the humanness of others, so necessary in the struggle for human rights language that attends to the humanness in all. To paraphrase Langer, if we are to imagine new humans, we must get us a whole world of new stories about them.

Both Dorothy Allison's *Bastard Out of Carolina* (1992) and Marjane Satrapi's *The Complete Persepolis* (2003) remake the *Bildungsroman,* in part because of both authors' insistence on linking issues of human justice and feminist consciousness, and in part through the depictions of their heroines' growing recognition that one is entailed by the other. The young women they follow through childhood in the typical, even positivist, innocence-to-experience path of the *Bildungsroman* exist in wildly different class, economic, religious, and cultural worlds. But their coming-of-age tales suggest the mutual implication of women's rights and human ones and offer stimuli for readers' imaginations to expand and complicate what it means to be human.

The narratives are at once both autobiographical and fictionalized. As readers learn from reading Allison's memoir *Two or Three Things I Know for Sure* (1995), the story the narrator tells in *Bastard* is poignantly close to the story of Allison's own growing up. Poor, humiliated, abused, and finally raped by a terrorist of a stepfather, abandoned by a mother weakened by poverty and hopelessness, the character in the novel and the one in the memoir share a haunting consciousness of the powerlessness of their class situation and, especially, of their gender. *Persepolis* is overtly, rather than implicitly, autobiographical, written, as Satrapi herself puts it in the preface to her memoir, with the didactic intent of countering the stereotypes of Iran and Iranians: "I believe that an entire nation should not be judged by the wrongdoings of a few extremists."[23] Yet, despite its author's claim to experiential verity, the book is fictionalized by Satrapi's choice of the graphic novel as her genre. The cartoon characters and simply rendered situations highlight and shade the realities of the cultural context in vibrantly stark black and white drawings, as well as symbolize the childish perspective of its narrator.[24] It is autobiography close to fiction as *Bastard* is fiction close to autobiography.

This simultaneous move toward and away from "the real story" suggests that the narratives of these two young girls carry both "real" cultural weight and symbolic cultural momentum.[25] Wayne Booth argues that reading narrative forces readers to see both the "reality" of the lived life (their own lives) and the alternative reality a text presents: "Whenever we embrace the patterns of desire of any narrative, we become figured . . . by cumulative interrelationships of figurings that make up the temporal narrative experience itself. It transforms the life we might have lived during the hours we spend with the narrative and it thus becomes . . . a replacement of, and consequently a radical criticism of—that unlived life."[26] Readers move from their temporal experience into another, abandoning their "unlived life" for the life the narrative offers: "It is clear that all narrative is metaphoric, in the sense of saying, 'All of life, the entire world, is *like* this piece of it'—not necessarily on the surface . . . but in the depths of the author's penetrating vision."[27] The simultaneity of the "real" Marjane and the graphically created one, and the essayist Allison who explains the story of the fictional Bone, deepens readers' awareness of Booth's contention that narrative is both experientially and metaphorically "true."

Bone, Allison's persona in *Bastard*, is a girl in the American South, growing up as "white trash" in her rural South Carolina community and the victim of poverty's results: poor housing and education; humiliation at her class station and mockery from her class "betters"; family alcoholism, violence, and despair. She must learn to live in a culture that places little value on her because of her "no-count" family and because of her gender. In fact, it's her status as a female that makes her especially worthless. "Lord!" Bone's grandmother grumbles early in the novel. "I've got five girls and they never seem to appreciate me. It's how girls are though, selfish and full of themselves. I shouldn't expect any better."[28] To be a girl is to be lacking both in character and worth. "Yarboroughs been drowning girls and newborns for surely two hundred years now," Aunt Alma hoots at a neighbor who makes fun of her family for not valuing its children.[29]

The girl child in *Persepolis* could hardly be more distant from Bone. She is wealthy, from an educated family with ties to Persian royalty and a long history of influence in contemporary Iran. As the repressive reign of the Shah ends and is heralded by the people, Marjane's family first rejoices at what appears to be freedom and then becomes increasingly dismayed by the despotic rule that replaces the Shah, a religious fundamentalism that suddenly insists on rigid adherence to strict behavioral codes, especially on women's retreat into the home and away from the public eye. What begins as an issue of human rights for Marjane becomes a growing understanding of the need for justice for women, who suffer a different kind of cruelty from their husbands and brothers.

In these widely variant venues and class situations, each young girl grows conscious of her own individuality and her own place in her community and culture, as in classic Enlightenment *Bildungsromane*. But the encounters that provoke such growth, the tools each uses, and the consequences for self and other proceed in dramatically, almost opposite ways from the paths of Wilhelm or Robinson. The girls in each of these narratives begin—not *end,* as in classic *Bildungsromane*—by knowing their place. That place is taught to them in these stories by a host of factors, and is for both unquestioned at the beginning of their tales. Males in the narratives teach civic and social lessons meant to guide their acceptance. Marjane learns the verities of public and private life from her father. When the Shah is deposed and repairs to Egypt at the invitation of Anwar Sadat, Marjane suggests that Sadat has taken the Shah in because of family ties: "Maybe Sadat welcomed the Shah because his first wife was Egyptian," she speculates to her father. He wags his finger at her: "Surely not! Politics and sentiment don't mix."[30] The father's lesson is at once a comment about Marjane's naiveté and a lesson about the gendered world of politics. Sentiment is women's work; politics doesn't mix with it.

Bone learns about her place in the family from her cousin Butch, a stand-in for the father who ran off before she was born. She asks if it's true that the Boatwright clan has intermingled with black people, as she has heard: "Colored. Oh, yes, we got colored. Boatwrights got everything—all colors, all types, all persuasions. . . . Boatwright babies look pretty much alike, like we been rinsed in bleach as we're born. 'Cept you of course, all black-headed and strange. But that because you got a man-type part of you. Rock hard and nasty and immune to harm."[31] Each young girl asks questions of the elder males whose definitive answers leave them dissatisfied—Marjane's expression is bewildered; Bone pauses and then says "Naah" back to Butch. The men's responses help each girl to recognize early in her story that what is individual and personal is embedded in community, and that the questions themselves are somehow both new and risky.

The recognition of the way in which community makes and shapes the individual, even the way that class position determines agency and must be confronted, is a part of the coming-of-age genre. Judith Butler's discussion of subjectivity and norms in terms of Adorno's work echoes the classic plot: "The epistemological frame is presupposed in this encounter, one in which a subject encounters moral norms and must find his way with them."[32] Butler questions that process by asking, "But did Adorno consider that norms also decide in advance who will and will not become a subject?"[33] Butler points to the criticism Slaughter offers of human rights discourse, that genre conventions presuppose subjects or humans, and the limitations of the norms limit the kinds of humans who are subjects. In asking new kinds of questions, Marjane and Bone begin questioning norms (as their authors question the genre they are working within). The enlightenment hero of Robinson Crusoe doesn't need to question his place in a world governed by others like him; he must find how to succeed among those others. Marjane and Bone question not only their place but the world they are born into.

For the authors of these texts, the primary rhetorical strategy is an authorial irony that overlays the naiveté and ultimately commonsensical logic employed by the main characters. The questions asked by both young women are logical. When her father chides her for writing love letters on behalf of the family's illiterate maid, saying that love between social classes is impossible, Marjane wails, "But is it her fault that she was born where she was born???" "Dad," she continues, "Are you for or against social classes?"[34] The following frame indicates that her father hasn't given a response that answers. Bone's logic follows the same path, illuminating the illogical construction of cultural and familial codes and creating critical commentary that Bone uses to forge a new kind of path toward maturity. When her stepfather Glen crushes her in an apologetic embrace to atone for his rage and squeezes so tight that he raises a bruise, Bone has to counter his comment with her own. "Bone knows I'd never mean to hurt her. Bone knows I love her," Glen says. "I stared up at him, Mama's hands on my shoulders, knowing my mouth was hanging open and my face was blank. What did I know? What did I believe?"[35]

The logic of experience and observation employed by both Bone and Marjane often runs exactly opposite to lessons taught the girls by male and female elders, by culture and community, and by books. As for Crusoe, whose discovery of a trunk of books washed up on the shore signals his reattachment to civilization and initiation into the responsibilities of his citizenship, books are important symbols for the young women in Iran and South Carolina. Marjane creates her own book, a prophet's book that solves all the problems she observes in the world around her: "rule number six: Everybody should have a car. Rule number seven: all maids should eat at the table with the others." She abandons her own book and her dream of becoming a prophet when she is given books "to enlighten me." "I knew everything about the children of Palestine. About Fidel Castro. About the young Vietnamese killed by the Americans. About the revolutionaries of my country. But my favorite was a comic book entitled dialectic materialism," a hint about the seriousness of her own comic.[36] Books prove unsatisfactory in explaining the violence she hears about and eventually witnesses for herself. "I didn't know what justice was. Now that the revolution was finally over once and for all, I abandoned the dialectic materialism of my comic strips."[37] Bone becomes an avid reader to escape her forlorn, fearful life. In the summer after Glen has broken Bone's shoulder for the second time, she finds a place in the woods where she reads: "the librarian gave me *Black Beauty, Robinson Crusoe,* and *Tom Sawyer.* On my own I found copies of *Not as a Stranger, The Naked and the Dead, This Gun for Hire,* and *Marjorie Morningstar.*[38] The *Bildungsromane* the librarian offers—young boys or men who learn the paths toward improvement and success—she supplements with books whose titles betray her own fears and hopes. To be connected, to uncover her hidden abuse, to punish, and to move toward a new day.

Slaughter argues that literacy itself represents a potential human rights issue, especially when literacy is reified as such an unproblematized virtue that illiteracy becomes a vice. In this way, the European nation-states "rewrite the nineteenth-century colonial missionary disposition of 'civilized' European nation-states toward 'savage' peoples in terms of intellectual, technical assistance, a humanitarian interventionist posture of the literate, industrialized worlds toward the illiterate peoples of the Third World."[39] As Slaughter shows, learning to read and interpret well is integral to the plot of the *Bildungsroman.* In fact, he notes, "the novel narrates the story of an individual's initiation into a modern society of readers."[40] Links among literacy, liberty, and citizenship are established in the *Bildungsroman,* which, as Slaughter says, tells a literacy narrative of progress, "a story about being empowered by books" through self improvement and cultural uplift. The fact that literacy is taken for granted implies that reading is neutral, without ideological intent except for human betterment. Slaughter shows that contemporary postcolonial fiction often sees the negative consequences of such reading, where it operates as obstacle to freedom as much as fulfillment.

But for the young women in the new *Bildungsromane* represented by *Persepolis* and *Bastard Out of Carolina,* reading books is not such an either-or proposition. Marjane and Bone read the works the culture offers them—they even perhaps take such literacy for granted—but they insist on rewriting those works in their own terms with their own experiences in mind. They make up their own stories—Marjane's prophet's book and Bone's wild storytelling—using what Paulo Freire called *generative words* that express their class, national, and gendered conditions. Freire's literacy program, initiated in the late 1960s in his native Brazil and expanded to many other developing nations and to the US in the late twentieth century, is premised on the notion that people learn to read the way they learn the world around them: "Reading the word is not preceded merely by reading the world, but a certain form of *writing* it or *rewriting* it, that is, of transforming it by means of conscious, practical work. This dynamic movement is central to the literacy process."[41] Generative words are those that come from the experiences and the cultural and class conditions of those learning to be literate; they are words that evoke worlds, express stories. Literacy learning proceeds from learners' use of generative words to read and write the worlds they live in and read. The problems Slaughter finds with literacy programs are in great measure resolved by Freire's understanding of the connection between *word* and *world* in his literacy plan. Bone and Marjane read the world and read the word for what it teaches them about the world they have questions about. They use their own words: writing their own books, or finding them, to make new knowledge. They make what they read generative for their own development rather than destructive of their subjectivity.

As part of their development as human and gendered selves, both girls "try out" the male *Bildungsroman* hero's strategy of attempting daring, stereotypically male deeds to help them to separate from their upbringings or provide possible answers to the hard lessons the culture is teaching them about humans and women. After the Shah's retreat, Marjane observes how what was revered is vilified, how neighbors eagerly turn on one another to accuse someone of suspect loyalty to the old regime. Marjane herself, hearing that a friend's father was part of the Shah's police, devises with two boys a scheme to torture the child: "My idea was to put nails between our fingers like American brass knuckles and to attack Ramin," she reflects. When her mother stops her by making her consider what it would feel like to have her own "ears nailed to the wall," Marjane learns a lesson about justice and forgiveness. "Your father is a murderer but it's not your fault so I forgive you," she says sanctimoniously.[42] She later learns the complications of fault and forgiveness, but she is immediately at least more critical of the black and white of right and wrong.

Bone's act is illegal rather than violent. Along with two boy cousins, she breaks into the Woolworth's store, ostensibly to loot it but actually to revenge herself on the manager who has humiliated her as "white trash." To allay suspicion when the three children run down Main Street carrying Five and Ten goods, she calls to the men sitting on the courthouse steps that the Woolworth's is open and people are helping themselves: "That was the thing that made me happy, the sound of those boots running down the street and the thought of what all those men would carry home."[43] She is never caught; her aunt's sudden death the next morning deflects any questioning. Her act ultimately is meaningless in the face of death and her uncles' discovery of the beatings her stepfather has been administering.

Bone and Marjane learn from their explicitly "unfeminine" acts—their male accomplices are agape at their boldness and ungirlishness—that they have to forge their own paths, not compliant and not stereotypically gendered male. For each, it is painful to separate themselves from the teachers their cultures and families offer, since they must move away from the place of "knowing their place" to another spot more like Crusoe's deserted island, forsaken by him once he takes on the responsibilities of citizenship that he has learned in isolation. Marjane leaves for Vienna to learn to see her own country and her own female position in new ways before she can return; Bone loses her mother to the man who has raped Bone. Each grows stronger as they link the human pain they witness and suffer to their positions as humans gendered female. Bone recognizes in her mother's actions the effect of human injustice and the need for equity in opportunity to live free from want. Marjane sees her ability to be a productive, contributing citizen in her country compromised by the limitations imposed by her gender upon her education, public freedom, and voice.

Interestingly, both stories have a sequel of sorts. Marjane's *Persepolis II* describes her continuing development as human and woman in Europe and as she returns home to study, marry, divorce, and leave once more. Bone's author Allison reflects on her story in *Two or Three Things I Know for Sure*, which has the adult describing how the child survived and developed as thinker and writer.[44] Thus, the *Bildunsgromane* they develop is a continual and open-ended process, these reflections and sequels suggest; not a completed act of becoming human and a citizen, but more a continuing audit of meaning, a readiness to alter ideas when new experience makes old ones seem unworkable.

It may seem naïve to propose the reading of alternative tales as a possible beginning solution to the problem of imagining women as humans, not to mention acting on that understanding in human rights documents and international law. Yet, as Slaughter, Butler, Freire, Anderson, and a host of reading theorists attest, reading narrative carries powerful persuasive force for its ability to foster imaginative possibilities in the minds of readers. Coleridge's definition of imagination, in fact, as the "forming power of mind" is echoed in the language of the UDHR, which places such symbolic weight on the story of a shipwrecked Britisher and his encounters with his "good man." Elaine Scarry's argument in her essay "The Difficulty of Imagining Other People" hinges on the primacy of the imagination to action. "The way we act towards others," she insists, "is shaped by the way we imagine them."[45] Reading theorist Louise Rosenblatt argues that readers' imaginations are not limited to a narrow "interpretive community," to use Stanley Fish's phrase that describes how meaning making is constrained by the limitations of community; instead, readers are invited to come to new understandings when underlying or tacit criteria (such as what constitutes human development or who counts as human) are made explicit by reading. "This creates the possibility of change in interpretation, acceptance of alternative sets of criteria, or revision of criteria," she offers. "Such self awareness on the part of readers can foster communication across social, cultural, and historical differences between author and readers, as well as among readers."[46]

How do such criteria get made explicit? Education is one important way, of course; Freire would say that such exposure to underlying ideas is the primary function of the educator.[47] But readers in and out of school, when they are exposed to a variety of narratives and more than one kind of human in the protagonist's role, will juxtapose and weigh narratives, will compare narratives with their own, and will deepen their understandings of underlying criteria as well as explicit thematic agendas. What if the framers of the UDHR document carried in their symbolic toolbox *Persepolis* as well as *Robinson Crusoe* as the coming of age of a young human person? Might the document have been from the first more explicit rather than tacit about its criteria for what constitutes *human* and what constitutes *development*?

Scarry notes that humans' ability to injure others comes precisely from our inability to imagine them or their suffering, and although she acknowledges literature's power to aid readers in imagination, she worries that the number of characters as well as readers' lack of tolerance "for imaginary features that are different from our own features" makes the healing power of literature limited. In a statement oddly similar to Marjane's father's comment about politics, she says, "The work accomplished by a structure of laws cannot be accomplished by a structure of sentiment."[48] Yet declarations such as the UDHR and the US Declaration of Independence suggest otherwise, based as they are on ideals of humans or sentiments.

Scarry's solution for cosmopolitan readers is to imagine ourselves differently, not by knowing others as well as we know ourselves but by "making [one] ignorant about oneself, and therefore as weightless as all others."[49] But the ability to make ourselves weightless comes to readers of narrative inescapably, as Wayne Booth points out in his description of how readers abandon—making weightless—the lives they live to enter the ones offered to them by narrative. Weightless, we are able to make the world we enter a symbolic and metaphoric one, where we can imagine the weight of others by escaping our own weight. "Surely," Booth says, "learning to meet 'the others' where *they* live is the greatest of all gifts that powerful fiction can offer us."[50]

The need to imagine others as human, to meet others 'where they live' is essential for human rights and for women's rights. It's essential for literacy as well as liberty. Louise Rosenblatt links this kind of reading and democracy: "It helps readers develop the imaginative capacity to put themselves in the place of others—a capacity essential in a democracy, where we need to rise above narrow self-interest and envision the broader human consequences of political decisions."[51] New, and more, stories of people learning about their own humanity and that of others around them suggest new lessons to readers about what it might be to be accounted a human, functioning agent in the world.

The new *Bildungsromane* illustrated here by *Persepolis* and *Bastard Out of Carolina* might include some of these alternative paths toward maturity and humanness:

- The private and public are not mutually exclusive arenas. Marjane and Bone demonstrate the ways in which the family and the culture become mutually reinforcing, and the way that limitations placed on women are often done so in the name of privacy.
- Empathy is a sign of maturity and human development. Bone and Marjane learn to forgive, learn to understand others, and come to terms with the cultural/economic factors that cause human failings.
- Experience is the test of the validity of a position or an idea, and experience must be connected to others and continually revised. Marjane and Bone question others and themselves when what they see and hear contradicts what the culture tells them, and they learn to use their own experiences as a guide to the possible truths of the ideas they're presented with, about culture, citizenship, and women's place in culture and as citizens.

The juxtaposition of Marjane's Iranian story with Bone's South Carolina one demonstrates the importance of reading stories that vary in cultural specifics, in genre and in thematic purpose. Reading the two together, readers imagine the very different life circumstances of these two young girls and the very similar paths they take toward self-knowledge and subjective agency. The stories end with the main characters neither opposed to or disillusioned by their gendered and social conditions, nor capitulating to them, as in traditional *Bildungsromane*. Instead, Marjane and Bone will remake what they must in order to exercise what they have learned about themselves. They will leave behind what they must as well. As readers read more coming of age stories that take a variety of paths, that do more than comment on the stereotypical western male one, but remake it in another image, female ones as well as male, they learn to symbolize and imagine ways to see humans that include human women more explicitly. Human rights discourse will begin to change as the stories that have provoked that discourse alter.

The deep-seated problems that Slaughter's work uncovers with a human rights discourse based on a generalizable logic of "what everybody knows," and the blind spots of human rights discourse that feminist thinkers expose as the omission of women's human rights, might be productively addressed together in an approach, both pragmatic and feminist, that values the contextual, the plural, and the revisable. As for the female *Bildungsromane* described here, and for feminist thought, the growth of the self is ongoing, never quite complete, always both social and contingent. As pragmatist philosopher John Dewey puts it, "Individuality is not originally given, but is created under the influences of associated life."[52]

"Let us treat the men and women well; treat them as if they were real," Emerson urged in his own declaration of human possibility, "Experience," in 1847. "Perhaps they are."[53] Imagining others by reading the world and the word in new, continually revisable, ways, human rights discourse might begin to treat more men and women well: as if they were real, as if they were human.

NOTES

1. Catharine MacKinnon, *Are Women Human? And Other International Dialogues* (Cambridge, MA: Harvard University Press, 2006), 3.
2. Charlotte Bunch, "Transforming Human Rights from a Feminist Perspective," in *Women's Rights, Human Rights: International Feminist Perspectives*, ed. Julie Peters and Andrea Wolper (New York: Routledge, 1994), 11.
3. Richard Rorty, "Feminism and Pragmatism," *Michigan Quarterly Review* 30, no. 2 (1991), 234.
4. Judith Butler and Gayatri Chakravorty Spivak, *Who Sings the Nation-State?* (New York: Seagull, 2007), 68.
5. Joseph R. Slaughter, *Human Rights, Inc.: The World Novel, Narrative Form, and International Law* (New York: Fordham, 2007), 3 (original emphasis).
6. Slaughter, *Human Rights, Inc.*, 3.
7. Slaughter, *Human Rights, Inc.*, 3.
8. Quoted in Charlotte Bunch and Niamh Reilly, *Demanding Accountability: The Global Campaign and Vienna Tribunal for Women's Rights* (New York: UNIFEM, 1994), v.
9. Quoted in Slaughter, *Human Rights, Inc.*, 43.
10. Slaughter, *Human Rights, Inc.*, 51.
11. There were dissenters. Charles Malik, Lebanese scholar and a framer of the UDHR, objected to the term "individual" for its connotations of radical autonomy, claiming, "There are no Robinson Crusoes here." Quoted in Mary Ann Glendon, *The World Made New: Eleanor Roosevelt and the Universal Declaration of Human Rights* (New York: Random House, 2001), 42.
12. Slaughter, *Human Rights, Inc.*, 57.
13. Slaughter, *Human Rights, Inc.*, 61.
14. Slaughter, *Human Rights, Inc.*, 111.
15. Slaughter, *Human Rights, Inc.*, 328.
16. Benedict Anderson, *Imagined Communities: Reflections on the Origin and Spread of Nationalism*, 1983, rev. ed. (London: Verso, 2006), 6.
17. Anderson, *Imagined Communities*, 36.
18. Anderson, *Imagined Communities*, 36.
19. Elissavet Stamatopoulou notes that the final provision of the "Elimination of Violence Against Women," adopted by the UN's General Assembly in 1993, is especially interesting for its statement: "physical, sexual and psychological violence perpetrated or condoned by the state, wherever it occurs." The state then is culpable for violence against women in both public and private spheres ["Women's Rights and the United Nations," in *Women's Rights/Human Rights*, ed. Julie Peters and Andrea Wolper (New York: Routledge, 1995), 36–50].
20. These texts include Christopher Hope, *A Separate Development* (Johannesburg: Raven, 1980) and Tsitsi Dangarembga, *Nervous Conditions* (London: Women's Press, 1988).
21. Slaughter, *Human Rights, Inc.*, 215.
22. Susanne Langer, *Philosophy in a New Key*, 3rd ed. (Cambridge, MA: Harvard University Press, 1957), 14.
23. Marjane Satrapi, *The Complete Persepolis* (New York: Pantheon, 2003), ii.
24. See Scott McCloud, *Understanding Comics* (New York: Harper Collins, 1993). The simplicity and understatement of the graphic contribute to its power and its connections to readers, he maintains. See also Hilary Chute, "Comics as Literature? Reading Graphic Narrative," *PMLA: Publications of the Modern Language Association of America* 123, no. 2 (2008): 452–465.

230   *Hephzibah Roskelly*

For a discussion of *Persepolis*'s use of the form see Nima Naghibi and Andrew O'Malley, "Estranging the Familiar: 'East' and 'West' in Satrapi's *Persepolis*," *ESQ* 31, no. 2–3 (June–Sept. 2005): 223–248.

25. Several critics point to the importance of memoir and autobiography for postcolonial nations and for women, as well as the contradictions in personal memoir. See, for example, Farzaneh Milani's *Veils and Words: The Emerging Voices of Iranian Women Writers* (Syracuse, NY: Syracuse University Press, 1992) and Afsaneh Najmabadi, ed., *Women's Autobiographies in Contemporary Iran* (Cambridge, MA: Harvard University Press, 1990).
26. Wayne Booth, *The Company We Keep: An Ethics of Fiction* (Berkeley: University of California Press, 1988), 339.
27. Booth, *The Company We Keep*, 340.
28. Dorothy Allison, *Bastard Out of Carolina* (New York: Plume, 1993), 18.
29. Allison, *Bastard Out of Carolina*, 54.
30. Satrapi, *The Complete Persepolis*, 43.
31. Allison, *Bastard Out of Carolina*, 54.
32. Judith Butler, *Giving an Account of Oneself* (New York: Fordham University Press, 2005), 5.
33. Butler, *Giving an Account of Oneself*, 9.
34. Satrapi, *The Complete Persepolis*, 37.
35. Allison, *Bastard Out of Carolina*, 70.
36. Satrapi, *The Complete Persepolis*, 12.
37. Satrapi, *The Complete Persepolis*, 53.
38. Allison, *Bastard Out of Carolina*, 119.
39. Slaughter, *Human Rights, Inc.*, 280.
40. Slaughter, *Human Rights, Inc.*, 285.
41. Paulo Freire and Donaldo Macedo, *Literacy: Reading the Word and the World* (South Hadley, MA: Bergin Garvey, 1987), 35.
42. Satrapi, *The Complete Persepolis*, 46.
43. Allison, *Bastard Out of Carolina*, 226.
44. Allison uses the visual in her memoir, in photographs that, like Satrapi's work, unsettle what is "true" and consistent in the cultural narrative and the memoir form.
45. Elaine Scarry, "The Difficulty of Imagining Other People," in *For Love of Country: Debating the Limits of Patriotism*, ed. Martha Nussbaum (Boston: Beacon Press, 1996), 78.
46. Louise Rosenblatt, *Making Meaning with Texts* (Portsmouth, NH: Heinemann, 2005), 23.
47. The educator "enters into dialogue" with the learner to aid in the development of consciousness about culture. This premise guides many of Freire's works. See especially Freire and Donaldo Macedo, *Education for Critical Consciousness* (New York: Seabury Press, 1973), 47 ff.
48. Scarry, "The Difficulty of Imagining Other People," 110.
49. Scarry, "The Difficulty of Imagining Other People," 105.
50. Booth, *The Company We Keep*, 414.
51. Rosenblatt, *Making Meaning with Texts*, xxxiii.
52. John Dewey quoted in James Livingston, *Pragmatism, Feminism and Democracy* (New York: Routledge, 2001), 10.
53. Ralph Waldo Emerson, "Experience," in *Heath Anthology of American Literature*, 5th ed., ed. Paul Lauter (Boston: Houghton Mifflin, 2006), 1659.

13 "Disaster Capitalism" and Human Rights

Embodiment and Subalternity in Indra Sinha's *Animal's People*

Alexandra Schultheis Moore

When an "airborne toxic event" impugns the putatively safe existence of a middle-class, Midwestern American community in Don DeLillo's *White Noise*, his protagonist, Jack Gladney, strains to understand himself and his family as victims: "These things happen to poor people who live in exposed areas. Society is set up in such a way that it's the poor and the uneducated who suffer the main impact of natural and man-made disasters."[1] Although early reviewers noted the tragic irony of the novel's appearance just a month after the December 1984 Union Carbide chemical gas leak in Bhopal, India, criticism of the novel has focused on its postmodern sensibilities rather than upon related material referents. Through play with forms of representation and representability, however, DeLillo's disaster serves as a metaphor for broader cultural malaise and anxiety including, but not limited to, technological risk.[2] Ursula K. Heise offers a clear articulation of how narrative form captures that risk for more than stylistic ends, despite the novel's satirical engagement with simulacra and the crisis of authenticity (the very traits that make the disaster in *White Noise* unbelievable to its characters). Using a "risk-theory approach to narrative," she argues that DeLillo's "destabilization of distinctions between the real and the nonreal can itself serve specific realist objectives" in mirroring readers' own continual need to evaluate the technological risks of daily life.[3]

Without minimizing the risks faced by readers whom the novel rightly reminds us are falsely secure, the distance between them (with Jack Gladney as the point of identification) and "those poor people who live in exposed areas," such as the victims of Bhopal, remains vast. Bridging that distance necessitates attention to the distribution of risk and its toxic effects, particularly when they affect those who lack access not only to the illusion of safety but also to the choices implicit in the evaluation of risk and the juridical and medical discourses which frame bids for compensation when risk turns to loss. Whereas much has been written about the paradox that human rights is aspirationally universal, yet practically tied to citizenship, the challenges posed by violations linked to transnational capital, whose interests often supercede national sovereignty, have received less attention. Unlike Jack Gladney, whose exposure to toxic gas from a leak at the train depot is framed by transience and chance, Bhopal's gas sufferers (those killed the night of the explosion, those who died later of illnesses from gas exposure, and those who continue to be poisoned by a toxic environment) were primarily residents of semi-legal slum neighborhoods abutting the pesticide plant. The exposed are those with the least rights and low standing as citizens, who bear the terrible costs of participation in industrial capitalism promoted by the state.

Among the poorest of Bhopalis, these residents possess(ed) neither the consumer and other material choices satirized in *White Noise* and implicit in risk theory nor the luxury of DeLillo's characters of remaining "unable to relate to their own situation unless it is amply covered by the media."[4] Instead, the Bhopalis who were immediately downwind of the plant can trace their exposure to the vagaries of chance, but more determinedly to their location in a web of political and economic relationships from the colonial era to the present: Union Carbide's operation in India since 1905; Cold War US international development policies and Ford Foundation support for India's Green Revolution and the resulting need for agrochemicals; political will to license Union Carbide India Limited's (UCIL) Bhopal pesticide plant in 1969 on state land under a long-term lease; asymmetrical regulatory codes that allowed UCIL to build and operate the plant without all of the safety precautions (including community awareness policies) mandated for Union Carbide's similar plant in West Virginia; an economic downturn and falling demand for pesticide that led to the implementation of cost-cutting measures linked to safe operations at the plant beginning in 1983; and political patronage battles between the Congress Party and Bharatiya Janata Party (BJP) before and after the leak that impacted (through land titles, "benign" neglect, and anti-encroachment policies) the distribution of Muslims and Hindus in Bhopal's slums as well as local government responsiveness to their needs.[5]

Drawing on his work on behalf of the Bhopal Medical Appeal since 1994, Indra Sinha in *Animal's People* (2007) imagines the subaltern's response to such a leak and the decades-long campaign for recognition and compensation in the fictional Khaufpur ("place of fear" or "Terror Town"). *Animal's People* poses the challenge of reading the violations of community members' human rights by "disaster capitalism," particularly when those violations are deeply embedded in colonial and neocolonial relations as well as contemporary national politics. How does the novel invite ways of reading the human rights of the subaltern at the intersection of multiple narratives—literary, legal, corporate—of transnational capital in industrial disaster? What theoretical approaches to human rights and literature illuminate violations that stem not solely from conflicts over national power and identity but from the pressures of both national and transnational development, when the subaltern subject is caught not in the paradox of human rights and citizenship but rather of human rights and industrial capitalist participation? Moreover, if in Inderpal Grewal's words, "human rights produced the liberal subject of transnational civil society," what might we learn from the subaltern subject who bears the brunt of the toxic effects of transnational neoliberal development that enables that civil society?[6]

Animating each of these questions is the need to account for the embodiment of suffering and subalternity. As Anna Grear insists, in order to "re-invigorate the protective potential of human rights for vulnerable human beings and communities against powerful disembodied legal persons (corporations)," we need "a space in which the living, embodied, situated person can be allowed to re-emerge and challenge those aspects of positive law (and its embedded ideological structures) that produce human suffering."[7] In *Animal's People*, Sinha imagines this space and the embodiment of suffering through its eponymous narrator. The insistence on the material (corporeal and otherwise) grounds of Animal's story offers an alternative to textuality alone in figuring the subaltern sufferer who bears the costs of industrial capitalism, although, as I will argue here, the normatively gendered terms of embodied desires in the novel constrain its potential.

In "Voices of Suffering and the Future of Human Rights," legal theorist Upendra Baxi writes that "[r]ecovery of the sense and experience of human anguish provides the only hope that there is for the future of human rights."[8] This project, articulated more fully in his subsequent book, *The Future of Human Rights*, responds to the "demise of human rights languages," wherein "[t]he generative grammars, as it were, of human rights dissipate human and social suffering, at times to a point of social illegibility" and human rights as a "moral language [. . .] is simply *exhausted*" (original emphasis).[9] Exacerbated by the turn he describes toward "trade-related, market-friendly human rights," the crisis in narration demands a response at once recuperative and productive of missing voices, voices which—as do his own vocabulary and metaphors—emphasize the intersections of literary and legal storytelling. Framing the future of human rights in terms of narration focuses attention on the subject constituted by and through her story, the efficacy of whose legal personhood—as one who "can act in law" as opposed to legal non-persons "who cannot act in law and who are generally thought of as property"[10]—rests not on the violation itself but on its narratability. Narratability confirms the subject's "inherent dignity and worth" set forth in the Preamble of the Universal Declaration of Human Rights. As a confirmation which appears to bridge the gaps between the "person" as a biological human, a subject endowed with rational agency, and an object of legal and moral concern, the subject's ability to tell his or her story seems all the more vital in cases pitting the interests of the human being against the accepted legal fiction of corporate personhood.[11] The gendered terms of the story seem all the more important when we consider that the legal personhood claimed by the corporation bears the

234 Alexandra Schultheis Moore

"characteristics of the male, white, property-owning, and hyper-rational calculator—identified by a range of theorists as a product of classical Western liberal philosophy."[12] Baxi underscores the legal and ethical import of the narrative self in such contexts, especially when capitalism's "'negative side-effects' become embodied selves": "How may we periodize the various births and rebirths of this narrative self in the archetypal situations of mass/social disasters from Bhopal to Ogoniland and beyond?"[13]

Recognizing the "incorporative effect" of storytelling for the way it locates the subject in the public sphere, Joseph Slaughter, in his exemplary *Human Rights, Inc.*, similarly addresses human rights as "a question of both literacy and legislation, as much matters of literature as of law."[14] Slaughter argues for a "narratological understanding of human rights" to "clarify some of the narrative assumptions that underwrite [. . .] human rights law and practice, as well as legal assumptions that sustain and are sustained by the modern novel and the *Bildungsroman* in particular."[15] The "sociocultural, formal, historical, and ideological conjunctions between human rights and [. . .] the coming-of-age genre" constitute them as "mutually enabling fictions that institutionalize and naturalize the terms of incorporation in (and exclusion from) an imagined community of readers and rights holders."[16]

Both Baxi and Slaughter draw our attention to the need to expand access to the public sphere and to "guarantee[e] the ability to self-narrate"[17] for the future of human rights. At the same time, they problematize the self-determining, stable subject at the imagined center of modern discourses of rights (and, for Slaughter, of the *Bildungsroman*) to argue not for his restitution, but for a more complex understanding of the imbrication of subjectivity, law, and narrative within the public sphere in order to reorient the political landscape of the struggle for rights. Slaughter, for instance, provides a detailed analysis of the ways in which the *Bildungsroman* may also signify dissensuality from normative codes of law, citizenship, and narrative plotting, although usually for their reform rather than for revolution. Limiting the potential for more radical narratological change are the demands of a predominantly western readership for a product circulating according to "the global market dynamics that have commodified both human rights and the *Bildungsroman* [and that] constitute part of the uneven international conditions of (im)possibility for human personality development and its novelistic form of expression."[18]

Animal's People is located precisely at this juncture. On one hand, the novel's short-listing for the Man Booker Prize guarantees a global readership. Yet the Prize's corporate sponsorship itself emerges out of a history of transnational capitalization: from the Booker Corporation's ownership of Guyana as a sugar plantation to India's Green Revolution—which created the demand and opportunity for Union Carbide's pesticide plant in Bhopal—to current sponsor the Man Group's global business in "alternative investment management."[19] On the other hand, the novel interrogates what full human personality development might mean for one who is "removed from lines of social mobility,"[20] lines ostensibly multiplied by economic globalization, poverty, tragedy, local politics, and physical impairment. Animal, whose exposure to the gas leak in infancy has left him able to walk only on all fours, provocatively begins with this conceit: "I used to be human once. So I'm told. I don't remember it myself, but people who knew me when I was small say I walked on two feet just like a human being."[21] And his successful development seems assured in the novel's final section when the activist leader, Zafar, confirms, "Animal, my brother, you are a human being. A full and true human being."[22]

Throughout the intervening narration, however, Animal refuses to engage fully in the religious, legal, medical, and aesthetic discourses that focus the lives of his humanitarian circle: the French nun, Ma Franci, who has raised Animal since infancy, predicts a post-leak "Apokalis," but has reverted solely to French since "that night"; the Hindi-speaking American doctor, Elli, who arrives unannounced to open a free medical clinic and tries unsuccessfully to translate her skills to a suspicious public; local leader of a poison relief committee, Somraj, a famous singer who lost his voice (and wife and son) the night of the explosion, and his beautiful daughter, Nisha, who teaches Animal to read; and, charismatic Zafar, who dropped out of college and rushed to Khaufpur to "organise the fight against the Kampani" immediately following the disaster.[23] Animal locates himself both within and outside of these competing discourses, his distinction marked by a profane voice tied to his physical impairment and an ability to read what other characters leave unsaid: "The world of humans is meant to be viewed from eye level. Your eyes. Lift my head I'm staring into someone's crotch. Whole nother world it's, below the waist."[24] As opposed to the abstract-able humanitarian discourses of the upright, Animal insists on the inseparability of loss and desire from the corporeal subject. To the voices in his head, he sneers, "You are all pathetic. Voices without bodies, what the fuck is the use of you? Without me you're nothing."[25] At the same time, the coding of desire through those voices is overtly masculine, as the plot develops out of Animal's desire for Nisha's attention, sexual fulfillment, and his hope that Elli will restore his spine.

Although Sinha asks that we not read *Animal's People* as "a polemic," insisting "[t]his is a book about people, not about issues,"[26] the novel nonetheless parallels events in Bhopal in significant and obvious ways and, perhaps more importantly, opens a space for exploration that was foreclosed in the immediate aftermath of the December 2/3, 1984 chemical gas leak. Five months after the toxin methyl isocyanate (MIC) escaped from Union Carbide India Limited's pesticide plant in the capital of Madhya Pradesh, one of India's poorest states, killing thousands outright and poisoning and disabling hundreds of thousands more over the short and the long term, the Indian Government enacted the Bhopal Gas Leak Disaster (Processing of Claims) Act—the Bhopal Act (1985). The legislation appointed the

Indian Government, already stakeholders in UCIL,[27] legal standing to act in *parens patriae* of the thereby juridically incompetent or *non sui juris* sufferers. Arguably protecting Bhopal victims, predominantly the impoverished squatters living in settlements just south/southeast of the plant, from potentially predatory and capricious practices of American lawyers arriving in Bhopal[28] and creating a more efficient mechanism for claims processing, the Bhopal Act "provided victims access to the law, but not to rights" by denying them the right to represent themselves as well as to "natural justice" through the choice to opt out of the settlement plan.[29] As Veena Das rightly notes, this "judgment creates a master discourse in which the various voices are appropriated in a kind of monologic structure" and which ironically designates the sufferers, rather than the corporation or the state, incompetent.[30] *Animal's People* attempts to disrupt that monologic structure, which "constituted [victims' suffering] purely as a verbal object, dissolving the concrete and existential reality of their being,"[31] through an insistence on an embodied and embedded subaltern voice of the one marked by "disaster capitalism."[32] The potential of that disruption is both enabled and limited by the novel's strict focalization on Animal. Whereas his name, impairment, and the emphasis placed on his physical survival mock the supposed reach of human rights discourses to those on the underside of neoliberal development, his consistent objectification of women stage his desire for full "incorporation," in Slaughter's words, in suspiciously normative terms. At the same time, the novel offers an alternative to the failure of the bureaucratized narratives of suffering recognized by the state.

The Bhopal Act positioned the state at the nexus of two competing discourses of human rights and duties of care, *simultaneously* representing its least viable citizens, those predominantly underemployed and illiterate victims whose suffering became abstracted through the Bhopal Act, *while* representing the interests of its broader citizenry as the beneficiaries of state agricultural policies and foreign investment.[33] Although a full description of the intricacies, insults, and ironies of the litigation, in both the US and India, against Union Carbide[34] exceeds the space available here, the novel does engage with two of its key moments: the initial struggle over the legal representability of suffering and the profound anger over the 1989 settlement. Among the many incontrovertible injustices of the Bhopal litigation, the failure of the state to imagine and register the suffering of Bhopalis is perhaps the most egregious. Not only did the Bhopal Act classify medical information under the Official Secrets Act[35], but the government actively sought to "safeguard its own interests" by minimizing the toxic effects of the gas leak as well as the treatments available.[36] Estimates of the numbers of people affected by the gas in the short and long terms by state and national government officials, the Indian Council on Medical Research, the International Medical Commission on Bhopal, a German toxicologist who was in Bhopal by December 4, 1984 (before being asked to leave three days later), and advocacy groups span an almost inconceivable range, varying in the thousands for immediate deaths and the hundreds of thousands for long-term effects. In the rush to dispose of bodies immediately after the explosion, no comprehensive count of the dead or of casualties took place. Moreover, the state contradicted the immediate findings of the local hospital that bodies showed signs of cyanide poisoning and survivors might benefit from the standard antidote, sodium thiosulphate (NaTS). Ten days later, the local Director of Health Services, under direct order from the Ministry of Health, effectively banned this treatment with the statement that "[u]nder no circumstances shall NaTS be given unless it is correctly and conclusively proved in the laboratory that it is cyanide poisoning."[37] Processing claims thus necessitated the creation of a system of medical documentation according to symptoms and causes determined by state interests for residents who had previously existed outside of such bureaucratic structures (and thus had no prior medical records against which to compare their current health). Whereas survivor testimony attests to both isolated and (multi-)systemic effects of toxicity—with the most common symptoms including pulmonary edema, gynecological and obstetric problems (gynecological pain, spontaneous abortion, and birth defects), blindness, exhaustion, and weakness, the framework developed for documenting victims' symptoms itemized injuries within a hierarchical scoring system and attributed systemic complaints to poverty and poor nutrition. In its rationale for the settlement, which provided victims who had proper documentation an estimated $400 per person in compensation, the court based its judgment on data provided by the State of Madhya Pradesh, which according to Kim Fortun, "placed only five percent of victims in compensatable categories."[38] Five years later, in 1994, the Indian Council of Medical Research ended its research on the long-term effects of the gas (despite the fact that no comprehensive environmental clean-up had been undertaken, nor were any official alternatives available for studying multi-generational effects of gas exposure).[39] A result of these trespasses is that the "desperate need for paper proof of victimization has become part of the legacy of Bhopal, as has a need for new idioms through which disaster can be represented, both textually and socially."[40] Perhaps in response to that need, as Sheila Jasanoff notes, "The language of suffering bodies still possesses in Indian political space an authenticity and a power to convince that cannot be matched by any number of published scientific articles."[41]

The character of Animal, regularly dismissive of paper proof and humanitarian discourses, yet propelled by the desire to walk upright, offers an alternative corporeal and verbal expression. The novel provides a transformative look at the disabled body, one that moves from the objectifying gaze to political engagement. This shift takes place through Animal's changing views of himself, although it requires ratification by others to take effect: "*You got angry,*" Animal scolds himself when he first meets Elli, "*because when you looked at her you thought sex, when she looked at you she thought cripple.*"[42] What begins as a competition between relative positions of objectification develops over the course of the novel into a more complex negotiation of Animal's and Elli's interrelationship in the context of Bhopal. For Elli, who has come to India apparently to atone for her failed marriage and ex-husband's work on behalf of the offending company, Animal is her first (and for much of the novel, only) patient. His disability serves as a synecdoche for the disaster itself, a symbol of human vulnerability to nefarious corporate interests and unintelligible technologies; however, the medical lens framing Animal's condition defines the impairment as a loss in need of restitution, an individualized problem which might be solved by expertise and treatment.[43] Animal's four-footedness, as too often happens with disability, "is a significant factor in the imagination of [his] right to have rights, but it serves . . . as a negative operator,"[44] and Elli's desire to cure him appears initially to be motivated by her needs and desires rather than in response to his.

To move from personal loss to political injustice, from "tragic circumstances" to the "link between global capitalism and local disabilities," requires shifts in both perspective and the ethics of recognition.[45] In place of a visual rhetoric of staring at the disabled body, a perspective that emphasizes distance frozen in time between (active) subject and (passive) object, we might cultivate an ethic of mutual regard that nonetheless acknowledges the "extraordinary bodies" at work.[46] In her reading of disability as "not so much a property of bodies as a product of cultural rules," Rosemarie Garland Thomson argues that "the meanings attributed to extraordinary bodies reside not in inherent physical flaws, but in social relationships in which one group is legitimated by possessing valued physical characteristics and maintains its ascendancy and its self-identity by systematically imposing the role of cultural or corporeal inferiority on others."[47] The extraordinary body as a site and source of competing interests, narratives, and practices allows for a richer reading of Animal in the context of the Bhopal disaster—one which makes visible the interplay of structures of (neo)colonial power, juridical-medical discourse, and the possibilities for resignifying subaltern and disabled people in the novel in political terms.

Sinha invokes the extraordinary body through the image of the "parapagus" to describe both Animal and his Khā-in-a-Jar, a two-headed fetus spontaneously aborted the night of the explosion, which Animal encounters on a childhood trip to the doctor. Khā-in-a-Jar becomes animated for Animal at the moment a childhood doctor says he cannot be cured and should be grateful to be alive, and the Khā functions as another interlocutor through most of the book. Both Animal and his Khā are divided between spectacle and selfhood. In the jar, Khā calls one of his heads "the clever one with ideas," and the other "dumb;"[48] for Animal, the division is between his bent body and "a second you who's straight, stands upright and tall [. . .], has been there all along, thinks, speaks and acts, but it's invisible."[49] Narrative logic demands the resolution of this divide into a single subject—embodied and visible—yet we must be wary of our own readerly desire for a stable protagonist (especially if the response to the disaster took the form of a single character's healing at the hands of a benevolent American doctor motivated by disappointment in her own love life).

Toward the end of *The Future of Human Rights*, Baxi argues for the "necessity for human rights entrepreneurs to commodify human suffering, to package and sell it in terms of what the markets will bear" in order to "titillate and scandalize for the moment at least, the dilettante sensibilities of the globalizing classes."[50] *Animal's People* is both complicit with and resistant to this effort. Its address to the implicated reader is made possible in the story through the conceit of Animal telling his story directly to "Eyes" (the reader) through a tape recorder left by an enterprising Australian "jarnalis" who already has negotiated a book contract based on Animal's life. At the same time, Animal mocks our "hunger" for his story,[51] is skeptical that its circulation will have any material effects, and appears motivated purely by self-interest and financial gain. Insisting that the book consist solely of complete transcripts of his own story, Animal agrees to speak: "This story has been locked up in me, it's struggling to be free, I can feel it coming, words want to fly out from between my teeth like a flock of birds making a break for it."[52] Freedom through self-representation seems to confirm the promise of an enlarged public sphere and to restore Animal to full humanity within it.

Although the novel in many ways fulfills the promise of self-narration (and the *Bildungsroman*) as the path to both selfhood and manhood, it also underscores the limitations of voice alone, to borrow again from Baxi, for the "recovery of the sense and anguish of human suffering."[53] The anticipated liberation proffered by the tape recorder is both literally and figuratively disembodied, an effect at odds with the material conditions of Animal's daily existence and thus constrained in both its descriptive and political potential. Voice alone risks reproducing a dualistic subjectivity all too familiar in colonial vestiges of the law and the novel and may contribute to a hierarchizing of human rights. As Slaughter recognizes in "A Question of Narration," "while civil and political rights might be the first guarantees for the right to narration, economic and social rights become important for understanding that an individual requires fair wages and safe working conditions to tell her story."[54]

Even as it conforms to certain narrative expectations in portraying the narrator's moral and political development, ending with the wish for marriage as the proof of incorporation as citizen and man, *Animal's People* dismantles the implicit hierarchy of civil and political over social, cultural, and economic rights. It gives voice to the subaltern residents of Khaufpur's poorest neighborhoods surrounding the pesticide plant and insists on that voice as both embodied and socio-economically embedded. Animal's often perverse and profane, engaging and alienating story is inseparable from his disabilities and functions as a "material rhetoric" in Wendy Hesford's definition: it "highlights the discursivity of the material world as well as the materiality of discourse [. . .], challenges the idea that corporeal bodies are overdetermined by discourse, and prompts consideration of how individual and collective struggles for agency are located at the complex intersections of the discursive and material politics of everyday life."[55] Although Hesford invokes the concept to warn against the danger of reading non-fiction testimony "solely as a cultural politics of representation," the contradictory impulses of the novel turn the reader relentlessly back to Bhopal. As *Bildungsroman* and political fable, the novel explores the dangers "disaster capitalism" poses to the sanctity of the human subject, as evidenced through the struggle of the characters for human rights in their daily lives, as well as the inadequacy of human rights discourse itself. As Animal tells the journalist dismissively, "You will bleat like all the rest. You'll talk of *rights, law, justice*. Those words sound the same in my mouth as in yours but they don't mean the same."[56] Sinha locates the struggle for rights at the intersection of corporate, juridical, medical, and literary operations and in the shadows of the twinned ideals of manhood and legal personhood. Given the assault on the corporeal, psychic, and social integrity of Bhopal's victims by the explosion and its aftermath, it is difficult to read Animal and "Animal's people" *without* nostalgia for notions of sovereign subjectivity, including those enshrined in the Universal Declaration of Human Rights and implied in compensatory claims. However, Animal insists, "On that night it was poison, now it's words that are choking us."[57]

Animal's participation in the public sphere, his decisions regarding his medical treatment, and his desire for marriage with Anjali—the childhood friend and prostitute with whom he fails, not for want of trying, to lose his virginity—confirm Elaine Scarry's argument concerning the grounding of all three forms of consent (political, medical, and conjugal) in the body.[58] The result, sustained until the final page of the novel, structures Animal as a bearer of human rights according to overlapping models of sovereignty and free will which are exercised through bodily consent, although the body itself is not always compliant. One reading of the body's resistance to will is that Animal is less than fully human because he lacks at key moments political will and sexual drive. If, as Scarry argues, "consent is a redistributive site,"[59] then it follows that Animal in this reading makes a powerful claim for personhood, citizenship, and legal standing abrogated by the Bhopal Act and the ensuing settlements, although he does so in normative terms of sovereign subjectivity through which he is also marginalized.

Particularly in his bid for marriage at the end of the novel, Animal seems to complete the teleology of the *Bildungsroman*. If, as Slaughter writes, "*Bildung* and modern human rights were both technologies of incorporation whose historical social work was to patriate the once politically marginal bourgeois subject as national citizen,"[60] then Animal moves swiftly from the underclass to the bourgeoisie, for whom the gas leak might appear to be a "necessary" cost of progress so long as those costs are borne by others.[61] His entry into the public sphere as story space manifests through literacy in English, such that Animal confirms his willing "incorporation into an international society of readers."[62] Notably this takes place when he refuses to read a political pamphlet Zafar has produced on the grounds that "I am not a child" and chooses instead to read what Zafar reads (as opposed to writes): "*It is a truth universally acknowledged, that a single man in position of good fortune, must be in want of a wife.*"[63] Of the two possible readings of the sentence, each problematic, but one more sexist than the other, Animal chooses the more generous at the end of the novel when he hopes that he can use the money raised for his operation to pay off Anjali's debts and release her from prostitution.

Animal's final words build on this momentum and shift the focus from the consent of the individual bearer of rights to the demands of the collective. The last section begins with Animal's demand that Eyes recognize him as unique. Although "[a]ll [he] ha[s] to do is sign a paper," Animal withholds his signature for the operation Elli promises, for Anjali and because he figures, "Stay four-footed, I'm the one and only Animal."[64] This bid for extraordinary singularity signifies his rejection of medicalized discourses of disability as confirmation of his inadequacy and, more radically, is simultaneously undone through the invocation of the subaltern in the novel's last lines: "Eyes, I'm done. Khuda hafez. Go well. Remember me. All things pass, but the poor remain. We are the people of the Apokalis. Tomorrow there will be more of us."[65] Gayatri Spivak's insight that literature teaches us "to learn from the singular and unverifiable"[66] suggests that Animal, as a narrator and extraordinary body, offers less an imaginative witness/proof of violation than an irreverent critique of "trade-related, market-friendly human rights" and the subjects they normalize. Animal's transformation of the meaning of his disability from personal loss to common struggle "disclose[s] how the 'physically disabled' are produced by way of legal, medical, political, cultural, and literary narratives that comprise an exclusionary discourse" in order "to move disability from the realm of medicine into that of political minorities."[67] Disability studies provides another avenue of critique of the subject at the center of liberal individualism and human rights[68], while the emergent field of human rights and literature, which is rarely confined to American studies, identifies new areas of inquiry for disability studies as well.[69]

By demanding that the reader acknowledge his shift from singular to plural, Animal makes three distinct claims: that the "politics of recognition are inseparable from the politics of redistribution;"[70] that consent in the body may have collective as well as singular force and meaning; and, that human rights claims articulated through disability may define a future politics in addition to or instead of a past loss. As Michael Bérubé argues, disability read in this way "compels us to understand embodiment in relation to temporality."[71] This temporal shift is central to the novel's ability to intervene in the discourses of Bhopal wherein both short- and long-term effects of gas exposure (not to mention the political climate, as well as religious and gendered factors that continue to influence the responses of national and local government) remain disputed. Even in the more immediate aftermath of the catastrophe, "[t]he space-time of the [Union Carbide Corporation] decision makers was intensely *global*; the space-time of those violated at Bhopal was irremediably *local*."[72] The imaginative production of multiple, co-existing conceptions of space-time may be precisely what literature can perform that advocacy cannot. Not only does the novel provide access to the subject's interiority, it does so by showing how Khaufpur is crucial in "the social production of (sexed) corporeality: the built environment provides the context and coordinates for contemporary forms of body" and it "provides the order and organization that automatically links otherwise unrelated bodies."[73] Khaufpur's destroyed factory offers remnants of the catalyst that brings the characters together in *Animal's People*; but it also plays an ever-present role in structuring Animal's sense of himself and his relationships with others. The image of the "HELL HOLE" is individually coded yet shared among the characters: it is foremost Animal's home; it provides Ma Franci with an apocalyptic reading of the explosion; it describes Elli's father's dangerous work in the depths of a Pennsylvania steel mill, her own immediate connection to the dangers of industrial development, where "[o]ne slip, you're history;"[74] it characterizes Animal's experience in a test of fire at the local mosque celebration of the story of Hussein at Karbala;[75] and it returns at the end of the novel when a fire at the dilapidated plant turns into an effective social protest, where the women "possessed by nothing's power, begin their chants, 'We are flames not flowers'" and the impending deal between the company and the local government is called off.[76]

Transforming the tools of violation into those of political action brings the competing narratives of the meaning of suffering together. Even within Animal's character, his ostensible passivity as the innocent bearer of injurious wrong, already presented ironically through his attempts to poison Zafar, his rival for Nisha's love, is translated in this reading into a catalyst for collective, political action. If "[m]ovement locates, rather than merely illustrates, the will,"[77] then Animal's foreboding statement—"Tomorrow there will be more of us"—presages a collective rather than an individual response, this time not to jealousy but to the inherently inequitable distribution of risk through industrial capitalism, inequities which are magnified in this post- and neo-colonial context. When the company lawyers attempt a second "shameful meeting" with local government officials to avoid appearing in court, their vulnerability to the toxic gas is treated with sardonic humor. A burqa-clad Elli, posing as a cleaner, releases a stink bomb that produces the same "evil burning sensation . . . a little like the smoke of burning chilies," that Bhopali survivors reported from the night of the explosion, and "[t]hese big shot politicians and lawyers, they got up in a panic, they reeled around, retching, everything they did just made the pain and burning worse [. . .] They rushed from the room, jostling in the doorway each man for himself, the buffalo it seems, being too bulky to rush, was left behind while the others scrambled to save their skins."[78] Within the confines of one sentence, their fear transforms these men into beasts. Rather than remind readers of the need to gauge technological risks more readily for themselves to avoid becoming like Animal, the book cautions that the large-scale social inequities guaranteed by transnational industrial capital development limit the humanity of us all. It does so "[t]hrough complex transactions between body and language," through the ability "to *voice* and to *show* the hurt done to [the immediate sufferers] and also to provide witness to the harm done to the whole social fabric—the injury was to the very idea of different groups being able to inhabit the world together."[79]

NOTES

1. Don DeLillo, *White Noise: Text and Criticism*, ed. Mark Osteen (New York: Penguin, 1989), 114.
2. See, for instance, the chapter on "toxic discourse" in Lawrence Buell, *Writing for an Endangered World: Literature, Culture, and Environment in the U.S. and Beyond* (Cambridge, MA: Harvard University Press, 2001) and Ursula K. Heise, "Toxins, Drugs, and Global Systems: Risk and Narrative in the Contemporary Novel," *American Literature* 74, no. 4 (2002): 747–778.
3. Heise, "Toxins, Drugs, and Global Systems," 756.
4. Heise, "Toxins, Drugs, and Global Systems," 750.
5. For a much more detailed look at the role of political patronage in Bhopal and its effects on gas sufferers, see Amrita Basu, "Bhopal Revisited: The View from Below," *Bulletin of Concerned Asian Scholars* 26, no. 1–2 (Jan.–June 1994): 3–14.
6. Inderpal Grewal, *Transnational America: Feminisms, Diasporas, Neoliberalisms* (Durham, NC: Duke University Press, 2005), 130.
7. Anna Grear, "Human Rights—Human Bodies? Some Reflections on Corporate Human Rights Distortion, the Legal Subject, Embodiment, and Human Rights Theory," *Law Critique* 17 (2006), 171, 193.
8. Upendra Baxi, "Voices of Suffering and the Future of Human Rights," *Transnational Law and Contemporary Problems* 8 (1998), 125.
9. Upendra Baxi, *The Future of Human Rights*, Second Edition (Oxford: Oxford University Press, 2006), xx, xvi, xxi.
10. Ngaire Naffine, "Who Are Law's Persons? From Cheshire Cats to Responsible Subjects," *The Modern Law Review* 66, no. 3 (2003), 347.
11. Jehns David Ohlin, "Is the Concept of the Person Necessary for Human Rights?" *Columbia Law Review* 105 (2005), 233–237. Ngaire Naffine, whose model Grear cites, organizes the three conceptions of legal personhood slightly differently: P1 as the "capacity to bear a legal right"; P2 as the biological human; and P3 as the rational actor and "responsible subject" (Naffine, "Who Are Law's Person's?" 350).
12. Grear, "Human Rights—Human Bodies?" 187.
13. Upendra Baxi, "The 'just War' for Profit and Power: The Bhopal Catastrophe and the Principle of Double Effect," *Responsibility in World Business: Managing Harmful Side-Effects of Corporate Activity*, ed. Lene Bowmann-Larsen and Oddny Wiggen (Tokyo and New York: United Nations University, 2004), 182, 183.

14. Joseph R. Slaughter, *Human Rights, Inc.: The World Novel, Narrative Form, and International Law* (New York: Fordham University Press, 2007), 3.
15. Slaughter, *Human Rights, Inc.*, 44.
16. Slaughter, *Human Rights, Inc.*, 3, 328.
17. Joseph R. Slaughter, "A Question of Narration: The Voice in International Human Rights Law," *Human Rights Quarterly* 19, no. 2 (1997), 430.
18. Slaughter, *Human Rights, Inc.*, 276.
19. For a thorough discussion of the history of the Booker Prize and its relationship to the novels it celebrates, see "Prizing Otherness: A Short History of the Booker," in Graham Huggan, *The Postcolonial Exotic: Marketing the Margins* (New York and London: Routledge, 2001), 105–123.
20. Gayatri Chakravorty Spivak, "Righting Wrongs," *The South Atlantic Quarterly* 103, no. 2/3 (2004), 531.
21. Indra Sinha, *Animal's People* (New York: Simon & Schuster, 2007), 1.
22. Sinha, *Animal's People*, 364.
23. Sinha, *Animal's People*, 27.
24. Sinha, *Animal's People*, 2.
25. Sinha, *Animal's People*, 44.
26. Sandhya, "Q&A with Indra Sinha, Author of the Booker Shortlisted 'Animal's People'," *Sepia Mutiny*, March 13, 2008, www.sepiamutiny.com/sepia/archives/005088.html.
27. At the time, the American corporation, Union Carbide, owned 50.99 percent of UCIL's stock. In 2001, the Dow Chemical Corporation purchased Union Carbide.
28. Baxi reports that the first mass tort claim was filed by American lawyers in the United States just five days after the gas leak, and identifies 145 actions filed on behalf of an estimated 200,000 plaintiffs in the following two months (Upendra Baxi and the Indian Law Institute, *Inconvenient Forum and Convenient Catastrophe: The Bhopal Case* [Bombay: N. M. Tripathi Pvt. Ltd., 1986], 36–37). Lawyers' contingency fee agreements led to widespread public debate about whether or not the lawsuits were exploitative.
29. Kim Fortun, *Advocacy after Bhopal: Environmentalism, Disaster, New Global Orders* (Chicago: University of Chicago Press, 2001), 37.
30. Veena Das, "Moral Orientations to Suffering: Legitimation, Power, and Healing," in *Health and Social Change in International Perspective*, ed. Lincoln C. Chen, Arthur Kleinman, and Norma C. Ware (Boston: Harvard School of Public Health and Harvard University Press, 1994), 154.
31. Das, "Moral Orientations to Suffering," 151.
32. To the extent that the novel's representation of Bhopal's subaltern is also a form of speaking for them, it raises the question of how the success of the novel impacts other forms of gas-sufferers' self-representation and activism. The relationship between the fictional narrative and the twenty-five years of complex advocacy work in Bhopal bears far more attention than is possible here. Kim Fortun's *Advocacy after Bhopal* provides an excellent starting point for such analysis, particularly in its attention to the instability of the meaning of Bhopal in advocacy work as well as its double-effects (10). See also Bridget Hanna et al.'s *The Bhopal Reader* (New York: The Apex Press, 2005); T. R. Chouhan's *Bhopal: The Inside Story* (New York: The Apex Press, 1994); and Radha Kumar's *The History of Doing: An Illustrated Account of Movements for Women's Rights and Feminism in India, 1800–1900* (New York and London: Verso, 1996). Sheila Jasanoff reads Bhopal activism in the context of competing "civic epistemologies" or those "shared understandings of what credible claims should look like, and how they ought to be articulated, represented, and defended in public

domains" (Sheila Jasanoff, "Bhopal's Trials of Knowledge and Ignorance," *New England Law Review* 42 [Summer 2008], 688). For Jasanoff, *Animal's People* "may have done more to revive international interest in Bhopal, and thus to touch the conscience of the world, than decades of medical or legal action" (692).

33. Fortun, *Advocacy after Bhopal*, 39. Arvind Rajagopal argues the related points, that "the State underplayed the disaster to minimize the political fallout; and that industrial accidents were seen as the price to be paid for 'progress'" ("And the Poor Get Gassed: Multinational-Aided Development and the State—The Case of Bhopal," *Berkeley Journal of Sociology* 32 (1987), 131).
34. See introduction to Upendra Baxi and the Indian Law Institute, *Inconvenient Forum and Convenient Catastrophe* for excellent summary of the first eighteen months of litigation.
35. Kumar, *The History of Doing*, 188.
36. Rajagopal, "And the Poor Get Gassed," 130.
37. Cited in Rajagopal, "And the Poor Get Gassed," 137.
38. Fortun, *Advocacy after Bhopal*, 146.
39. Jasanoff, "Bhopal's Trials of Knowledge and Ignorance," 4.
40. Fortun, *Advocacy after Bhopal*, xvi.
41. Jasanoff, "Bhopal's Trials of Knowledge and Ignorance," 691.
42. Sinha, *Animal's People*, 72.
43. Tobin Siebers, "Disability in Theory: From Social Constructionism to the New Realism of the Body," *American Literary History* 13, no. 4 (2001), 738.
44. Tobin Siebers, "Disability and the Right to Have Rights," *Disability Studies Quarterly* (Winter/Spring 2007). www.dsq-sds.org.
45. Ato Quayson, *Aesthetic Nervousness: Disability and the Crisis of Representation* (New York: Columbia University Press, 2007), 3, 4.
46. In "Seeing the Disabled: Visual Rhetorics of Disability in Popular Photography" (in *Disability Studies: Enabling the Humanities*, ed. Sharon L. Snyder, Brenda Jo Brueggmann, and Rosemarie Garland Thomson [New York: Modern Language Association, 2002]), Rosemarie Garland Thomson identifies four visual rhetorics of disability: wondrous, sentimental, exotic, and realistic (339). Whereas the sentimental and exotic are most frequently mobilized by humanitarian discourses, the realist mode "suggests that the viewer must become concerned or involved [. . .] because the disabled viewer is like the viewers—socially level with them—rather than different from them" (344), although of course the medium itself ensures that difference remains.
47. Rosemarie Garland Thomson, *Extraordinary Bodies: Figuring Physical Disabilities in American Culture and Literature* (New York: Columbia University Press, 1997), 6, 7.
48. Sinha, *Animal's People*, 59.
49. Sinha, *Animal's People*, 139.
50. Baxi, *The Future of Human Rights*, 223.
51. Sinha, *Animal's People*, 4.
52. Sinha, *Animal's People*, 12. Animal's phoneticisms and mongrelization of key terms in rights discourse—eyes, jarnalis, Apokalis—also signify his alienation from normative structures of rights.
53. Baxi, "Voices of Suffering."
54. Slaughter, "A Question of Narration," 430.
55. Wendy Hesford, "Rape Stories: Material Rhetoric and the Trauma of Representation," in *Haunting Violations: Feminist Criticism and the Crisis of the 'Real,'* ed. Hesford and Wendy Kozol (Urbana and Chicago: University of Chicago Press, 2001), 18.

56. Sinha, *Animal's People*, 3.
57. Sinha, *Animal's People*, 3.
58. Elaine Scarry, "Consent and the Body: Injury, Departure, and Desire," *New Literary History* 21 (1990), 886.
59. Scarry, "Consent and the Body," 883.
60. Slaughter, *Human Rights, Inc.*, 114.
61. See, for instance, the division in the responses to Bhopal that Rajagopal documents in "And the Poor Get Gassed" between the "leaders of the activists (who, with few exceptions, were all young, middle-class men and women from outside Bhopal)" (142) and the responses received by Dr. Vinod Raina who tried to mobilize local college students' to join advocacy efforts: "There was little enthusiasm among his audience. At the fifth college he visited, he was confronted by a question from a student in the crowd. Hadn't Malthus already predicted that, once the population expanded beyond its resources, disasters would occur and reduce the population level? So what was all the fuss about?" (n. 131).
62. Slaughter, *Human Rights, Inc.*, 143, 276.
63. Sinha, *Animal's People*, 36.
64. Sinha, *Animal's People*, 365, 366.
65. Sinha, *Animal's People*, 366.
66. Spivak, "Righting Wrongs," 532.
67. Thomson, *Extraordinary Bodies*, 6.
68. Thomson, *Extraordinary Bodies*, 16.
69. Most of the scholarship cited here from the field of disability studies is explicitly located in the context of cultural productions of the United States. An exception is Ato Quayson's cross-cultural analysis in *Aesthetic Nervousness*. Foundational work by Siebers, Bérubé, and Garland Thomson nevertheless develops key methodologies and concepts—of visual and textual rhetorics, the link between disability as physical impairment and social construct, and more broadly about the politics of representation—that open up readings in other locations.
70. Michael Bérubé, "Citizenship and Disability," *Dissent* (Spring 2003): 53.
71. Michael Bérubé, "Disability and Narrative," *PMLA* 120, no. 2 (2005): 570.
72. Baxi, "The 'Just War' for Profit and Power," 184.
73. Elizabeth Grosz, *Space, Time, and Perversion* (New York: Routledge, 1995), 104.
74. Sinha, *Animal's People*, 201.
75. Sinha, *Animal's People*, 219–222.
76. Sinha, *Animal's People*, 311.
77. Scarry, "Consent and the Body," 875.
78. Sinha, *Animal's People*, 360.
79. Veena Das, "The Act of Witnessing: Violence, Poisonous Knowledge, and Subjectivity," in *Violence and Subjectivity,* ed. Das, Arthur Kleinman, Mamphela Remphele, and Pamela Reynolds (Durham, NC: Duke University Press, 1997), 205–06.

14 Do Human Rights Need a Self?
Buddhist Literature and the Samsaric Subject

Gregory Price Grieve

From the spot where I did dwell
Issued forth a fearful "thud";
What it was I could not tell,
Nor what caused it understood.
> —"The Timid Hare and the Flight of the Beasts," *The Jataka*

Ethics and politics—as well as literature—are evaded when we fall
back on the conceptual priority of the subject, agency, or identity as
the grounds of our action.
> —Thomas Keenan, *Fables of Responsibility*

There I saw the body and the head of the dove lying on the ground. I
felt no shock or surprise. What I had witnessed was a clear glimpse into
the mind of a man who had been kept away from his home for many
years. Could I claim that such a thing was not latent inside me, too?
> —Bijay Malla, "The Prisoner and the Dove"

There has been a long debate on whether human rights can be founded on
authentic Buddhist concepts, or whether they are, as James Dietrick writes,
"the infusion of Euro-American thought into the veins of Buddhist Asia."[1]
These questions center on Engaged Buddhism, a movement founded by
the Vietnamese monk and peace activist Thich Nhat Hanh, which applies
insights from meditation practice and *dharma* teachings to situations of
political, social, and economic injustice. The difficulty has revolved around
the ideology of the subject: is the "individual" who has "rights" a western (ultimately Protestant) cultural artifact, or can human rights co-exist
with the Buddhist concept of the "no-self" (*anatman*)? The no-self doctrine
argues that whereas a conventional Self—empirical, subject to conditional
phenomena, and responsible, in the causal-moral sense—exists, no ultimate metaphysical Self can be apprehended.[2]

Because the debate clings to the philosophic point that no metaphysical Self can be apprehended, it often ignores the more prosaic side of the doctrine that describes the conventional samsaric self which is the bearer of morality. In this chapter I maintain that the debate on whether Buddhist human rights need a self has missed the mark, because it has centered on philosophy rather than literature. What Buddhologists often forget is that even if Siddhartha Gautama wore the robes of a monk, he was a good storyteller. As Ralph Flores suggests in *Buddhist Scriptures as Literature*, we need "to read [Buddhist] texts not as primarily philosophy, doctrine, theory, or even advice for better living, but rather as literature."[3] There is no doubt a connection between human rights, literature, and subjectivity. As Joseph Slaughter argues in *Human Rights, Inc.: The World Novel, Narrative Form, and International Law,* there is an ideological conjunction between documents, such as the Universal Declaration of Human Rights, and the coming-of-age narrative of the *Bildungsroman,* a plot structure in which an individual is socialized through the process of learning for him- or herself what is ostensibly universally already known.[4] As Slaughter indicates, this coming-of-age narrative buttresses weak international law by offering a conceptual vocabulary, a humanist social vision, and a narrative grammar for human rights discourse.

One of the main wellsprings of Buddhist literature is the *Jataka Tales*—literally "birthlets"—that are fables that narrate the Buddha's previous births as bird, animal, supernatural creature, and human being.[5] In their descent into the prosaic domestic sphere of animals and other lesser beings, the *Jataka Tales* engage in a curious mix of fiction and seriousness. Through various types of embodiment, these birth tales trace the life and acts that, in the Buddha's final incarnation, blossom into enlightenment or awakening. For the majority of Buddhists, it is from such allegory that they receive their moral training. Such allegory also plays a part in contemporary literature, such as Bijay Malla's 1978 short story, "The Prisoner and the Dove" ("*Pareva ra Kaidi*")—a Nepali narrative that extends the moral function of allegory to modern fiction.[6] Bijay Malla is one of Nepal's leading writers, political critics, and literati. "The Prisoner and the Dove" takes place among a group of political prisoners locked up in a jail known as the Round House and revolves around the killing of a dove by one of the prisoners. Although there were differences among the prisoners, they were forced by their circumstances into a show of unity, which made their daily relations like those of a family. They lacked the facilities for reading and writing, and so their days centered on domestic chores. The most important responsibility was the care of four pairs of doves, with whom they came to identify closely, and which were at the center of the this-worldly domestic space that made prison life easier to tolerate.

What makes these texts "Buddhist literature," however, is neither that they were written by Buddhists, nor even that they discuss explicitly Buddhist topics. As Thomas Keenan reminds us in *Fables of Responsibility,* literature "is not simply a matter of poems, not a given body of work, but a question of reading, its strategies, difficulties, and conditions."[7] For Keenan, reading literature exposes one to the singularity of a text, whose complexities cannot be organized in advance. Buddhist literature is *literary* because it exposes the reader to the complexities of Emptiness (*shunyata*), which on an ultimate level describes the observation that no phenomenon possesses essential, enduring identity. Yet, on an everyday conventional level, Emptiness is *samsara*, the whirl of perpetual flux, that flowing on, that designates the entire cycle of transmigration and more down to earth, everyday existence in the world. In contemporary Nepali, *samsara* connotes the world of birth, death, and transmigration. In more classical texts, the term simply denotes empirical phenomenological existence: the conditioned and ever-changing phenomenological world, as opposed to the unconditioned, eternal, and transcendent state of nirvana. *Samsara* is not so much a place where one is, however, but rather a process or a practice of doing. As we interact with others, we all play a part in the creation of worlds. In a samsaric fashion, through material, everyday worldly relations, people make themselves and are made, in turn, by others.

Like Malla's short story, the *Jataka Tales* tell about love, sacrifice, and the qualities of friendship, but most of all about this responsibility toward others. Unabashedly fabulous, these stories articulate a subjectivity most clearly exposed as what Thich Nhat Hanh defines as "Interbeing"—the ideology that all "phenomena are interdependent . . . endlessly interwoven."[8] Yet, these stories do not represent the grounds of such ethics, but rather attempt to shake the reader's foundations so as to make apparent one's latent responsibility to others. A Buddhist literary theory, then, cannot be the application of a more or less mechanical agenda, because "Buddhist literature" happens when a text breaks our rules, and thus dislodges our expectations and exposes us to our responsibility. To pun off a famous saying by the Zen Master Linji, "when you meet Buddhist literature on the road, kill it." The point of such ungrounding is not a quest for philosophic mysticism (or self-realization) but rather that the realization of our codependence will end the suffering by leading the reader towards compassion and responsibility towards others. As Keenan argues for the genre of the fable, the dissolution of certainty does not simply deconstruct essentialized ethico-political discourses, but demonstrates "that what we call ethics and politics only come into being or have any force of meaning thanks to this very ungroundedness."[9]

From this perspective, such Buddhist fables as *The Jataka Tales* are moral because they teach responsibility through such moments of difficulty—a crocodile that wants to eat a monkey's heart, an over-talkative turtle, and a timid rabbit (just to name a few). These are moments that, as Keenan maintains about Aesopian narratives, are not stable entities but are "rigorous paradoxes or enigmas of this ethico-political tradition."[10] Malla's short story should also be read in this light. The central point in Malla's "The

Prisoner and the Dove" is just such a destabilizing moment. The prisoners become sad and angry because they discover one of the doves decapitated and flung to the ground. They blame the prison orderlies, and their relations with them sour. One hot afternoon, while the prisoners are resting quietly on their cots, the protagonist goes to the outhouse. From his seat, he sees one of his fellow prisoners pick up a dove, caress it, kiss it, and then suddenly force the bird into his mouth and suffocate it. The prisoner then blankly tosses the bird's bloody body to the ground, and walks off.

BUDDHISM AND HUMAN RIGHTS: ENGAGED COMPASSION OR "SCRIPTURAL LIBERATION"?

Few would deny that Engaged Buddhism has done "good work" in the world. The question that plagues the movement is whether it maintains continuity with traditional Buddhism, or whether it is a "new" form of Buddhism forged in the crucible of modern, global concerns. Thich Nhat Hanh states that Buddhism has always been socially engaged, so that today's Engaged Buddhism is nothing new. Critics claim, however, that whereas social ideals may have been latent in Buddhist teachings, they have not been actualized until modern times; therefore, Engaged Buddhism constitutes a major departure from traditional forms. Many, in fact, claim that the Buddhist concern with social reform is, at least in part, inspired by liberal Protestant notions of social service. This debate centers on two main issues, the first of which is ecology. Engaged Buddhism is posed by many to be more environmentally friendly than other religious traditions, and thus a stark contrast is drawn between it and the Christian notion of human dominion over the Earth. Unlike the Book of Genesis, where the world was created by God, to which he appointed man the steward, Buddhism teaches that people and the natural world evolved together.

The second element of the debate is human rights. On the contemporary world stage, "human rights" have become the common currency of debates surrounding social, political, and ethical issues. A right can be defined as an exercisable power invested in the enlightenment—ultimately Protestant—conception of the individual. This power allows the right-bearer to impose a claim upon others. Even if declared universal, few would deny that human rights emerged in the west from a particular combination of social and historical events. That is, human rights are a recent product of the modern Western European common law traditions, and the concept stemmed from the religious wars of the sixteenth and seventeenth centuries, was refined during the Enlightenment, and came to fruition as a response to the genocide of the Second World War. Still, even if human rights were generated in the West, there is no direct conflict between Buddhism and human rights. For instance, none of the rights mentioned in the thirty-nine articles of the Universal Declaration of Human Rights, proclaimed by the

General Assembly of the United Nations, contradicts Buddhist teachings. The problem is that traditional Buddhist sources do not pose moral questions in this form. For instance, there is no word in early Buddhist sources that corresponds to the notion of "rights" as understood in the West.

The debate, then, is more than *can* Buddhism engage in "rights talk," but *should* it if human rights have no genuine foundation in Buddhist doctrine? As stated above, that question pivots on the subject of the "self." We can trace the roots of this debate to how early European Orientalist Buddhologists ultimately perceived the tradition as a "world-denying" set of philosophic texts, and how current Engaged Buddhists stress the more conventional this-worldly aspects of the tradition. One of the largest translational changes that occurred when Buddhism was brought to the west during the colonial period was the foregrounding of elite monastic philosophic texts that meshed with the Enlightenment ideology of individual freedom. For instance, as Robert Sharf depicts in "Buddhist Modernism and the Rhetoric of Meditative Experience," the colonial encounter refashioned Buddhism as a post-Enlightenment Christianity that emphasized individualism, rational instrumentalism, universalism, and scripture.[11]

The privileging of the "world-denying" set of philosophic texts leads to what I have called "scripturalism," a pattern of mediation that forces religious phenomena into the "Protestant bed" of the printed text and then reifies these texts, and their readers, as ahistorical.[12] Whether wielded as critique or apology, the leitmotif of scripturalism runs through the study of Buddhism and often "stretches" or "cuts" religious phenomena to fit a romanticized quest for salvation and transcendence, a form of therapy, or even just philosophy. This "one-size-fits-all" scriptural approach, which metamorphosizes phenomena to fit a preconceived ideal, is reinforced by the interplay between a "puritan model" of religion and the logocentric academic fetishization of the book. The emphasis on scriptural liberation fails to account, however, for how the majority of lay Buddhists live in *samsara* on a conventional everyday level. For the majority of Buddhists in the world, the key is not individual liberation, but the well-being of the family. Because scripture tended to be written by monks for monks, it often tends to be anti-family. In "The Prisoner and the Dove," this domestic sphere is emphasized as Malla writes, "The daily relations of [the prisoners] inside the Round House were like those of a family."[13] The conception of the family that Malla narrates is one based on an orthopraxic religious model, which, as in a typical Nepali family, is centered on the domestic sphere of the kitchen: "We collected together the 'offerings' they gave us in jail. We also divided up the various jobs among us. We twelve young men ran our kitchen like this. . . . [D]omestic chores helped the time to pass without [us] being aware of it."[14]

This debate between engaged worldly compassion and scriptural liberation is exemplified in the exchange found between Damien Keown's article "Are There Human Rights in Buddhism?" and Derek S. Jeffreys's "Does

Buddhism Need Human Rights?"[15] Answering his title query in the negative, Jeffreys argues that "a human rights ethic is incompatible with [the
Buddhist] no-self doctrine," and that one should abandon "the pursuit of
an elusive Buddhist human rights theory" so that one can "appreciate Buddhism's fascinating understanding of the mind, a philosophical gem that
has much to teach us."[16] Similarly, Peter Junger argues that the Buddha,
having wisdom and compassion, has no need for rights in themselves.[17]
On the other side of the debate are those who seek to merge human rights
discourse with Buddhism, an argument that can take the form of seeking a moral foundation from within Buddhism. For instance, as Keown
maintains, one can translate the Five Precepts (*Panca-Sila*)—the basic Buddhist code of ethics—into a human rights ethic. Craig Ihara argues that
human rights can be used as a form of expedient means (*upaya*) for the
overall elimination of suffering.[18] As he notes, the elimination of suffering
is embedded in "Interbeing," as stated above, a word coined by Thich Nhat
Hanh to employ the concept of Emptiness for human rights.

BUDDHIST LITERATURE: TELLING THE SAMSARIC SUBJECT

According to Buddhism, like the prisoners in the round house, humans are
trapped in *samsara*, which is created from our co-dependent material actions
(*karma*). Because of how *karma* reverberates with Protestant notions of the
Earthly sins, the term is often understood negatively in western literature
and theorized in purely philosophic and soteriological terms as this-worldly
actions that are the opposite of a pious mystic "enlightenment." Conflating
karma with sin, however, poses *karma* as individual intention and enlightenment as salvation, and thus misses the crucial, procreative practices by
which human beings collectively construct the lived world. In Buddhism,
this interdependency is clearest in the doctrine of dependent origination
(*pratityasamutpada*)—literally "this being given, that follows," which has
been called the central doctrine of Buddhism, one that also at the center of
the concept of "Interbeing."

Keeping in mind our co-dependency, samsaric this-worldly conventional
selves are defined less from thinking and intention and more from their
material, methods, and social relations. They are a thing done rather than
a thing believed. This samsaric self is fluid—ready and open to be constituted by and to constitute other selves and other signs. It is tied together
through a complex web of giving and receiving of both goods and favors,
which Nepalis often speak of as a net. For Nepalis, then, the self is not
bounded, but is created by a net of social relations. As I was told many
times during my fieldwork in Nepal between 1995 and 2000, "Life is not
just for ourselves, but for relatives and family. You can't live only by yourself. I am a different person to different people. To my father I am a son, to
my son and daughters I am a father, to my teacher I was a student, to you

I am a teacher."[19] The Buddha's *Birth Stories* are based upon the form of the traditional saga, which includes tales of courage, audacity, and loyalty to family and clan, and usually narrates a central figure and a hero's battle against the group's enemies. *The Jataka Tales* re-narrate the traditional epic to focus on a central figure who is heroic because of his or her kindness, compassion, and generosity, which are based upon an attitude of detachment and a view of the interconnectedness of the world. Detachment does not mean that one does not live in the world, but that one is not invested egotistically in the outcome of one's actions. Such heroic detachment allows for one to be concerned not just for oneself, or for one's "tribe," but rather for sentient beings in general.

This heroic compassion is narrated through generosity. Giving (*dana*) is one of the foundational elements of Buddhist practice and is recognized by most Buddhists as one of the most basic human virtues that testifies to the depth of one's capacity for self-transcendence. Giving is one of the six perfections (*paramitas*) and for the laity centers on giving to the monastic members of the community. In Buddhist *dharma,* the *danakatha*, "the story of giving," was always the first topic to be discussed. Only after appreciating this virtue would the Buddha introduce other aspects, such as morality and *karma*. Strictly speaking, giving does not appear as part of the Eightfold Path (the moral principles at the heart of Buddhism), nor is it a prerequisite for enlightenment. Instead, giving underlies and quietly supports the entire endeavor to be free of attachments by actualizing one's latent responsibility towards others.

This attitude of heroic compassion is no better exemplified than by the act of extreme giving. For instance, the final *Jataka Tale*, "Vessantara's Sacrifice," which narrates the Buddha's penultimate life, is the story of a Great Prince Vessantara, who was known for his generosity. As the Prince's fame for *danaparamita* (perfection of charity) spread, whatever was asked of him he gave. As his life went on, he married an honorable lady called Maddi who bore him two children, Jali and Kanhajina. One day, eight Brahmins came to beg for his white elephant, which had guaranteed rain in the kingdom. The prince happily gave it away. The people were so outraged by this gift that they forced the king to banish Vessantara from the kingdom. Before setting forth with his wife and two children, the Great Prince held an alms-giving ceremony where he gave away seven hundred pieces of seven hundred kinds of things to the needy people.

Vessantara left with his family in a royal chariot drawn by four horses. On the way, four Brahmins begged for his horses, which he gave them. Soon afterward a Brahmin beggar asked for the carriage, which again the Prince gave away. The family arrived in the deepest forest, where they built hermitages, and with nothing more to give lived happily for many months. One day, however, an old Brahmin with hairy armpits came to the hermitage and begged for the Prince's children. The children clung to their father, asking to wait at least until the arrival of their mother. But shrewd and mean, the Brahmin fastened the children's hands with vines and forcibly dragged them away. When his wife returned, she asked Vessantara of the children's whereabouts, but the Prince kept silent. She then repeated the same question several times. Finally, he told what he had done. Surprisingly, she praised Vessantara's great act of charity. Again, the Brahmin returned, and this time asked for the Prince's wife.

What is important about such gifts is not so much their value, but rather how they undermine and destabilize the protaganist's life, leaving him or her groundless. For instance, giving away the rain-making elephant undermined Vessantara's position as a monarch, and giving away his family undermined his position as a householder. As such, Buddhist fables do not create moral rules to follow, but teach responsibility by generating a feeling of groundlessness. Similarly, at stake in the heroic giving of the dove in Malla's story is the illumination of the responsibility towards others through the creation of groundlessness. The dove both points out and destabilizes those social and material transactions that hold a home, and ultimately one's lived world, together.

NEPALI LITERATURE, THE MODERN SAMSARIC SUBJECT, AND THE HEROIC GIFT OF RESPONSIBILITY

Nepali literature is clearly a twentieth-century phenomenon, and thus stands in a strategic location for blending traditional narratives with modern political concerns. A late starter to the world's literatures, Nepal quickly developed a rich and unique tradition. Modern Nepali, however, is essentially hybrid, and stems from four distinct influences: Sanskrit classical tradition, the indigenous folk tradition, developments in Hindi literature, and the influence of the west. The founding of modern Nepali literature can be traced to Motiram Bhatta (1866–1896). Yet, even Bhatta's style remained poetic, largely Sanskritized, strictly metrical, and exclusively the purview of educated Brahmin males. It is only in the early 1930s that the first overtly modern short stories appeared, closely resembling current developments in Hindi fiction. During the 1960s, self-consciously modernist literary movements appeared in Darjeeling and Kathmandu.

Yet, whereas Nepali literature is "modern," because of its hybrid nature it borrows heavily from an oral folk tradition, which consists of songs, tales, proverbs, and riddles. Because it is grounded in these traditional fables, "The Prisoner and the Dove" offers an alternative literary model for human rights than the one exemplified in the *Bildungsroman*. The characters in Buddhist literature are not individuals seeking self-discovery. The Buddha's stories are populated by a cluster of sentient beings who react compassionately toward each other. In these stories the Buddha is shown not as withdrawing from the world, but as acting with compassion toward all living beings. Such compassion is often shown in "heroic" acts of giving.

In the *Jatakas*, taking the form of a Deer King, the Buddha risked his own life to free all creatures; as a monkey he saved an ungrateful hunter; as a lion he saved all the frightened beasts of the jungle; as a parrot he flew unselfishly through flames to save those trapped in a burning forest; as an elephant he offered his life so that starving men might live; as a king he offered his own flesh so that a dove might live.

In Malla's story, the prisoners take such good care of the doves that even the orderlies become more compassionate. But things start to change when they find one of the doves beheaded. What is ungrounding in Malla's narrative is not the death of the dove—something that seems inevitable once the birds are introduced into the story—but instead the protagonist's reaction: he "feels no shock or surprise," and instead expresses compassion and responsibility toward the killer: "Could I claim that such a thing was not latent inside me, too?" [20] Malla does not give us an ethical rule to follow but sets up a situation in which latent responsibility emerges. It is these samsaric responsibilities, and even the burden of this net of relations, that the dove in Malla's short story symbolizes. The prisoners do not choose to have the doves: "they had been cared for by a prisoner who was transferred shortly after our arrival." [21] Yet, as the narrator explains, while "we feared that the doves might be a burden on us," we "played with the simple domestic creatures, [and] they became quite attached to us." [22] Like the samsaric relations described above, this attachment revolves around the kitchen: "At mealtimes, and when we scattered grain for them, the doves would congregate." [23] The prisoners come to identify closely with the doves. Yet, it is not the doves' freedom that they are attached to, but rather that "the hardships of life in prison weighed less heavily on us because of them." [24] The doves, then, do not represent the possibility of escape from the world, but samsaric responsibility: "We would toss the adult birds into the air, and they flew across the sky above the compound, mounting higher and higher. . . . But they always flew back inside to come and settle on our shoulders. . . . The jail was truly their home." [25]

CONCLUSION: DO HUMAN RIGHTS NEED BUDDHIST LITERATURE?

I am not arguing that "literature" offers a hidden treasure, "an elusive Buddhist human rights theory," but rather something more prosaic: Buddhist literature offers a responsible way to read the subject. As this chapter has demonstrated, in Buddhist literature, the moral subject differs at an essential level from the individual ideal subject who is the protagonist of the *Bildungsroman* that narrates human rights. Both in the *Jataka Tales* and in the "The Prisoner and the Dove," we do not find a subject who is a stable, bounded, integrated, dynamic center of awareness and judgment. Instead, we find the "samsaric subject"—a this-worldly conventional self who is tied to others through love, compassion, and a duty of responsibility. Samsaric responsibility is not grounded in the recognition of the other individual's inherent rights but in the compassion and responsibility of a radically destabilized subject dependent on others.[26] In Thich Nhat Hanh's words, the responsibility comes from being in the middle. Being in the middle does not guarantee security, or cognitive certainty. Instead, as Keenan argues for fables in general, it masks a complex "no man's land" of responsibility that sits uneasily between ethics and politics. This responsibility rests not "on the search for a lesson or a rule to be applied," but rather in the exposure "to something that [is] irreducible to ourselves and what we already know." [27] Effective human rights literature does not create responsibility by preaching to the converted. Buddhist literature is important to human rights because it removes the ground from under our feet. As Keenan argues: "It is when we do not know exactly what we should do, when the effects of conditions of our actions can no longer be calculated, and we have nowhere to turn, not even back onto our 'self,' that we encounter something like responsibility."[28]

If this is the case, can human rights be founded on the selfless self of the no-self doctrine? In a typical Buddhist answer the best response may be both "no" and "yes." No, if this "self" is a bounded abstract individual who is the bearer of rights, the historical product of the European Enlightenment, and the subject of a Protestant ideology. Yet, such a simple refusal does not reflect Buddhism's whole story; it leaves out the tales that Buddhists tell. What is at stake in marginalizing Buddhist literature is not simply that we leave out many voices in the tradition; it also leaves out an entire subjectivity. Attending to how literature plays a part in constructing such selves is crucial, because selves are not natural. They are produced and not given, and therefore one must attend to the role of ideology in constituting concrete individual subjects. So pervasive is ideology in relation to how literature constructs subjects that it forms our very frame and thus appears as not only undeniably "true" but overwhelmingly "obvious."

Reading Buddhist literature allows other ways of constituting subjects to traverse the narrative structure of the *Bildungsroman*, thus enabling one to imagine other ways of engaging with suffering beyond the *telos* of the development of a bounded individual. The Buddhist literary quality of stories such as "The Prisoner and the Dove" and the literary quality of the tradition's early fables expand the subject of human rights by constituting the samsaric subject as a conceptual alternative to the normative western model of the individual. Buddhist literature is crucial for the study of human rights, then, because human rights discourse often presupposes an "atomistic" individual who is the bearer of rights, who is more or less an isolated, free-standing entity with little connection to other people, at least inasmuch as he or she is recognized as a subject of human rights law. If, as Slaughter suggests, human rights discourse inevitably relies on literary narratives, then Buddhist literature offers a way to reinvigorate this field by expanding the stories we tell, and thus our conception of human subjects, and by proxy human rights.

If Buddhist literature expands the notions of subjects and liberation, it also magnifies the concept of human rights to include a compassionate responsibility toward others which, like the gift of the dove, or Vessantara's children, is a heroic gesture which undermines one's own world and leaves one groundless. The Buddhist self is a selfless self, which is narrated through heroic stories that destabilize the reader's conventional subject position, and leads to a particularly this-worldly conception of moral responsibility based on our "interbeing" with others. As such, a Buddhist human rights should be founded not in timeless philosophic doctrine. Instead, its purview lies in the everyday conventional responsibility that springs from our dependent origination with other selves right here right now. Such responsibility is conveyed not in grand narratives, but rather in the space where literature leaves the reader in a no-man's land with no where to hide. Paradoxically, samsaric subjectivity is grounded in this everyday groundlessness. Once one empties a metaphysical "Self," what is left is a responsibility toward others. Accordingly, focusing on the samsaric subject, and the net of social interconnectedness which supports it, foregrounds the human impulse of responsibility, giving, and forgiving that expands human rights discourses beyond the rhetoric of individual entitlement.

So do human rights need a self? Yes, if the "self" is a this-worldly conventional samsaric subject who is responsible for others, the historical product of Asian notions of *karma*, and the subject of Buddhist literature. The doves are a symbol of the prisoner's "liberation." Yet, the doves' "liberation" does not signify individual freedom—the power to act or speak or think without externally imposed restraints—which implies immunity from duty. Instead, the doves speak to that responsibility that burdens each of us toward others. The dove, in a sense, indicates the role of the *bodhisattva*, a "Buddha to be" or "enlightenment being." This type of human being is a model of virtue that holds off entering final individual liberation out of the realization that we are interconnected—how can I be free if you are not?—and attempts the heroic task of leading all sentient beings to complete, perfect enlightenment. In short, human rights discourse needs Buddhist literature, because the stories it tells expand the human subject beyond the egocentricism of the "bearer of human rights" by highlighting the responsibility that stems from the interrelatedness and interdependency of sentient beings in the everyday lived world.

NOTES

1. James Deitrick, "Engaged Buddhist Ethics: Mistaking the Boat for the Shore," in *Action Dharma. New Studies in Engaged Buddhism*, ed. Damien

Keown, Charles Prebish, and Christopher Queen (New York: Routledge, 2003), 253.

2. Peter Harvey, *The Selfless Mind: Personality, Consciousness and Nirvana in Early Buddhism* (New York: Curzon Press 1995), 33.

3. Ralph Flores, *Buddhist Scriptures as Literature: Sacred Rhetoric and the Uses of Theory* (New York: SUNY Press, 2008), 3.

4. Joseph Slaughter, *Human Rights, Inc.: The World Novel, Narrative Form, and International Law* (New York: Fordham University Press, 2007).

5. Redactions of these "birthlet" stories are located throughout much of Buddhist literature and Asian visual culture. The stories presented in the canon are probably just a small sample of a much larger oral tradition. The popularity of this tradition is evident in that many of Buddhism's greatest monuments are covered in carvings that depict such scenes. For these birth stories see E. B. Cowell, ed., *The Jataka*, trans. Robert Chalmers, 1985, which can be found online at http://www.sacred-texts.com/bud/j1/index.htm (accessed October 7, 2010).

6. Bija Malla, "Parevā ra Kaidī," in *Parevā ra Kaidī* (Kathmandu: Sākjhā Prakāshan, 1978) [bi sa 2034]. *Parevā* literally means pigeon. So translating the title with "dove" is a poetic choice—or in a Benjaminian sense, dove is a better "truth content" than "subject matter." "Dove" works better here for a western context, because in Nepal, pigeons rather than doves are flown as signs of peace. A translation can be found in Michael James Hurt's *Himalayan Voices: An Introduction to Modern Nepali Literature* (Berkeley: University of California Press, 1991), http://www.escholarship.org/editions/view?docId=ft729007x1;brand=ucpress (accessed Feb 10, 2010). I have indicated where my translation differs from Hurt's.

7. Thomas Keenan, *Fables of Responsibility: Aberrations and Predicaments in Ethics and Politics* (Stanford, CA: Stanford University Press, 1997), 1.

8. Thich Nhat Hanh, *Love in Action: Writings on Nonviolent Social Change* (Berkeley, CA: Parallax Press, 1993), 129.

9. Keenan, *Fables of Responsibility*, 3.

10. Keenan, *Fables of Responsibility*, 2.

11. Robert Sharf, "Buddhist Modernism and the Rhetoric of Meditative Experience," *Numen* 42 (1995), 252.

12. Gregory Price Grieve, *Retheorizing Religion in Nepal* (New York: Palgrave Macmillan, 2006).

13. Malla, "The Prisoner and the Dove."

14. Malla, "The Prisoner and the Dove."

15. Damien Keown, "Are There Human Rights in Buddhism?" in *Buddhism and Human Rights*, ed. Damien Keown, Charles Prebish, and Wayne Husted (Surrey: Curzon Press, 1998), 15–41; Derek Jeffreys, "Does Buddhism Need Human Rights," in *Buddhism and Human Rights*, ed. Damien Keown, Charles Prebish, and Wayne Husted (Surrey: Curzon Press, 1998), 270–285.

16. Jeffreys, "Does Buddhism Need Human Rights," 282.

17. Peter Junger, "Why the Buddha has no Rights," in *Buddhism and Human Rights*, ed. Damien Keown, Charles Prebish, and Wayne Husted (Surrey: Curzon Press, 1998), 86.

18. Craig Ihara, "Why There Are No Rights in Buddhism: A Reply to Damien Keown," in *Buddhism and Human Rights*, ed. Damien Keown et al. (Surrey: Curzon Press, 1998), 44–51.

19. Personal interview, August 10, 1995.

20. Malla, "The Prisoner and the Dove."

21. Malla, "The Prisoner and the Dove."

22. Malla, "The Prisoner and the Dove."

23. Malla, "The Prisoner and the Dove."
24. Malla, "The Prisoner and the Dove."
25. Malla, "The Prisoner and the Dove."
26. For the relation between Emmanuel Levinas's thought and the samsaric self see Gregory Grieve, "Symbol, Idol and *Murti:* Hindu God-images and the Politics of Mediation," *Culture, Theory and Critique* 44 (2003): 57–72.
27. Keenan, *Fables of Responsibility,* 175, 189.
28. Keenan, *Fables of Responsibility,* 2.

Epilogue

*Elizabeth Swanson Goldberg
and Alexandra Schultheis Moore*

The challenge at the core of this volume has been exploring the expressions of human rights as material, theoretical, and literary practice. Our contributors may take a cue from novelist J. M. Coetzee, who insists that the "dignity" at the root of human rights "is not our essence but a foundational fiction to which we more or less wholeheartedly subscribe, a fiction that may well be indispensible for a just society."[1] Or, they may respond to the definition provided by scholar James Dawes in "Human Rights in Literary Study" that "human rights work is, at its heart, a matter of storytelling."[2] If human rights pursuits are modeled upon *and* shape stories, as Joseph Slaughter also argues in the Foreword to this volume, then those pursuits—literary or otherwise—open themselves to the theoretical, interpretative techniques of literary studies. Theoretical perspectives can chart various routes through the five paradoxes shared by human rights and literary practices that Dawes identifies: the paradoxes of beauty (the aesthetic), truth, description, suffering, and witnessing. Such paradoxes mean, in other words, that stories written or interpreted on behalf of the alleviation of suffering or the pursuit of justice from human rights abuses may "promote human dignity" or mask its threats; present contesting and contested truths in language that at once stays and/or frees the subject; represent and/or re-traumatize sufferers of abuse whose voice in this process is possibly both "rescu[ed] and usurp[ed]."[3] Our introductory chapter charts the history of the interdiscipline of human rights and literature as it emerges in relation to other theoretical developments in the academy. The contributors in this volume have navigated the tricky terrain between essentializing the role of literary discourses in human rights work, particularly in autobiographical or testimonial forms, and, alternatively, instrumentalizing literature in service to theory. As Dawes reminds us, "even at this level of high theory, the most basic concern (and, indeed, ethical impulse) is the same: what are the ethical risks and obligations of our language practices?"[4]

Dawes answers this question with a turn to literature, not to recoup any "purity of the text's intention"[5] but to explore the conditions through which literature of human rights emerges. This turn reminds us of the rich dialectic between human rights literature and theory. In the case of Emmanuel Dongala's *Johnny Mad Dog*, Dawes notes, the author's suffering in the Congolese civil war and eventual removal to safety are conditions that made the novel possible: "Dongala knew . . . that he was trading his story for his life" in appealing to humanitarian workers to remove him from the war; and perhaps in response, one of his characters insists instead on the right to the privacy of suffering the war's effects.[6] In other words, Dongala's necessary sacrifice of his personal or autobiographical privacy paradoxically creates the possibility of the imagination of such silence as a basic right in his fiction. The paradox of rights emerges here as product of the exchange of genres and generic expectations between, first, the author and the humanitarian workers who rescue him from Congo and, second, the fictional characters of an African woman and outsider journalist who would report her suffering caused by the novelized civil war. Dawes's discussion of the relationship between Dongala's life story and fiction frames an ethical position for the reader of this combinatory story of civil war as the possibility of readership is founded in the first instance, only to be deferred in the second. That precariousness of the possibility of narration underscores the stakes of readers' and authors' "responsibility to the story" in conditions of extremity.[7]

It is no surprise that the question of the role of theory in human rights and literary studies leads to the paradoxes at the heart of both. Theory often comes up against the limits of its own terms, and in its familiar academic forms may seem complicit with a kind of Euro-American imperializing approach to human rights and humanitarian discourses. Although one legacy of arguments during the 1980s and 1990s over the role of theory, as in Barbara Christian's "The Race for Theory" (1987) and Donald Goellnicht's "Blurring Boundaries: Asian American Literature as Theory" (1997), may echo the debate over universal versus culturally specific human rights, another may unleash questions about what counts as human rights literature and practice.

Such questions would push human rights oriented literary theory past the more obvious testimonial and autobiographical forms of witness literature, to embrace literatures of protest—that is, literature that tells stories of ongoing abuses, as opposed to establishing the truth of past violations—as well as postmodern narratives and satires. Two particularly fine recent examples of the latter are John Edgar Wideman's *Fanon* (2008) and Percival Everett's *The Water Cure* (2007). Of course, such questions would also press literary theorists to attend to the role of drama and poetry of all kinds—currently underrepresented in human rights–oriented literary criticism, with its near singular focus on story in the novel form—in representing human rights events and claims. Similarly, such questions about "what counts," or "what gets heard," could employ literary and narrative theories to push human rights practice beyond the valorization of civil and political rights, especially those publicized by media driven focus upon particular disaster zones, to attend to the chronic abuses of global poverty, identified as a new status quo in the work of sociologists such as Mike Davis in *Planet of Slums* (2007), and left essentially untouched inside the vacuum where the economic (not to mention literary) counter-discourse of Marxism once was. We hope that this collection offers a range of approaches to the dynamic exchange between literature, theory, and human rights, an exchange that continually produces new discourses, ways of reading, and readers and writers.

In "Ethics and Narrative: The Human and the Other," Chris Abani, poet, novelist, essayist and former political prisoner, writes, "Let us not begin with definitions. With academic references. With proof that many books have been studied on the subject. With the notion that for an idea to be singular, purposeful, or even useful it must be backed up by the research of others. Let us begin with a smaller gesture [. . .] a story, perhaps."[8] The story that he begins here, of his learning to kill a goat in a rite of passage, expands to weave a social fabric of family, language, belief, masculinity, war, shame, and finally acceptance of a shared responsibility for and complicity in violent acts. Quoting his cousin, a former child soldier in Nigeria whose "simple gestures" of intervention allowed Abani to complete the sacrifice, he considers: "Perhaps it is enough, as Emmanuel said, to know that it will always be hard."[9] Abani couches the story within a larger meditation on what fiction requires of both reader and writer, rendering that conclusion an address to his readers as well as to himself. To those who would read stories of human rights abuses with simple compassion, he dismisses sentimentality entirely and asks: "What if compassion, true compassion, requires not the *gift* to see the world as it is, but the *choice* to be open to seeing the world as it really is, or as it can be?"[10] We perceive human rights–oriented literary criticism to be just such a choice, a conscious decision to enact an engaged theoretical practice that accepts the responsibility of the witness-interpreter-theorist-producer to recognize both the untold ugliness and incalculable beauty of the world. That accepts the responsibility of theorizing not only our own pain but also the pain of others, not only the actions of others but also our own complicities. That accepts the responsibility of seeing and imagining not only what is but also the possibilities for difference within the whirlwind of everyday global life.

NOTES

1. J. M. Coetzee, *Giving Offense: Essays on Censorship* (Chicago: University of Chicago Press, 1997), 14.
2. James Dawes, "Human Rights in Literary Study," *Human Rights Quarterly* 31, no. 2 (2009), 394.
3. Dawes, "Human Rights in Literary Study," 395–396.
4. Dawes, "Human Rights in Literary Study," 409.

5. Allen Thiher, "A Theory of Literature, or Recent Literature as Theory," *Contemporary Literature* XXIX, no. 3 (1988), 339.

6. Dawes, "Human Rights in Literary Study," 409.

7. Paul Gready, "Introduction—'Responsibility to the Story'," *Journal of Human Rights Practice* 2, no. 2 (June 2010), 177. Gready attributes the phrase to Brian Phillips.

8. Chris Abani, "Ethics and Narrative: The Human and the Other," *Witness* XXII (2009), 167.

9. Abani, "Ethics and Narrative:," 168, 173.

10. Abani, "Ethics and Narrative," 170.

Contributors

Elizabeth Susan Anker is assistant professor of English at Cornell University, where she teaches courses in contemporary world literature and law and literature. She holds a J.D. from the University of Chicago and a Ph.D. from the University of Virginia. She has published essays in *Modern Fiction Studies*, *James Joyce Quarterly*, *Theory & Event*, *New Literary History*, and *American Literary History*, as well as different edited collections. She is currently completing a book, *Fictions of Dignity: Human Rights and the Postcolonial Novel.*

Stephanie Athey is associate professor of English and Director of Mexico Shoulder to Shoulder and the Honors Program at Lasell College in Massachusetts. Her edited volume, *Sharpened Edge: Women, Resistance and Writing* (2003), studies transnational feminism and human rights in a global context, and she has published on eugenics, race and colonial discourse in *Genders*, *American Literature*, and *Narrative*, among other publications. She held a 2006 appointment as Visiting Scholar at the Columbia University Center for the Study of Human Rights, and her recent scholarship has been on U.S. torture.

Carolyn Forché is a poet, translator and editor of the ground-breaking anthology *Against Forgetting: Twentieth-Century Poetry of Witness* (1993). A human rights activist for over thirty years, she was presented the Edita and Ira Morris Hiroshima Foundation Award for Peace and Culture in Stockholm, 1998, for her work on behalf of human rights and the preservation of memory and culture. She has received fellowships from The John Simon Guggenheim Foundation, The Lannan Foundation and The National Endowment for the Arts. She has held The Lannan Chair of Poetry at Georgetown University, where she also directs The Lannan Center for Poetics and Social Practice.

Elizabeth Swanson Goldberg is associate professor of English and Mandell Family Term Chair at Babson College, where she teaches postcolonial literature and human rights. Author of *Beyond Terror: Gender, Narrative, Human Rights* (2007), she has published articles in edited collections and in journals including *Callaloo* and *The South Atlantic Quarterly*. She recently edited a special issue of the transnational journal *Peace Review* devoted to the subject of literature, film, and human rights (2008).

Gregory Price Grieve is associate professor of Religious Studies and the Director of MERGE: A Network for Interdisciplinary and Collaborative Scholarship at the University of North Carolina at Greensboro. He is the author of *Retheorizing Religion in Nepal* (2006) and the co-editor of *Historicizing Tradition in the Study of Religion* (2005). Grieve has been a research fellow at the Asia Research Institute, National University of Singapore, and the Center for Religion and Media at New York University.

Wendy Kozol is professor of Comparative American Studies at Oberlin College. She teaches courses on visual culture, citizenship and nationalism, and comparative feminist theories and activism. She is the author of *Life's America: Family and Nation in Postwar Photojournalism* (1994) and has co-edited two anthologies (with Wendy Hesford): *Haunting Violations: Feminist Criticism and the Crisis of the 'Real'* (2001) and *Just Advocacy: Women's Human Rights, Transnational Feminism and the Politics of Representation* (2005).

Nick Mansfield is Professor in Critical and Cultural Studies and Dean of Higher Degree Research at Macquarie University in Sydney. He is the author of several books including *Theorizing War: From Hobbes to Badiou* (2008) and *The God Who Deconstructs Himself: Subjectivity and Sovereignty Between Freud, Bataille and Derrida* (2010). He is one of the founding general editors of the journal *Derrida Today,* published by Edinburgh University Press.

Alexandra Schultheis Moore is associate professor of English, program faculty for Women's and Gender Studies, and founding co-coordinator of the Human Rights Research Network at the University of North Carolina at Greensboro. She is the author of *Regenerative Fictions: Postcolonialism, Psychoanalysis, and the Nation as Family* (2004) as well as numerous essays on contemporary postcolonial studies and human rights in literature and film.

Greg Mullins is a member of the faculty at The Evergreen State College, where he teaches comparative literature, American Studies, and human rights. He is the author of *Colonial Affairs* (2002), a study of colonialism and sexuality in American expatriate literature. His essays on literature, sexual rights, and human rights have been published in *Callaloo, MELUS,* and *Peace Review,* as well as in journals in Morocco and Brazil.

Julie Stone Peters, H. Gordon Garbedian Professor of English and Comparative Literature at Columbia University, is a specialist in early modern comparative drama and the literary and cultural dimensions of the law. She was the Founding Director of the Columbia College Human Rights Program, and served for many years on the board of the Columbia Center for the Study of Human Rights. Her publications include *Theatre of the Book: Print, Text, and Performance in Europe 1480–1880* (2003; winner of the ACLA's Harry Levin Prize, English Association's Beatrice White Award, and honorable mention from ASTR for the best book in theatre history), the co-edited *Women's Rights, Human Rights: International Feminist Perspectives* (1995), and numerous articles on the history of drama and performance and the cultural history of law and rights.

Hephzibah Roskelly is professor of English at the University of North Carolina Greensboro, where she teaches courses in rhetoric and composition, American literature, and women's and gender studies. She holds the Carlisle Professorship in Women's and Gender Studies. Her latest book is *Everyday Use: Rhetoric in Reading and Writing*, and her latest project is a study of pragmatic philosophy and women's activism in late nineteenth century U.S. culture.

Joseph R. Slaughter is associate professor of English and Comparative Literature and member of the Institute for the Study of Human Rights at Columbia University. His book, *Human Rights, Inc.: The World Novel, Narrative Form, and International Law* (2007), was awarded the 2008 René Wellek prize for the best book in comparative literature and cultural theory.

Domna Stanton is Distinguished Professor of French at the Graduate Center of the City University of New York, where she also teaches feminist theory and human rights. The author of essays on linguistic human rights and cosmopolitanism, Stanton's co-edited volumes on seventeenth-century philosopher, Gabrielle Suchon, and on female fairy tale writers for *The Other Voice* series appeared in 2010. Her book, *Women Writ, Women Writing: Gendered Discourse and Differences in Seventeenth-Century France* is forthcoming from University of Chicago Press. Stanton is now completing a book on *The Monarchy, the Nation and its Others in the Reign of Louis XIV*.

Meili Steele, professor of English and Comparative Literature at the University of South Carolina, has published numerous essays and four monographs: *Hiding from History: Politics and Public Imagination*, *Theorizing Textual Subjects: Agency and Oppression, Critical Confrontations: Literary Theories in Dialogue, and Realism*, and *The Drama of Reference: Strategies of Representation in Balzac, Flaubert, and James*. He is the recipient of three awards from the National Endowment for the Humanities.

Bibliography

Abani, Chris. "Ethics and Narrative: The Human and Other." *Witness* XXII (2009): 167–173.

Abel, Elizabeth, Marianne Hirsch, and Elizabeth Langland. "Introduction." In *The Voyage In: Fictions of Female Development*, edited by Elizabeth Abel, Marianne Hirsch, and Elizabeth Langland, 3–19. Hanover, NH: University Press of New England, 1983.

Agamben, Giorgio. *Homo Sacer: Sovereign Power and Bare Life*. Meridian: Crossing Aesthetics. 1995. Translated by Daniel Heller-Roazen. Edited by David E. Wellbery. Stanford, CA: Stanford University Press, 1998.

Agosin, Marjorie, ed. *Women, Gender, and Human Rights: A Global Perspective*. New Brunswick, NJ: Rutgers University Press, 2001.

Akhmatova, Anna. *Poems of Akhmatova*. Selected, translated, and introduced by Stanley Kunitz with Max Hayward. New York: Houghton Mifflin, [1967] 1973.

Alcoff, Linda. "The Problem of Speaking for Others." *Cultural Critique* 20 (1991): 5–32.

Allison, Dorothy. *Bastard Out of Carolina*. New York: Plume, 1993.

———. *Two or Three Things I Know For Sure*. New York: Plume, 1995.

Amnesty International. "Amnesty International and Portugal: A Long Relationship." August 9, 1999. http://asiapacific.amnesty.org/library/Index/ENGORG 500201999?open&of=ENG-PRT.

———. "'They Come in Shooting': Policing Socially Excluded Communities." London: Amnesty International. http://www.amnesty.org/en/library/info/ AMR19/025/2005.

Anderson, Amanda. "Cosmopolitanism, Universalism and the Divided Legacies of Modernity." In *Cosmopolitics: Thinking and Feeling Beyond the Nation*, edited by Pheng Cheah and Bruce Robbins, 265–289. Minneapolis: University of Minnesota Press, 1998.

Anderson, Benedict. *Imagined Communities: Reflections on the Origin and Spread of Nationalism*. 1983. Revised ed. London: Verso, 2006.

An-Na'im, Abdullahi A. "The Legal Protection of Rights in Africa: How to Do More with Less." In *Human Rights: Concepts, Contests, Contingencies*, edited by Austin Sarat and Thomas R. Kearns, 89–116. Ann Arbor: University of Michigan Press, 2001.

Appaduri, Arjun. "Comparison and the Circulation of Forms." Plenary Address. American Comparative Literature Association Annual Conference. Ann Arbor, Michigan. 17 Apr. 2004.

Arendt, Hannah. *On Revolution*. Middlesex: Penguin Books, 1973.

———. *The Origins of Totalitarianism*. [1951] 1968. New with added prefaces edition. New York: Harcourt Brace and Co., 1973.

Arias, Arturo. *After the Bombs.* 1979. Translated by Asa Zatz. Willimantic, CT: Curbstone Press, 1990.

Asad, Talal. *Formations of the Secular: Christianity, Islam, and Modernity.* Stanford, CA: Stanford University Press, 2003.

———. "What Do Human Rights Do? An Anthropological Enquiry," *Theory and Event* 4, no. 4 (2000). http://muse.jhu.edu/journals/theory_and_event/v004/4.4asad.html.

Athey, Stephanie. "Torture Alibi and Archetype in US News and Law Since 2001." In *Culture, Trauma, and Conflict: Cultural Studies Perspectives on War,* edited by Nico Carpentier, 135–160. Newcastle-upon-Tyne: Cambridge Scholars Press, 2007.

———. "The Terrorist We Torture: The Tale of Abdul Hakim Murad." In *On Torture,* edited by Thomas C. Hilde, 87–104. Baltimore: Johns Hopkins University Press, 2008.

Auerbach, Erich. *Mimesis: The Representation of Reality in Western Literature.* 1946. Translated by Willard Trask. Garden City, NY: Doubleday, 1957.

Avelar, Idelber. "Five Theses on Torture." *Journal of Latin American Cultural Studies* 10, no. 3 (2001): 253–271.

———. *The Untimely Present: Postdictatorial Latin American Fiction and the Task of Mourning.* Durham, NC: Duke University Press, 1999.

Azoulay, Ariella. *The Civil Contract of Photography.* Translated by Rela Mazali and Ruvik Danieli. New York: Zone Books, 2008.

Bacon, Francis. *The Philosophical Works of Francis Bacon.* Edited by John Robertson. Freeport, NY: Libraries Press, 1905.

Baker, Peter, ed. *Onward: Contemporary Poetry & Poetics.* New York: Peter Lang, 1996.

Bakhtin, M. M. "The *Bildungsroman* and Its Significance in the History of Realism (toward a Historical Typology of the Novel)." Translated by Vern W. McGee. In *Speech Genres and Other Late Essays,* University of Texas Press Slavic Series, No. 8, edited by Caryl Emerson and Michael Holquist, 10–59. Austin, TX: University of Texas Press, 1986.

Balfour, Ian, and Eduardo Cadava. "The Claims of Human Rights: An Introduction." *South Atlantic Quarterly* 103, no. 2/3 (Spring/Summer 2004): 277–296.

Balibar, Étienne. "Ambiguous Universality." *differences: a journal of feminist cultural studies* 7, no. 1 (1995): 48–76.

———. "Citizen Subject." Translated by James B. Swenson, Jr. In *Who Comes after the Subject?* edited by Jean–Luc Nancy, 33–57. New York: Routledge, 1991.

———. *Masses, Classes, Ideas; Studies on Politics and Philosophy Before and After Marx.* New York: Routledge, 1994.

Balkin, Jack. *What Brown v. Board of Education Should Have Said.* New York: New York University Press, 2001.

Balousha, Hazem, and Rory McCarthy. "'As I ran I saw three of my children. All dead.'" *The Guardian,* January 6, 2009. http://www.guardian.co.uk/world/2009/jan/06/gaza–israel.

Bandele-Thomas, 'Biyi. *The Sympathetic Undertaker and Other Dreams.* Oxford: Heinemann, 1993.

Barsamian, David. "Edwidge Danticat Interview." *The Progressive* (October 2003). http://www.progressive.com/mag_intvdanticat.

Basu, Amrita. "Bhopal Revisited: The View from Below." *Bulletin of Concerned Asian Scholars* 26, no. 1–2 (Jan.–June 1994): 3–14.

Baxi, Upendra. *The Future of Human Rights.* Oxford: Oxford University Press, 2006.

———. *Human Rights in a Posthuman World: Critical Essays.* New Delhi: Oxford University Press, 2007.

———. "The 'Just War' for Profit and Power: The Bhopal Catastrophe and the Principle of Double Effect." In *Responsibility in World Business: Managing Harmful Side–Effects of Corporate Activity*, edited by Lene Bomann-Larsen and Oddny Wiggen, 175–202. Tokyo and New York: United Nations University, 2004.

———. *Mambrino's Helmet? Human Rights for a Changing World*. New Delhi: Har-Anand Publications, 1994.

———. "Voices of Suffering and the Future of Human Rights." *Transnational Law and Contemporary Problems* 8 (1998): 125.

Baxi, Upendra and the Indian Law Institute. *Inconvenient Forum and Convenient Catastrophe: The Bhopal Case*. Bombay: N. M. Tripathi Pvt. Ltd., 1986.

Bello, Walden. "Humanitarian Intervention: The Evolution of a Dangerous Doctrine." *Focus on the Global South*. January 19, 2006. FocusWeb.org.

Bénabou, Marcel. *To Write on Tamara?* 2002. Translated by Steven Randall. Lincoln: University of Nebraska Press, 2004.

Benenson, Peter. "The Forgotten Prisoners." *The Observer*, May 28, 1961. http://www.amnestyusa.org/about–us/the–forgotten–prisoners–by–peter–benenson/page.do?id=1101201.

Benhabib, Seyla, Judith Butler, Drucilla Cornell, and Nancy Fraser. *Feminist Contentions: A Philosophical Exchange*. New York: Routledge, 1995.

Benitez-Rojo, Antonio. *The Repeating Island: The Caribbean and the Postmodern Perspective*. Translated by James E. Maraniss. Durham, NC and London: Duke University Press, 1992.

Benjamin, Walter. "Theses on the Philosophy of History." In *Illuminations*, edited by Hannah Arendt, translated by Harry Zohn, 253–264. New York: Schocken, 1969.

Bennett, Jill. *Empathic Vision: Affect, Trauma, and Contemporary Art*. Stanford, CA: Stanford University Press, 2005.

Berberien, Viken. *The Cyclist*. New York: Simon & Schuster, 2003.

Bérubé, Michael. "Citizenship and Disability." *Dissent* (Spring 2003): 52–57.

———. "Disability and Narrative." *PMLA* 120, no. 2 (2005): 568–576.

Beti, Mongo. *Mission to Kala*. 1957. Translated by Peter Green. London: Heinemann Educational Books, 1964.

Bettega Barbosa, Amilcar. *Os lados do círculo*. São Paulo: Companhia das Letras, 2004.

Beverley, John. *Testimonio: On the Politics of Truth*. Minneapolis: University of Minnesota Press, 2004.

Bhabha, Homi K. "Literature and the Right to Narrate," University of Chicago lecture, October 28, 2000. http://www.uchicago.edu/docs/millennium/bhabha/bhabha_a.html (part of *The Right to Narrate*, New York: Columbia University Press, forthcoming).

———. *The Location of Culture*. New York: Routledge, 1994.

Blanchot, Maurice. *The Writing of the Disaster*. Translated by Ann Smock. Lincoln: University of Nebraska Press, 1995.

Bloch, Ernst. *Natural Law and Human Dignity*. Studies in Contemporary German Social Thought. 1961. Translated by Dennis J. Schmidt. Edited by Thomas McCarthy. Cambridge, MA: MIT Press, 1986.

Boltanski, Luc. *Distant Suffering: Morality, Media, and Politics*. Translated by Graham Burchell. Cambridge: Cambridge University Press, 1999.

Booth, Wayne. *The Company We Keep: An Ethics of Fiction*. Berkeley: University of California Press, 1988.

Boraine, Alex. "Truth and Reconciliation in South Africa: The Third Way." In *Truth v. Justice: The Morality of Truth Commissions*, edited by Robert I. Rotberg and Dennis Thompson, 141–157. Princeton, NJ: Princeton University Press, 2000.

Bourdieu, Pierre. *Distinction: A Social Critique of the Judgement of Taste*. Translated by Richard Nice. Cambridge, MA: Harvard University Press, 1984.

———. *The Field of Cultural Production: Essays on Art and Literature*. Edited by Randal Johnson. Cambridge: Polity Press, 1993.

Bowden, Mark. "The Dark Art of Interrogation: The Most Effective Way to Gather Intelligence and Thwart Terrorism Can Also Be a Direct Route Into Morally Repugnant Terrain." *Atlantic Monthly* 292, no. 3 (October 2003): 51–70.

Bowers, Maggie Ann. *Magic(al) Realism*. New York: Routledge, 2004.

Braendlin, Bonnie Hoover. "*Bildung* in Ethnic Women Writers." *Denver Quarterly* 17, no. 4 (1983): 75–87.

Braziel, Jana. "Re-Membering Défilée: Dédée Bazile as Revolutionary *Lieu de Mémoire*." *Small Axe* 18 (Sept. 2005): 57–85.

Brennan, Timothy. *Salman Rushdie and the Third World*. New York: St. Martin, 1989.

Brison, Susan J. "Outliving Oneself: Trauma, Memory, and Personal Identity." In *Gender Struggles: Practical Approaches to Contemporary Feminism*, edited by Constance L. Mui and Julien S. Murphy, 137–165. Lanham, MD: Rowman and Littlefield, 2002. .

Brontë, Emily, and William M. Sale, Jr. *Wuthering Heights: An Authoritative Text, with Essays in Criticism*. 2nd ed. New York: Norton, 1972.

Brown, Wendy. *Edgework: Critical Essays on Knowledge and Politics*. Princeton, NJ: Princeton University Press, 2005.

———. "The Most We Can Hope For: Human Rights and the Politics of Fatalism." *South Atlantic Quarterly* 103 (Spring/Summer 2004): 451–463.

———. *Politics out of History*. Princeton, NJ: Princeton University Press, 2001.

———."Suffering the Paradoxes of Rights." In *Left Legalism/Left Critique*, edited by Wendy Brown and Janet Halley, 420–434. Durham, NC: Duke University Press, 2002.

B'Tselem. *The Interrogation of Palestinians During the Intifada: Ill-Treatment, "Moderate Physical Pressure" or Torture?* March 1991. http://www.btselem.org/English/Publications/Summaries/199103_Torture.asp.

Buell, Lawrence. *Writing for an Endangered World: Literature, Culture, and Environment in the U.S. and Beyond*. Cambridge, MA: Harvard University Press, 2001.

Buergenthal, Thomas. "United Nations Truth Commission for El Salvador." *Vanderbilt Journal of Transnational Law* 27, no. 3 (Oct. 1994): 497–544.

Bunch, Charlotte. "Women's Rights as Human Rights: Toward a Re-Vision of Human Rights." *Human Rights Quarterly* 12 (1990): 486–498.

———. "Transforming Human Rights from a Feminist Perspective." In *Women's Rights, Human Rights: International Feminist Perspectives*, edited by Julie Peters and Andrea Wolper, 11–17. New York: Routledge, 1994.

Bunch, Charlotte, and Niamh Reilly. *Demanding Accountability: The Global Campaign and Vienna Tribunal for Women's Human Rights*. New York: UNIFEM, 1994.

Bürger, Peter. *The Theory of the Avant–Garde*. Translated by Michael Shaw. Minneapolis: University of Minnesota Press, 1984.

Butler, Judith. *Bodies that Matter: On the Discursive Limits of "Sex."* New York: Routledge, 1993.

———. "Competing Universalities." In *Contingency, Universality, Hegemony*, edited by Judith Butler, Ernesto Laclau and Slavoj Zizek, 136–181. New York: Verso, 2000.

———. *Giving an Account of Oneself*. New York: Fordham University Press, 2005.

———. *Precarious Life: The Powers of Mourning and Violence*. New York: Verso, 2004.

———. "Restaging the Universal: Hegemony and the Limits of Formalism." In *Contingency, Universality, Hegemony*, 11–44. New York: Verso, 2000.

————. *Undoing Gender.* New York: Routledge, 2004.

————. "Universality in Culture." In *Comparative Political Culture in the Age of Globalization: An Introductory Anthology*, edited by Hwa Yol Jung, 357–362. Lanham, MD: Lexington Books, 2002. Also in *For Love of Country: Debating the Limits of Patriotism; Martha Nussbaum with Respondents*, edited by Joshua Cohen, 45–52. Boston: Beacon Press, 1996.

Butler, Judith and Domna C. Stanton, eds. "The Humanities in Human Rights: Critique, Language, Politics." Special issue of *PMLA* 121, no., 5 (October 2006): 1526-1557.

Butler, Judith, and Gayatri Chakravorty Spivak. *Who Sings the Nation-State?* New York: Seagull, 2007.

Campbell, David. "Horrific Blindness: Images of Death in Contemporary Media." *Journal for Cultural Research* 8, no. 1 (January 2004): 55–74.

Casanova, Pascale. *The World Republic of Letters.* 1999. Translated by M. B. DeBevoise. Convergences: Inventories of the Present. Edited by Edward W. Said. Cambridge, MA: Harvard University Press, 2004.

Chakrabarty, Dipesh. *Provincializing Europe: Postcolonial Thought and Historical Difference.* Princeton, NJ: Princeton University Press, 2000.

Chakravorty, Pinaki. "The Rushdie Incident as Law-and-Literature Parable." *The Yale Law Journal* 104, no. 8 (June 1995): 2213-2247.

Charters, Mallay. "Edwidge Danticat: A Bitter Legacy Revisited." *Publishers Weekly* 245, no. 33 (17 August 1998): 42-43.

Cheah, Pheng. *Inhuman Conditions: On Cosmopolitanism and Human Rights.* Cambridge, MA: Harvard University Press, 2007.

————. *Spectral Nationality: Passages of Freedom from Kant to Postcolonial Literatures of Liberation.* New York: Columbia University Press, 2003.

"Cheney's Speech on Bush Era Security Policies." Washington Wire. *Wall Street Journal*, May 21, 2009. http://blogs.wsj.com/washwire/2009/05/21/cheneys-speech-on-bush-era-security-policies.

Chouhan, T. R. *Bhopal: The Inside Story.* New York: The Apex Press, 1994.

Chow, Rey. "Where Have All the Natives Gone?" In *Contemporary Postcolonial Theory: A Reader*, edited by Padmini Mongia, 122–147. New York: St. Martin's Press, 1996.

Christian, Barbara. "The Race for Theory." *Cultural Critique* 6 (Spring 1987): 51–63.

Chute, Hillary. "Comics as Literature? Reading Graphic Narrative." *PMLA: Publications of the Modern Language Association of America* 123, no. 2 (2008): 452–465.

Clark, Elizabeth B. "The Sacred Rights of the Weak: Pain, Sympathy, and the Culture of Individual Rights in Antebellum America." *The Journal of American History* 82, no. 2 (Sept. 1995): 463–493.

Clark, Roger Y. *Stranger Gods: Salman Rushdie's Other Worlds.* Montreal: McGill-Queen's, 2001.

Cocalis, Susan L. "The Transformation of Bildung from an Image to an Ideal." *Monatshefte: Fur Deutschen Unterricht, Deutsche Sprache und Literatur* 70, no. 4 (1978): 399–414.

Coetzee, J. M. *Giving Offense: Essays on Censorship.* Chicago: University of Chicago Press, 1997.

————. "Into the Dark Chamber: The Novelist and South Africa." *New York Times Book Review*, January 12, 1986: 13.

————. *Waiting for the Barbarians.* London: Secker and Warburg, 1980. New York: Penguin, 1982.

Cohen, Stanley. *States of Denial: Knowing about Atrocities and Suffering.* Cambridge: Polity, 2001.

Cohen, Stanley, and Bruna Seu. "Knowing Enough Not to Feel Too Much: Emotional Thinking about Human Rights Appeals." In *Truth Claims: Representation and Human Rights*, edited by Mark Philip Bradley and Patrice Petro, 187–201. New Directions in International Studies. New Brunswick, NJ: Rutgers University Press, 2002.

Cornell, Drucilla. "Bodily Integrity and the Right to Abortion." In *Identities, Politics, and Rights*, edited by Austin Sarat and Thomas R. Kearns, 21–84. Amherst Series in Law, Jurisprudence, and Social Thought. Ann Arbor: University of Michigan Press, 1995.

———. *Just Cause: Freedom, Identity, and Rights*. Lanham, MD: Rowman & Littlefield Publishers, 2000.

Cowell, E. B., ed. *The Jataka*. Translated by Robert Chalmers. 1895. http://www.sacred-texts.com/bud/j1/index.htm.

Cubilié, Anne. *Women Witnessing Terror: Testimony and the Cultural Politics of Human Rights*. New York: Fordham University Press, 2005.

Dangarembga, Tsitsi. *Nervous Conditions*. London: Women's Press, 1988.

Danticat, Edwidge. *The Farming of Bones*. New York: Penguin Books, 1998.

Darnton, Robert. *The Literary Underground of the Old Regime*. Cambridge, MA: Harvard University Press, 1982.

Das, Veena. "The Act of Witnessing: Violence, Poisonous Knowledge, and Subjectivity." In *Violence and Subjectivity*, edited by Veena Das, Arthur Kleinman, Mamphela Remphele, and Pamela Reynolds, 205–225. Durham, NC: Duke University Press, 1997.

———. "Moral Orientations to Suffering: Legitimation, Power, and Healing." In *Health and Social Change in International Perspective*, edited by Lincoln C. Chen, Arthur Kleinman, and Norma C. Ware, 139–167. Boston: Harvard School of Public Health and Harvard University Press, 1994.

Davis, Mike. *Planet of Slums*. London: Verso, 2007.

Davis, Todd F., and Kenneth Womack, eds. *Mapping the Ethical Turn: A Reading in Culture, Ethics, and Literary Theory*. Charlottesville: University of Virginia Press, 2001.

Dawes, James. "Human Rights in Literary Study." *Human Rights Quarterly* 31, no. 2 (May 2009): 394–409.

———. *That the World May Know: Bearing Witness to Atrocity*. Cambridge, MA: Harvard University Press, 2007.

Dayan, Colin. *The Story of Cruel and Unusual*. Cambridge, MA: MIT Press, 2007.

Defence for Children International. Palestinian Section. "Palestinian Child Prisoners." 2007. http://www.dcipal.org/english/publ/research/2008/PCPReport.pdf.

Deitrick, James. "Engaged Buddhist Ethics: Mistaking the Boat for the Shore." In *Action Dharma. New Studies in Engaged Buddhism*, edited by Damien Keown, Charles Prebish, and Christopher Queen, 252–269. New York: Routledge, 2003.

DeLillo, Don. *White Noise: Text and Criticism*. Edited by Mark Osteen. New York: Penguin, 1989.

Derrida, Jacques. "Beyond: Giving for the Taking, Teaching, and Learning to Give, Death" ["Au-delà: donner à prendre, apprendre à donner—la mort"]. In *The Gift of Death*, translated by David Wills. Chicago and London: University of Chicago Press, 1995.

———. "Force of Law: The 'Mystical Foundation of Authority'." In *Acts of Religion*, edited by Gil Anidjar, 228–298. New York and London: Routledge, 2001.

———. *Of Grammatology*. Translated by Gayatri Chakravorty Spivak. Baltimore: Johns Hopkins University Press, 1976.

————. "Poetics and Politics of Witnessing." In *Sovereignties in Question*, edited by Thomas Dutoit and Outi Pasanen. New York: Fordham University Press, 2005.

Dewey, John. *Logic: The Theory of Inquiry*. New York: Irvington Publishers, 1982.

Diaz, Junot, and Edwidge Danticat. "The Dominican Republic's War on Haitian Workers." *The New York Times*, November 20, 1999. http://query.nytimes.com/gst/fullpage.html?res=9F05EFD7143CF933A15752C1A96F958260&sec=&spon=&pagewanted=all.

Dilthey, Wilhelm, Rudolf A. Makkreel, and Frithjof Rodi. *Selected Works, Vol. 5: Poetry and Experience*. 1910. Princeton, NJ: Princeton University Press, 1985.

Dongala, Emmanuel. *Johnny Mad Dog*. Translated by Maria Louise Ascher. New York: Picador, 1996.

Donnelly, Jack. *International Human Rights*. Boulder, CO: Westview Press, 2008.

————. *Universal Human Rights in Theory and Practice*. 2nd ed. Ithaca, NY: Cornell University Press, 2002.

Dorfman, Ariel. *Death and the Maiden*. New York: Penguin, 1991.

Douzinas, Costas. *The End of Human Rights: Critical Legal Thought at the Turn of the Century*. Oxford: Hart Publishing, 2000.

————. *Human Rights and Empire: The Political Philosophy of Cosmopolitanism*. New York: Routledge-Cavendish, 2007.

————. "Human Rights, Humanism and Desire." *Angelaki* 6, no. 3 (2001): 183–206.

Dow, Unity. *Juggling Truths*. North Melbourne: Sinifex Press, 2003.

Drinan, Robert F. *The Mobilization of Shame: A World View of Human Rights*. New Haven, CT: Yale University Press, 2001.

Du Toit, André. "The Moral Foundations of the South African TRC: Truth as Acknowledgment and Justice as Recognition." In *Truth v. Justice: The Morality of Truth Commissions*, edited by Robert I. Rotberg and Dennis Thompson, 122–140. Princeton, NJ: Princeton University Press, 2000.

Eagleton, Terry. *Literary Theory: An Introduction*. 2nd ed. Minneapolis: University of Minnesota Press, 1996.

Edgell, Zee. *Beka Lamb*. Caribbean Writers Series 26. London: Heinemann, 1982.

Eiselein, Gregory. *Literature and Humanitarian Reform in the Civil War Era*. Bloomington: Indiana University Press, 1996.

Ellison, Ralph. *Invisible Man*. New York: Vintage, 1981.

————. *The Collected Essays of Ralph Ellison*. Edited by John Callahan. New York: Modern Library, 1995.

Emerson, Ralph Waldo. "Experience." In *Heath Anthology of American Literature*, 5th ed., edited by Paul Lauter, 1653–1668. Boston: Houghton Mifflin, 2006.

Encyclopédie, ou Dictionnaire raisonné des sciences, des arts et des métiers. 28 vols. Paris: Briasson, 1751–1780.

Engblom, Philip. "A Multitude of Voices: Carnivalization and Dialogicality in the Novels of Salman Rushdie." In *Reading Rushdie: Perspectives of the Fiction of Salman Rushdie*, edited by D. M. Fletcher, 293–304. Amsterdam: Rodopi, 1994.

Escobar, Arturo. *Encountering Development: The Making and Unmaking of the Third World*. Princeton, NJ: Princeton University Press, 1995.

Evans, Gareth J., and Mohamed Sahnoun, eds. *The Responsibility to Protect: Report of the International Commission on Intervention and State Sovereignty*. Ottawa: International Development Research Center, 2001.

Everett, Percival. *The Water Cure*. Minneapolis: Graywolf Press, 2007.

Faris, Wendy B. "Scheherazade's Children: Magical Realism and Postmodern Fiction." In *Magical Realism: Theory, History, Community*, edited by Lois

Parkinson Zamora and Wendy B. Faris, 163–190. Durham, NC: Duke University Press, 1995.

Farmer, Paul. *The Uses of Haiti*. Monroe, ME: Common Courage Press, 1995.

Fauré, Christine, ed. *Les déclarations des droits de l'homme de 1789*. 2nd ed. Paris: Payot, 1992.

Feitlowitz, Marguerite. *A Lexicon of Terror: Argentina and the Legacies of Torture*. New York: Oxford University Press, 1998.

Felman, Shoshana, and Dori Laub. *Testimony: Crises of Witnessing in Literature, Psychoanalysis, and History*. New York: Routledge, 1992.

Felski, Rita. *Beyond Feminist Aesthetics: Feminist Literature and Social Change*. Cambridge, MA: Harvard University Press, 1989.

Ferguson, Robert. *Law and Letters in American Culture*. Cambridge, MA: Harvard, 1984.

Ferrara, Alessandro. "Universalisms: Procedural, Contextualist and Prudential." *Philosophy and Social Criticism* 14, no. 3/4 (1996): 243–269.

Ferry, Luc, and Alain Renaut. *Philosophie politique: Des droits de l'homme à l'idée républicaine*. Paris: Presses Universitaires de France, 1985.

Fiering, Norman S. "Irresistible Compassion: An Aspect of Eighteenth-Century Sympathy and Humanitarianism." *Journal of the History of Ideas* 37, no. 2 (April–June 1976): 195–218.

Finkielkraut, Alain. *In the Name of Humanity*. Translated by Judith Friedlander. New York: Columbia University Press, 2000.

Fiss, Owen. "Another Equality." *Issues in Legal Scholarship. The Origins and Fate of Antisubordination Theory*. Article 20, 2004. http://www/.bepress.com/ils/1552/art20.

Flores, Ralph. *Buddhist Scriptures as Literature: Sacred Rhetoric and the Uses of Theory*. New York: SUNY Press, 2008.

Forché, Carolyn. "El Salvador: An Aide Memoir." *American Poetry Review* (July–Aug. 1981): 3–7.

Forsdick, Charles. "Situating Haiti: On Some Early 19th Century Representations of Toussaint L'Ouverture." *International Journal of Francophone Studies* 10, no. 1/2 (2007): 17–34.

Fortun, Kim. *Advocacy after Bhopal: Environmentalism, Disaster, New Global Orders*. Chicago: University of Chicago Press, 2001.

Foucault, Michel. *The Care of the Self*. New York: Vintage Books, 1986.

———. *Discipline and Punish*. 2nd ed. Translated by Alan Sheridan. New York: Vintage, 1995.

———. *Foucault Live: Interviews 1966–84*. Translated by John Johnston. Edited by Sylvère Lotringer. New York: Semiotext(e), 1989.

Fourth World Conference on Women. Beijing Declaration. United Nations, 1995. Un.org/womenwatch/daw/Beijing/platform/declar.htm.

Franklin, Benjamin. *The Papers of Benjamin Franklin*. 37 volumes. Edited by L. W. Labaree and W. J. Bell, Jr. New Haven, CT: Yale University Press, 1959.

Freire, Marcelino. *Angu de sangue*. 2nd ed. São Paulo: Ateliê Editorial, 2005.

Freire, Paulo, and Donaldo Macedo. *Literacy: Reading the Word and the World*. South Hadley, MA: Bergin Garvey, 1987.

———. *Education for a Critical Consciousness*. New York: Seabury Press, 1973.

Frye, Northrop. *Anatomy of Criticism*. Princeton, NJ: Princeton University Press, 1957.

Gadamer, Hans Georg. *Truth and Method*. Translated by Garrett Barden and John Cumming. New York: Seabury Press, 1975.

Gaffield, Julia. "Complexities of Imagining Haiti: A Study of National Constitutions, 1801–1807." *Journal of Social History* 41, no. 1 (Fall 2007): 81–103.

Garber, Marjorie. *Academic Instincts*. Princeton, NJ: Princeton University Press, 2001.

Garber, Marjorie, Beatrice Hanssen, and Rebecca L. Walkowitz, eds. *The Turn to Ethics*. New York: Routledge, 2000.

Geertz, Clifford. "The Impact of the Concept of Culture on the Concept of Man." In *The Interpretation of Cultures: Selected Essays*, 33–54. New York: Basic Books, 1973.

Gilmore, Leigh. *The Limits of Autobiography: Trauma and Testimony*. Ithaca, NY: Cornell University Press, 2001.

Glendon, Mary Ann. *A World Made New: Eleanor Roosevelt and the Universal Declaration of Human Rights*. New York: Random House, 2001.

Glissant, Edouard. *Caribbean Discourse: Selected Essays*. Charlottesville: University Press of Virginia, 1992.

Glover, Jonathan. *Humanity: A Moral History of the Twentieth Century*. New Haven, CT: Yale University Press, 1999.

Goellnicht, David. "Blurring Boundaries: Asian American Literature as Theory." In *An Interethnic Companion to Asian American Literature*, edited by King-Kok Cheung, 338–365. New York: Cambridge University Press, 1997.

Goethe, Johann Wolfgang von. *Wilhelm Meister's Apprenticeship and Travels*. 1824. Translated by Thomas Carlyle. 2 vols. London: Chapman & Hill, 1894.

Goldberg, Elizabeth Swanson. *Beyond Terror: Gender, Narrative, Human Rights*. New Brunswick, NJ: Rutgers University Press, 2007.

Gorra, Michael. "'This Angrezi in which I am forced to write': On the Language of *Midnight's Children*." *Critical Essays on Salman Rushdie*. Edited by M. Keith Booker. New York: G.K. Hall, 1999.

———. *After Empire: Scott, Naipaul, Rushdie*. Chicago: University of Chicago Press, 1997.

Gourevitch, Philip. *We Wish to Inform You That Tomorrow We Will Be Killed with Our Families: Stories from Rwanda*. New York: Farrar Straus and Giroux, 1998.

Gramsci, Antonio. *Selections for the Prison Notebooks*. Translated by Quintin Hoare and Geoffrey Nowell Smith. Edited by Quintin Hoare and Geoffrey Nowell Smith. New York: International Publishers, 1971.

Gready, Paul. "Introduction—'Responsibility to the Story'." *Journal of Human Rights Practice* 2, no. 2 (June 2010): 177–190.

Grear, Anna. "Human Rights—Human Bodies? Some Reflections on Corporate Human Rights Distortion, the Legal Subject, and Embodiment of Human Rights Theory." *Law Critique* 17 (2006): 171–199.

Grewal, Inderpal. *Transnational America: Feminisms, Diasporas, Neoliberalisms*. Durham, NC: Duke University Press, 2005.

Grieve, Gregory Price. *Retheorizing Religion in Nepal*. New York: Palgrave Macmillan, 2006.

———. "Symbol, Idol and *Murti*: Hindu God-images and the Politics of Mediation." *Culture, Theory and Critique* 44 (2003): 57–72.

Grimshaw, Patricia, Katie Holmes, and Marilyn Lake, eds. *Women's Rights and Human Rights*. New York: Palgrave, 2001.

Grosz, Elizabeth. *Space, Time, and Perversion*. New York: Routledge, 1995.

Guillory, John. *Cultural Capital: The Problem of Literary Canon Formation*. Chicago: University of Chicago Press, 1993.

Gunesekera, Romesh. *Reef*. London: Granta Books, 1994.

Habermas, Jürgen. *Between Facts and Norms: Contributions to a Discourse Theory of Law and Democracy*. Translated by William Rehg. Cambridge, MA: MIT Press, 1996.

———. "Further Reflections on the Public Sphere." *Habermas and the Public Sphere*. Edited by Craig Calhoun. Cambridge, MA: MIT Press, 1992.

———. *Inclusion of the Other*. Translated by Ciaran Cronin. Cambridge, MA: MIT Press, 1998.

———. "On Legitimation Through Human Rights." In *Global Justice and Transnational Politics*, edited by Pablo De Greiff and Ciaran Cronin, 197–214. Cambridge, MA: MIT Press, 2002.

———. *The Structural Transformation of the Public Sphere: An Inquiry into a Category of Bourgeois Society*. Studies in Contemporary German Social Thought. 1962. Translated by Thomas Burger and Frederick Lawrence. Cambridge, MA: MIT Press, 1991.

———. *Truth and Justification*. Translated by Barbara Fultner. Cambridge. MA: MIT Press, 2003.

Haight, Amanda. *Anna Akhmatova: A Poetic Pilgrimage*. Oxford: Oxford University Press, 1976.

Hamad, Turki al-. *Adama*. 1998. Translated by Robin Bray. St. Paul, MN: Ruminator Books, 2003.

Hanna, Bridget, Ward Morehouse, and Satinath Sarangi, eds. *The Bhopal Reader*. New York: The Apex Press, 2005.

Harlow, Barbara. *Barred: Women, Writing, and Political Detention*. Hanover, NH: University Press of New England, 1992.

Harman, Danna. "Haitian Cane-Cutters Struggle." *The Christian Science Monitor*, February 1, 2006: 13.

Harvey, David. *A Brief History of Neoliberalism*. Oxford: Oxford University Press, 2005.

Harvey, Peter. *The Selfless Mind: Personality, Consciousness and Nirvana in Early Buddhism*. New York: Curzon Press, 1995.

Haskell, Thomas L. "Capitalism and the Origins of the Humanitarian Sensibility." *American Historical Review* 90, no. 2 (April 1985): 339–361 (Part 1) and 90, no. 3 (June 1985): 547–566 (Part 2).

Hasso, Frances Susan. *Resistance, Repression, and Gender Politics in Occupied Palestine and Jordan*. Syracuse, NY: Syracuse University Press, 2005.

Hatzfeld, Jean. *Machete Season: The Killers in Rwanda Speak*. Translated by Linda Coverdale. New York: Farrar, Straus and Giroux, 2005.

Haynes, Priscilla B. *Unspeakable Truths: Confronting State Terror and Atrocity*. New York: Routledge, 2001.

Heise, Ursula K. "Toxins, Drugs, and Global Systems: Risk and Narrative in the Contemporary Novel." *American Literature* 74, no. 4 (2002): 747–778.

Henkin, Louis. "Human Rights: Ideology and Aspiration, Reality and Prospect." In *Realizing Human Rights: Moving from Inspiration to Impact*, edited by Samantha Power and Graham Allison, 3–39. New York: Palgrave Macmillan, 2006.

———. *The Rights of Man Today*. Boulder, CO: Westview Press, 1978.

Hesford, Wendy. "Rape Stories: Material Rhetoric and the Trauma of Representation." In *Haunting Violations: Feminist Criticism and the Crisis of the "Real,"* edited by Wendy Hesford and Wendy Kozol, 13–46. Urbana and Chicago: University of Illinois Press, 2001.

Hesford, Wendy S., and Wendy Kozol, eds. *Haunting Violations: Feminist Criticism and the Crisis of the "Real."* Urbana and Chicago: University of Illinois Press, 2001.

———. *Just Advocacy? Women's Human Rights, Transnational Feminisms, and the Politics of Representation*. New Brunswick, NJ: Rutgers University Press, 2005.

Higgins, Tracy. "Anti-Essentialism, Relativism and Human Rights." *Harvard Women's Law Journal* 89 (1996): 89–126.

Hinderliter, Beth, et al., eds. *Communities of Sense: Rethinking Aesthetics and Politics*. Durham, NC: Duke University Press, 2009.

Hinton, Mercedes S. *The State on the Street: Police and Politics in Argentina and Brazil*. Boulder, CO: Lynne Rienner, 2006.

Hirsch, Marianne. "The Novel of Formation as Genre: Between Great Expectations and Lost Illusions." *Genre* XII, no. 3 (1979): 293–311.

Holland, Sharon Patricia. *Raising the Dead: Readings on Death and (Black) Subjectivity*. Durham, NC: Duke University Press, 2000.

Holston, James. *Insurgent Citizenship: Disjunctions of Democracy and Modernity in Brazil*. Princeton, NJ: Princeton University Press, 2008.

Hope, Christopher. *A Separate Development*. Johannesburg: Ravan Press, 1980.

Huggan, Graham. "Postcolonial Ecocriticism and Green Romanticism." *Journal of Postcolonial Writing* 45, no. 1 (2009): 3–14.

———. *The Postcolonial Exotic: Marketing the Margins*. New York and London: Routledge, 2001.

Huggan, Graham, and Helen Tiffin, eds. *Postcolonial Ecocriticism*. New York: Routledge, 2009.

Human Rights Clinic of Columbia Law School. *In The Shadows of The War on Terror: Persistent Police Brutality and Abuse in the United States. A Report Prepared for the United Nations Human Rights Committee on the Occasion of its Review of the United States of America's Second and Third Periodic Report to the Human Rights Committee*, New York, December 2007. http://www2. ohchr.org/english/bodies/cerd/docs/ngos/usa/USHRN15.pdf.

Human Rights Watch. "Torture and Ill-Treatment: Israel's Interrogation of Palestinians from the Occupied Territories." June 1, 1994. http://www.hrw.org/ legacy/reports/1994/israel/.

Humboldt, Wilhelm von. *Humanist without Portfolio: An Anthology of the Writings of Wilhelm Von Humboldt*. Translated by Marianne Cowan. Detroit, MI: Wayne State University Press, 1963.

———. *The Limits of State Action*. 1792. Translated by J. W. Burrow. London: Cambridge University Press, 1969.

———. *Linguistic Variability and Intellectual Development*. 1836. Translated by Frithjof A. Raven. Philadelphia: University of Pennsylvania Press, 1971.

———. *Über Die Verschiedenheit Des Menschlichen Sprachbaues Und Ihren Einfluß Auf Die Geistige Entwicklung Des Menschengeschlechts*. Darmstadt: Claassen & Roether, 1949.

Hume, David. *A Treatise of Human Nature*. Edited by L. A. Selby-Bigge and P. H. Nidditch. 2nd ed. Oxford: Clarendon Press, 1978.

Humphrey, John P. "The Magna Carta of Mankind." In *Human Rights*, edited Peter Davies, 31–39. New York: Routledge, 1988.

Hunt, Lynn. *Inventing Human Rights: A History*. New York: W. W. Norton and Company, 2007.

Hurt, Michael James. *Himalayan Voices: An Introduction to Modern Nepali Literature*. Berkeley: University of California Press, 1991.

Hutcheon, Linda. *A Poetics of Postmodernism*. New York: Routledge, 1988.

Ibhawoh, Bonny. "Restraining Universalism: Africanist Perspectives on Cultural Relativism in Human Rights." In *Human Rights, The Rule of Law and Development in Africa*, edited by Paul Tiyambe Zelera and Philip J. McConnaughay, 21–39, notes 257–259. Philadelphia: University of Pennsylvania Press, 2004.

Ignatieff, Michael. *Human Rights as Politics and Idolatry*. Princeton, NJ: Princeton University Press, 2001.

Ihara, Craig. "Why There Are No Rights in Buddhism: A Reply to Damien Keown." In *Buddhism and Human Rights*, edited by Damien Keown, Charles Prebish, and Wayne Husted, 44–51. Surrey: Curzon Press, 1998.

Intelligence Science Board. *Educing Information: Interrogation, Science and Art*. Washington, DC: National Defense Intelligence College, 2006. http://www.fas. org/irp/dni/educing.pdf.

International Committee of the Red Cross. *The ICRC Report on the Treatment of Fourteen "High Value Detainees" in CIA Custody.* February 2007. http://www.nybooks.com/icrc-report.pdf.

International Covenant on Civil and Political Rights. G.A. res. 2200A (XXI), 21 U.N.GAOR Supp. (No. 16) at 52, U.N. Doc. A/6316 (1966), 999 U.N.T.S. 171, entered into force March 23, 1976. http://www1.umn.edu/humanrts/instree/b3cppr.htm.

International Covenant on Economic, Social, and Cultural Rights. G.A. res. 2200A (XXI), 21 U.N.GAOR Supp. (No. 16) at 49, U.N. Doc. A/6316 (1966), 993 U.N.T.S. 3, entered into force Jan 3, 1976. http://www1.umn.edu/humanrts/instree/b2esc.htm.

Irigaray, Luce. *J'aime à toi: Esquisse d'une félicité en histoire.* Paris: Grasset, 1992.

———. *Sexes et parentés.* Paris: Editions de Minuit, 1987.

———. *thinking the difference: for a peaceful revolution.* Translated by Karin Montin. New York: Routledge, 1994.

James, C. L. R. "French Capitalism and Caribbean Slavery." In *Caribbean Slave Society and Economy,* edited by Hilary Beckles and Verene Shepherd, 130–135. New York: The New Press, 1993.

———. *The Black Jacobins.* 2nd ed. New York: Random House, 1989.

Jameson, Fredric. "On Literary and Cultural Import–Substitution in the Third World: The Case of the Testimonio." *Margins* 1 (1993): 11–34. Rpt. In *The Real Thing: Testimonial Discourse and Latin America,* edited by Georg M. Gugelberger, 172–191. Durham, NC: Duke University Press, 1996.

———. "Third-World Literature in the Era of Multinational Capitalism." *Social Text* 15, no. 3 (1986): 65–88.

Jasanoff, Sheila. "Bhopal's Trials of Knowledge and Ignorance." *New England Law Review* 42 (Summer 2008): 679–692.

Jefferson, Thomas. *The Writings of Thomas Jefferson.* Edited by Andrew Lipscomb and Albert Ellery Bergh. Washington, DC: Thomas Jefferson Memorial Association, 1904.

Jeffreys, Derek. "Does Buddhism Need Human Rights?" In *Buddhism and Human Rights,* edited by Damien Keown, Charles Prebish and Wayne Husted, 270–285. Surrey: Curzon Press, 1998.

Johnson, Kelli Lyon. "Both Sides of the Massacre: Collective Memory and Narrative on Hispaniola." *Mosaic: A Journal for the Interdisciplinary Study of Literature* 36, no. 2 (June 2003): 75–91.

Johnson, M. Glen. "A Magna Carta for Mankind: Writing the Universal Declaration of Human Rights." *The Universal Declaration of Human Rights: A History of Its Creation and Implementation, 1948–1998.* Edited by UNESCO, 19–75. Paris: UNESCO Publishing, 1998.

Johnson, Samuel. *A Dictionary of the English Language.* London: J. and P. Knapton et al., 1755.

Junger, Peter. "Why the Buddha Has No Rights." In *Buddhism and Human Rights,* edited by Damien Keown, Charles Prebish, and Wayne Husted, 53–96. Surrey: Curzon Press, 1998.

Kaldor, Mary. *Global Civil Society: An Answer to War.* Cambridge and Malden, MA: Polity Press, 2003.

Kant, Immanuel. *Perpetual Peace.* Edited by Lewis White Beck. Indianapolis: Liberal Arts Press, 1957.

Kaplan, Robert D. "Rereading Vietnam." *The Atlantic Monthly,* August 24, 2007. http://www.theatlantic.com/doc/200708u/kaplan–vietnam.

Kass, Stephen L. "Integrated Justice." *Transnational Law & Contemporary Problems* 18 (2009): 115–138.

Kaufman, Michael T. "What Does the Pentagon See in the 'Battle of Algiers'?" *The New York Times*, September 7, 2003, Section 4, 3.

Keenan, Thomas. *Fables of Responsibility: Aberrations and Predicaments in Ethics and Politics.* Stanford, CA: Stanford University Press, 1997.

———. "Mobilizing Shame." *South Atlantic Quarterly* 103, no. 2/3 (2004): 435–449.

Kennedy, David. *The Dark Sides of Virtue: Reassessing International Humanitarianism.* Princeton NJ: Princeton University Press, 2004.

Keown, Damien. "Are There Human Rights in Buddhism?" In *Buddhism and Human Rights*, edited by Damien Keown, Charles Prebish, and Wayne Husted, 15–41. Surrey: Curzon Press, 1998.

Kerber, Linda. "The Stateless as the Citizen's Other: A View from the United States." In *Migrations and Mobilities: Citizenship, Borders, and Gender*, edited by Seyla Benhabib and Judith Resnick, 76-213. New York: New York University Press, 2009.

Kermode, Frank. *The Sense of an Ending.* New York: Oxford University Press, 1966.

Khadra, Yasmina. *The Attack.* New York: Doubleday, 2005.

Khan, Shahnaz. "Reconfiguring the Native Informant: Positionality in the Global Age." *Signs: Journal of Women in Culture & Society* 30, no. 4 (2005): 2017–2035.

King, Adele. *Rereading Camara Laye.* Lincoln: University of Nebraska Press, 2002.

King, Sallie. "Human Rights in Contemporary Engaged Buddhism." In *Buddhist Theology: Critical Reflections by Contemporary Buddhist Scholars*, edited by Roger Jackson and John Makransky, 293–311. London: Routledge Curzon, 1999.

Kiss, Elizabeth. "Moral Ambition Within and Beyond Political Constraints: Reflections on Restorative Justice." In *Truth v. Justice: The Morality of Truth Commissions*, edited by Robert I. Rotberg and Dennis Thompson, 68–98. Princeton, NJ: Princeton University Press, 2000.

Klein, Naomi. *The Shock Doctrine: The Rise of Disaster Capitalism.* New York: Metropolitan Books/Henry Holt, 2007.

Kontje, Todd Curtis. *The German Bildungsroman: History of a National Genre.* Columbia, SC: Camden House, 1993.

Koshy, Susan. "From Cold War to Trade War: Neocolonialism and Human Rights." *Social Text* 58 (1999): 1–32.

Kramnick, Jonathan Brody. *Making the English Canon: Print-Capitalism and the Cultural Past, 1700–1770.* Cambridge: Cambridge University Press, 1998.

Kumar, Radha. *The History of Doing: An Illustrated Account of Movements for Women's Rights and Feminism in India, 1800–1900.* New York and London: Verso, 1993.

LaCapra, Dominick. *Writing History, Writing Trauma.* Baltimore: Johns Hopkins University Press, 2001.

Lacey, Michael J., and Knud Haakonssen, eds. *A Culture of Rights: The Bill of Rights in Philosophy, Politics, and Law 1791–1991.* Cambridge: Cambridge University Press, 1991.

Laclau, Ernesto. *Emancipation(s).* London: Verso, 1996.

———. "Universalism, Particularism and the Question of Identity." *October* 61 (1992): 83–90.

Laclau, Ernesto, and Chantal Mouffe. *Hegemony and Socialist Strategy: Towards a Radical Democratic Politics.* London: Verso, 1985.

Lacoue-Labarthe, Philippe. *Poetry as Experience.* Translated by Andrea Tarnowski. Stanford, CA: Stanford University Press, 1999.

Laferrière, Dany. *Dining with the Dictator.* Toronto: Coach House Press, 1994.

Lagouranis, Tony, and Allen Mikaelian. *Fear Up Harsh: An Army Interrogator's Dark Journey Through Iraq.* New York: New American Library, 2007.

La Harpe, Jean-François de. *Adresse des auteurs dramatiques a l'assemblé nation-ale, Prononcée par M. de la Harpe, dans la Séance du mardi soir 24 Août.* Paris: n.p., 1790.

Langer, Lawrence. *The Holocaust and the Literary Imagination.* New Haven, CT: Yale University Press, 1975.

Langer, Susanne. *Philosophy in a New Key,* 3rd ed. Cambridge, MA: Harvard University Press, 1957.

Laqueur, Thomas W. "Bodies, Details, and the Humanitarian Narrative." In *The New Cultural History,* edited by Lynn Hunt, 176–204. Berkeley: University of California Press, 1989.

Laub, Dori. "Bearing Witness: or the Vicissitudes of Listening." In *Testimony: Crises of Witnessing in Literature, Psychoanalysis, and History,* edited by Shoshana Felman and Dori Laub, 57–74. New York: Routledge, 1992.

Lauren, Paul Gordon. *The Evolution of Human Rights: Visions Seen.* Pennsylvania Studies in Human Rights. 2nd ed. Philadelphia: University of Pennsylvania Press, 2003.

Layoun, Mary. "The Trans-, the Multi-, the Pluri-, and the Global: A Few Thoughts on Comparative and Relational Literacy." *Passages: A Journal of Transnational & Transcultural Studies* 1, no. 2 (1999): 182–188.

Lazarus, Neil, Steven Evans, Anthony Arnove, and Anne Menke. "The Necessity of Universalism." *differences: a journal of feminist cultural studies* 7, no. 1 (1995): 75–137.

Levinas, Emmanuel. *Ethique et infini: Dialogues avec Philippe Nemo.* Paris: Fayard, 1982.

———. *Proper Names.* Translated by Michael B. Smith. Stanford, CA: Stanford University Press, 1996.

———. *Time and the Other and Additional Essays.* Translated by Richard A Cohen. Pittsburgh: Duquesne University Press, 1987.

Lewis, Neil A. "Red Cross Finds Detainee Abuse in Guantánamo." *The New York Times,* November 30, 2004. http://www.nytimes.com/2004/11/30/politics/30gitmo.html?

——— and Thom Shanker. "As Chaplain's Spy Case Nears, Some Ask Why it Went so Far." *The New York Times,* January 4, 2004. http://www.nytimes.com/2004/01/04/us.

Lionæs, Aase. "Award Ceremony Speech." Presented at the Nobel Peace Prize Ceremony, Oslo, Norway, December 10, 1977. http://nobelprize.org/nobel_prizes/peace/laureates/1977/press.html.

Littman, David. "Universal Human Rights and Human Rights in Islam." *Midstream* (1999): n.p. http://www.dhimmi.org/Islam.html.

Littré, Paul-Emile. *Dictionnaire de la langue française.* Versailles: Encyclopaedia Britannica France, 1994.

Livingston, James. *Pragmatism, Feminism and Democracy.* New York: Routledge, 2001.

Lloyd, David. *Anomalous States: Irish Writing and the Post-Colonial Moment.* Dublin: The Lilliput Press, 1993.

———. "Arnold, Ferguson, Schiller: Aesthetic Culture and the Politics of Aesthetics." *Cultural Critique* 2 (Winter 1985–1986): 137–169.

Lloyd, Moya. *Judith Butler: From Norms to Politics.* Cambridge and Malden, MA: Polity Press, 2007.

Loh, Vyvyane. *Breaking the Tongue.* New York: W. W. Norton, 2004.

London School of Economics, Centre for Civil Society. "What is Civil Society." http://www.lse.ac.uk/collections/CCS/what_is_civil_society1.htm. Accessed October 10, 2006.

Lukács, Georg. *Goethe and His Age.* 1947. Translated by Robert Anchor. London: Merlin Press, 1968.

————. *Goethe Und Seine Zeit*. Bern: A. Francke, 1947.

————. *The Theory of the Novel: A Historico-Philosophical Essay on the Forms of Great Epic Literature*. 1920. Translated by Anna Bostock. Cambridge, MA: MIT Press, 1971.

Lyotard, Jean-François. *The Postmodern Condition*. Translated by G. Bennington and B. Massumi. Minneapolis: University of Minnesota Press, 1984.

MacCormick,Neil. *Legal Reasoning and Legal Theory*. New York: Oxford University Press, 1978.

Mackey, Chris (pseudonym), and Greg Miller. *Interrogator's War: Inside the Secret War Against Al Qaeda*. Boston: Little Brown, 2004.

MacKinnon, Catherine. *Are Women Human? And Other International Dialogues*. Cambridge, MA: Harvard University Press, 2006.

Maclear, Kyo. "The Limits of Vision: Hiroshima Mon Amour and the Subversion of Representation." In *Witness and Memory: The Discourse of Trauma*, edited by Ana Douglass and Thomas A. Vogler, 233–248. New York: Routledge, 2003.

Malla, Bijay. "*Parevā ra Kaidī.*" *Parevā ra Kaidī*. Kathmandu: Sākjhā Prakāshan, 1978 [bi sa 2034].

Mamdani, Mahmood. *When Victims Become Killers: Colonialism, Nativism, and the Genocide in Rwanda*. Princeton, NJ: Princeton University Press, 2001.

Mangonés, Frederick. "The Citadel as Site of Haitian Memory." *Callaloo* 15, no. 3 (Summer 1992): 857–861.

Maran, Rita. *Torture: The Role of Ideology in the French–Algerian War*. New York: Praeger, 1989.

Maritain, Jacques. *The Rights of Man and Natural Law*. Translated by Doris C. Anson. New York: Scribner's Sons, 1943.

Markandaya, Kamala. *Nectar in a Sieve*. New York: J. Day Co., 1954.

Marx, Karl. *Capital: A Critique of Political Economy*. 1867. Translated by Ben Fowkes. Vol. I. New York: Vintage, 1977.

Maslan, Susan. "The Anti-Human: Man and Citizen before the Declaration of the Rights of Man and of the Citizen." *South Atlantic Quarterly* 103, no. 2/3 (2004): 357–374.

McClennen, Sophia A. "Human Rights, the Humanities, and the Comparative Imagination." *Comparative Literature and Culture* 9, no. 1 (March 2007). http://docs.lib.purdue.edu/clcweb/vol9/iss1/13.

McClennen, Sophia A., and Joseph R. Slaughter. "Introducing Human Rights and Literary Forms; or, The Vehicles and Vocabularies of Human Rights." *Comparative Literary Studies* 46, no. 1 (2009): 1–19.

McCloud, Scott. *Understanding Comics*. New York: Harper Collins, 1993.

McCoy, Alfred W. *A Question of Torture: CIA Interrogation, from the Cold War to the War on Terror*. New York: Metropolitan Books, 2006.

McDermott, Patrice and Amy Farrell. "Claiming Afghan Women: The Challenge of Human Rights Discourse for Transnational Feminism." In *Just Advocacy: Women's Human Rights, Transnational Feminisms, and the Politics of Representation*, edited by Wendy Hesford and Wendy Kozol, 33–55. New Brunswick, NJ: Rutgers University Press, 2005.

McGreal, Chris. "Ban on Foreign Journalists Skews Coverage of Conflict." *The Guardian*, January 10, 2009. http://www.guardian.co.uk/world/2009/jan/10/gaza–israel–reporters–foreign–journalists.

Meister, Robert. "Forgiving and Forgetting: Lincoln and the Politics of National Recovery." In *Human Rights in Political Transitions: Gettysburg to Bosnia*, edited by Carla Hesse and Robert Post, 135–176. New York: Zone Books, 1999.

Merry, Sally Engle. "Women, Violence and the Human Rights System." In *Women, Gender and Human Rights: A Global Perspective*, edited by Marjorie Agosín, 83–97. New Brunswick, NJ: Rutgers University Press, 2001.

Milani, Farzaneh. *Veils and Words: The Emerging Voices of Iranian Women Writers*. Syracuse, NY: Syracuse University Press, 1992.

Miller, Charles. "Forget Haiti: Baron Roger and the New Africa." *Yale French Studies* 107. *The Haiti Issue: 1804 and Nineteenth-Century French Studies* (2005): 39–69.

Minden, Michael. "The Place of Inheritance in the *Bildungsroman*: Agathon, Wilhelm Meister's Lehrjahre, and Der Nachsommer." In *Reflection and Action: Essays on the Bildungsroman*, edited by James Hardin, 254–292. Columbia: University of South Carolina Press, 1991.

Mohanty, Satya. "Epilogue: Colonial Legacies, Multicultural Futures: Relativism, Objectivity and the Challenge of Otherness." *Colonialism and the Postcolonial Condition*, special issue of *PMLA* 110, no. 1 (1995): 108–118.

More, Hannah. *Strictures on the Modern System of Female Education*. 2 vols. London: T. Cadell and W. Davies, 1799.

Moretti, Franco. *The Way of the World: The Bildungsroman in European Culture*. 1987. Translated by Albert Sbragia. New ed. London: Verso, 2000.

Morgan, Ellen. "Human Becoming: Form and Focus in the Neo–Feminist Novel." In *Images of Women in Fiction: Feminist Perspectives*, edited by Susan Koppelman Cornillon, 183–205. Bowling Green, OH: Bowling Green University Popular Press, 1972.

Morgan, William. *Questionable Charity: Gender, Humanitarianism, and Complicity in U.S. Literary Realism*. Durham, NH: University Press of New England, 2004.

Morris, Rosalind C. "Images of Untranslatability in the US War on Terror." *Interventions: The International Journal of Postcolonial Studies* 6, no. 3 (2004): 401–423.

Morsink, Johannes. *The Universal Declaration of Human Rights: Origins, Drafting, and Intent*. Pennsylvania Studies in Human Rights. Philadelphia: University of Pennsylvania Press, 1999.

Moyn, Samuel. *The Last Utopia: Human Rights in History*. Cambridge, MA: Harvard University Press, 2010.

Munro, Martin, ed. *Reinterpreting the Haitian Revolution and Its Aftershocks*. Kingston, Jamaica: University of West Indies Press, 2006.

Mutua, Makau. *Human Rights: A Political and Cultural Critique*. Pennsylvania Studies in Human Rights. Philadelphia: University of Pennsylvania Press, 2002, 2008.

Naffine, Ngaire. "Who Are Law's Persons? From Cheshire Cats to Responsible Subjects." *The Modern Law Review* 66, no. 3 (2003): 346–367.

Naghibi, Nima, and Andrew O'Malley. "Estranging the Familiar: 'East' and 'West' in Satrapi's *Persepolis*." *ESQ* 31, no. 2/3 (June–Sept. 2005): 223–248.

Najmabadi, Afsaneh, ed. *Women's Autobiographies in Contemporary Iran*. Cambridge, MA: Harvard University Press, 1990.

Nesbitt, Nick. "The Idea of 1804." *Yale French Studies* 107. *The Haiti Issue: 1804 and Nineteenth–Century French Studies* (2005): 6–38.

———. "Troping Toussaint, Reading Revolution." *Research in African Literatures* 35, no. 2 (Summer 2004): 19–33.

Needham, Anurandha Disngwaney. "The Politics of Post-Colonial Identity in Salman Rushdie." In *Reading Rushdie: Perspectives on the Fiction of Salman Rushdie*, edited by D.M. Fletcher, 145–158. Amsterdam: Rodopi, 1994. Reprinted from *Massachusetts Review* 29 (1988–1989): 609–624.

Nhat Hanh, Thich. *Love in Action: Writings on Nonviolent Social Change*. Berkeley, CA: Parallax Press, 1993.

Nussbaum, Martha C. *Cultivating Humanity: A Classical Defense of Reform in Liberal Education*. Cambridge MA: Harvard University Press, 1998.

———. *For Love of Country: Debating the Limits of Patriotism*. Boston: Beacon Press, 1996.

Ohlin, Jehns David. "Is the Concept of the Person Necessary for Human Rights?" *Columbia Law Review* 105, no. 1 (2005): 209-249.

Oliver, Kelly. *Witnessing: Beyond Recognition*. Minneapolis: University of Minnesota Press, 2001.

Organisation of the Islamic Conference. Report and Resolutions on Political, Muslim Minorities and Communities, Legal and Information Affairs. http://www.oic–cio.org/english/conf/fm/27/27th–fm–political(3).htm.

Orwell, George. "Politics and the English Language." *Horizon* (1946). http://www.netcharles.com/orwell/essays/politics–english–language1.htm.

Osiel, Mark. *Mass Atrocity, Collective Memory, and the Law*. New Brunswick, NJ: Transaction Publishers, 2000.

Owen, Nicholas, ed. *Human Rights, Human Wrongs: Oxford Amnesty Lectures*. Oxford: Oxford University Press, 2003.

Paine, Thomas. *Thomas Paine Reader*. Edited by Michael Foot and Isaac Kramnick. Middlesex: Penguin Books, 1987.

Parra, Teresa de la. *Mama Blanca's Memoirs*. 1929. Translated by Harriet D. Onís. Revised by Frederick H. Fornoff. Pittsburgh Editions of Latin American Literature. Edited by Doris Sommer. Critical edition. Pittsburgh: University of Pittsburgh Press, 1993.

Pereira, Anthony W. "Public Security, Private Interests, and Police Reform." In *Democratic Brazil Revisited*, edited by Peter R. Kingstone and Timothy J. Power, 185–208. Pittsburgh: University of Pittsburgh Press, 2008.

Perlman, Janice E. "Redemocratization Viewed from Below: Urban Poverty and Politics in Rio de Janeiro, 1968–2005." In *Democratic Brazil Revisited*, edited by Peter R. Kingstone and Timothy J. Power, 257–280. Pittsburgh: University of Pittsburgh Press, 2008.

Perlmutter, David D. *Photojournalism and Foreign Policy: Icons of Outrage in International Crises*. Westport, CT: Praeger, 1998.

Perniola, Mario. *Enigmas: The Egyptian Moment in Society and Art*. Translated by Christopher Woodall. London: Verso, 1995.

Pestalozzi, Johann Heinrich, et al. *How Gertrude Teaches Her Children; Pestalozzi's Educational Writings*. Significant Contributions to the History of Psychology 1750–1920. Washington, DC: University Publications of America, 1977.

Peters, Julie Stone. "Law, Literature, and the Vanishing Real: On the Future of an Interdisciplinary Illusion." *PMLA* 120, no. 2 (2005): 442–453.

Peters, Julie, and Andrea Wolper, eds. *Women's Rights, Human Rights: International Feminist Perspectives*. New York: Routledge, 1995.

Phelps, Teresa Godwin. *Shattered Voices: Language, Violence, and the Work of Truth Commissions*. Philadelphia: University of Pennsylvania Press, 2004.

Phillips, Anne. "Universal Pretensions to Political Thought." In *Destabilizing Theory: Contemporary Feminist Debates*, edited by Michèle Barrett and Anne Phillips, 10-30. Stanford, CA: Stanford University Press, 1992.

Pierce, Charles Sanders. *The Collected Papers of Charles Sanders Pierce*. Edited by Charles Hartshorne and Paul Weiss. Cambridge, MA: Harvard University Press, 1932–1935.

Piquet Carneiro, Leandro. "Democratic Consolidation and Civil Rights: Brazil in Comparative Perspective." In *Brazil Since 1985: Economy, Polity and Society*, edited by Maria D'Alva Kinzo and James Dunkerley, 232–250. London: Institute of Latin American Studies, 2003.

Pollis, Adamantia, and Peter Schwab. "Human Rights: A Western Construct with Limited Applicability." In *Human Rights: Cultural and Ideological Perspectives*, edited by Adamantia Pollis and Peter Schwab, 1–18. New York: Praeger, 1979.

Pope, Alexander, ed. *The Works of Shakespeare.* 6 vols. London: Jacob Tonson, 1725.

Popkin, Margaret. *Peace without Justice: Obstacles to Building the Rule of Lavy in El Salvador.* University Park: Pennsylvania State University Press, 2000.

Post, Robert. *Prejudicial Appearances.* Durham, NC: Duke University Press, 2001.

Pratt, Mary Louise. "Harm's Way: Language and the Contemporary Arts of War." *PMLA* 124, no. 5 (2009): 1515–1531.

Priest, Dana and Barton Gellman. "US Decries Abuse but Interrogations." *The Washington Post,* December 26, 2002, A1, 14, 15.

Puta-Chekwe, Chisanga, and Nora Flood. "From Division to Integration: Economic, Social, and Cultural Rights as Basic Human Rights." In *Giving Meaning to Economic Social and Cultural Rights,* edited by Isfahan Merali and Valerie Oosterveld, 39–51. Philadelphia: University of Pennsylvania Press, 2001.

Puttenham, George. *The Arte of English Poesie, 1859.* English Linguistics, 1500–1800—A Collection of Facsimile Reprints. Edited by R. C. Alston. Menston: Scholar, 1968.

Quayson, Ato. *Aesthetic Nervousness: Disability and the Crisis of Representation.* New York: Columbia University Press, 2007.

Queen, Christopher, Charles Keown, and Damien Keown, eds. *Action Dharma: New Studies in Engaged Buddhism.* New York: Curzon Press, 2003.

Qurush, Emram. "Misreading 'The Arab Mind': The Dubious Guidebook to Middle East Culture That's on the Pentagon's Reading List," *The Boston Globe,* May 30, 2004. http://www.boston.com/news/globe/ideas/articles/2004/05/30/misreading_the_arab_mind.

Radnóti, Miklos. *Under Gemini: A Prose Memoir and Selected Poetry.* Translated by Kenneth McRobbie, Zita McRobbie, and Jascha Kessler. Athens, OH: Ohio University Press, 1985.

Rajagopal, Arvind. "And the Poor Get Gassed: Multinational-Aided Development and the State—The Case of Bhopal." *Berkeley Journal of Sociology* 32 (1987): 129–152.

Rawls, John. *A Theory of Justice.* Cambridge, MA: Harvard University Press, 1971.

———. *Political Liberalism.* New York: Columbia University Press, 1993.

"The Red Berets." Review of The Centurions, by Jean Lartéguy. *Time,* January 19, 1962. http://www.time.com/time/magazine/article/0,9171,895876-1,00.html.

Redfield, Marc. *Phantom Formations: Aesthetic Ideology and the Bildungsroman.* Ithaca, NY: Cornell University Press, 1996.

Rejali, Darius. "Modern Torture as a Civic Marker: Solving a Global Anxiety with a New Political Technology." *Journal of Human Rights* 2, no. 2 (2003): 153–171.

———. *Torture and Democracy.* Princeton, NJ: Princeton University Press, 2007.

———. "Torture Makes the Man." In *On Torture,* edited by Thomas C. Hilde, 165–183. Baltimore: Johns Hopkins University Press, 2008.

Ricchiardi, Sherry. "Missed Signals." *American Journalism Review* (Aug.–Sept. 2004). http://findarticles.com/p/articles/mi_hb3138/is_4_26/ai_n29113376/?tag=content;col1.

Rieff, David. *A Bed for the Night: Humanitarianism in Crisis.* New York: Simon and Schuster, 2003.

Risse, Thomas, and Kathryn Sikkink. "The Socialization of International Human Rights Norms into Domestic Practices: Introduction." In *The Power of Human Rights: International Norms and Domestic Change,* edited by Thomas Risse, Stephen C. Ropp, and Kathryn Sikkink, 1–35. Cambridge: Cambridge University Press, 1999.

Robbins, Bruce. *Secular Vocations: Intellectuals, Professionalism, Culture.* New York: Verso, 1993.

Roos, Bonnie, and Alex Hunt, eds. *Postcolonial Green: Environmental Politics and World Narratives*. Charlottesville and London: University of Virginia Press, 2010.

Roosevelt, Eleanor. "The Promise of Human Rights." *Foreign Affairs* 26 (1948): 470–477.

Rorty, Richard. "Feminism and Pragmatism." *Michigan Quarterly Review*. 30, no. 2 (1991): 231–258.

Rosenblatt, Louise. *Making Meaning with Texts*. Portsmouth, NH: Heinemann, 2005.

Rotberg, Robert I., and Dennis Thompson, eds. *Truth v. Justice: The Morality of Truth Commissions*. Princeton, NJ: Princeton University Press, 2000.

Rousseau, Jean-Jacques. *On the Social Contract with Geneva Manuscript and Political Economy*. Edited by Roger D. Masters. Translated by Judith R. Masters. New York: St. Martin's Press, 1978.

Roy, Arundhati. *The God of Small Things*. New York: Random House, 1997.

Ruffato, Luiz. *Eles eram muitos cavalos*. 6th ed. Rio de Janeiro: Editora Record, 2007.

Rushdie, Salman. *Imaginary Homelands*. New York: Penguin, 1982.

———. *Midnight's Children*. New York: Penguin, 1981.

———. *Shalimar the Clown*. New York: Random House, 2005.

———. *Step Beyond This Line: Collected Nonfiction 1992–2002*. New York: Modern Library, 2003.

Saar, Erik, and Viveca Novak. *Inside the Wire: A Military Intelligence Soldier's Eyewitness Account of Life at Guantánamo*. New York: Penguin, 2005.

Sacco, Joe. *Palestine*. Foreword by Edward W. Said. Seattle: Fantagraphic Books, 2001.

Said, Edward W. *Culture and Imperialism*. New York: Knopf, 1993.

———. "Nationalism, Human Rights and Interpretation." In *On Human Rights: The Oxford Amnesty Lectures, 1993*, edited by Stephen Shute and Susan Hurley, 175–214. New York: Basic Books, 1994.

———. *Orientalism*. New York: Pantheon, 1978.

Salamon, Lester M., S. Wojciech Sokolowski and Associates. *Global Civil Society: Dimensions of the Nonprofit Sector*. Bloomfield, CT: Kumarian Press, 2004.

Sammons, Jeffrey L. "The Mystery of the Missing *Bildungsroman*; or, What Happened to Wilhelm Meister's Legacy?" *Genre: Forms of Discourse and Culture* 14, no. 2 (1981): 229–246.

Sanders, Mark. "Introduction: Ethics and Interdisciplinarity in Philosophy and Literary Theory." *Diacritics* 32 (2002): 3–16.

Sandhya. "Q&A with Indra Sinha, Author of the Booker Shortlisted 'Animal's People'." *Sepia Mutiny*, March 13, 2008. http://www.sepiamutiny.com/sepia/archives/005088.html.

Sarat, Austin. "Toward Something New or Maybe Something Not So New: Is There Room for Legal Scholarship in Law Schools? A Review of Paul Kahn, *The Cultural Study of Law: Reconstructing Legal Scholarship*." *Yale Journal of Law and Humanities* 12 (2000): 129–144.

Sarat, Austin, and Thomas Kearns. "The Unsettled Status of Human Rights: An Introduction." In *Human Rights*, edited by Austin Sarat and Thomas Kearns, 1–24. Ann Arbor: University of Michigan Press, 2001.

Satrapi, Marjane. *The Complete Persepolis*. New York: Pantheon, 2003.

Scarry, Elaine. "Consent and the Body: Injury, Departure, and Desire." *New Literary History* 21 (1990): 867–896.

———. "The Difficulty of Imagining Other People." In *For Love of Country: Debating the Limits of Patriotism*, edited by Martha Nussbaum, 98–110. Boston: Beacon Press, 1996.

———. *The Body in Pain: The Making and Unmaking of the World.* New York: Oxford University Press, 1985.

Schaffer, Kay, and Sidonie Smith. *Human Rights and Narrated Lives: The Ethics of Recognition.* New York: Palgrave, 2004.

Schiller, Friedrich. *On the Aesthetic Education of Man in a Series of Letters.* Translated by E. M. Wilkinson and L.A. Willoughby. New York: Oxford University Press, 1983.

Scholes, Robert E., and Robert Kellogg. *The Nature of Narrative.* New York: Oxford University Press, 1966.

Schor, Naomi. "French Feminism Is a Universalism." *differences: a journal of feminist cultural studies* 7, no. 1 (1995): 15–47.

Schwarz, Roberto. *Misplaced Ideas: Essays on Brazilian Culture.* Translated by John Gledson. Edited by James Dunkerley, Jean Franco, and John King. London: Verso, 1992.

Sen, Amartya. *Development as Freedom.* New York: Anchor Books, 2000.

Shane, Scott and Mark Mazzetti. "In Adopting Harsh Tactics, No Look at Past Use." *The New York Times,* April 21, 2009.

Sharf, Robert. "Buddhist Modernism and the Rhetoric of Meditative Experience." *Numen* 42 (1995): 228–283.

Siebers, Tobin. "Disability and the Right to Have Rights." *Disability Studies Quarterly* (Winter/Spring 2007). http://www.dsq-sds.org.

———. "Disability in Theory: From Social Constructionism to the New Realism of the Body." *American Literary History* 13, no. 4, Winter 2001: 737-754.

Siegfried, Charlotte Haddock. *Pragmatism and Feminism: Reweaving the Social Fabric.* Chicago: University of Chicago Press, 1996.

Singer, Marcus George. *Generalization in Ethics.* New York: Alfred A. Knopf, 1961.

Sinha, Indra. *Animal's People.* New York: Simon & Schuster, 2007.

Skinner, Quentin. "Who Are 'We'? Ambiguities of the Modern Self." *Inquiry* 34 (1991): 133–153.

Slaughter, Joseph R. "*Clef à Roman*: Some Uses of Human Rights and the *Bildungsroman.*" *Politics and Culture* 4, no. 3 (2003). http://aspen.conncoll.edu/politicsandculture/page.cfm?key=244.

———. "Enabling Fictions and Novel Subjects: The *Bildungsroman* and International Human Rights Law." *PMLA* 121, no. 5 (2005): 1405–1423.

———. *Human Rights, Inc.: The World Novel, Narrative Form, and International Law.* New York: Fordham University Press, 2007.

———. Slaughter, Joseph R., "Narration in International Human Rights Law." *Comparative Literature and Culture* 9. 1 (2007). http://docs.lib.purdue.edu/clcweb/vol9/iss1/19/.

———. "A Question of Narration: The Voice in International Human Rights Law." *Human Rights Quarterly* 19, no. 2 (1997): 406–430.

Slemon, Stephen. "Magical Realism as Postcolonial Discourse." In *Magical Realism: Theory, History, Community,* edited by Lois Parkinson Zamora and Wendy B. Faris, 407–426. Durham, NC: Duke University Press, 1995.

Smith, Adam. *The Theory of Moral Sentiments.* Edited by D. D. Raphael and A. L. Macfie. Oxford: Clarendon Press, 1976.

Smith, Anne. "The Unique Position of National Human Rights Institutions: A Mixed Blessing?" *Human Rights Quarterly* 28 (2006): 904–946.

Smith, John H. *The Spirit and Its Letter: Traces of Rhetoric in Hegel's Philosophy of Bildung.* Ithaca, NY: Cornell University Press, 1988.

Sontag, Susan. *Regarding the Pain of Others.* New York: Farrar, Straus and Giroux, 2003.

Soysal, Mümtaz. "Nobel Lecture." Presented at the Nobel Peace Prize Ceremony, Oslo, Norway, December 11, 1977. http://nobelprize.org/nobel_prizes/peace/laureates/1977/amnesty–lecture.html.

Spender, Stephen. "Catastrophe and Redemption: O *the Chimneys*. By Nelly Sachs." *The New York Times Sunday Book Review*, October 1967, 5, 34.

Spivak, Gayatri Chakravorty. "Can the Subaltern Speak?" In *Marxism and the Study of Culture*, edited by Cary Nelson and Lawrence Grossberg, 271–312. Urbana: University of Illinois Press, 1988.

———. Preface to *Of Grammatology* by Jacques Derrida, ix–lxxxvii. Translated by Gayatri Chakravorty Spivak. Baltimore: Johns Hopkins University Press, 1976.

———. *In Other Worlds: Essays in Cultural Politics*. New York: Methuen, 1987.

———. "Righting Wrongs." In *Human Rights, Human Wrongs: Oxford Amnesty Lectures 2001*, edited by Nicholas Owen, 168–227. Oxford: Oxford University Press, 2003. Also in *The South Atlantic Quarterly* 103, no. 2/3 (2004): 523–581.

———. "Terror: A Speech After 9–11." *boundary 2* 31, no. 2 (Summer 2004): 81–111.

Spurr, David. *The Rhetoric of Empire: Colonial Discourse in Journalism, Travel Writing, and Imperial Administration*. Durham, NC: Duke University Press, 1993.

Sreberny, Annabelle. "Unsuitable Coverage: The Media, the Veil, and Regimes of Representation." In *Global Currents: Media and Technology Now*, edited by Tasha G. Oren and Patrice Petro, 171–185. New Brunswick, NJ: Rutgers University Press, 2004.

Stamatopoulou, Elissavet. "Women's Rights and the United Nations." In *Women's Rights, Human Rights: International Feminist Perspectives*, edited by Julie Peters and Andrea Wolper, 36–50. New York: Routledge, 1995.

Stanton, Domna C. "Foreword: ANDs, INs, and BUTs." Special Issue on The Humanities in Human Rights: Critique, Language, Politics. Edited by Domna C. Stanton and Judith Butler. *PMLA* 121, no. 5 (October 2006): 1518–1524.

Steele, Meili. *Hiding from History: Politics and Public Imagination*. Ithaca, NY: Cornell University Press, 2005.

Stein, Robert. "The French West Indian Sugar Business." In *Caribbean Slave Society and Economy*, edited by Hilary Beckles and Verene Shepherd, 94–101. New York: The New Press, 1993.

Steiner, George. *Language and Silence: Essays on Language, Literature, and the Inhuman*. London: Faber and Faber, 1958.

Steiner, Henry J., and Philip Alston, eds. *International Human Rights in Context*. New York: Oxford University Press, 2006.

Stoler, Ann Laura. *Carnal Knowledge and Imperial Power: Race and the Intimate in Colonial Rule*. Berkeley: University of California Press, 2002.

Sundquist, Eric J. *Strangers in the Land: Blacks, Jews, Post-Holocaust America*. Cambridge, MA: Harvard University Press, 2005.

Tal, Kali. *Worlds of Hurt: Reading the Literatures of Trauma*. Cambridge: Cambridge University Press, 1995.

Tanner, Laura. *Intimate Violence: Reading Rape and Torture in Twentieth Century Fiction*. Indianapolis: Indiana University Press, 1994.

Taylor, Charles. *The Ethics of Authenticity*. Cambridge, MA: Harvard University Press, 1992.

———. *Language and Human Agency*. Cambridge: Cambridge University Press, 1985.

———. *Modern Social Imaginaries*. Durham, NC: Duke University Press, 2004.

————. *Philosophy and the Human Sciences.* Cambridge: Cambridge University Press, 1985.

————. *Sources of the Self.* Cambridge, MA: Harvard University Press, 1989.

Taylor, John. *Body Horror: Photojournalism, Catastrophe, and War.* New York: New York University Press, 1998.

Teson, Fernando. "International Human Rights and Cultural Relativism." *Virginia Journal of International Law* 25, no. 4 (1985): 869–898.

Thiher, Allen. "A Theory of Literature, or Recent Literature as Theory," *Contemporary Literature* XXIX, no. 3 (1988): 337–350.

Thomson, Rosemarie Garland. *Extraordinary Bodies: Figuring Physical Disability in American Culture and Literature.* New York: Columbia University Press, 1997.

————. "The Politics of Staring: Visual Rhetorics of Disability in Popular Photography." In *Disability Studies: Enabling the Humanities*, edited by Sharon L. Snyder, Brenda Jo Brueggemann, and Rosemarie Garland-Thomson, 56–75. New York: Modern Language Association, 2002.

————. "Seeing the Disabled: Visual Rhetorics of Disability in Popular Photography." In *The New Disability History: American Perspectives*, edited by Paul K. Longmore and Lauri Umansky, 335–374. New York: New York University Press, 2001.

Tierney, Brian. *The Idea of Natural Rights: Studies on Natural Rights, Natural Law, and Church Law, 1150–1625.* Atlanta: Scholars Press, 1997.

Todorov, Tzvetan. *On Human Diversity: Nationalism, Racism and Exoticism in French Thought.* Cambridge, MA: Harvard University Press, 1993.

Trotter, Catharine. *The Unhappy Penitent.* London, 1701.

Tsvetaeva, Marina. *Art in the Light of Conscience: Eight Essays on Poetry.* London: Bloodaxe Books, 2010.

Tuck, Richard. *Natural Rights Theories: Their Origin and Development.* Cambridge: Cambridge University Press, 1979.

Turits, Richard Lee. "A World Destroyed, A Nation Imposed: The 1937 Haitian Massacre in the Dominican Republic." *Hispanic American Historical Review* 82, no. 3 (August 2002): 589–635.

Turner, Bryan. *Vulnerability and Human Rights.* University Park: The Pennsylvania State University Press, 2006.

Twenty-Five Human Rights Documents. New York: Center for the Study of Human Rights, Columbia University, 1994.

Umansky, Eric. "Failures of Imagination." *Columbia Journalism Review* (Sept. 2006): 16–31.

United Against Torture Coalition. *Alternative Report for Consideration Regarding Israel's Fourth Periodic Report to the UN Committee Against Torture.* September 1, 2008. http://www2.ohchr.org/english/bodies/cat/docs/ngos/UAT_Israel42_1.pdf.

Universal Declaration of Human Rights, G.A. res. 217A (III), U.N. Doc A/810 at 71 (1948). http://www.unm.edu/humanrts/instree/bludhr.htm.

United Nations. *Third Session, Proceedings of the Third Social and Humanitarian Committee.* New York: United Nations, 1948.

United Nations Economic and Social Council, Resolution 1994/54, "National Institutions for the Promotion and Protection of Human Rights," March 4, 1994. http://www.nhri.net/pdf/HRCres1994.pdf.

United Nations General Assembly. "World Summit Outcome Document." September 15, 2005. http://www.who.int/hiv/universalaccess2010/worldsummit.pdf.

United Nations High Commissioner for Human Rights. *Office of the United Nations High Commissioner for Human Rights Handbook.* Professional Training Series, no. 54. New York: United Nations, 1995.

Vargas Llosa, Mario. *The Storyteller.* 1987. Translated by Helen Lane. New York: Farrar Straus Giroux, 1989.

Villey, Michel. *La formation de la pensée juridique modern.* Paris: PUF, 2003.

Vollmann, William T. *Europe Central.* New York: Penguin, 2005.

Vondung, Klaus. "Unity through *Bildung*: A German Dream of Perfection." *Independent Journal of Philosophy* 5/6 (1988): 47–55.

Wachtel, Eleanor. "Conversation with Edwidge Danticat." *Brick* 65 (Fall 2000): 106–119.

Waldron, Jeremy, ed. *'Nonsense upon Stilts': Bentham, Burke and Marx on the Rights of Man.* London: Methuen, 1987.

War Photographer. Produced and directed by Christian Frei with James Natchway. New York: Christian Frei Film Productions, 2001.

Watt, Ian. *The Rise of the Novel: Studies in Defoe, Richardson, and Fielding.* Berkeley: University of California Press, 1957.

Weiss, David, ed. *In the Act: Essays on the Poetry of Hayden Carruth.* Geneva, NY: Hobart and Williams Smith Colleges Press, 1990.

Weiss, Thomas, Gareth J. Evans, and Don Hubert. *The Responsibility to Protect: Research, Bibliography, Background.* Ottawa: International Development Research Center, 2001.

Weissbrodt, David, and Clay Collins. "The Human Rights of Stateless Persons." *Human Rights Quarterly* 28, no. 1 (2006): 24–76.

Weyrauch, Walter O. "On Definitions, Tautologies, and Ethnocentrism in Regard to Universal Human Rights." In *Human Rights*, edited by Ervin H. Pollack, 198–201. Buffalo, NY: Jay Stewart Publications, 1971.

Whitlock, Gillian. "Autographics: The Seeing 'I' of the Comics." *Modern Fiction Studies* 52, no. 4 (Winter 2006): 965–979.

Wideman, John Edgar. *Fanon.* New York: Houghton Mifflin Harcourt, 2008.

Williams, Raymond. *Keywords: A Vocabulary of Culture and Society.* 2nd ed. New York: Oxford University Press, 1983.

———. *Marxism and Literature.* Oxford: Oxford University Press, 1977.

Wilson, Richard Ashby, and Richard D. Brown, eds. *Humanitarianism and Suffering: The Mobilization of Empathy.* Cambridge: Cambridge University Press, 2008.

Witte, W. "Alien Corn—The 'Bildungsroman': Not for Export?" *German Life and Letters* 33, no. 1 (1979): 87–96.

Wollstonecraft, Mary. *Vindication of the Rights of Woman.* Edited by Miriam Brody Kramnick. Middlesex: Penguin, 1982.

Wright, Laura. *Wilderness into Civilized Shapes: Reading the Postcolonial Environment.* Athens, GA, and London: University of Georgia Press, 2010.

Yee, James. *For God and Country: Faith and Patriotism under Fire.* New York: Public Affairs, 2005.

Zamora, Lois Parkinson and Wendy B. Faris, eds. *Magical Realism: Theory History Community.* Durham, NC: Duke University Press, 1995.

———. "Introduction: Daiquiri Birds and Flaubertian Parrot(ie)s." In *Magical Realism: Theory, History, Community*, edited by Lois Parkinson Zamora and Wendy B. Faris, 1–11. Durham, NC: Duke University Press, 1995.

Zeleny, Jeff and Thom Shanker. "Obama Moves to Bar Release of Detainee Abuse Photos." *New York Times*, May 13, 2009.

Zirilli, Linda M. G. "This Universalism Which Is Not One." *Diacritics* 28, no. 2 (1998): 3–20.

Zobel, Joseph. *Black Shack Alley.* 1950. Translated by Keith Q. Warner. Washington, DC: Three Continents Press, 1980.

Index

foundations of, 5, 23–24, 36–37; history of, 3–4, 9; "human" in, 68–72; humanitarianism and, 14, 31, 121; indivisibility of, 103–119; interdiscipline of, 1–16, 260; international human rights, 41–64, 73, 78, 121, 216, 218; literature helping with, 201–214, 260–261; narrating, 149–164; neoliberalism and, 120–132; news media and, 167–170; normativity of, 6, 88–95; obligations of, 23, 260–261; paradox of, 120–132, 260–262; politics of, 201–214; problematic for, 87–102; protecting, 121–122; role of theory in, 260–263; "self" and, 247–259; social imaginary and, 87–102; transcendental view of, 90–93; universalism in, 65–86; violations of, 149–164; as violence, 201–214; witnessing, 167–170; women's rights, 8, 172, 215–230. *See also* rights of man
Human Rights: A Political and Cultural Critique, 9
human rights activism, 7, 74, 122–123
Human Rights and Narrated Lives: The Ethics of Recognition, 8
human rights culture, 33–37, 56
Human Rights in a Posthuman World: Critical Essays, 13
"Human Rights in Literary Study," 260
Human Rights, Inc., 216, 248
human rights law: *Bildungsroman* and, 41–64, 234; contemporary concept of, 45–46, 51–52; structure of, 51–52
human rights movements, 31, 71, 104–105
human rights regime, 72–74
humanitarian discourses, 30, 235–237, 261
humanitarian narrative, 30, 35
humanitarian principles, 23–24
humanitarian rights, 37
humanitarianism: compassion and, 30–31, 34–36; description of, 34; doctrines of, 23; human rights and, 14, 31, 121; international humanitarianism, 56; politics and, 121, 209; suffering and, 34

Humanitarianism and Suffering: The Mobilization of Empathy, 14
"Humanities in Human Rights: Critique, Language, Politics," 2
Humboldt, Wilhelm von, 55
Hume, David, 36
Humphrey, John, 51
"Hunger Camp at Jaslo," 143
Hunt, Lynn, 4–5
Hutcheon, Linda, 149
Hutcheson, Francis, 23

I
I/Thou, 137
Ibhawoh, Bonny, 67–68
Ignatieff, Michael, 67
Ihara, Craig, 252
In the Name of Humanity, 34
In the Time of the Butterflies, 108
indivisibility of rights, 103–119
Infinite Jest, 212
Instead of a Preface, 135–136
Insurgent Citizenship, 120
"Interbeing," 249, 252, 257
interdisciplinary field: of human rights, 1–16, 260; of literature, 1–16, 260; mapping, 14–15
International Committee of the Red Cross, 188
International Covenant on Civil and Political Rights, 43, 70
International Covenant on Economic, Social, and Cultural Rights, 43, 69
international human rights, 41–64, 73, 78, 121, 216, 218
international tribunals, 19
Intifada, 165, 167, 172–174
Intimate Violence: Reading Rape and Torture in Twentieth Century Fiction, 8
"Into the Dark Chamber," 182
Inventing Human Rights, 4
Invisible Man, 97
Irigaray, Luce, 66, 71

J
James, C. L. R., 109
James I, 21
Jameson, Fredric, 48
Jataka Tales, 247–249, 253, 255–256
Jefferson, Thomas, 23, 52
Jeffreys, Derek S., 251–252
Jin, Ha, 184